Table of Contents

Chapter 6
Physical Database Implementation. 245

Chapter 7
The master Database Is Special 261

Chapter 8
SQL Server Recovery 275

Preface

This book discusses the issues that anyone involved with the DBA team supporting a large multiserver environment needs to be aware of. Here we cover what is and is not discussed in the text.

This book discusses the issues that anyone involved with the DBA team supporting a large multi-server environment needs to be aware of. Here we cover what is and is not discussed in the text.

Purpose
Who Is This Book For?
What You Need to Know to Use This Book
What You Will Learn From This Book
Conventions
Terms
Versions of SQL Server
SQL Server System 11
Versions of Replication Server

Purpose

This book is intended for those persons who will take a small Sybase SQL Server 4.9.x or System 10 to a large Sybase SQL Server® 4.9.x or System 10 multiserver environment that will be administered by a team of DBAs.

Who Is This Book For?

Clearly, the DBA is one person that this book is intended for, but so is the manager who is trying to plan such growth and the financial officer who will have to pay for staff and hardware to support the system. The experiences described here will benefit DBAs with less experience, while the checklists and procedures will save the experienced DBA time.

It is assumed that the reader is familiar with the Sybase SQL Server and the commands used to control the server. The book does not provide a complete syntax for any of the server commands and as such is not intended as a beginning training text. The Sybase courses are very good for this purpose, and this book is an excellent companion to the course material as it expands on, explains, and underscores the practical impacts of many things described in the course and the manuals.

What You Need to Know to Use This Book

This book is based on experiences with the Sybase SQL Server running on Sun® hardware using SunOS™ 4.1.3. The descriptions of the server and the procedures will work with the Sybase SQL Server on other UNIX® operating systems. Every attempt has been made to make the discussion relevant to any Sybase SQL Server installation. When needed, commands or procedures that are specific to SunOS are identified as such.

You probably won't use and don't need to use all of the material presented all at once. Certain sections will be immediately relevant to your current situation. When a crisis hits, you can use the other sections as checklists of things to review as a way to isolate and fix the problems your system is experiencing.

What You Will Learn From This Book

The DBA who is responsible for the administration of a Sybase SQL Server will find the information directly applicable to his or her job. While portions of the discussions relate directly to the SunOS UNIX environment, the commands used are described in sufficient detail that the equivalent commands for virtually any UNIX platform could be readily identified.

With the growth in the databases themselves comes an increase in the number of database servers as well. While a single server was fine for the pilot project, you now need to consider the implications of a single server failure and how to implement a standby system. Users in various parts of your growing business will want their data on their own server, located near the primary users and maintained by their own DBA. All of this causes more servers, oftentimes containing much of the same data, that must all communicate with each other. The DBA must learn about the new issues relevant to dealing with multiple servers.

This book is designed for use in the real world. Procedures are laid out to be followed step-by-step. Sufficient detail is included to ensure the procedures can be used on a variety of systems by all members of the DBA staff, from the most senior to the latest recruit. Further, these procedures make the process of training a new person much easier.

Real-world observations are included throughout the text and are denoted by the ;-) symbol. These observations are included to provide motivation to readers to pay attention to the subject and apply what is presented to their own systems. Viewed another way, these observations provide stark evidence of the price you may well pay if you choose to avoid the advice presented. Without these observations it is easy to dismiss the instruction as too detailed and perhaps even paranoid.

;-)   Disasters do happen and real people get fired over them.

The manuals included with the Sybase SQL Server (including the CD-based products SyBooks and AnswerBase) are excellent and cover the topic of a single server very well. This is their purpose and their duty. However, as your system grows to even two servers, there are new problems that just aren't addressed in the manuals. This book covers these issues in detail and as such provides a bridge between the manuals with their server-centric view of the world to your multiserver environment. While the manuals are invaluable for documenting and describing all the options for a given command, they won't even begin to help you understand the large database environment.

As your business grows and expands, you will need to be familiar with the System 10 family of Sybase products. Whether you upgrade your existing servers from 4.9.x to System 10 or install a new server at System 10, you will face the hurdles of upgrading and installing. System 10 has many new features, and the upgrade process is more involved than simply installing another EBF. This book will cover the upgrade process in detail and will cover the important differences between the 4.9.x and System 10 versions of the Sybase SQL Server.

As with the many Sybase products available, there are an endless number of permutations of hardware, operating system software, middle-ware, and so on, that you may have in your environment. We make no attempt to address the issues that would arise in any given multivendor environment. We cover in great detail the issues relevant to administering a Sybase multiserver environment running UNIX. While the examples are taken from a SunOS environment, care has been taken to make these examples useful in any UNIX environment. Wherever possible, we avoid the use of commands or tools that are only available in the SunOS environment. Further, the function of the SunOS commands used is covered in sufficient detail that it should be easy to determine the equivalent commands or options in the UNIX environment that you are using.

This book does not cover any theory of databases, nor does it compare the functionality of any competing products. We assume you have (or were hired into an environment that already has) selected Sybase SQL Server. If you are in the process of selecting the DBMS for your environment, this book will assist you in determining what you need to have in place to maintain a large, multiserver Sybase system, but, it will not provide any comparisons to other DBMS vendors or their products. We assume you are at a point where you need information relevant to administering a Sybase environment, not in need of a survey of DBMS products.

Conventions

Sybase SQL Server commands are shown in the text in the following font:

disk init

Sybase SQL Server command syntax is shown in the following font:

```
sp_helpdb database_name
```

```
sp_helpuser sa

sp_addsegment segment_name, server_device

sp_addsegment myseg0, server_device_1
```

Stored procedures supplied by Sybase as part of the SQL Server product are referred to as

sp_<stored_procedure_name>

sp_helpdevice

Stored procedures not supplied (or supported) by Sybase (described in Chapter 15 "Scripts") are referred to as

p_<stored_procedure_name>

p_devspace

The names of databases, segments, tables, and columns are shown in the following font:

master database

system segment

syslogins table

segmap column

Operating system (OS) commands are shown in the following font:

dkinfo

Real-world experiences that you need to think about are preceded by

;-)

Terms

There are many terms that are used in the description of the Sybase SQL Server and its environment. Listed below are some terms that will be used throughout the book. These terms are defined here to provide a standard set of definitions for the discussions that follow.

server

Within this book a server is a Sybase Server, and almost all the time it refers to a SQL Server. Occasionally the term "server" may refer to a Sybase Open Server such as the Backup Server that is part of the System 10 SQL Server.

server machine

Refers to the CPU, memory, disks and network interfaces that form the computer that actually executes the SQL Server.

server logical device (tape or disk)

A device as seen by the SQL Server. Note that SQL Server only knows about devices that are assigned to it and there isn't necessarily any direct correlation between a SQL Server device and a physical disk for example.

server device

Same as server logical device

spindle

Another term for a physical disk.

physical device

Refers to a physical disk or tape drive as opposed to a logical device, such as a partition of a physical disk that is assigned to a server device.

SQL Server user 'sa'

The SQL Server login that has ultimate authority and is used by the DBA.

server machine SA

The person who installs, maintains, and repairs the hardware and operating system software that supports the SQL Server and its associated products.

database system

The entire collection of server machines, SQL Servers, networks, clients, backup systems, and so on, that work together to support a business.

failover

The process of moving from a primary to a standby SQL Server. Also, the process of moving from a server device to its mirror.

Versions of SQL Server

While there are many differences between SQL Server 4.9.x and System 10, almost all of the material presented here applies to both versions. With the exception of the material that is specific to installing or upgrading 4.9.x (or System 10) specifically, all the other topics are applicable to both versions. Whether you are running 4.9.x or System 10, you need to be concerned with the issues and solutions regarding documenting a server, capacity planning, assigning segments to server devices, partitioning disks, and recovery. Further, few environments support only 4.9.x or System 10 SQL Server. The typical environment supports both versions at the same time with new servers of both kinds being installed and some 4.9.x servers being upgraded to System 10.

SQL Server System 11

The next major release of the SQL Server is System 11. Although the details of the new features and command syntax are not official at this time, the important changes to the server are well established. We discuss the new features of System 11 that will affect the DBA and show how these new features relate to the material presented throughout this book. There will be many sources of the details of any new system tables or stored procedures once the product is officially released, but you can prepare for the new server version now by considering the important changes that are being made.

System 11 incorporates changes to the SQL Server to support thousands of concurrent users, high OLTP transaction volumes, very large databases, and the ability to add resources and see immediate improvements in performance for a server running on multiprocessor hardware. SQL Server System 11 is a performance release specifically aimed at improving SQL Server performance on Symmetric Multiprocessor (SMP) server machines. There is little new functionality but many changes to improve server performance. We review the changes listed in the table below, as well as the upgrade path to System 11.

Cache
Size of Disk I/O Units
Transaction Log
Table Slicing
Lock Management
Engines
Updates to Tables
Query Optimizer
Dirty Reads
Upgrading to System 11

Cache

SQL Server performance improves when more of the data pages needed to satisfy a query are already in the data cache. This caching reduces the amount of physical I/O the server must do. With the current server design, there is only one data cache for the entire server. Data pages that are needed for the current query(s) are brought in from disk, and pages that have been in cache are moved back to disk to make room. If more pages are needed from disk than the cache has room for, then all of the data pages currently in cache will be moved back to disk, for example, when a large table is scanned. Thus, the data pages for frequently accessed tables, or other objects, are all back on disk and need to be reloaded into cache. This requires lots of physical I/O, which reduces server performance.

System 11 introduces named or dedicated caches. Instead of one cache for the server, you can create individual caches dedicated to specific database objects. That is, you can isolate objects that are most often accessed by an application and dedicate a portion of cache to store the objects. So, even if the server needs to load more pages into cache than there is room for, the dedicated caches that you have established will not be flushed from cache. This feature allows you to optimize cache much more than you can now. Also, you can set up dedicated caches with different buffer sizes depending on the needs of the objects to be stored in the cache. You will be able to specify smaller buffers for a cache supporting OLTP activity and larger buffers for cache that supports queries needing larger amounts of data. All of this reduces the physical I/O needed for your most important queries and prevents other users/applications from moving critical database objects out of cache.

Size of Disk I/O Units

Currently the server does all I/O in chunks of 2 Kb. Further enhancing the dedicated cache scheme, the System 11 server can support I/O in chunks up to 16 Kb. This scheme will improve server performance by reducing the physical I/O needed to move data from disk to cache and back.

Transaction Log

The existing SQL Server sends all entries for the transaction log through one process to be written to the transaction log for the database, so that multiple transactions in the database might be waiting for the one and only process to write their changes to the transaction log. The System 11 server will dedicate a portion of memory to storing the transaction log records of each transaction in the database. When a transaction actually commits, the transaction log records that have been created in memory will be written to the database transaction log on disk. This process is transparent to the users and applications and can be performed by multiple processors at the same time. This feature will greatly reduce the performance bottleneck created by contention for the transaction log.

Table Slicing

Whenever a new row is inserted into a table, the current server places the new row on the end of the table on disk. All applications that are making inserts will therefore be contending for the last pages of the table on disk as they wait for locks to make their inserts. With System 11, as you create a new table, you can specify a number of partitions or slices for that table. Then, as rows are inserted, they can be inserted into each of the slices, not just at the end of the table; multiple processors can each insert into the same table at the same time. This improves performance by eliminating contention and blocking for the last pages of the table.

Note that this new approach may require that you dump, drop, and recreate tables to benefit from this performance improvement.

Lock Management

Another bottleneck in the current server design is the way locks are managed. Since all locks are controlled by a single utility, all server users that need locks are forced to deal with, and wait for, the single lock manager to get to their request. In SQL Server 11, the process of lock management is done in parallel. The parallel lock manager will allow parallel access to various types of locks to further reduce contention among users within the server.

Engines

While the current server can utilize multiple engines, one engine was always assigned to dealing with all the network duties. This meant that there could be contention among the other engines as they waited for network access. System 11 is more flexible in that all the engines will be able to deal with network I/O requests, eliminating the contention for network access.

Updates to Tables

Currently, there are very limiting restrictions on the conditions under which the server will perform a row update in place. (Update in place means that under certain circumstances the server will make a row update without moving the row out on disk.) When these conditions are not met, the server performs a row update by deleting the existing row and reinserting the row with the updated value(s); the row will be added to the end of the table, just like a new row. The System 11 server removes all restrictions on update in place, which allows the server to avoid all the I/O involved with deleting existing rows and inserting them (moving them) at the end of the table.

Query Optimizer

The query optimizer is now more efficient in its need for and use of temporary tables to store intermediate results, that is, the server creates fewer and smaller temporary tables to satisfy subqueries. Further, the reports generated by the optimizer that tell you what the query plan is will be enhanced to better aid performance and tuning efforts.

Dirty Reads

When many concurrent users need to read and write to the database, lots of locks are held and many users are blocked, waiting for locks to be released. To reduce this contention, SQL Server 11 will allow you to specify ANSI SQL 92 Isolation Level 0, which means reads do not acquire locks of any kind. Users that need to read from a table won't acquire locks and, therefore, won't block users that need to write. The reverse would also be true. Depending on the application, this can greatly reduce the contention caused by locks held and users blocked.

Note the implications for your users. The fact that reads don't acquire locks means the table may be updated while you are reading; if you were to read from the table again, there is no mechanism to ensure that you will see the same results of the read. That is why the change is called allowing "dirty" reads, that is, reads from data pages that have changed but have not been committed. Since the read acquires no locks, it isn't clear whether or not a data page reflects a committed transaction. You must be sure that this ambiguity is acceptable for the applications that will read from the database.

Upgrading to System 11

Users will be able to upgrade from SQL Server 4.9.2 directly to System 11, but the upgrade path will involve the same steps and procedures that are currently involved with upgrading from 4.9.2 to System 10 (see "Upgrading SQL Server, Upgrading 4.9.x to System 10"). Since a database dump made from a 4.9.2 server can't be loaded into a System 10 server, the same situation will apply to upgrading a 4.9.2 server to System 11.

Versions of Replication Server

Chapter 8 "Replication Server" reflects the way the product was up to version 10.0.3, using rs_install and rs_setup_db for installation and adding databases to the replication system. With Replication Server Release 10.0.3, you use sybinit for installation and adding databases.

This change can be confusing, especially when you are using a 4.9.2 SQL Server as part of the replication system. In such a system, the SQL Server is installed and reconfigured (if needed) with sybconfig, but sybinit is used for Replication Server. If a System 10 SQL Server is also a part of your database system, then you would use sybinit for the System 10 SQL Server as well.

Replication Server Release 10.1 now uses rs_init for installation and addition of databases. The 10.1 release supports encrypting Replication Server user passwords. Note, however, that if you are upgrading to Replication Server 10.1, the upgrading process, which can encrypt the passwords, does not delete any existing configuration files that contain the unencrypted passwords. You must manually delete any such files. Further, once you have used this feature of Replication Server 10.1 you cannot regress to a previous release of the product.

Acknowledgments

This book is dedicated to Scott Vu, the only person who really understands what I went through. This book is a testament to those who suffered as we did. Scott believed in me and I could not have survived the experience without him. I continue to try to help him as he helped me. I doubt I will ever succeed.

This book should have had a very different and more meaningful title, but the publisher had more mundane and important goals in mind. The title I wanted was "Sybase DB—Life on the Streets" but that was too harsh for the marketing department. Anyway, that would have been a more accurate title for the material presented here and the experiences that it represents.

Many times an author will simply list the names of people that have helped inspire or produce a book. I think, though, that if you are grateful, you should let people know exactly why. Life is short and while there is always time for criticism, there never seems to be any time left for gratitude. I intend to remedy that situation.

Michael Hushour was the instructor for my Sybase DBA class and is perhaps the one person most responsible for my obsession with the job. He inspired me to pursue what I enjoyed no matter how unconventional. He also taught me to question the manuals and document my own experiences well enough to learn what was really happening, the official explanation notwithstanding.

Benjamin von Ullrich has always been the senior technical wizard in my universe. While the innovation award was fine, my most meaningful achievement (after never losing any production data) was that I never received a Ben-o-gram. I prefer to think I knew how to look before leaping, especially when the data of other departments was involved.

Jody Dworzak and Amy Bowers are among a very few people who understood and remembered why I had started all this and actually took an interest in it all. They have both been an inspiration and have provided vital support when the world seemed to be coming apart. It is my wish that they both find the personal and professional rewards they deserve. Persons of their abilities and sophistication are very rare. They should be revered, if not idolized, and I'm sure that soon they both will be. I hope they don't give up the wait.

Sheryl Hooper is, like Jody and Amy, one of the few who actually took an interest in this project and was instrumental in keeping me from quitting. She also kept me sane while forces several levels above me tried every trick they could to make me do something stupid. I owe her more than can be expressed. She allowed me to go to the desert many years ago to pursue my dream of working on the Space Shuttle, and she worked as a miner in a Borax plant to make it all happen. I can't ever completely make up for what she sacrificed for my dream—but I continue to try.

Helen Ruth deserves credit for encouraging me to pursue my interests even though they were not ones she shared. She often went out of her way to provide the environment I needed to arrive at this point. I can still remember the first book on engineering she ever gave me, a book now lost in the mists of time, but never forgotten.

Eric Robert and Christopher Noah also put up with a lot during the creation of this work. They both spent a great deal of time entertaining themselves while I struggled with the explanation of one server concept or another. I hope that the results of this project will directly assist them in whatever it is they choose to do. Through their fascination with anything on a prerecorded video tape, they also caused me to learn the words to many of Disney's greatest hits. Eric would often catch me watching one of these when I should have been writing. He would then get up, turn my chair towards my own screen and remind me "You just have to write!!" I'm convinced the publisher has been sending him something in return for this very personal vigilance.

Francis Griswold took the time to support my interests over the years, and this project was no exception. I would not have survived the process that gave me the experiences described here without his understanding.

Linda Halloran reviewed and debated many of the subtle points of server recovery and provided the kind of real-world feedback that only her years of experience could provide. As she enters the world of replication, I hope she will continue to include me in her adventures.

Mark Taub was instrumental in this work ever being contemplated, let alone created. During my most oppressed times at work he never let me give up on this project, a project that provided a critical continuity as my professional life came apart. Through him I found a whole new aspect to my professional development, one that allowed me to see the rest of what went on in my professional life over the last year for what it really was: irrelevant and largely infantile.

Liz Marin was the one person without whom I never would have gained the experiences that are reflected in these pages. The most important changes in one's life are too often made by people you deal with once or twice and then never have any contact with again. Liz is one of these people. She radically altered my life for the better by working hard to allow me to find the right work environment at the right time in my life. She performed this service twice, and both times my professional life improved dramatically. People spend their lives trying to make a difference. In my opinion Liz already has, at least for me.

Donna Ringer was always supportive and took an interest in my progress throughout the project.

Robert Hitchcock, without knowing it at the time, prepared me for this opportunity by showing me the books written by my father, grandfather, and great-grandfather. Through his encouragement, I became the fourth generation of my family to publish.

Nes Albano, Marcia Barrie, Cindi Beckett, Linda Halloran, Pedro Lay, and Karen Learn all worked to bring me to Sun Microsystems. Terry Brown befriended me in my new environment, making it seem like I had come home. Sienna Apis has been inspirational by maintaining a very positive attitude, no matter what the situation. Steve Lucchesi has encouraged me to take on new projects, something I had not had the opportunity to do in a long time. Without their efforts I would not have had the environment I needed to finish this project, and I am grateful to them all.

I understand better than most what it is like to do the very best you know how and only get attention when things beyond your control bring the system down. To get only negative reviews is part of the DBA job. It is also this way for the persons who helped me so much in Sybase Technical Support and Call Coordination. They supported me so many times and I rarely had the chance to return the favor. Theirs is a thankless job, but I am thankful they were always there for me and always helped me out.

Finally, I survived the Cold War, McCarthyism, and the Silence of the Lamb, but I did not survive the period of Grand Larceny. It is ironic but also completely normal that the greatest threats come from within any organization. Given the cost of hiring and training people for this sort of work, dispensing with those same people as a form of sport is a bigger drain on any organization than any loss the stockholders might worry about. The relentless desire to motivate your best people to leave is a strange way to build an organization. But so it goes, and life is also ultimately very fair. The painful process led to a much better existence. You just have to keep going, pursuing what you know to be true.

Psycho, somewhere in the East Bay, July 1995.

Chapter 1

Standard Server and Server Machine Environment

Now that we have established that we are dealing with a large database system, we discuss the many things you need to establish to form a maintainable and efficient environment for your database system.

Unlike a small, single server system, your large database system will involve many server machines, see Figure 1.1. To administer this more complex environment, you must establish and enforce standards. We discuss various things you will need at the organizational, operating system, and server levels.

1.1	You Are Not Alone Anymore
1.2	The Multiserver Environment
1.3	Why You Should Have a Standard Configuration
1.4	Standard for Overall Environment
1.5	Standard Configuration for All Server and DBA Machines
1.6	Standard Configuration for Servers

1.1 You Are Not Alone Anymore

You alone can't even begin to take care of a large multiserver database system. You will need a team of DBAs. While you will certainly be a member of this team, you can't look at your job the way you have in the past. Previously, you alone controlled and were responsible for all aspects of database administration. Now you must consider the organization needed to keep up with the more complex system you now have. This can be a big change for the existing DBA(s) that are used to the small database system outlook. You must change or you will not survive. Those DBAs that

1

can't or won't change will need to find another small environment to move to, or they will be seen as incompetent and after a time a threat. As your business grows, the support required by the database system simply outgrows any one DBA.

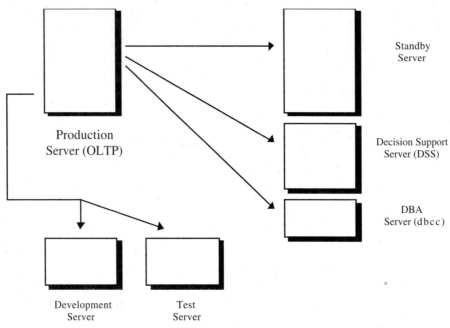

Data on other servers distributed from Production Server via database and transaction log dumps, see Chapter 8. All servers connected by network LAN and/or WAN.

Figure 1.1   Multiserver database system -

You will be part of a team of DBAs. In order to be a successful member of this team, you must realize how to keep the team moving forward. Note that "success" refers not only to the success of the business you are supporting but also to your own individual success. There will be DBAs on different shifts and with different backgrounds. Each DBA will approach things a little differently. This diversity requires very clear and ongoing communication among the DBAs, the server machine SA(s), application design and support persons, network specialists, and project managers to ensure that the whole database system is supporting the business.

The members of the team need to have a consistent way to communicate among themselves. While email is very important, it is only a part of the solution. You need to set up a mail queue that you will use for mail messages generated by various scripts that you will have running to monitor and maintain your system. Further, you should have another mail queue set up for messages that are intended for the entire DBA team. This queue is used for messages documenting actions taken, problems encountered, and other notices that should be put in a central location so all DBAs can access these messages as they need them to do their jobs.

Along with email, you need to establish a log file or diary. This file can be as simple as an operating system file and vi used as the editor. While vi is not a user-friendly editor, it is widely available and is accessible from character-based dumb terminals that you are likely to have for off-site work. This file should contain only important events that all DBAs need to know about. These events should be listed in chronological order in some standard format. For example, each entry in this file should begin with the time the event occurred, the name of the server involved, and the description of the event. At the end of the event description, the person making the entry should put their login name or email name. This makes it very easy for others of the DBA team to reply with email for questions or comments related to the event. As events are entered for a new day, the date should be entered as well. This diary file provides a good way to communicate important events and the order in which they occurred as well as to record who performed the work. This diary file should exist on one machine in your system, preferably the same machine that you will use to run all of your DBA-related scripts and cron jobs that aren't run on each individual server machine.

The DBA team must document what they do and how they do it. As new members of the DBA team need to be trained they can use the documentation to come up to speed. The diary file is one piece of the documentation that will greatly help you when training new DBAs. Other documentation must include a set of procedures that describe the details of day-to-day duties that the DBA team must carry out, such as adding database space, adding or dropping user accounts, clearing common error conditions, and so on. These procedures should be stored online in a central location that is accessible by all members of the team. Along with these procedures you will also need to store the documentation of each server, that is, the individual server-maps. See Chapter 5 for details of how to prepare the servermaps.

;-)

> You can't control the actions of the other DBAs on the team. Think about how you will handle the problems that will come up as one DBA partitions a new disk one way and another DBA sets up a new database assuming a difference partitioning. What will you do when the users come after you?

Finally, there is another aspect of being a member of a DBA team that you must understand. You can't control the actions of the other DBAs on the team. This doesn't mean that anyone on the team is going to do things that are stupid or dangerous. What it does mean is that you must realize no one is going to do anything exactly the way you would. You need to understand the issues involved with maintaining your system so that you can see the impacts of your actions and the actions of the other DBAs and be prepared to deal with whatever comes up. You can't survive assuming all of your fellow DBAs are going to take care of you. This isn't an indictment of your coworkers. Rather, a fact of life. This is the motivation for the communication and documentation discussed above. The simpler and more consistent your database system environment can be, the less time you will have to spend arguing about how to do things and how to cure problems.

Your system needs a team of DBAs to support it. At the same time, the duties that are performed by the DBAs are more narrowly defined than for a small system. The following breakdown of the work needed to support the database system is highly flexible; for any given installation you may not need each of these functions performed by a distinct set of people; see Figure 1.2. Still, you must realize that all of these functions need to be performed, and, as your system grows, you may well need individuals (and eventually groups) for each of the following functions.

As with application development, the responsibility for the logical design of your databases and maintenance of the schemas will be taken from the DBA group and placed with a group of data analysts (DA). You (DBA) won't have time to track the new applications as they come along, let alone know what all the design goals and objects are, so there is no way you can take care of the logical and physical design of these systems. Again, DBA will be involved with the installation of the physical design once it is done and will assist the DAs with the logical design whenever needed. You (DBA) will no longer have either knowledge, or control, of what objects are being created and deleted or changed on your database system, or why.

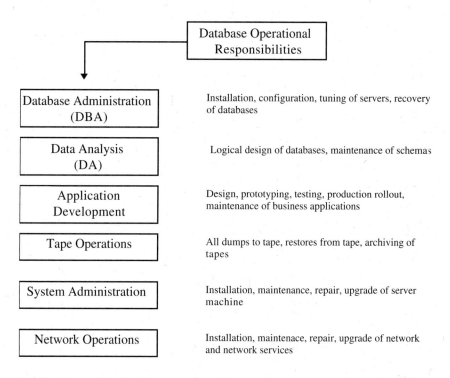

Figure 1.2   Database functions -

The application developers will also be in a separate group. This may or may not reflect a significant change in your environment. The persons that design and code applications will become separate from the DBAs. This is a natural result of the applications becoming far too complex and far too important to the success of the business to leave in the hands of a group that has any other responsibilities. While DBAs will continue to be involved with the applications that run on their database systems, DBA will not develop applications, nor should DBA be responsible for detailed change requests regarding these applications. The role of the DBA becomes more and more one of ensuring security and quality of the data while striving to provide that data faster and more easily. As your database system grows, DBA will not be able to know what is going on inside the many applications that the databases support.

In a small database system, you as the DBA may have been doing the database (and transaction log) dumps yourself. You may have been doing this through cron jobs, and so on. Now, with a large database system, the number of dumps to be made at each dump cycle grows quickly. The need to archive, provide off-site storage, and to guarantee dumps each and every dump cycle regardless of employee vacations, and so on, requires the creation of a separate group of tape operators that does nothing else but make and monitor database dumps.

This group will probably be making dumps for the entire business and will make the file system dumps for the machines that support your servers. You must plan your backup strategy and provide the operators with the scripts and schedule(s) needed to make the backups you require without getting in the way of the business. You must also establish a system to monitor the dumps. Monitoring the dumps for errors is vital but so is the timing information such monitoring provides. Knowing how long your dumps take will be needed as your business grows to require support around the clock.

1.2   The Multiserver Environment

The servers in the multiserver environment support different functions that together provide the basic database operation and the various reporting, maintenance, and recovery operations necessary to keep the database(s) current, accurate, and secure. We discuss each of the types of servers you will need in your database system:

Production Servers
Development Servers
Standby Production Servers
Decision Support Server (Reporting Server)
DBCC Server
Dedicated DBA Machine
Databases On All Servers To Contain Shared Company Data

Production Servers

Each of the production servers in your database system must be running on a separate machine. This machine must be dedicated to only one application, the SQL Server. Production servers always need as much of the machine as possible, and any other application or process that runs on the server machine will slow down the server. Further, you don't want your server to be at risk that some other process or application might crash the server machine. There will always be some reason to run more than just the SQL Server on a given server machine, but you should resist this pressure. You and your users will be happier in the long run if each production SQL Server is on a dedicated server machine.

Development Servers

Each of the development servers in your database system should be on a dedicated machine. This is desirable so that a crash of the development server will not bring down another development server. You need to know that a given server can be tested to the extreme, including looking for known bugs that may lock or crash the machine. If you don't have each development server on a dedicated machine, you must always be concerned about the impact of your testing on other servers and their development work should your development work interfere with the server machine. As was the case for the production SQL Server, there will always be some reason to run more than just the SQL Server on a given server machine, but you should resist. You and your users will be happier in the long run if each development SQL Server is on a dedicated server machine.

You also need a dedicated development server for trying out server upgrades before installing them in the production environment.

If this is not feasible, at the very least you must not have a development server running on a machine on which a production server is running.

Standby Production Servers

Depending on the needs of your business, you will likely require a standby system to support production business applications in the event your primary production server(s) go down. This standby server must be treated as another production server and must be the only process running on a dedicated machine. When the need arises and you switch to the standby server, you will want very similar performance and reliability as you require of the primary server. Which production servers require a standby server and how to establish and maintain such a server is discussed in Chapter 8.

Decision Support Server (Reporting Server)

You will need a dedicated decision support server for running queries and reports that would interfere with the production server(s) performance. The production servers that support your business should be set up and tuned for maximum OLTP performance; all other activity should run against a decision support server. See Chapter 9 "Performance/Tuning" for discussion of OLTP versus decision support server.

DBCC Server

You will need a dedicated server on a dedicated machine for running **dbcc** checks of your large production databases. As the size of your databases grows, so does the time needed to run **dbcc** checks. Soon you can't run all of the recommended **dbcc**s on all of your production databases during the downtime you have each day, week, or month. At that point you must begin running **dbcc**s in parallel with the production systems.

As you load tape dumps of your large databases from your production server, you are also verifying that the dump tape is good. For databases where you are dumping to and loading from disk to perform **dbcc** runs, this dedicated DBCC server should also be used to periodically verify the dump tapes by loading a database and running **dbcc** checks on that load. See Chapter 8 "SQL Server Recovery" for a discussion of **dbcc** runs.

You will also need this dedicated DBCC server for loading dumps of production data to retrieve data and/or objects that have been accidentally dropped or modified from the production server. Sometimes you will be asked to retrieve a row of data, a table, or other objects so that the application developers can see if recent modifications to their applications are deleting or corrupting data. Since SQL Server does not allow you to recover anything smaller than the entire database from a dump, you need to create and load the entire database in question. This is best done on a server that is separate from the production server. See Chapter 8 "SQL Server Recovery" for a discussion of logical dumps that allow retrieval of individual objects or data without the need to load the entire database dump.

If the need for such retrieval of data and objects comes up often, you will need a dedicated server on a machine separate from the server used for **dbcc** runs. You don't want the **dbcc** runs slowed down by the creating, loading, and querying of these restored databases.

Dedicated DBA Machine

You will need a set of cron jobs for each server machine for various maintenance and monitoring needs. These cron jobs will do things like check for database space, scan **dbcc** output for errors, and so on. Since you must have your servers each on a dedicated machine, you will also need a dedicated machine for running these cron jobs. You don't want to run these cron jobs on a machine with other users or processes, because these cron jobs will often require the server user 'sa' password and other users could see the password as part of the process. Note that this machine does not have a SQL Server running on it. This machine is also useful as a central place on the system to store the DBA scripts, documentation, and so on.

Databases on All Servers to Contain Shared Company Data

There will be certain pieces of data that will be needed by virtually all the applications your system supports. The set of tables that contain the data on all the employees of your business are a good example. You can improve performance of each application by supplying this common or shared data on each server. You accomplish this by creating a database on each server to house whatever common business data the application(s) on each server require. Designing and maintaining such a common database is very dependent on the specifics of your business. You will need to identify the primary location of each table of common data and provide a system to keep the copies on other servers up-to-date with the changes made at the primary, see Chapter 2 "Replication Server."

1.3 Why You Should Have a Standard Configuration

There are many reasons you will need a standard configuration for both your servers and the machines that support them. You will be forever upgrading and migrating servers and their associated machines. Without standards you must document the exact setup of each machine and server down to the last detail, or you must recall these details as you need them, or worst of all, you must explore each server to determine the configuration each time you do something. Further, each DBA on the team will have the same problem at some point. By standardizing configuration, you can save a great deal of time and frustration. The number of servers and machines that you and the DBA team will be supporting will grow quickly. You will find it is far easier to direct the server machine SAs when you have a standard configuration for the file systems on your server machines. Similarly it makes communication between the DBA team members more efficient if you don't have to recall and specify the details of each machine involved in a problem. Finally, training new DBAs or server machine SAs is dramatically easier if such standards are in place.

We discuss such standards for the overall environment, each server, and the machine that each server runs on. Such standards are highly dependent on your individual system. The discussion that follows suggests various things that should be standardized on your system. Only you can determine which areas of your system will benefit from the imposition of standards, but the point is that you must recognize the need for and benefits of such standardization.

1.4 Standard for Overall Environment

In this section, we discuss the following overall environment standards:

Naming Conventions for Servers
Naming Conventions for Objects
Interfaces File
User Passwords
Documentation of System Components
Consistent User *Suid* across Servers

Naming Conventions for Servers

You and your team will be working with many servers. You will waste a great deal of time if you don't adopt some simple naming conventions for your servers. We discuss an example here, but the specifics aren't important. You must choose a naming convention that works for you and your environment. The goals are the same as for many other aspects of the multiserver environment, more efficient use of the DBAs time, fewer mistakes due to miscommunication, and so on.

Your naming convention needs to be clear to you and the other DBAs. You can always add extra entries in the interfaces file to allow users to use whatever server name they want. However, you need to have your own DBA name for the servers you support. These names don't have to be clear to the users, and they can't be long enough to make the name clear to everyone. You will be typing these names many times each day so you need to keep them short, seven or eight characters at most.

Start by making it clear in your server names which servers are production and which are not production. Servers in the "not production" group include development and test servers and any other system component that will appear in the interfaces file. This distinction is useful because the way you deal with a production server is much more critical to your business than is a given development server. When training new DBAs, it is easy for you to tell them to work with one of the experienced DBAs if they need to work with any server whose name indicates it is a production server.

Next, the server name should describe the part or your business that the server supports. Examples for this would be servers for engineering, operations, sales and marketing, finance, human resources, and so on.

Finally, you have two more factors to consider. First, you need to decide how to handle multiple servers that support the same business function and are all production or development, and so on. Up to this point the server names for such servers would be identical. Appending a number for each server is an obvious approach. Second, you may want to identify the physical location of each server in the name. As with multiple servers, you can identify physical areas or regions and associate a number or other character with each such area. The server name would then help the DBAs with the question of where the server is located physically.

Taking this all into consideration you could construct the following server naming convention:

XXXYYY#A

where XXX is

PDS FOR PRODUCTION DATA SERVER
PRS FOR PRODUCTION REPORT SERVER (DECISION SUPPORT SERVER)
PSS FOR PRODUCTION STANDBY SERVER
DDS FOR DEVELOPMENT DATA SERVER

and YYY is any set of three characters that describe the group or application that uses the server. Examples could include SHP for shipping, INV for invoicing, and so on, DBA for database administration, or DEV for development work.

And # is for each of the geographic regions that have separate servers within your database system. Examples would include, 1 for North America, 2 for South America, and so on, or, 1 for West Coast, 2 for Midwest, 3 for East Coast, and so on. The choice would depend on how your database system is spread out across the state, country, or world.

And a is

1 FOR THE FIRST SERVER IN THIS SERIES
2 FOR THE SECOND SERVER IN THE SERIES

and so on.

Using all this you could build the following server names:

PDSOPS11—for the first production server supporting operations in North America. The next server supporting operations in the same region would be PDSOPS12.

DDSDEV1—for the only development server in North America supporting development.

DDSTST21—for the first development server in Europe supporting testing.

Naming Conventions for Objects

You and your team will be working with many more objects than servers, so the arguments for naming conventions for objects are the same. In a large database system, as discussed in Chapter 12, you as one of the DBAs will not have any way of knowing all the objects on the system. While you won't be naming objects, the application developers and the DAs you work with must be using object naming conventions. You, the DBA, will need these conventions when a user has trouble with an application and you need to find all the stored procedures on the system. You will want to tell just from the object name if the object is a trigger, a stored procedure, or whatever. As with server names, the specifics of your convention aren't important.

A related concept is that you must not change the stored procedures that are supplied with the Sybase SQL Server. If you want to use modified versions of these procedures, you must ensure that the original versions are still in the server. You must not give these modified versions the same name as the original, that is, don't overwrite the stored procedures supplied with the SQL server or any other Sybase product. You don't know when you will need the original versions to get through some crisis, so you should not throw them away by making modifications to the originals.

;-)

> The stored procedure **sp_addlogin** was modified with no documentation and no communication to the other DBAs. Instead of copying the original to a stored procedure of another name and modifying that, someone modified the original. The modifications involved checking that the user password was the same on several other servers when adding a new login. Everything was fine until one of those servers was moved to a different machine in a different region with a new server name. The modified version of **sp_addlogin** began to fail and none of the remaining DBAs knew why. Once the modifications to **sp_addlogin** had been identified as the cause of the problems, the original was restored. As always, this all occurred in the middle of an unrelated system crash, a time when adding a login should have been a simple operation.

Interfaces File

Now that you are dealing with a large database system, you will have entries in the interfaces file for many servers (see Chapter 11 for details of how the interfaces file works). These servers will need to know about each other, and that means each server must have access to the interfaces file entries for all the other servers. You need to have an interfaces file on each server machine, but maintaining all these separate files would be inefficient and error-prone. Instead, you should set up one master copy of the interfaces file and copy this file out to all the server machines.

You will need to set up two versions of the master interfaces file. One version, the server version, will be copied out (distributed or "pushed") to each server machine and contains the full interfaces file entry for each and every server and related services (open servers and so on) for your entire system. The other version, the client version, will be copied out to any and all file servers that support all the users of your database system. The client version of the interfaces file is maintained by DBA but is not distributed by DBA. Rather, DBA will make changes to the client version of the interfaces file and request the distribution to the client file servers by the organization that supports the file servers. When the client version of the interfaces file is distributed, it should be done such that the file is read-only on the client file servers. This prevents end users from changing their interfaces file and improves security by preventing users from accidentally or maliciously changing things that could result in their access to other servers. It also prevents endless calls to DBA about each interfaces file on each file server having problems as users make changes to the file.

The client version of the interfaces contains entries only for those servers and related services that DBA wants the end users to have access to. For example, the end user does not need, and should not be allowed to have, access to the server dedicated to DBA for running **dbcc** checks. The entries in the client version of the interfaces file consist of only one line for each server, which is all that a user needs to communicate with the servers.

Having two separate interfaces file is something you need. When installing a new server, you make entries in the server version of the interfaces file. This allows you as DBA to test and check out the server and its communication with other servers, but does not provide access to the end user. When the server is ready for end-user access, the one-line entry for the server is put into the client version of the interfaces file and the file is distributed to the file servers. Further, when a server needs repair or upgrade, you frequently need to lock out any user access. This is easy to do if you have these two separate versions of the interfaces file (see Chapter 11).

User Passwords

You must ensure that user passwords are the same on all the servers that a given user needs to access. This is required by the way SQL server allows remote server access. When a user on server A makes a remote procedure call (RPC) to another server B, server B checks the user's password on server B; it must agree with the user's password on server A for the request to be processed. You can set up servers so that they don't do this password checking, but you will then have a security risk.

Documentation of System Components

You need to have the various components of your environment documented. These components include your overall database system structure as well as the procedures involved in the setup and maintenance of servers, server machines, user logins, the server user sa password, user passwords, and so on.

Consistent User Suid across Servers

For various reasons you should maintain the server user ID (*suid*) of each user across all the servers in your database system. This means you need to have all the server logins added to all the servers that need to talk to each other, and those server logins need to be added in the same order on each server. Note that *suid* problems also impact remote servers since the local server will compare passwords based on the *suid* of the remote server. If the *suid* values between the local and remote server do not line up, the access will not be allowed. Further, when you add or drop a server login from any of these servers you must repeat the operation on all the other servers to keep the *suid* values in line. For any group of servers on your system that will share data, you should ensure that the users of the databases involved all have the same *suid* on all the servers. If you do not maintain the same *suid* for each of these users on all the servers involved, then, as you copy objects from one server to another, the object permissions, and so on, which are based on the server login *suid* will be confused. Suddenly, a user who could update a table on server1 can't even select from the table after the database was dumped from server1 and loaded into server2.

1.5 Standard Configuration for All Server and DBA Machines

We discuss various things that you should set up on each and every machine that is dedicated to DBA use. Most of these machines will be those dedicated to supporting a SQL Server, but most of the items also apply to those machines that are dedicated to DBA but that don't have a server running on them.

Hardware Configuration
No End-user Access to Server Machines
DBA Machine That Doesn't Have Server But Still Has Standard Configuration
UNIX User "DBA" Password Same as Server User "sa" Password
DBAs Have su on All DBA Machines
File System Structure
Don't Use UNIX User 'sybase'
Interfaces File Locations
Cron Jobs
Server User "sa" Password File
Tape Drive Compatibility

Hardware Configuration

You should have a basic hardware configuration that all of your server machines meet. Your server machines will not all be identical. The basic hardware configuration of each server machine consists of the processor(s), memory, and the disk system, see Figure 1.3.

Your standard server machine configuration will make ordering new server machines much easier. You will also need it when asked to take over other server machines from other parts of your business. Note that you may want to have two standards, one for server machines that support production servers and another for machines that support development or test servers. Having both standards makes it easy for you to upgrade a development machine when needed. Further, if your database system consists of several different kinds of hardware, you should establish standards for each kind of server machine you will be using. This exercise alone will convince you of the benefits of standardizing on one vendor's hardware. We cover the following hardware configuration:

Processor(s)
Memory
Disks on controllers
Disk usage across controllers
Partitions for server logical devices

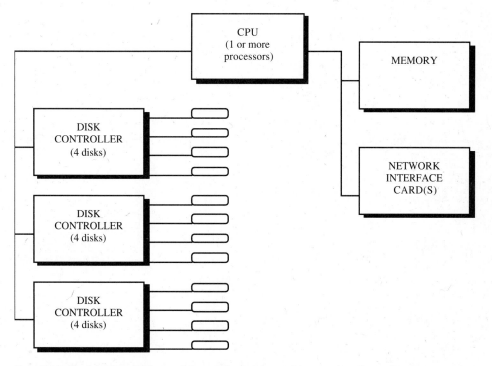

Note: The optimal number of disks per disk controller and the maximum number of controllers that a server machine can accommodate is platform specific. Three disk controllers are shown for illustration only.

Figure 1.3   Server machine components -

Processor(s)

There are many factors in choosing and configuring a multiprocessor system, and we don't cover them here. You need to select the processing capacity of each server individually, based on the applications and user load that is planned for each server. You do need to establish a minimum processing capacity for your servers, perhaps one that is as simple as a set number of transactions-per-second (TPS). This minimum processor standard should be selected with an eye to the future. You need to ask if the minimum processor of today will be of any use to your overall database system in two or five years. Consider what you will do with machines as they are replaced with new more powerful processors and disk systems. You may find that your current machines can be used as development or test server machines, or even as individual workstations, after they have served their useful life as server machines.

Memory

You should establish a minimum amount of memory for your server machines. You won't perform a detailed analysis of the performance trade-offs between various amounts of memory; it is just too inexpensive these days to justify much thought. Your standard can be as simple as 200 Mb of RAM as the minimum RAM for any server on your system.

Disks on controllers

You should establish the maximum number of disks that can be attached to a single controller before overall performance suffers. You will need to confer with your server machine SA for your particular hardware. This number will drive your capacity planning when specifying a new server machine.

Disk usage across controllers

You should spread out over the controllers the disks that will support file systems and those that support the server (see Figure 1.4). You should establish standard sizes for the various standard file systems. Overall, you need a standard approach to this. You need to have different segments of the most important databases on different disks on separate controllers for maximum performance. You need to have the server devices and their mirrors on separate disks on separate controllers for maximum security. If one controller fails, it won't corrupt both your primary device and

the associated mirror. You should spread your file system disks across all of the controllers also in order to have your server disks on as many different controllers as
possible, but be careful that your database dumps to disk are not made to file systems
that are on the same physical disk(s) as the database itself. See Chapter 10 "Capacity
Planning" for details of the process of determining how many disks and controllers
you need for each server machine.

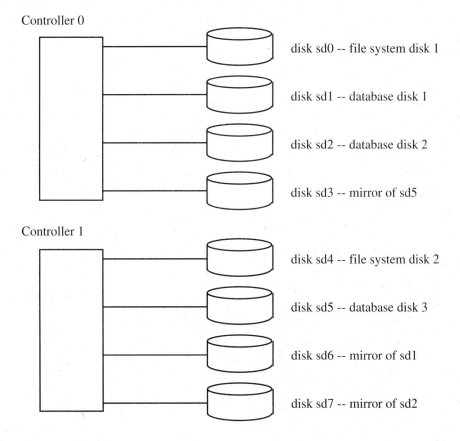

This example is for a server machine with eight disks — 1/4 of the disk space is given over to file system
space. The remaining six disks are split among server devices and their mirrors. Note that each physical disk
is used only for one purpose, file system, server devices, or mirrors of server devices. Each server device
and its mirror are on disks attached to separate controllers. The disks that support server devices are spread
across all the available controllers.

Figure 1.4   Spreading disks across controllers -

Partitions for server logical devices

You should have a standard for partitioning each disk on your server machines. Consult your server machine SA person before trying to establish this standard. While you can argue for different partitioning schemes for different server machines, it is much easier if you can simply specify a simple set of partitioning information for all disks. You should start with a basic scheme like this. First, the file system disks are partitioned as needed to support the file systems specified by your standard server machine configuration. Second, for all the disks allocated to the SQL server, you want a very simple partitioning scheme as shown in Table 1.1 and in Figure 1.5.

Your server machine SA person will find it takes much less time to set up and verify a partitioning scheme like this than worrying about different partitioning for each disk on each server machine. In times of crisis you will want to simply ask the server machine SA person to verify the standard partitioning of a disk rather than trying to recall what the partitioning for a given disk was or should be. Further, you will greatly reduce your already onerous documentation chores with a standard partitioning scheme. With a standard like this, you will not have to worry about keeping track of the partitions of all disks. And you will spend a great deal less time explaining such a standard partitioning scheme to the other DBAs you work with or train.

Table 1.1   Standard Disk Partitioning

Partition	Description/Recommendation
a	Never to be used by a server. It simply serves to hold the disk label, which is cylinder 0 of each disk. By putting cylinder 0 in partition 'a' and specifying that DBA never uses it for supporting a server, you will save yourself a great deal of trauma.
c	Refers to the entire disk and should not be used, since you need to have more than one partition per disk for performance and data security.
h	Should be a relatively small size, for example 30 MB. Each server you install will need several small databases. These 30-MB partitions provide a very convenient location for the server logical devices that will support these small databases and their mirrors. You will need more such partitions as you migrate to System 10 (see Chapter 13). While you may not need a 30-MB partition on every disk, it is much easier for you to specify one partitioning scheme for all disks.
b, d, e, f, and g	All the same size, and each of these partitions is 1/5 of the remaining disk space.

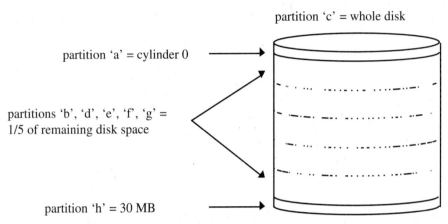

partition 'c' = whole disk

partition 'a' = cylinder 0

partitions 'b', 'd', 'e', 'f', 'g' = 1/5 of remaining disk space

partition 'h' = 30 MB

Figure 1.5   Standard disk partitions for server devices and their mirrors - - - - - - - - - - - -

No End-User Access to Server Machines

The machines dedicated to DBA use should be very secure. The only UNIX user that should have an account on these machines is the UNIX user 'dba.' All access to the machines should be through 'dba' or 'root.' Even though end users may not have an account on a SQL Server, if they can log in to the server machine, they can see cron job processes running that contain the SQL server user 'sa' password. You must not allow any other users to have access to the DBA machines.

DBA Machine That Doesn't Have Server Still Has Standard Configuration

Remember that even though a machine does not support a server, it should still follow the standards you set up for the machines in your database system. You may have a machine dedicated to supporting a Sybase Open Server, and while this isn't a SQL Server, the machine should be set up just like all the other server machines. Note that some of the configuration parameters discussed for server machines may not apply (mirroring doesn't apply to an Open Server).

UNIX User 'dba' Password Same as Server User 'sa' Password

You should set up the UNIX user 'dba' password to be the same as the SQL server user 'sa' password. The fact is that if anyone has either password, your system is in deep trouble. Making the UNIX-level 'dba' password the same as the SQL server 'sa' password makes life easier for the DBAs.

DBAs Have su on All dba Machines

Each member of the DBA team should have su privileges on all the DBA machines. This includes the individual workstations used by the DBAs for their routine work. This access is vital for changing permissions on devices, specifically devices used as logical devices for the server, and for killing processes on server machines. For example: The server machine SA, who is always 'root' when working on a server machine, may not see the harm in leaving open files and devices owned by 'root.' You will need su privilege so you can become 'root' to correct this problem, or your production system will be down while you wait for the SA to return.

;-)

You're on the pager that night. It's late. Europe is working away when you get paged. The European users are all blocked and their business is halted. You investigate and find one of the DBAs has left an isql session going that was holding locks on a system table that is causing all the blocking. You have su and you can kill the offending process at the UNIX level. The server won't always let you kill a process. Normally, you would identify the blocking process and kill it within the server. But, depending on the *status* (in the output of **sp_who**) of the process, you may not be able to kill it from within the server. You then need to kill the client host process at the UNIX level. If you have su privilege on the DBA machines, you can kill any process that is running on those machines.

File System Structure

Each of the machines dedicated to DBA use should have the same basic file directory structure, see Figure 1.6.

There will always be reasons to deviate from the standard you set up. You should resist these changes. The more consistent the DBA environment, the fewer errors you will have to fix and explain to management and your users. The specifics are not relevant. It is the idea of a standard structure that is important, followed by the DBA team putting the same kind of files in the same locations on all the servers. We will discuss the standard file system directories as an example of how you should set up the files systems (see Table 1.2). For discussion of sizing these directory structures, see Chapter 10, "Capacity Planning."

Table 1.2   Standard File System Structure

Directory	Description/Recommendations
/dba	The top-level directory for the server on the machine. Since you should be dedicating a machine to each SQL server, you should not have many other top-level directories. You want to have all the files relating to the installation, startup, and logging of the server in a directory structure separate from all the other files on the machine, because you will need to allocate space for this file structure separately from the other major file systems you will need on the machine. You should not dump everything into a single huge file system. Doing so makes it very difficult to locate individual files and requires training unique to each machine. In /dba you will have a subdirectory for each server running on the machine. While only one server should be on the machine, you may need a subdirectory to store files that relate to other servers. The Sybase SQL Monitor Server is a good example. The Monitor Server would have a separate subdirectory for the files needed to start and maintain the product.
/dba/sybase	The root directory of the Sybase installation file structure. Here you will put the standard set of Sybase files and subdirectories when you install the server. This is also the location of any other products that you install, such as Monitor Server.
/dba/software	Contains a subdirectory for each set of product files you load from tape or copy from another server machine. You will need to have a set of product files separate from those in the Sybase installation directory when you upgrade the server (see Chapter 13).
/dba/<servername>	The directory for each server or related product. In this directory you place the RUN_<servername> script, which starts the server and performs any related tasks such as starting the Monitor Server (and Backup Server for System 10). See Chapter 15 for discussion of these scripts.
/dba/<servername>/bin	Contains all the binaries or executables for the server. All the EBFs should be located here, as well as the current server binary that you are actually executing.
/dba/<servername>/sql	Stores all the SQL scripts that you need to install, maintain, and rebuild the server. The scripts you store here should be almost entirely SQL, as opposed to shell scripts that perform many other functions in addition to some SQL statements. The SQL scripts in this directory are frequently executed by cron jobs running on the machine.

Table 1.2   Standard File System Structure (Continued)

Directory	Description/Recommendations
/dba/<server-name>/scripts	Stores all the shell scripts that you need for the installation, maintenance, and rebuilding of your server. The scripts you store here may update statistics on tables in the server, dump databases and transaction logs, bulk copy data between servers, and so on. The shell scripts in this directory are frequently executed by cron jobs running on the machine.
/dba/<server-name>/diagnostics	Holds the output of any scripts that pertain to the configuration, maintenance, and performance of the server. This is where you should periodically dump the server configuration. Other outputs that should be put here are results of **dbcc** runs.
/dba/<server-name>errorlog	Stores the current and old server errorlogs. This is the directory that the server errorlog should be directed to in the server startup script.
/logdump	The directory where transaction log dumps are placed. Note that this assumes all transaction logs are dumped to disk. (See Chapter 8 "SQL Server Recovery," for discussion of the reasons you should be dumping transaction logs to operating system files.) You may need an entire physical disk dedicated to this file system in order to store log dumps from an active database for any length of time. You want this directory to be very large, because the transaction log dumps for your largest databases grow to be very large themselves. For all of the databases on your server that need to have transaction logs dumped regularly, all of the transaction logs for all these databases should be placed in this directory. To dump the transaction logs, you should be using a script that will handle the naming of the dumps to make it easy to find a dump for a particular database.
/diskdump	Stores all database dumps made to operating system files. This directory needs to be very large, which may require placing it on a physical disk separate from the other directories. Dumping databases to disk is very useful for many maintenance and recovery scenarios (see Chapter 8).
/usr	Stores all the files for UNIX user 'dba' including the.login file needed to set up the UNIX user 'dba' when you log in to the machine.
/usr/dba	Contains the server user 'sa' password file. You need to have one such file for each server that is involved with the cron jobs running on that server machine.

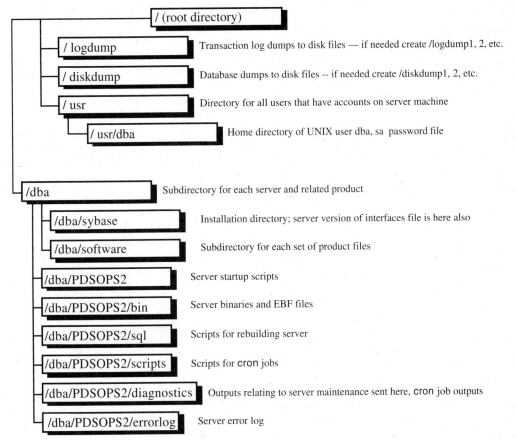

Figure 1.6   Standard server machine file system structure- -

Don't Use UNIX User 'sybase'

You do not want to use the UNIX user 'sybase' for anything relating to the operation of your server(s). Anyone within your company who must install, test, and use any of the Sybase product set will need access as UNIX user 'sybase' to the machine(s) they are using. The UNIX user 'sybase' account and password will have been set up in the distant past, and many users will know the password for that UNIX user. In a large system of many user machines, it will be difficult for DBA to set up UNIX user 'sybase' on the DBA machines with a different password from that used by the rest of the user community. Even if you can do this, it isn't worth the bother. You simply set up the UNIX user 'dba' for all the DBA machines and avoid the many potential security problems you'll have with the UNIX user 'sybase' account.

Note that for some scripts, such as sybconfig (sybinit for System 10) you must be UNIX user 'sybase' to run them. This is fine, you simply run chown on any files or devices you need, use su to become 'sybase' to run the script, and, when done, change owner of the files or devices back to 'dba.'

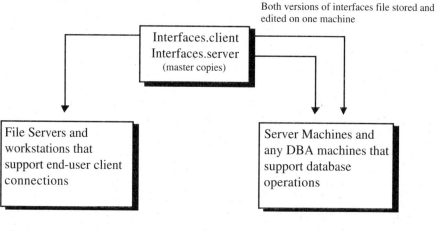

Both versions of interfaces file stored and edited on one machine

Interfaces.client
Interfaces.server
(master copies)

File Servers and workstations that support end-user client connections

Server Machines and any DBA machines that support database operations

The file interfaces.client is copied to each and every file server machine that supports end-user client connections. The only entries in this version of the interfaces file are the query entries for the servers and related products in the database system that end users are allowed to have access to.

The file interfaces.server is copied to each and every server machine as needed by DBA. The entries in this version of the interfaces file include master and query (and console for 4.9.x) entries for all servers and related products in the database system.

Each server machine should also get a copy of the interfaces.client file as part of the distribution of the file to all file server machines.

Figure 1.7   Interfaces file for clients vs. servers -

Interfaces File Locations

The need for two versions of the interfaces file was discussed previously; see also Figure 1.7. On each server machine you need to have a copy of both versions. The server version should be stored in /dba/sybase, and the client version should be stored in the same directory as it is on all the client (user) file servers. A good example would be /usr/local/sybase. Whenever the client version of the interfaces file is "pushed out" (copied) to all the client file servers, it will also be copied out to the server machines. Having the client version stored on each server machine is useful when making changes to the server version. Having both versions allows you to check what the end users have to work with and allows you to verify that you have restored the server version correctly after making changes.

Cron Jobs

Cron jobs are executed by the machine, based on entries made in the crontab for each user. For your purposes that means entries made in the crontab for UNIX user 'dba.' When you log in remotely to one of your machines as UNIX user 'dba' and execute crontab -l, you will get a listing of the crontab entries showing what jobs are set to run at what times on the machine. If you need to make changes, execute crontab -e to bring up the crontab entries within the default editor on your system.

You must ensure that the cron jobs running on each server machine don't conflict with each other. If one cron job runs **dbcc** checks for several hours on a weekend, make sure you aren't trying to run a cron job that does **update statistics** at the same time. Otherwise, the two cron jobs will at best slow each other down, and perhaps neither job will finish before your users need the system again, or at worst one or both of the cron jobs will die because of this conflict.

Your cron jobs must provide some way to check that they ran, what the results were, and how long they took to run. You must be able to check that various tasks are getting done on a regular basis. You must also check the timing information to verify that the cron jobs are not conflicting with each other. A good way to do this is to have each cron job send mail to an email alias that is created just for this purpose. A good email alias would be dba_cronjobs. This means you need to set up an email alias dba_cronjobs, and then add each member of the DBA team to this alias. Then, each of your cron jobs will be written to send email to this alias.

Each of the cron jobs that runs on each server machine should contain the same basic structure. First, the cron job must output to a file that is stored somewhere on the machine—/dba/<*servername*>/diagnostics is the best place. This file would contain any error messages that occurred during execution. The number of output files from each cron job that you save will vary with the cron job and how often it runs. Generally, saving the most recent output is sufficient. This most recent output file coupled with the email sent for each run of the cron job will allow you to track down what the problem is and how long the cron job has been failing. Second, each cron job must output the time and date that it starts and finishes. You use this information to verify that the cron jobs aren't conflicting and as a planning tool when deciding when to run each cron job. Third, each cron job must send email to the dba_crontabs alias. This email doesn't need to be much, just a message that the cron job succeeded or failed.

You will need to decide which of the standard set of cron jobs should run on each server machine and which should run on a single machine controlled by DBA and dedicated to running cron jobs for the maintenance of DBA servers and server machines. The decision you must make boils down to a trade-off between convenience and reliability. It is more convenient to have a single machine that contains one version of each standard cron job script and then runs each cron job against all of the server machines. This makes it easy to maintain one copy of each cron job script. However, if anything goes wrong with this machine or the network, none of your standard cron jobs will get done and you will have to manually run them on all of your server machines as soon as possible. The other approach is to have all of the standard cron jobs running on each server machine. This means any change to a cron job script has to be propagated to all the server machines.

Table 1.3   Standard Cron Jobs

Dump transaction logs
Dump databases depending on your backup plan
Dump system tables to disk file
Run **dbcc**s of smaller databases
update statistics/sp_recompile on objects
Report on database size and free space
Report on machine file system size and free space

Each server machine should have a set of cron jobs running to perform certain maintenance and monitoring functions. While each individual server may need additional cron jobs running from time to time, you should set up a standard set of cron jobs and make sure they are all running on all of your server machines. Your standard set of cron jobs should consist, at a minimum, of those listed in Table 1.3. We assume here that the machine in question is supporting a SQL Server. See Chapter 15 "Scripts" for examples of each of these scripts. How often each of these cron jobs should run depends on your recovery plan and the load on each server (see Chapter 8).

Dump transaction logs

You must determine your recovery plan for each server before you can determine how often you need to dump the transaction log of a given database. Your plan may well be different for different databases on each server. Further, your recovery plan will determine whether the transaction log dumps are made to disk files, to tape, who makes the dumps, and so on.

Dump databases depending on your backup plan

As with transaction log dumps, you need a recovery plan to determine how best to dump databases. You will need a script to dump databases, but you will have to decide which databases are dumped by a cron job versus by an operator and which databases will be dumped to disk file or to tape.

Dump system tables to disk file

You will need to dump the system tables for each server regularly, perhaps daily. You must have this information available in case you need to rebuild the server. You should run this cron job once a day, every day.

Run **dbcc**s of smaller databases

You will need to have a cron job to run **dbcc** checks on the smaller databases on each server. The term "smaller" here means the **dbcc** checks for all the "small" databases on the server can be run within the maintenance time available for that server. Note that as time passes and databases grow, you will need to move the **dbcc** runs for some databases off the primary server and onto a dedicated DBCC server.

update statistics/sp_recompile on objects

You want to be executing **update statistics** and **sp_recompile** for as many tables as possible in each database as often as possible. Which tables to do this to and how often, you must determine from a study of the activity on each table and the impact on your business of slow performance caused by old statistics.

Report on database size and free space

You need a cron job report on database space regularly in order to become proactive about providing your users with database space. You should run this cron job once a day, every day. See Chapter 15 "Scripts" for discussion of the stored procedure **p_devspace** that will provide a report of free space on all server devices.

Report on machine file system size and free space

As with database space, you need to stay ahead of the demand for disk space on the server machine. You should run this cron job once a day, every day.

Server user 'sa' password file

Each server machine should have a file that contains the server user 'sa' password for the server running on that machine. This file should be owned by UNIX user 'dba' and only be accessible by this user. This file is specified in the execution of scripts in the crontab file. This removes the need to type in the server user 'sa' password as part of each crontab entry. These crontab entries appear as an active process, that is, in the output of the ps command, and the password would appear with the process entry. This means that any UNIX user that can log in to the server machine could see the server user 'sa' password.

This file should be in the same location on all server machines. To allow for different server user 'sa' passwords on different servers, each server should have a different 'sa' password file. Recall that servers that need to communicate with each other should have the same 'sa' password unless special remote login arrangements are made (see Chapter 11). The filename should simply be .<*servername*> where the '.' is used as part of the filename to suppress the display of such files in the ls output. Each server machine will need an 'sa' password file for each server that is involved in the cron jobs running on the server machine.

Tape drive compatibility

You must ensure that the tape drives installed on all your server machines are compatible. This doesn't mean that all of the tapes drives have to be compatible with all the others. It means that you must determine the way your database system is going to operate both normally and in time of disaster recovery and determine which server machines will need to move tape dumps to other server machines. The tape drives on these server machines must be compatible. Note that "compatible" does not just mean the size of the media or the manufacturer's model number. For example, a 10-GB tape drive can use various levels of compression to have an effective capacity of 2.0, 5.0, and 10.0 GB of data on the same tape. You must understand the capacities being employed on each server machine. Further, you must determine if the different levels of compression are compatible between tape drives on different systems. If you need to move tapes between server machines, the only real way to verify that it works is to do it. Make a dump on one server machine and load it on the other server machine. Also note that it is difficult to determine what compression your tape drive(s) are using. When you dump to a device (e.g., /dev/nrst0 or nrst8) how do you know what level of compression is being employed? Check with the server machine SA, but make the dump and load to be sure. Remember this when you order new machines. You must make sure the new machine with new tape drives can read the dumps from your existing machine.

;-)
> The new server machines were delivered with 10-GB tape drives that could read 5-GB dumps. The existing server machines had 5-GB tape drives. So, the dumps should be compatible. However, the existing drives were being used to make dumps without any compression at all, that is, a tape capacity of 2 GB. Are you sure the new drives will read a 2-GB tape?

1.6   Standard Configuration for Servers

You need to set up many things when installing a new SQL server. You should standardize as many of these as possible and then apply these standards to your existing servers. We discuss the following:

Overall Server Setup
Model Database
Standard Set of Databases
Standard Set of Options on Databases
Scripts to Create or Rebuild Server
Scripts to Create or Rebuild Databases
Scripts to Maintain Server
Permissions on Databases
Ownership of Databases and Objects by Server User 'sa'

Overall Server Setup

The standardization of the configuration of your servers involves many things, from the detailed configuration of the server operating parameters (output of **sp_configure** and buildmaster -yall), to the databases, logins, users, and permissions established within the server. We discuss the following:

Port numbers
Device names
User passwords
Basic server configuration
Server use of whole disks
No disk devices 'default' especially not master device
Default sort order and character set

Port numbers

You should set up a set of port numbers that the SQL Server and any associated products will use on each of your server machines. These are the port numbers that are specified in the interfaces file for each server (see Chapter 11 for details of how the interfaces file works). A standard set of port numbers saves you time and confusion. When building a new server, you don't have to think what port numbers to use.

You can check a server errorlog and tell immediately if it is running on the standard port or not, which would tell you if someone (another DBA, we assume) has restarted the server on another port to isolate the server from the user community. You can detect errors in a user version of the interfaces file when you use a standard set of port numbers. Depending on the operating system you are using, a standard set of port numbers may save you a considerable amount of work when setting up or maintaining the interfaces file. You can tell the server machine SAs that this standard set of port numbers will be needed on all server machines so they can ensure that no other processes are assigned to those ports.

A standard set of port numbers is shown in Table 1.4:

Table 1.4   Standard Server Machine Port Numbers

Server or related product	port #
SQL Server master and query	1025
SQL Server console (4.9.x only)	1026
Backup Server (System 10 only)	1030
SQL Monitor	1035
DataTools SQL BackTrack license manager	1050
Replication Server	1070
Replication Server Log Transfer Manager(s)	1071, 1072, 1073, ...

Device names

You must have a simple and consistent server logical device naming convention to apply to disk devices and tape devices.

For disk devices you should name the logical device after the physical disk and partition where the logical disk device is located. This makes it much easier for you to determine which physical disk is having problems when errors occur, since the server machine name for each disk is how the hardware errors are logged in the machine's errorlog. You are assured that you won't specify duplicate device names if you follow the names the machine uses for the disks. When you need to determine the physical size of a disk partition, you will need to use the machine name for the disk, so you should use this name for the logical devices as well.

Your approach to naming the server logical disk devices should be as simple as this. For server machine disk /dev/rsd1 and partition 'd' the server logical disk device would be: rsd1d.

You need a standard set of dump devices that you install on all the servers in your system. While such a set of dump devices will not cover all the special needs of all your servers, it will provide a common set of devices that will be available on all servers. This set of dump devices should include a disk and a tape device at a minimum. Also, you need to establish a naming convention for these devices so it is easy to determine which dump device does what. For example, the dump device called diskdump dumps to a file called diskdump on the server machine file system, and ntapedump8 is a nonrewinding tape device known to the server machine as /dev/nrst8. By following conventions like these, it is easy for any of the DBAs to know which dump device to use.

User passwords

When the server was installed, two users were in the system table *syslogins*, the server user 'sa' and the user 'probe.' More importantly, both of these users are set up initially with a NULL password. The probe user is used in the two-phase commit process. If you don't use two-phase commit for the server in question, you should drop the probe user from *syslogins*. You must not have the server user 'sa' password set to NULL. Further, the passwords for all users need to be the same on all servers they need to access. This means that the server user 'sa' password must be the same on all servers. This is related to how servers allow remote access. See Chapter 11 for a discussion of how servers regulate remote access through the *sysservers* system table.

Basic server configuration

While each server in your database system will have unique requirements and therefore a unique configuration, all of your servers should have a baseline configuration that you use when installing a server. Further, you will need the checklist in Table 1.5 to periodically verify that each of your servers is configured properly.

Table 1.5   Basic Server Configuration Checklist

Action	Description/Recommendations
allow updates is set to 0	Verify that **allow updates** is set to 0 in the output of the **sp_configure** server command. If this configuration option is set to 1, it means updates to the system tables can be made directly. You must not have this configuration option set unless you are actually working on system tables, and as soon as you are done, you must set this option back to 0.
sysservers entries are correct	Verify that each entry in *sysservers* is correct. Make sure you want all of the listed servers to be communicating with the server in question both for security and performance questions. A site-handler problem caused by an RPC between servers can cause blocking that brings your system to a halt.
sysremotelogins entries are correct	Verify that each of the entries in *sysremotelogins* is correct. You must understand what the entries in *sysremotelogins* mean. See Chapter 11 for details of how the entries in *sysservers* and *sysremotelogins* function. You should make sure you understand who is logging in to each server from other servers, and make sure you want this going on. The default arrangement for remote server logins is the most secure, that is, the server checks the remote user's server login password against the local server's password for the same login, and if the two passwords are not identical, the RPC fails. This is why maintaining user passwords to be consistent across all servers involved in an RPC is something the DBA must worry about. Anything other than this default arrangement needs to be thoroughly explained, justified, and documented so that it can be turned off as soon as the need for this less secure configuration goes away.
Local server entry in *sysservers* is correct	Verify that the local server entry in *sysservers* is correct. This is the name that will be returned when you execute `select @@servername` within the server. This is valuable as a quick and easy way to verify which server you are on. This 'name' also appears in various error messages from the server. You should 'name' each server in your system.
Server startup scripts	Periodically check the scripts RUN_*<servername>* for each server to ensure that they are executing the proper server binary and that the proper trace flags are being enabled whenever the server is started. See Chapter 15 for a discussion of these scripts.

Server use of whole disks

Each of your server machines should be set up so that for all physical disks that are part of the machine, each disk is dedicated to either the SQL Server running on that machine or to something else. In other words, you must not combine SQL Server logical devices with any other type of device on the same physical disks. This is important for several reasons. You will find it easier to maintain mirrors by mirroring an entire physical disk to another whole disk of the same size. When you do have a problem with a disk, it is easier to determine whether the SQL Server or a file system is affected, which simplifies the recovery process. You will also make your documentation and other maintenance procedures less error-prone if you can tell the server machine SA that a set of whole disks is used by your server and nothing else. This prevents DBA and the server machine SA person from trying to use the same disk partition for two different things.

No disk devices 'default' especially not master device

You must not have any of the server logical disk devices defined as "default" disks. The server maintains a pool of default disk space that is used for databases that are created or altered without specifying logical devices. You don't want the users to be creating or altering databases in any of your servers in the first place. And, you don't want anyone, not even other DBAs, creating or altering databases without locating those databases on specific disk devices. The placement of each database segment on specific server disk devices is a big part of improving and controlling the performance of your server. Make sure none of the server disk devices are marked as default disks! You must be especially careful about the master device. If it is left marked as a default disk device, then anyone who creates or alters a database and doesn't specify a disk device will be filling up the master device. You should not allow anything to be created on the master device other than the *master, model,* and the first portion of *tempdb.* You can see if any of your devices are marked as default by running **sp_helpdevice** without specifying a particular device. If any of the devices are marked as 'default,' use the **sp_diskdefault** stored procedure to drop the default designation. Note that the master device is marked as a default device when you first install the SQL server. Unless you remove this designation manually, the master device will remain a default device. See Chapter 7 for more details about the *master* database and the master device; see Chapter 11 for details of checking for any disk devices marked as default.

Default sort order and character set

You must establish what the default sort order and character set(s) are for all the servers in your database system. You may not need to select anything other than the defaults that are applied during installation of the SQL Server through sybconfig (sybinit for System 10). Any servers that need to share data, including dumps, must have similar sort order and character set. While there are some combinations of sort order and character set(s) that are compatible with other combinations, it is much easier if you simply set up all the servers the same way. If you deviate from this, you should have a very good reason and you must document any deviations clearly for all the other DBAs. Incompatibilities between servers due to differing sort orders or character sets can cause a great deal of grief later on. You can verify the default sort order and character set that is in place for a given server by examining the output of **sp_configure**.

Model Database

You should establish a standard for the *model* database on all your servers. Ideally, you do this and make the changes to *model* before you create any of the other databases on the server. This way all the changes are automatically made to the *model* database (including permissions) in each database you create after that. Add users to the *model* database for any users that will need to dump the databases on the server. You also need to grant permission to these users to execute the **dump database** command so they can dump the databases.

Further, you need to determine if the size of the *model* database is sufficient for your needs. The size of the *model* database can affect you in two ways. First, if you need lots of objects (users, permissions, and so on) in *model*, it is possible to fill it up. You would then have to increase the size of *model*. Second, if you had to extend the *model* database then any other database that you create after that will have a minimum size equal to the size of the *model* database. Normally this isn't a problem, but you should be aware that anything you do to *model*, such as increasing its size, will affect every database created after that point.

Recall that the *model* database default size is 2 MB. Note that this should not be a question for most of the databases that you create, since you should be placing most of the databases on specific devices and segments. However, if you will be creating a number of small databases on your servers, you should make sure the *model* database size is sufficient for these databases.

Standard Set of Databases

You should examine your database system to determine an appropriate set of standard databases that should be on every server in your system, see Figure 1.8. By establishing these databases on each server, you make it easier to maintain the servers. You can create these standard databases whenever you install a new server, thus saving time. You can plan for the capacity needs of these standard databases. It is easier to move applications and data between servers if the servers have more structure in common. These standard databases should include those shown in Figure 1.8, although the databases you need on your servers may be very different.

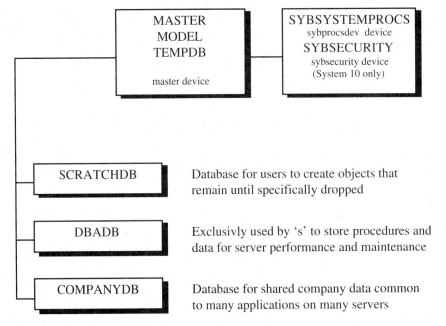

Figure 1.8   Standard server databases -

First, you should have a database that is a place for users to create objects that are not part of the production system. *Tempdb* certainly allows for the creation of temporary objects but users will need to create objects that will remain on the server longer than will *tempdb*. Also, from a performance perspective, you don't want *tempdb* used for anything but the most short-lived, transient user objects possible. You need a database with a name like *scratchdb* to serve this purpose.

Second, you need to have a database that is dedicated to use by DBA. This database is where you locate any and all data and stored procedures that are the tools of the DBA team. You need a database like this so that DBA can create, experiment, and develop new tools and techniques. Because DBA completes many tools, you don't want to fill up the *master* database with such tools, so you need to keep them in their own database. This database should not be accessible by anyone other than members of the DBA team. This database is also useful for setting up tables to store performance data and other diagnostics. A good name for this database would be *dbadb*.

Third, you should create a database that provides a common place to store data that is needed by many applications and users. For example, you may want to have your *customer* database on every server in your system because almost all of your applications need to retrieve parts of this dataset all the time. Note that this database does not need to be identical on each server, just that it exists on each server to provide a place for such data. You will simplify the process of application development if you create this database on all servers. It allows the developers to know ahead of time that there is a consistent place to put such data. Note that this approach results in improved performance, since the data is local, as opposed to making a call to a remote server each time the data from this common dataset is needed. Also, you can increase the availability of each server if it has a copy of this common dataset locally. If the primary source of the common dataset goes down, the local server can still function by using the local copy. You should determine what data the applications on each local server need from this common dataset and copy that data to the local server.

Further, this database also provides a logical place to put data that is copied from one place to another. A good name for this database is *<businessname>db*.

Standard Set of Options on Databases

Once you have set up the databases you need on a server, you need to apply a standard set of database options. While you will change database options for various short-term reasons, you must have a baseline set of database options and understand why they are needed before you can control your servers.

First, determine which of the databases on the server are indeed production databases that must be recovered as completely as possible (see Chapter 8 for details of designing your recovery strategy). For these databases you must not set, or allow to be set, the following options: **select into/bulkcopy, truncate log on checkpoint.**

For databases on your server that are not critical as far as recovery is concerned, you should set **truncate log on checkpoint** to prevent the transaction log from filling, and set **select/into bulkcopy** so that users can use bcp to copy data into the database. The databases that you are not setting up to be recoverable (other than from the most recent dump tape) are databases that are there for the support of users and their applications as temporary storage locations or the like. Hence, you should allow users to use these databases with bcp for moving large datasets in and out. Note that you shouldn't need to dump the transaction log of these databases and for that reason you should set **truncate log on checkpoint** so that you don't have to worry about the transaction log filling. See Chapter 8 for more details regarding recovery.

Finally, setting a standard set of database options serves another purpose: It makes it easier for you and the other DBAs to see which databases are production databases on the server. In times of crisis it is very useful that any DBA can isql into the server, run **sp_helpdb,** and see from the database options which databases must have their transaction logs preserved and which ones need not preserve the transaction logs.

It is useful to print out a hardcopy of various server configuration information *before* you have a problem that requires rebuilding the server. Information, such as database options that were set up, is very hard to remember, and if the server is not available, the hardcopy is all you have to work with. See Chapter 5 "Documenting a Server" for discussion of the information you should be recording, and Chapter 15 "Scripts" for discussion of the dump_systables script that will dump much of this information for you.

Scripts to Create or Rebuild Server

You must have a set of SQL scripts that will allow you to recreate the server on short notice. You need these if the server has a serious problem and you have to rebuild the basic structure of the server and reload the databases from dumps. Further, these scripts are necessary when you need to move a server from one machine to another or to set up a new server that is basically the same as an existing server.

While you should maintain these scripts to keep them current, you will have many other things to do that seem more important at the time. A more practical approach is this. When you install a server, write and execute each of the following scripts. These scripts form the base set of scripts that you can build on. You must be dumping the system tables that will tell you the current configuration of the server (see Chapter 15). With this up-to-date data, you can add to the base scripts to rebuild your server. Note that no matter how careful you are to manually or automatically keep these scripts up-to-date, you must have a current dump of the system tables to verify that your scripts will reconstruct the server completely.

We list the various scripts in Table 1.6 that you must have ready to run and then discuss the scope and purpose of each one. Note that we list these scripts in the order that you should execute them to rebuild the server.

Table 1.6   Scripts to Rebuild Server

Server startup
configure
add_dumpdevices (4.9.x only)
disk_init
disk_mirror
add_servers
add_users

Server startup

RUN_<*servername*> is not a script you would execute until you had the server installed and ready to run. You must keep the RUN_<*servername*> script current, however, since it will document the size and location of the master device as well as how the server is being started.

configure

configure is a script that will allow you to quickly bring the server back to the same configuration. Apply this script with care. If you are rebuilding the server after a repair to the server machine or rebuilding the server on another machine, be aware that you must ensure that the server machine can handle the previous configuration. If the server machine does not have the file descriptors or the physical memory needed, the server may not start after being configured by this script.

add_dumpdevices (4.9.x only)

add_dumpdevices is a script that documents the tape and disk dump devices that were existing on the server. In times of crisis, you don't want to try to remember if your server machine's 5-GB tape drive is /dev/nrst8 or /dev/nrst9. This script allows you to be ready to load from dump quickly. Note that with System10 you can use the Backup Server to make dumps and loads directly to file system files without using server dump devices.

disk_init

disk_init is a script that contains the size and location of each server logical disk device. This script is very important. If you don't have this information, you can't be sure that you can recreate the databases as they existed on the server before the crisis. If the devices aren't the same size (or bigger) than the original, you may not be able to recreate the database segments in the same size as the original, which can prevent you from successfully loading from dump.

disk_mirror

disk_mirror is a script that you can live without, but it is a tedious process to remember where you wanted to mirror each server logical disk device and why. You can reconstruct the mirroring easily if you follow the standard, discussed earlier, of dedicating entire physical disks of the same size to server disk devices and their mirrors, and applying the same partitioning scheme to all the disks. You can then document your whole server mirroring scheme by simply noting which disks are primaries and which are mirrors.

add_servers

add_servers is another script that isn't necessary to restore the server itself, but it is vital to restoring the server's business function within your database system. Without restoration of the entries that were in the *sysservers* system table, the server can't communicate with any of the other servers in your system. Note that this script must also contain the commands needed to recreate the entries in the *sysremotelogins* table as well.

add_users

add_users is a script that will recreate all the users that were in the *model* database and set up their permissions. Normally, you don't allow any users of the *master* database. The users described in this script are only those that need to dump the database, and their permissions should reflect that. By having this script and executing it, you ensure that every database created later on will contain these users, since each database created copies the *model* database. By doing this you ensure that all the databases on the server can be dumped by the same group of people. This saves time for you and makes it easier to ensure that all the databases can be dumped when needed.

Scripts to Create or Rebuild Databases

You need a set of scripts to create the databases on the server. This does not mean a script to create each and every object on the server. As discussed previously, it isn't practical for DBA to maintain a script for every object on all servers in the system (see Chapter 8 for details of recovering objects and databases). However, you must maintain a set of scripts that will allow you to quickly and accurately create the databases themselves, so you can then load the databases from dump. When the need to reload a database from dump occurs, you do not want to be worrying about which device had the log segment and how big it was. This is why you must maintain such a script for each database. Note that these scripts should be written to create the database with the **for load** option. This option means that the server does not go out and clear every page that is allocated for the database, so the creation of the database is much faster. Since this whole process is usually needed in times of crisis, you need to get this process done as fast as possible. See Chapter 15 for a discussion of such a script (**p_dbcreate**) and see Chapter 8 for details of recovering a database using the **for load** option.

Scripts to Maintain Server

You need to have a standard set of scripts that you use to maintain each server in your system. This set of scripts, listed in Table 1.7, will allow you to automate various database maintenance tasks such as dumping databases and their transaction logs, updating statistics, and performing **dbcc** runs on the databases (see Chapter 15 for details). In Table 1.7 we discuss the maintenance scripts.

Table 1.7   Server Maintenance Scripts

Script	Description/Recommendation
RUN_<*servername*>	Starts up the SQL Server. This script provides a good place for you to put other functions that should be automated and are part of the server startup procedure, such as renaming the errorlog. Note the simplicity that such a standard script provides. For each and every server on your system, there should be a RUN_<*servername*> script in the standard location within the server machine file system. This makes it much easier to train new DBAs and much easier to build new servers.
dumplog	Dumps the transaction log for any databases on the server that need to be recoverable to a more recent state than the last database dump. This script should be executed as a cron job at some interval you determine to be sufficient. The interval that is sufficient depends on how much data your business can afford to lose (see Chapter 8).
dumpdb	Dumps the databases on the server. You should have almost all the databases on the server in this script, except for *tempdb* and any databases that are static and can be recovered from other sources. You should have this script run by your tape operators. Or, if you are dumping to disk files which are then dumped to tape with the rest of the server machine file systems, execute this script as a cron job. How often you dump the databases, like the transaction logs, depends on the cost to your business of lost data (see Chapter 8).
update_statistics_all_tables	Should run regularly to update the statistics on all tables in the server. You don't have a good way to determine which tables need this done or how often. The best approach is simply to run **update statistics** and **sp_recompile** as often as you can, and if possible run them against all the tables in the server. At the very least, identify which tables get the most use and **update statistics** for those tables as often as you can. For the rest of the tables on the server, update them less frequently, but don't let any table go without a regular **update statistics** being run. Anytime you run **update statistics** you should run **sp_recompile** for the object(s) as well.
checkdb (**dbcc**)	Runs the **dbcc** checks against your databases on the server. How often you run **dbcc** against which databases is a complicated question. For the largest databases, you may not be able to run **dbcc** against them during the system downtime that your business can afford. In that case, you must dump that database and load it into another server on a separate server machine and run the **dbcc**s there. For any databases on the server that are not so large as to require this, this script should run a full **dbcc** on each of these smaller databases regularly. The point is to make sure all of your databases get a **dbcc** run on some regular basis.

Table 1.7   Server Maintenance Scripts (Continued)

Script	Description/Recommendation
dump_systables	Dumps many of the server system tables. This information is vital to recovering from various disasters. You must execute this script as a cron job to run frequently, so that it dumps the state of the server often enough that you catch all changes. You should run this script every night. You may think you know the server configuration and you may have a hardcopy somewhere, but, all too often, one of your fellow DBAs will make a configuration change that you won't know about. You can remove this painful mystery by dumping the system tables as a script regularly (see Chapter 8).

Permissions on Databases

You need to determine a standard approach to granting permissions on databases. You need to know which users (SQL server logins, or entries in *syslogins*) are made users of which databases. You then need to establish a relatively simple scheme for granting permissions on objects in the databases. The best way to do this is to set up groups, assign various permissions on database objects to these groups and then assign users to these groups. For many objects, such as stored procedures, you can simply grant execute to group 'public' and avoid having to grant permissions on these objects to other groups at all. Of course, you need to ensure that you really want all server logins to be able to execute the stored procedure in question, since every entry in *syslogins*, or every server user, is automatically made a member of the group 'public.' Finally, recall that each server user can only belong to one group in addition to being in the group 'public.' Keep this in mind when determining what groups you need for each server.

One of the most contentious permissions questions you as DBA must deal with concerns who can and will be aliased to 'dbo' in any database. DBA can off-load many database change requests to users by aliasing the user to 'dbo.' However, remember that once you set this up, that user continues to have full control over the database. You must decide on a policy regarding this. You must be sure that the users that are given this privilege will take responsibility for their actions. You must remember that you as DBA will get the call (and page) in the dead of night demanding that you repair the damage that can be done by someone, acting as 'dbo,' who modified or dropped an object in a database.

Ownership of Databases and Objects by Server User 'sa'

On all the servers in your database system, all the databases should be owned by server user 'sa.' This implies that only 'sa' creates databases, which is exactly what you want. This is necessary because only the DBA team should be allowed to determine where a database is located, how big it is, what options are set up, how the new database gets added to the backup and recovery plan, and so on. Further, there are problems with RPC requests between databases that occur when the databases in question are not owned by the same server user. You will prevent many problems by making server user 'sa' the owner of all databases.

This same logic applies to the objects within the databases, that is, that all objects in a database should be owned by 'sa.' Users that need objects created or changed should prepare a script for the DBA to execute as server user 'sa.' This also provides the DBA with a way to see what is being done.

Chapter 2

Replication Server

Replication Server is a relatively new Sybase product that works with the SQL Server to move data from a primary SQL Server to a replicate or target SQL Server. You will probably have one or more applications that need to distribute data throughout your database system, and you probably have various manual techniques for moving that data as needed. Replication Server can replace most of these manual techniques and provide a more reliable method of distributing data.

In the past, when you needed to keep data at multiple sites in sync, you would think of using two-phase commit. In two-phase commit, all the servers involved must be on the network at the same time. Through a process of one server (the master server) polling all the others, each individual transaction would either commit at all servers or be rolled back on all servers. The problems with this process are severe. First, all the servers involved in each transaction must be available in order for any transaction to commit. If even one server is off the network, the entire process stops and none of the involved servers can commit any transactions. This is not the way to run a business, that is, to be completely dependent on having all servers online all the time. Second, the two-phase commit functionality requires custom programming to identify the master server as well as the other servers and to specify how the polling, and so on, will proceed. This leads to systems that are very unique, hard to maintain, and even harder to troubleshoot. For these reasons, Replication Server was developed; it provides a more realistic alternative for keeping remote servers in sync.

You must understand what Replication Server does and does not do before you begin to use it. Further you must recognize that Replication Server does not provide an immediate capability that can replace your home-grown systems overnight. Replication Server is not a simple product that you just install and leave alone. In fact Replication Server requires much planning and design effort before it can be used beyond the most rudimentary functionality.

We discuss the basics of what the product does and what it takes for you to use it. Note that Replication Server is maturing rapidly and many new features are promised in future releases. We discuss the product as it is today.

;-)

Please encourage your many bosses to buy Replication Server. With its many subtleties and overall complexity, if enough businesses install it, the Sybase DBAs of the world will have even better job security than they (we?) already enjoy.

2.1	Overview
2.2	What Replication Server Does
2.3	What Replication Server Doesn't Do
2.4	Example of the Process of Replicating Data
2.5	Configuration Issues
2.6	Installing Replication Server
2.7	Creating a Subscription
2.8	Users and Passwords
2.9	How Replication Server Links With the SQL Servers
2.10	Affects on Existing and New Applications
2.11	Capacity Planning
2.12	Administration Using Replication Server Manager
2.13	Failure Modes
2.14	Function Strings

2.1 Overview

As a DBA, you need to know about Replication Server so you can determine if it would be beneficial to your business. Further, you need to have some idea what it will and won't do before somebody else in the organization decides they have to have it. You don't need to deal with being blamed for some marketing promises that the product can't really deliver on. Better for you to know what the product is about as soon as possible. The whole issue of distributed databases is very popular at this time, and there is a lot of desire among the users of your database system to make use of the many benefits of Replication Server. You will probably be asked about it soon, so you should learn about it now.

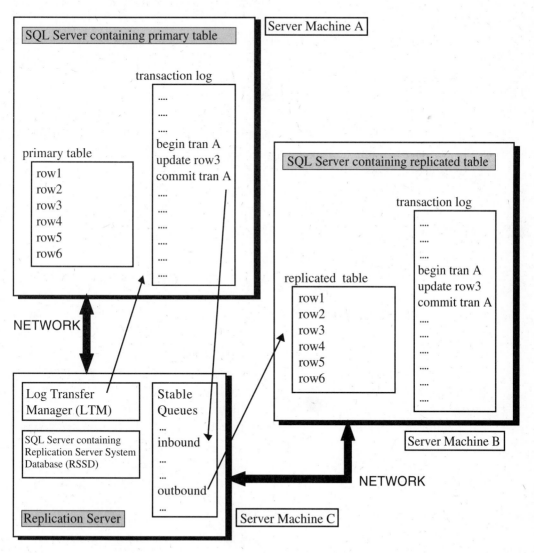

Figure 2.1   Replication server configuration -

Replication Server functions by scanning the transaction log of a given database. When it sees a transaction that affects the primary table in a replication definition and subscription, it sends the transaction off to the Replication Server, which then sends it to the replicate database, which can be in the local or remote SQL Server, where the transaction is then applied. Figure 2.1 illustrates the concept.

Replication Server requires a SQL Server to support various databases required for the basic functionality of the product itself. You can modify the product so that it works with other vendor's databases, but for the discussion here we will assume the primary and replicate databases are on SQL Servers.

By using Replication Server you can have applications run against local copies of primary data that is maintained at a remote server. This can improve performance for the local application because it will be running against a local set of databases. A local copy of the data will also remain available when the network goes down.

2.2   What Replication Server Does

Replication Server consists of several processes that together provide the basic functionality. Replication Server copies (replicates) rows of the primary table and applies them to the replicate table. Note the terminology, in that there is a primary data server that contains the primary database that contains the primary table. Similarly, there is a replicated table in a database on the same or another data server. Throughout the following discussion, we will refer to the source of any replicated data as the primary table, database, and data server. The destination of this data will be referred to as the replicated table. We will assume that the primary and replicated tables are on separate SQL Servers just to make the discussion easier, but this is not required by the product. Note that it is not required that the replicated table be in a database that is a complete copy of the primary database. Replication Server replicates (copies) data from a primary table to a replicated table. The replicated table can be in any database on any SQL Server that is on the network and set up to communicate with Replication Server.

Replication Server consists of the Replication Server itself, the Log Transfer Manager (LTM), and the Replication Server System Database (RSSD). We discuss each of these components below.

The Replication Server itself coordinates all the components of the product. It provides and maintains the stable queues where the incoming transactions from a primary table are stored until they are moved out to the replicated table. Replication Server keeps track of which replicated tables are supposed to get which data from which primary tables.

The basic operation of the Replication Server revolves around the transaction log of the primary database in the primary data server. The LTM scans the transaction log of the primary database looking for any committed transactions that affect the primary table (see Figure 2.5). The LTM knows which table(s) in the primary database it cares about, based on "subscriptions" that are created and maintained by the Replication Server. You must set up an LTM for each primary database. There is only one LTM for a primary database, no matter how many or how few tables in the database are being replicated. You don't have to replicate all the rows or columns of a primary table. The replication definition that you create on the primary table will determine which columns are eligible for replication. The subscription that is defined for each replicated table can contain a where clause that will determine which rows of the primary table are sent to each replicated table.

Because the whole process revolves around transactions in the transaction log and transactions affect one or more rows in a table, the Replication Server is all about replicating rows, or changes to rows, in the primary table to the replicated table. You need to realize that Replication Server doesn't replicate tables, or databases or entire servers, just rows in one table being copied to another table.

You can also set up a replicated stored procedure that can be executed at the SQL Server that supports the replicated table in one of the server's databases. This replicated stored procedure does not modify any of the data (replicated data) that is stored in the replicated table on the remote server. What happens is this: Replication Server knows about this replicated stored procedure; when it is executed, the execution is replicated through the system back to the primary data server. The corresponding stored procedure on the primary data server is executed. The changes made to the data in the primary table due to this stored procedure (that has been replicated to the data server where the replicated table is) will then be replicated out to the replicated table through the normal replication process. Figure 2.2 illustrates this process.

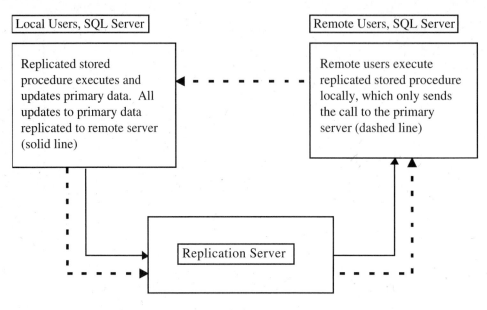

Figure 2.2   Replicated stored procedure -

As a DBA you are used to thinking in terms of adding users, committing transactions, and other activities in the data server that happen more or less immediately. You execute **sp_who** and you expect to see results very quickly or you know the users will be calling to complain about performance. You will enter a new and very different world with Replication Server. The product is asynchronous, which is a big word meaning that things don't happen right away. With the SQL Server, if **sp_who** didn't return results in a very short time, you would be concerned. With Replication Server, you need to develop a great amount of patience. Various events in Replication Server will start and then show no signs of going anywhere for a while. It becomes a very different process, dealing with processes that may or may not be running normally but appear to be dead.

There are many applications where Replication Server is ideal. As discussed previously, there are many reasons to have a reporting or decision support server with a recent copy of the data from the primary (OLTP) server. Such a reporting server does not have to be completely in sync with the primary server; it can, in fact, be one or more days out of sync and still support most if not all the needs of users for decision support queries. In such a system Replication Server is very good. It will relieve you of the burden of dumping and loading all the databases every day. In fact, Replication Server could improve the time delay between the servers from a day or more to a few seconds.

Another ideal use for Replication Server is distributing reference data or other data that is not immediately needed for online processing. For example, the data that represents the sales at the end of the week for each remote office could easily be replicated from each field office to the main office, and the main office could easily replicate the summary results back out to all the field offices. Replication Server in such an application would save you a great deal of time and effort and provide much improved service to your customers.

2.3   What Replication Server Doesn't Do

First, you must again think about the fact that Replication Server does not replicate anything other than transactions affecting one table within one database to another table in the same or in a remote server.

You would think that Replication Server would be a good choice for implementing a hot standby server. You would simply replicate all the tables in one database on the primary SQL Server to a database on the hot standby server. You could repeat this for all the databases on the primary data server. You would think this is appropriate, but you would be wrong. The asynchronous nature of Replication Server is very good in that operations on the primary don't have to wait for anything as they move along. Replication server simply catches the appropriate pieces of the transaction log and takes care of everything else.

But the other side of this approach is that there is a period of time between the transaction committing on the primary data server and the replicated data appearing in the replicated table(s). This means you can't predict exactly when any given replicated transaction will be applied at the replicated table. Hence, if your primary data server fails, you don't have any assurance that the hot standby server is in any given state. The replicated tables will be in sync with the primary within a few seconds perhaps, but the product does not guarantee to deliver all of the transactions to the replicated table(s) in any set amount of time. Although Replication Server will keep track of the pending transactions, you must realize that until the primary data server is restored, there may be transactions that have not made it out of the primary to be passed on by Replication Server.

Another problem with using Replication Server is that it doesn't replicate all the components of a database or a data server. Note again that it only deals with transactions in a database and doesn't deal with system tables at all. Hence, you can't replicate *syslogins* to keep the user logins on a standby system in sync with the primary server. This also means you can't use Replication Server to keep the stored procedures or triggers or other database objects up-to-date between two servers. In fact, you should not have any triggers on the replicated tables that affect the data within the replicated table. All changes happen at the primary table, and only the rows of data within the table are replicated as they are added, deleted, or updated. All of this means you can't really replicate a database or a data server. You can only "replicate" data within user tables.

Replication Server is very good at keeping track of the transactions in the primary database that affect the primary table and passing them along to the replicated table. If the link between the primary and replicated tables is not working, whether it be network problems or something else, Replication Server will store the pending transactions while it waits for the link to be restored. You must understand what this means for users at a remote server that are working from replicated data. Unless the replicated data is read-only data, the users will need to make updates to the data. The basic Replication Server functionality requires that users of replicated data can update that data only by sending a request (or using a replicated stored procedure) to the primary data server, which will update the primary table; the changes made to the primary table will then be replicated out to the remote users (see Figure 2.3).

The whole idea here is that Replication Server will allow for the link going down, so that remote users are not stopped by any one piece of the system. However, the users of the replicated data can't even make the request to update the primary data while the link is down. You will need to somehow allow the users to update their local data; when the link is restored, your applications must remember all the updates that were made, request those same updates to the primary data, and then be able to resolve any problems that come up. Note that while the link is down and the users of the replicated data were making their own local updates, the users of the primary data may well have made updates of their own (see Figure 2.4). You will need to develop a process for resolving the conflicts that will arise between the two sets of updates. Depending on the application, these conflicts could be very costly to your business and very difficult and time consuming to resolve.

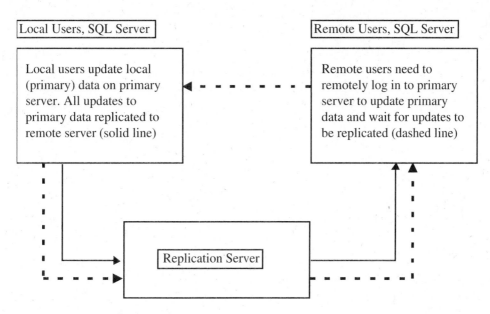

Figure 2.3   Remote users updating primary data -

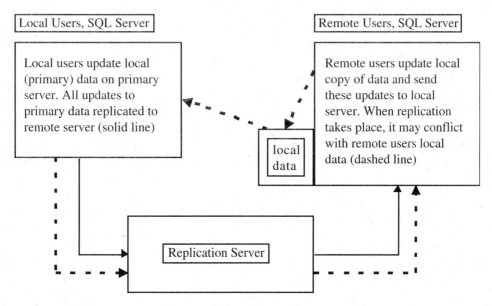

Figure 2.4   Remote users update local data while waiting for replication - - - - - - - - - - - - -

All of this should make you sensitive to what Replication Server will and won't do for you. It is very good at replicating data from one table to another. To completely realize a hot standby or an application with truly distributed databases requires more than Replication Server alone can provide. The product does not perform its replication immediately and therefore is not the final answer for applications that really need to be sure a given transaction has been distributed to all sites before any other processing goes on.

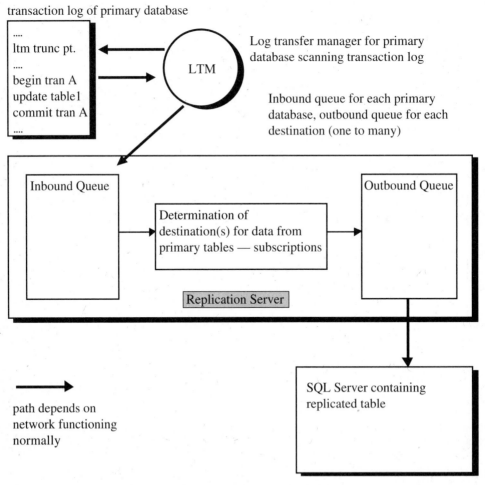

Figure 2.5   Details of replication process -

2.4   Example of the Process of Replicating Data

You need to see the process of replication in detail to appreciate all the components that are involved. We assume that all the components of Replication Server have been installed and configured and are operating normally.

A transaction commits in the database that supports the primary table. The Log Transfer Manager for the database captures the transaction and passes it along to the Replication Server, which places it in a stable queue. The Replication Server reviews all the subscriptions that apply to the replication definition that is defined on the primary table and determines where any and all replicated tables are.

Now, the transaction is passed to another queue to wait to be sent to the SQL Server that supports the database that supports the replicated table, as shown in Figure 2.5. For each destination, the queued transactions are applied to the replicated table just as if any other server user had logged into the server and executed the same commands that were executed against the primary table.

2.5   Configuration Issues

You will need to plan where you will run the various components of Replication Server: the Replication Server itself, the LTM for each database that will serve as a primary database (note that a database can be both primary for some data and a replicated database for other data), and the database that supports the Replication Server.

Replication Server can be installed on the same server machine as the primary database, on the same server machine as the replicated database, or on a server machine that is separate from both. Replication Server can use significant resources, depending on what you are doing with it; therefore, the best plan is to treat it as you would any other production server and give it a separate, dedicated server machine. Further, if the Replication Server is replicating data to and from databases that are all on the LAN, then only one Replication Server is needed with LTMs going out to the various databases involved.

You may have to experiment to see what configuration gives you the best performance among the various servers and server machines that are involved in replication on the LAN. You could run each LTM on the server machine that supports the

SQL Server that contains a primary (or replicated) database, with the Replication Server, its RSSD, and the LTM for the RSSD runs on a dedicated server machine or on a server machine that is not heavily used. However, whether or not the LTM is running on an individual SQL Server, it still has to communicate with the Replication Server over the network, so it may not be any worse to have all the components of the Replication Server running on the one dedicated (or lightly used) server machine. From the DBA point of view, this is much easier to maintain because you will have all the startup scripts, errorlogs, source files, and so on, all on one server machine. With the number of components that you will have for even a moderately complex Replication Server application, you need to plan how you will keep track of them.

As soon as a WAN is involved, you should install a Replication Server at each end. The Replication Server that is installed at each end will then gather or distribute the replicated data to the databases on the LAN at each end of the WAN. The communication between Replication Servers is more efficient than that from the LTM to a Replication Server, so it is better to have the slower and more expensive WAN communication take place between Replication Servers.

Note that you can set up rather complicated routes through Replication Servers. You don't have to have a WAN link directly between each pair of Replication Servers. You can have Replication Server in San Francisco that communicates over a WAN with New York but also needs to replicate data to London. The data to be replicated to London can be sent to the Replication Server in New York, which will then send it on to London.

2.6   Installing Replication Server

The process of installing Replication Server is more involved than installing a SQL Server. Note that you will find installing each component quite easy, but there are many components, each requiring names and ports and server machines. And after all that, you haven't really done anything because you haven't actually started to replicate anything.

To begin with, you will need to create an installation parameters file for each of the Replication Servers. This file specifies which Replication Server in the system of Replication Servers will be the ID Server, the name of the Replication Server, the name of the RSSD, the raw disk partition that will support the stable queues, parameters for the RSSD LTM, and the passwords and user logins for all these processes. Note that the passwords stored in the RSSD for Replication Server are not encrypted, even if you are using System 10 SQL Server. You must apply the appropriate security measures to the installation parameter files and the logins to the Replication Server(s) and LTM(s). If the SQL Server user 'sa' login password is used by the Replication Server and/or the LTM, then anyone who has access to these Replication Server components could gain access to the 'sa' password for the SQL Server(s).

The RSSD needs an LTM of its own because the RSSD holds the information about the associated Replication Server and the replication definitions that have been set up for tables in the SQL Servers involved in replication that are managed by this Replication Server. This information itself is then replicated out to all the other Replication Servers in the system, so that they all know about the replication definitions available on the SQL Servers managed by this Replication Server.

You can now see what the ID Server is all about. The ID Server is the first Replication Server in the system to be installed. The ID Server must be running when any other Replication Server is added to the system and whenever a database or a route between Replication Servers is added, because the ID Server keeps track of all the Replication Servers, databases, and routes in the entire system. Note that the ID Server generates unique numbers to identify each of these components of the Replication Server System. There can only be one ID Server in the system.

You should create the RSSD database manually on server devices of your own choosing. The configuration file can be set up so that the RSSD is created automatically, but then the RSSD will be created on the master device, and you don't want that.

The raw disk partition that will support the stable queues must be chosen carefully. You must think about how much space you will need to hold the expected transaction volume during any downtime for the Replication Server.

Along with all this, you must add entries to the interfaces file for the Replication Server that you are installing, and you must add the LTM associated with the RSSD for the Replication Server.

Once the installation parameters file is complete, you run rs_install, which actually installs and starts the Replication Server. It also generates the scripts needed to start up the Replication Server and the RSSD LTM and creates the errorlog files for each.

This process must be repeated for each Replication Server that you install. At this point, you would also define any routes needed between the Replication Servers that you have installed. Recall that these routes define what a Replication Server does with transactions that are sent to it but that are meant for another Replication Server. Note that the process of creating a route is asynchronous; again, that means it doesn't complete immediately. It may take some time before you can tell if the route(s) were created successfully or ran into an error condition.

You must now create a database parameters file for each database that will participate in the replication process. Each database that contains a primary or replicated table must have a parameters file. This file specifies which Replication Server manages the database, the name of the SQL Server that manages the database, the name of the database, and the various users and passwords needed for these components to communicate with each other. The database parameters file also includes information about the LTM that will read the transaction log of the database. If the database contains only replicated data (tables) and will not be initiating any replicated stored procedures, you don't have to create an LTM for it. Each LTM that is created for a database will need an entry in the interfaces file. Now, you can run rs_setup_db, which will load stored procedures into the database so that it can participate in the replication process, create the link between the database and the specified Replication Server, create scripts to start the LTM for the database, and start the LTM running.

Once you have executed rs_setup_db, you have started the process of the LTM scanning the transaction log of the database, looking for committed transactions to pass along to the Replication Server. This occurs even though you have not told the Replication Server to replicate anything yet, but the LTM doesn't know that and will simply transfer the transaction log records to the Replication Server. This has implications for the transaction log filling, and so on. See Section 2.9, "How Replication Server Links with SQL Servers."

2.7   Creating a Subscription

You now start defining what it is that will be replicated. In the Replication Server itself you will create a replication definition that defines what part of the primary table is available for replication; see Figure 2.6.

You can look at the replication definition as a form of security on the primary table. Only the columns that are in the replication definition are available to be sent to replicated tables. The replication definition requires the base datatypes of each column that will be eligible for replication. This can be tedious for you because any user-defined datatypes must be translated to the underlying datatypes. The replication definition also requires that you specify the primary key for the primary table; if the primary table doesn't have a primary key, you have to create one before you can complete the replication definition. The replication definition that you create is stored in the RSSD for the Replication Server and is then replicated out to all the other Replication Servers, so that they all know that this table in this database is available as a source for replication.

You must now create the table that will hold the replicated data. This table must have columns that match those of the replication definition on the primary table.

Now you can create a subscription in the Replication Server that manages the database that will hold the replicated table. When you create a subscription, you refer to an existing replication definition; you can use a where clause to select a subset of the rows of the primary table to be replicated. You must have set up the replication definition to allow this, using the searchable columns syntax of the **create replication definition** command.

Once the subscription is defined, it needs to be "materialized," which simply means populating the replicated tables with data from the primary table. Until this process is complete, the subscription will not be finished. There are several methods of materializing a subscription. The default method is to simply have Replication Server send all the rows of the primary table to the replicated table. For very large tables, this is not always the best choice, and you may want to bulk copy the data between primary and replicated tables. The method of materialization is specified in the **create subscription** command.

Once the process of materialization of the subscription is complete, the normal process of replication should begin. This means that as soon as there is a committed transaction in the transaction log of the primary table's database, the transaction should be captured by the LTM and passed to the Replication Server. The Replication Server will log in to the SQL Server that has the replicated table and will apply the transactions by executing the appropriate insert, update, or delete statements just as they were executed against the primary table.

At this point you are replicating. Note that you need to repeat (replicate?) this process of defining a subscription for each and every primary table, and you need to repeat the process of subscribing for each and every replicated table. If the data in one primary table is to be replicated to five different replicated tables, then you must define the replication definition once but you must create the subscription five times.

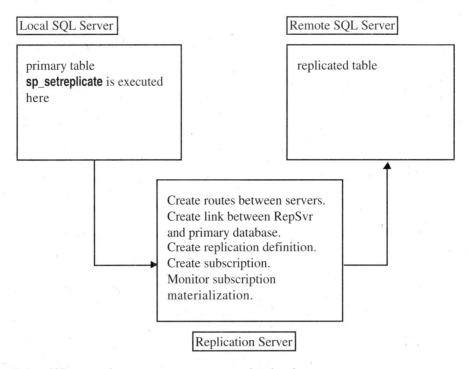

Local SQL Server

primary table
sp_setreplicate is executed
here

Remote SQL Server

replicated table

Create routes between servers.
Create link between RepSvr
and primary database.
Create replication definition.
Create subscription.
Monitor subscription
materialization.

Replication Server

Figure 2.6   Where various components are maintained- -

2.8   Users and Passwords

Replication Server consists of several components; for any practical installation, there will be multiple instances of each component. Each component has to interact with the others through a user login and password. When one Replication Server needs to pass along transactions to the next Replication Server on the route, it will log in and use a password that you specified when installing. Note that this means there are a lot of passwords and users floating around. More important to you is the fact that some of these components need the server user 'sa' password in order to do their job, such as the Replication Server itself when it needs to log in to the SQL Server that supports the RSSD of the Replication Server. This means that the 'sa' password is being stored at multiple locations around your database system. When you need to change the 'sa' password, you need to remember all these locations to prevent any failures among the many components of the Replication Server. Note that while using SQL Server System 10 will get you password encryption, Replication Server does not encrypt the passwords even though the product will work between 4.9.x and System 10 SQL Servers.

A good example of the confusion that can be generated by all this is the fact that while the passwords for user logins used by the Replication Server are stored in the RSSD, the passwords for the users used by the LTM are stored in the LTM configuration file that is used when the LTM starts up. To change one of these passwords for the Replication Server, you change entries in a table in the RSSD, but for the LTM, you have to change the configuration file and then restart the LTM.

;-)

It's late at night, do you know who is looking at your LTM configuration files? Do you know what the password is for the maintenance user for Replication Server 2 of 4? Can you recall how to find out the password or the user login for the LTM that monitors the primary data server? These are all questions that will come up while you are setting up the system and especially when something goes wrong. You must get on top of these issues early by setting up standards for naming components and user logins, and so on.

2.9 How Replication Server Links with SQL Servers

The Log Transfer Manager is the primary link between the Replication Server and the primary database. The LTM scans the transaction log of the database, looking for transactions of interest to the associated Replication Server. The LTM needs to make sure it doesn't miss any transactions, so it places a marker, called an LTM truncation point, in the transaction log. The LTM truncation point marks how far the LTM got through the transaction log the last time it was scanning the transaction log. You care about this because the database transaction log can't be truncated beyond the LTM truncation point. This makes sense because you don't want to truncate the transaction log beyond the LTM truncation point or else the process of replication would be broken. But, you need to realize the implications for your SQL Server that houses the primary database. Suppose the Replication Server is unavailable, for whatever reason. This means the LTM can't return anything from the database transaction log, so the LTM stops which means the LTM truncation point in the database transaction log stops moving. This has the same effect as an open transaction in the transaction log. Even if you are dumping the transaction log regularly, it continues to fill, and eventually you will get 1105 errors (with System 10 and thresholds you would get suspended transactions, see Chapter 14). Once that happens, the database is effectively lost because it can't write to the transaction log. Note that this problem can also come up if the Replication Server stable device fills up. If another Replication Server on the route from the local Replication Server has a problem or the network between the Replication Servers goes down, the transactions for that Replication Server begin to pile up on the stable device in the local Replication Server. If the stable device fills up, it can't accept any transactions from any of the LTMs that are connected to the local Replication Server, and you get the same effect of filling the transaction log in the SQL Server.

At this point you must get the Replication Server running again so that it can receive transactions from the LTM and so that the LTM truncation point can move through the SQL Server transaction log. You would then need to dump the transaction log; if that is successful, the whole operation can resume. If you can't get Replication Server running soon enough, you must break the replication process by turning off the LTM truncation point. The command for this is shown below:

```
use <database_name>

go

dbcc settrunc(ltm, ignore)

go
```

Now the LTM truncation point is ignored and the SQL Server can truncate the transaction log past the LTM truncation point. At the same time, this also means the Replication Server can't tell how many transactions have been lost, so it will mark the subscriptions to the primary table in the server as invalid. You will have to restore the LTM truncation point in the SQL Server by using dbcc settrunc(ltm, valid). Then you must either rematerialize each subscription that is based on tables in this SQL Server or run rs_subcmp, which compares the primary and replicated tables row by row and brings the replicated table into agreement with the primary.

Once you have executed rs_setup_db to link a database with a Replication Server, the LTM truncation point is set as valid in the transaction log for the database that supports the primary table, and the database is at risk of having the transaction log fill because of a stuck LTM truncation point. Anytime you are having trouble truncating a transaction log, remember to check the LTM truncation point. Even if *you* haven't set up replication, someone else may have. If nothing else is working, check the LTM truncation point for the database.

2.10 Affects on Existing and New Applications

Using Replication Server with an existing application requires a great deal of planning. Replication Server is based on replicating the transactions of one database. Depending on how your application works, you may need to have data in one database in sync with data in another database. Using Replication Server to copy the data to a remote server and allowing users to run the application against this copy of the primary data may run into trouble if all the tables in all the databases are not in the required state, as they would be on the primary data server. The latency between the time that changes are made to the primary data and when those changes appear at the replicated tables may also cause problems. As we said, users will want to update a local copy of the application's data, and the whole idea of having the data closer to the users is to prevent downtime at a remote site causing downtime at the user's site; however, their updates to their local, replicated data need to be reconciled with the primary data at some point. This process of reconciliation is not automated and is not part of the Replication Server product. You will need to plan for these situations, and you may find it is harder to modify an existing application than it would be to simply start fresh.

Overall, you need to review your applications and decide if you can use Replication Server effectively. If possible, you should start planning for Replication Server in any new applications you are currently developing. It is much easier to build in the logical and physical design needed to take full advantage of Replication Server while the application is in the early stages of development. You should clearly identify what data needs to be replicated; make sure you minimize the number of tables to be replicated and place them all in one database. You also need to consider the implications of latency on your business, since local users will see changes to the data before the remote users do.

2.11 Capacity Planning

As with all the other parts of your database system, Replication Server takes up resources. You need to plan ahead to support the installation and growth of your replicated data system.

You will need space for the source files for the product as well as room for the configuration files and errorlogs of the Replication Server and the LTMs. The biggest resource you must provide is the stable device, which is a raw disk partition that supports the stable queues of the Replication Server. You must allow room for the stable queues of each Replication Server and try to estimate the volume of transactions and the size of each transaction in order to estimate the required disk space for the stable device. You need enough disk space to store all the transactions that you expect to come through the Replication Server during the longest period of SQL Server downtime the Replication Server is expected to carry you through. Also, note that each Replication Server requires an RSSD, which is a database in a SQL Server. If, as recommended previously, you place one Replication Server and all its associated LTMs on one dedicated server machine, you must install a SQL Server on that server machine. Whether or not the RSSD is part of a dedicated SQL Server on a dedicated server machine, the RSSD must be dumped and the transaction log must be dumped as well, just like any other database that you must be prepared to recover in the event of failure.

You will also need more CPU cycles to support Replication Server. Even with a dedicated Replication Server machine, the LTMs log in to the SQL Server supporting the primary table and scan the transaction log, which takes away from whatever else the server machine is doing. And, as with all of this, you will need the people to design, install, configure, initialize, maintain, and troubleshoot this complex product. You will need to train all the persons that will need to start up and recover all the components of the Replication Server. Just from this overview, it should be apparent that you can't just buy the product, install it, and leave it alone.

2.12 Administration Using Replication Server Manager

Once you have all the components of Replication Server up and running, you need to think about administration of all these different pieces. You will have to check that all the components are running, you should check the errorlogs of all the components regularly, and you will need a startup script for each component. Further, you need to remember what piece is executed on which machine, which is an argument for putting all the components of the local Replication Server on one dedicated server machine, as shown in Figure 2.7.

To help you with the task of Replication Server administration is another piece of the product, Replication Server Manager. This product provides a graphical display of the status of each Replication Server, LTM, route between Replication Servers, partitions used for stable queue storage, and connection between a Replication Server and a database, as well as the status of each SQL Server that supports a primary or replicated table. This display is very helpful in that components that are functioning normally appear as green, and the icon for each component of the Replication Server system will turn red if it fails. During normal operation, you can reduce this whole display to a single icon. The icon will change color if anything fails, alerting you to open the window and determine the components that are causing the problem. From there, you can examine the errorlog(s) of the components involved and enter commands for that component. Replication Server Manager also allows you to group icons for components into summary icons to simplify the process of troubleshooting the system.

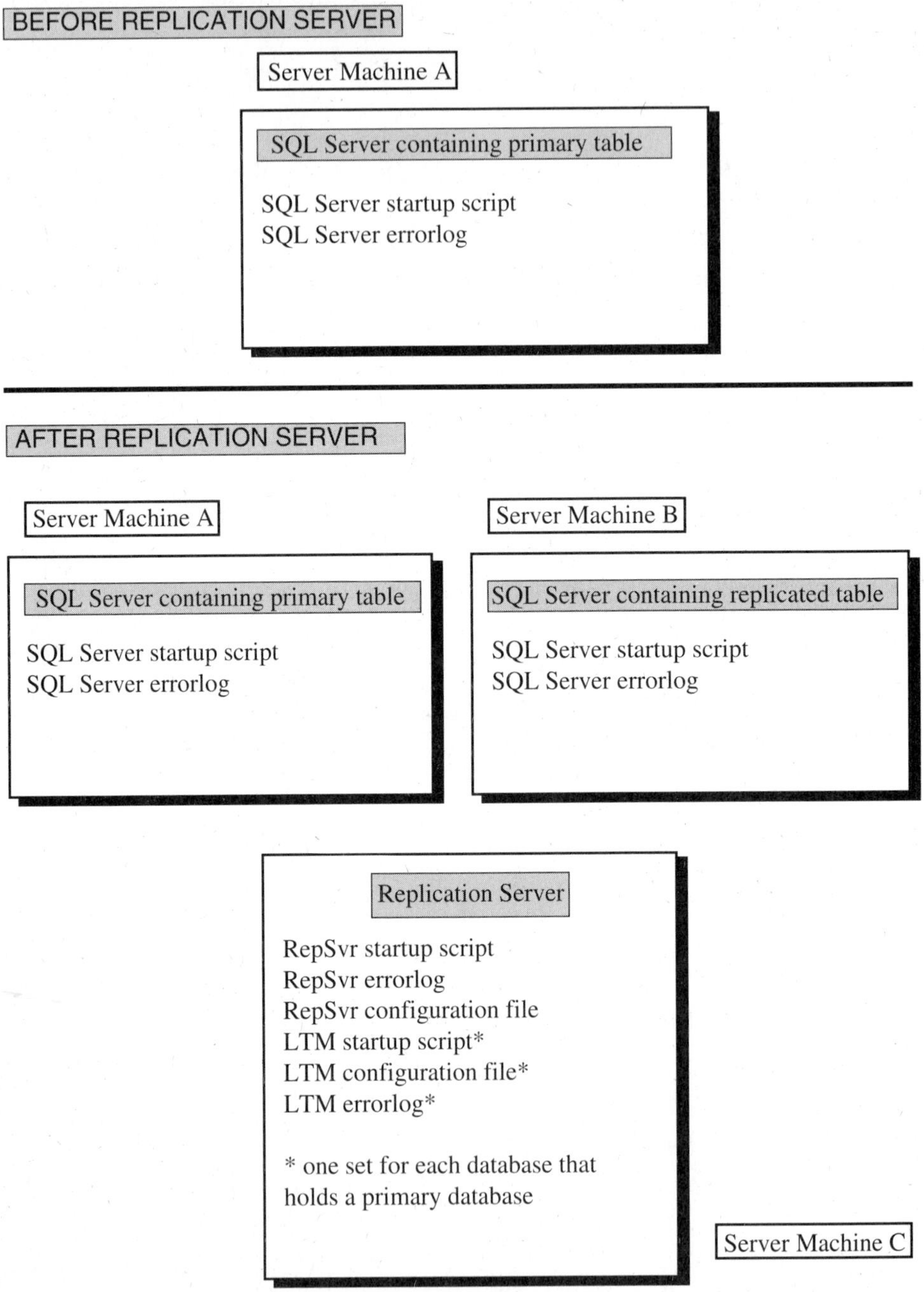

BEFORE REPLICATION SERVER

Server Machine A

SQL Server containing primary table

SQL Server startup script
SQL Server errorlog

AFTER REPLICATION SERVER

Server Machine A

SQL Server containing primary table

SQL Server startup script
SQL Server errorlog

Server Machine B

SQL Server containing replicated table

SQL Server startup script
SQL Server errorlog

Replication Server

RepSvr startup script
RepSvr errorlog
RepSvr configuration file
LTM startup script*
LTM configuration file*
LTM errorlog*

* one set for each database that
holds a primary database

Server Machine C

Figure 2.7   Replication server components and administration- - - - - - - - - - - - - - - - - - -

Another very interesting feature of Replication Server Manager is that it will create and monitor what is called a "heartbeat." At a regular interval, a message is sent from the primary database to the replicated database; Replication Server Manager measures the time it takes and displays a chart of this time delay over time. This is a very good way to tell that replication is indeed functioning and how long the latency is between a change to the primary data and the same change being applied to the replicated table.

You need to lay out a plan for what you will do when (not if) a Replication Server failure causes a SQL Server transaction log to fill up. You need a detailed plan, down to the exact syntax of the commands, where they are to be executed and in what order. Although you may be a fan of Replication Server and therefore revel in its many idiosyncrasies, not everyone that has to deal with it will share your obsession. All of your disaster recovery plans must be clear and understandable by the other DBAs on the team.

You not only need to plan for these contingencies, but you must also test them. You must consider the impacts these failures will have. For example, consider a table of 100,000 rows being replicated from San Francisco to New York. For whatever reason, the replication has to be broken and you will need to restart it. You need to determine the best way to restart the replication and how long it will take. The users of the replicated data will want to know as well. You could truncate the replicated table, drop the subscription and resubscribe, but how long will it take before all 100,000 rows are at the replicated table? You could use the rs_subcmp utility, but that will have to compare each and every row of the primary table to the replicated table. The only way to know what to do is to test both options. Keep track of the time it takes to perform the original subscription and try rs_subcmp for the same table. This sort of failure testing should be part of your project plan for installing Replication Server. Certainly, you may need to do this testing in a development environment since the users don't want you to experiment with their 100,000 rows of data. This again points to the process of capacity planning. To do this sort of testing in a meaningful way, you would need to have a development server machine on each end of the same (or similar) network that the production Replication Servers will use. You need to recreate the production Replication Server system in the development environment, and that takes significant hardware and network resources. Until you time the process of subscribing (you may need to time all four methods of materializing the subscription), you don't have a credible disaster recovery plan.

If you are supporting a Replication Server system where the remote users can update their local copy of the replicated data, how will you resolve the conflicts that will arise between their local updates and those made at the primary site? This problem will only grow during a disaster because the number of updates made at the remote site will grow, and as time moves along, those remote updates are being made on older and older data. You must have a plan for these situations. All of this takes time and resources.

2.13 Failure Modes

The Replication Server product is designed to tolerate and recover from many system failures. Specifically, if the network between components fails or if a SQL Server involved with replication is not available, the Replication Server can detect these situations and will wait until the network is repaired, at which time replication will continue. In the case of the SQL Server that holds the replicated table being unavailable, the transactions that have accumulated in the Replication Server will be forwarded to the replicated table. During this time, the stable queue that holds transactions that are destined for the SQL Server that is down will fill up. If it runs out of room, the SQL Server that holds the primary table won't be able to truncate its transaction log and may suffer 1105 errors. Replication Server does not automatically handle this error condition.

The Replication Server can automatically resume replication with no loss of transactions for server machine crashes as long as the disks supporting Replication Server are not involved—for example, network failures, SQL Server crashes that don't result in losing transactions from the transaction log, and Replication Server or LTM shutdown (not crash).

You also need to know that there are several situations from which Replication Server will not automatically recover. These include interfaces file problems, a full stable device, a stable device failure, truncation of the transaction log for the database containing the primary table, and errors that do result in the loss of transactions from the transaction log.

Errors from the SQL Server that holds the replicated table are not automatically handled by Replication Server. For example, if the attempt by the Replication Server to insert a row into the replicated table resulted in a SQL Server message about duplicate entries, the default action would be to suspend the connection between the Replication Server and the SQL Server. This means no further replication would go on until the connection was resumed manually. When the connection is resumed, the Replication Server will again try to execute the transaction. Hence, if you can deduce and cure the problem with the SQL Server, then Replication Server will handle the details of reapplying the transaction once you resume the connection.

If you don't want the connection suspended when the SQL Server that holds the replicated table returns an error, you can define an Error Class that will be associated with a connection. Then, depending on the action you specify, the Replication Server will retry, ignore, or the transaction will be placed into the Replication Server exceptions log where it will remain until you manually intervene. Understand that if you tell Replication Server to ignore SQL Server errors, you can't be sure of the data integrity on the replicated table because some transactions were not applied and others were.

Finally, you need to think about what to do if the Replication Server itself crashes. Depending on what it was doing at the time of the crash, you may have to recreate replication definitions, subscriptions, or any other item that was being processed. Further, you may find various components of the system in an indeterminate state, that is, it won't be obvious where the errors are. You will have to check the errorlog for each component to determine what the impact of the crash is.

2.14 Function Strings

The Replication Server product has been created to be very flexible. As such, it has been designed so that you can use it to interface with almost any other vendor's database. The way this is done is by writing a custom LTM. Note that writing your own LTM is no small effort. Recall that the LTM scans the transaction log of the primary SQL Server and passes the relevant transactions on to the Replication Server. The Replication Server looks up the subscriptions to the replication definition defined on the primary table and determines where the replicated tables are. The Replication Server then logs into the SQL Server that holds the replicated table and applies the transactions that were first applied to the primary table.

This process assumes that the primary and replicated tables are both stored in SQL Servers. If this is not the case, then you need to write your own LTM that can somehow interface with whatever database holds the primary data, detect changes to that data, and convert that into a set of commands (insert, update, delete, select) that can be passed to the Replication Server. Next, depending on the database that stores the replicated database, you need to write commands that will convert what the Replication Server sends (select, insert, update, delete) into commands that perform the appropriate commands in the target database. Here is where function strings come in. For each replication definition, there will be associated function strings. If you do not define these function strings, the defaults will be used. For example, if the Replication Server passes an insert command to the target SQL Server, then the default function string for insert will be the Transact-SQL **insert** command. If the database that holds the replicated table is another type of database, you need to redefine the function insert (for this one replication definition) so that it is converted into the proper commands to insert the data into the replicated table.

The fact that these function strings must be defined for each replication subscription may seem tedious, but the benefit is that one replication definition, based on the type of database that holds the primary table, can be subscribed to by any and all types of target database, since each target will have its own subscription and therefore its own set of function strings.

Chapter 3

Installation of SQL Server from Scratch

The process of installing an SQL Server is very simple if done properly. Part of the mystery of installing a server is that for a normal site you don't install the server very often. When you do need to install a server, it has often been a long time since you last installed one. The documentation that is supplied with the product is very good, but it assumes you have the disks installed and partitioned before you start. You also need to realize that the documentation stops after the very basic installation is done. We will cover the more detailed and complex real-world process of installing a server and configuring it for use.

We cover the preparatory work that must be done before installation begins and then go over the output of a sybconfig (sybinit for System 10) session for installation of both a 4.9.x server and a System 10 server. The differences are not great, but it is good to see what the process looks like before you begin. We discuss the following topics:

3.1	Preparing for Installation
3.2	sybconfig for SQL Server 4.9.x
3.3	sybinit for SQL Server System 10
3.4	Post sybconfig (sybinit for System 10)
3.5	sybconfig (sybinit for System 10) Errors

You need to understand that sybconfig (sybinit for System 10) can be rerun if you make a mistake or change your mind. However, you also need to realize that sybconfig (sybinit for System 10) completely wipes out any and all data regarding any server that was previously installed on the raw partitions where sybconfig is creating the master device (sybinit for System 10 and the sysprocsdev and sybsecurity device). You can rerun as often as needed to get it right, but once you are settled on the basic

73

installation of the server, you need to be very careful about running sybconfig (sybinit for System 10) again. Note that you may need to run sybconfig (sybinit for System 10) again to change the configuration of the server, but you must realize that by choosing the wrong options in the program, you can wipe out the existing server.

3.1 Preparing for Installation

Before you can begin the actual installation of a Sybase SQL Server you must prepare the server machine. This involves the steps listed in Table 3.1. We will discuss each of these steps:

Table 3.1   Checklist for Server Installation Preparation

Obtain and Read the *Installation Guide*, Release Notes, and Administration Supplement
Verify Sybase Technical Support Arrangements
Verify Server Machine SA Support
Inform Users and Management
Establish su Privileges
Create a Servermap
Complete the Server Machine Installation
Verify Sybase Setting
Load SQL Server Product Set Files
Run sybconfig (sybinit for System 10)

Obtain and Read the Installation Guide, Release Notes, and Administration Supplement

Before you do anything else, you absolutely must order, obtain, and read the *Sybase SQL Server Installation Guide*, Release Notes, and the System Administration Guide Supplement that should have been included when you ordered the product. These documents contain important information that is specific to the hardware and operating system platform you will be using to support SQL Server. These documents are not shipped with every update to the SQL Server, so make sure you keep these documents available at all times. If you are supporting servers on multiple platforms, you need to build up a small library of installation guides and the like for each SQL Server version on each platform and operating system

;-)   If you are a real DBA, you'll actually find reading these documents inter-
       esting and entertaining. The information they contain is what makes you
       marketable, and the lack thereof is what causes your fellow DBAs to take
       a sick day whenever a server needs to be installed. You will also find that
       these documents are as valuable as gold-pressed latinum, that is, seem-
       ingly worthless now but, trust me, they will be very valuable in the future.
       You should lock them up somewhere since they are specific to the plat-
       form and you will need them in the event of a disaster that requires a com-
       plete server installation. Do not skip this step. You will be sorry. The tips in
       these documents will make you a guru without really trying.

Verify Sybase Technical Support Arrangements

Verify what level of support you have with Sybase Technical Support. You must not wait until your installation has gone sour to find out the bean-counters didn't pay for Technical Support. If you don't have 24 hour 7 day a week support, you should con-sider the wisdom of installing during off-hours unless you can wait until the next day to get support. Before beginning the installation, you should call Sybase Technical Support and verify that they know about your support arrangements as well. You should verify that all the proper persons in your organization are known to Sybase Technical Support as persons authorized to call in cases and verify that your current phone and fax numbers are accurate as known to Sybase.

Verify Server Machine SA Support

You must verify that you have the server machine SA support you need. Verify that there is an SA assigned to support your server machine and that the person is aware of the impending server installation. Be nice to this person. Discuss your needs well ahead of time. From reading the installation guides discussed above, you should be able to point out what specific UNIX kernel parameters should be set up and verified to support SQL Server. Ask the SA person about operating system patches, which are needed—are they readily available? and is all the hardware installed and config-ured? Make sure you give the SA person sufficient lead time to fix any problems before you begin installation. Note that you may be both the DBA and the SA person for this server machine. That is fine, but make sure you understand everything you will need for this server installation. Perhaps you know some other SA persons that are more experienced with the hardware and especially with installing SQL Server on the platform. If so, you should query them now before you are stuck. Further, you must verify what sort of arrangements have been made for technical support from the hardware/software vendors supplying the platform you are installing on. This should include any third-party hardware and/or software that needs to be operational to support the SQL Server. An example of this is SQL BackTrack, a third-party software product that supplies logical and physical backup and recovery of database objects. If you need to have such a product installed and operational as part of the server installation, you must clarify the technical support arrangements for the product.

;-)   Be nice to the server machine SA person(s) and all the people you deal with in Technical Support. Making cookies works well. Visit them if at all possible and distribute the cookies. Call it a "Goodwill Tour." It works. They are so accustomed to being ignored and/or treated like dirt that they will be stunned by your kindness. They will remember and they will help you when your ass is out over the edge and the CIO is perched in your cubicle cawing "when will the server be up, when will the server be up..."

;-)   For reasons best known to themselves, the managers of your department, without involving any technical person, decide that moving to a new hardware platform will improve the throughput of your business applications by 1000 percent (10x). They make this decision with no benchmarks or other testing of any kind. The hardware arrives and you are told to install the SQL Server on all machines. There are only two SA persons in your organization that are experienced with this new hardware platform. One of them is going to Tokyo next week to install machines for your company. The other will be on vacation for two weeks a week from now. You have been given a deadline two weeks from now to have all four new machines installed and configured with SQL Servers installed and all user databases created and loaded. Don't you wish you had a window office so you could make decisions like this? Make sure you have the SA support you need.

Inform Users and Management

Make sure your users and your management know how long the server installation will take and what the possible problems may be. If you are installing a new server on the same hardware and operating system as other servers you have installed before, you can make promises. Don't underestimate the time needed for installing and testing a new server on either a new hardware or operating system platform. In either case, you should identify or have someone else identify a test plan that will provide some objective way of determining that the newly installed server is doing what it was installed to do. This may involve running business applications against the new server for some period of time before the business switches to the new server. If the new server will be supporting an existing application, you need to support both the old and new servers through the installation and testing of the new server.

Establish su Privileges

Make sure you have su privilege on the server machine or that someone who does will be available to you throughout the server installation process. Note that due to the way the sybconfig (sybinit for System 10) software functions, you must be able to perform su - sybase successfully on the server machine. Each of the DBAs that will support the server must have these privileges.

Create a Servermap

You should create a servermap for the server machine. This servermap will be filled in as you install the server and create the user databases. Therefore, the servermap at this point will consist of only the physical disks, which controllers they are attached to, their partitions, the size of each partition, and which will be server devices and which will be mirrors. This information is very useful during installation to verify that the master device and the mirror of the master device are on different physical disks and preferably on different controllers.

Complete the Server Machine Installation

Before you can begin the installation of a server, you need to complete the tasks of installing the server machine, connecting the server machine to the network, installing the physical disks, and partitioning the physical disks that will support server devices. The specific outputs shown below are taken from a SunOS environment. The steps needed are shown in Table 3.2.

Table 3.2   Server Machine Installation Checklist

Install server machine
Check installed disks
Partition disks
Compute size of partitions for server devices
Verify file system availability
Verify permissions on devices and /dba/sybase directory

Install server machine

The first steps are, of course, to install the server machine. You need to have the server machine installed and checked out by the server machine SA. You also need to ensure that the server machine is on the network and that it can communicate with the other server machines in your database system. Finally, the physical disks must be installed. As a part of your capacity planning effort, you should have a very clear idea of how many physical disks are required for the server devices and file systems needed to support the server you will be installing.

Check installed disks

Check that all the disks you think are installed are known to the server machine. You need to become superuser (root) and execute the format command. This is one of the reasons that each DBA must have su privilege on all the server machines. Note that you must not be creative with the format command. Further, you should inform the server machine SA that you need the output of the format command (and others, as we shall see) and that you intend to execute these commands as you need to. If the server machine SA objects, then that person will have to supply these outputs when-ever you need them. After executing the format command, exit from it by typing control-D (^D); don't try anything else with the format command.

The output of the format command tells you three things. First, the names of all the physical disks that the server machine is aware of. Second, which physical disks are attached to which controllers. This information is vital to properly spreading data-base segments over controllers. Third, how many physical disks are attached to any one controller. As discussed previously, you must determine the maximum number of physical disks that can be attached to one controller on your particular hardware platform before I/O bottlenecks are created. For the Sun machine used here, the max-imum number of physical disks that should be attached to one controller is four. In the output shown below the server machine is machine1.

After becoming the root user via the su command and running the format command, you see the output that displays each of the physical disks and the controller it is attached to. Looking at the output for one physical disk

```
0. sd0 at esp0 slave 24
        sd0: <SUN0424 STD cyl 1151 alt 2 hd 9 sec 80>
```

we see that the first physical disk is sd0 and that it is attached to controller esp0. The second line is information about the physical disk sd0. From looking at the entire output of the format command, we see that there are 12 physical disks (sd0 through sd11) and three controllers (esp0, esp1, esp2), and that there are four physical disks attached to each controller.

```
machine1% su
Password:
machine1% format
Searching for disks...done

AVAILABLE DISK SELECTIONS:
        0. sd0 at esp0 slave 24
            sd0: <SUN0424 STD cyl 1151 alt 2 hd 9 sec 80>
        1. sd1 at esp0 slave 8
            sd1: <FALCON 2.1GB-ST42100N cyl 2098 alt 2 hd
            15 sec 117>
```

```
 2. sd2 at esp0 slave 16
    sd2: <Micropolis 1598-15 cyl 1892 alt 3 hd 15
    sec 71>
 3. sd3 at esp0 slave 0
    sd3: <ANDATACO 120S5 Seagate ST41200N cyl
     1929 alt 2 hd 15 sec 69>
 4. sd4 at esp1 slave 24
    sd4: <FALCON 2.4GB-ST12400N cyl 2626 alt 2 hd
    19 sec 84>
 5. sd5 at esp1 slave 8
    sd5: <FALCON 2.4GB-ST12400N cyl 2626 alt 2 hd
    19 sec 84>
 6. sd6 at esp1 slave 16
    sd6: <FALCON 2.4GB-ST12400N cyl 2626 alt 2 hd
   19 sec 84>
 7. sd7 at esp1 slave 0
    sd7: <FALCON 2.4GB-ST12400N cyl 2626 alt 2 hd
    19 sec 84>
 8. sd8 at esp2 slave 24
    sd8: <FALCON 2.4GB-ST12400N cyl 2626 alt 2 hd
    19 sec 84>
 9. sd9 at esp2 slave 8
    sd9: <FALCON 2.4GB-ST12400N cyl 2626 alt 2 hd
    19 sec 84>
10. sd10 at esp2 slave 16
    sd10: <FALCON 2.4GB-ST12400N cyl 2626 alt 2
    hd 19 sec 84>
11. sd11 at esp2 slave 0
    sd11: <FALCON 2.4GB-ST12400N cyl 2626 alt 2
    hd 19 sec 84>
Specify disk (enter its number): ^D
```

Partition disks

Once you have verified the physical disks and controllers on the server machine, you must decide which physical disks will be used for server devices, mirrors of server devices, and file systems. As discussed in Chapter 1, as part of your standard environment you should apply your standard disk partitioning to all of the physical disks that will support server devices and the mirrors of server devices. The physical disks that will support file systems are partitioned as needed for the individual file systems. You must work with the server machine SA to work out the partitioning for file system disks.

The standard disk partitioning for physical disks that support server devices or their mirrors has been presented previously. In summary, it is as follows:

- Assign cylinder 0 of the physical disk to partition 'a' and never use partition 'a.' Have the server machine SA change the permissions on the files that control partition 'a' (/dev/ *<disk_name>*a and /dev/r*<disk_name>*a) so that UNIX user 'dba' can't access them.

- Assign enough cylinders to partition 'h' to provide 30 MB of space. You won't be able to assign exactly 30 MB but get as close as you can.

- Assign 1/5 of the remaining disk space to each of the partitions 'b,' 'd,' 'e,' 'f,' 'g'—the space given to each partition should be identical. If needed to create five equal partitions, add any leftover space to partition 'h.'

- Don't use partition 'c' at all. Have the server machine SA change the permissions on the files that control the 'c' partition so that UNIX user 'dba' can't access the 'c' partition.

- Have the server machine SA change the ownership of all files that control the raw partitions of physical disks that will support server devices to UNIX user 'dba'— except for partitions 'a' and 'c.' Note that the need to change file permissions to access disk partitions and file systems is another reason the DBA must be able to become superuser (root) on the server machine.

Compute size of partitions for server devices

Once you have the disks partitioned, check each partition to determine the exact size of each partition that you will be using to support server devices. Execute the dkinfo command for each physical disk that will support server devices. The output of the dkinfo command for one physical disk is shown below. For each partition that will support a server device, convert the number of sectors to megabytes. The number of megabytes is then rounded down to the nearest whole number and then converted into the equivalent number of 2K pages that you need to use when creating the server device on the partition by means of the **disk init** command. This is another advantage of establishing and applying a standard disk partitioning scheme. Most of the partitions will be the same size, greatly reducing the number of times you need to convert the number of sectors to megabytes.

```
machine1 % dkinfo sd3
sd3: SCSI CCS controller at addr f8800000, unit # 0
1929 cylinders 15 heads 69 sectors/track
a: 1035 sectors (1 cyls)
   starting cylinder 0
b: 387090 sectors (374 cyls)
   starting cylinder 1
c: 1996515 sectors (1929 cyls)
   starting cylinder 0
d: 387090 sectors (374 cyls)
   starting cylinder 375
e: 387090 sectors (374 cyls)
   starting cylinder 749
f: 387090 sectors (374 cyls)
   starting cylinder 1123
g: 387090 sectors (374 cyls)
   starting cylinder 1497
h: 60030 sectors (58 cyls)
   starting cylinder 1871
```

Note that you are only concerned with determining the size of partitions that will support server devices. As discussed in Chapter 6, you can greatly simplify your life by assigning whole physical disks to server devices and other whole physical disks to supporting the mirrors or server devices. Still, you only need to determine the exact size of a partition that will support a server device.

For this example, using physical disk sd3, the partitions that will be used to support server devices are partitions 'b,' 'd,' 'e,' 'f,' 'g,' all of which have 387090 sectors, and partition 'h,' which has 60030 sectors. You convert the number of sectors to the size of the partition in bytes by multiplying the number of sectors by 512 bytes per sector (this value is for the SunOS environment—verify the correct value for your environment). Once you have the partition size in bytes, use that value for two things. First, convert the partition size in bytes to megabytes by dividing the partition size in bytes by 1024 * 1024, which is one MB. You don't want to divide by one million. Second, convert the partition size in bytes to the equivalent number of 2K pages. One data page for SQL Server running in the SunOS environment is 2048 bytes or 2K. Again, you must verify the size of a data page in bytes for the server running on your specific environment.

For the two specific partition sizes of our example, the numbers work out like this.

sectors	# of bytes	MB	2K pages
387090	198190080	189.01	96772.5
60030	30735360	29.31	15007.5

# of bytes = sectors * 512 (bytes/sector for SunOS)

MB = # of bytes / 1024 * 1024 (bytes per MB)

2K pages = # of bytes / 2048 (bytes/data page for SQL Server for SunOS)

Now, recall from Chapter 4 that there are several things about physical disk partitions and server devices that come up now. You can have only one server device assigned to one physical disk partition. If you assign a 30-MB server device to a 500-MB partition, you are wasting 470 MB of disk space. That is why you need to have a small physical partition of 30 MB for the master device.

For a System 10 SQL Server, you need to have the master device, the sysprocsdev device, and the sybsecurity device on separate server devices; all three of these devices should be around 30 MB. You will need to provide small partitions for all three of these devices, preferably on different physical disks.

Once you have computed the actual size of each partition, you should round this size down to the nearest whole number of megabytes. You don't want to execute **disk init** with a size that is anything other than a whole number of megabytes. You will need to execute **disk init** later on for each server device you need to support the server and the databases, except for the master device. The master device is created for you when you run sybconfig (sybinit for System 10) or buildmaster—which you should not use unless you know what you are doing or are instructed to do so by Sybase Technical Support.

For a System 10 SQL Server, sybinit will also create the sysprocsdev and sybsecurity device for you while you are running sybinit.

You must not run **disk init** for the master device. You must know the size of the partition that will support the master device and be prepared to tell sybconfig (sybinit for System 10) how big the master device should be: The master device size is the largest whole number of MB that will fit on the partition. Note that for System 10 you also must not run **disk init** for the sysprocsdev or the sybsecurity device.

Verify file system availability

You need to verify the file systems that are available on the server machine. You get this information from the command df. Sample output for the df command is shown below. Note that the file systems should be set up by the server machine SA. Hence you don't need to check the partitions of the disks that support the file systems. Avoid mixing file systems and server devices on the same physical disk.

```
machine1 % df
Filesystem      kbytes     used   avail capacity  Mounted on
/dev/sd0a       20175      5380   12778    30%    /
/dev/sd0g       81103     64588    8405    88%    /usr
/dev/sd0h       30271      2202   25042     8%    /var
/dev/sd2a      945059    257686  592868    30%    /dba
/dev/sd1a     1730096     47069 1510018     3%    /diskdump1
/dev/sd9a     1968809         9 1771920     0%    /logdump1
/dev/sd10a    1968809         9 1771920     0%    /diskdump2
/dev/sd11a    1968809         9 1771920     0%    /logdump2
```

Check that the directory where you will install the server and its associated products has sufficient space. For this example, the Sybase home directory (also called the installation directory) will be machine1:/dba/sybase. The Sybase home directory is the directory where you load all the server files from the product tape, or where you copy such files from another machine. Whenever possible, it is better to load the product tape. That way, you have all the optional files that may be needed for configuring the server. Check the Sybase installation guide for your platform and operating system to verify the disk space needed for loading all the server files. You must also ensure that all the file systems that you need for installation and support of the SQL Server must be owned by UNIX user 'dba,' the UNIX user who will be starting and shutting down the server and making dumps to tape and to file systems.

Verify permissions on devices and /dba/sybase directory

You must verify that you and any other DBAs that will support this server have su privilege on the server machine. Further, you must also have the ability to execute the command su - sybase. You must execute this command to become the UNIX user 'sybase' as required in order to run the sybconfig (sybinit for System 10) program to install SQL Server. Since you will install the server as UNIX user 'sybase,' you need to change the ownership of various files to 'sybase' before you run sybconfig (sybinit for System 10) and then change the ownership back to UNIX user 'dba' after the server installation is complete. See Chapter 1 for more discussion of UNIX user 'sybase' and 'dba.'

You must verify that you have changed the ownership of the installation directory which means changing the ownership of all the files in /dba/sybase and all the subdirectories to UNIX user 'sybase.' Because sybconfig (sybinit for System 10) will create the master device, you also need to change the ownership of the file controlling the raw partition that will support the master device. Change the ownership to UNIX user 'sybase.' For a System 10 installation, sybinit (not sybconfig) will create the sysprocsdev and sybsecurity devices in addition to the master device, so you also need to change the ownership of the files controlling the raw partitions that will support these devices. When the installation process is complete, reset the ownership of all these files to UNIX user 'dba.'

Verify Sybase Setting

You must verify that the environment variable SYBASE is set to point to the Sybase installation directory, which is /dba/sybase. You can check this by executing echo $SYBASE; if needed, you can set this environment variable by executing setenv SYBASE /dba/sybase. If you don't have this variable set correctly, sybconfig (sybinit for System 10) won't be able to complete the server installation or it won't run at all.

Load SQL Server Product Set Files

You must have all the SQL Server product set files in the installation directory /dba/sybase. You can load these files from the product tape or, if you are installing a version of the SQL Server that is already running on a server machine in your database system, you can copy the files over the network. You are better off to load the files from the original product tapes, because that will ensure that you have all the files needed to support all the installation and configuration options. On an existing server, you may find that someone deleted various files to make space for other needs.

;-)
It's late, your manager says you can't take a lunch hour, you can't take a sick day (you've been sick for two weeks), your previously approved vacation has been revoked (in violation of all company policy), and you have to stay until the server is installed on the new platform. You think you are in good shape. Since no one bothered to inform you of the project plan (there isn't one), you don't have time to order the latest product tape for the server. Not to worry, you just copy the installation directory from another server in your database system. You begin sybconfig (sybinit for System 10), and things start to fail. You investigate and find some of the subdirectories of the installation directory (/dba/sybase) don't contain files, only links to other directories. Of course, those other directories don't exist on your new server machine so you don't have the files. You don't know why anyone would have moved parts of the product set to other directories on the other server machine, and you don't know exactly which machine does in fact have these linked subdirectories. The fun begins. You should have all the files of the product set on the server machine before you start installing.

10) *Run sybconfig (sybinit for System 10)*

Now you are ready to run the sybconfig (sybinit for System 10) program. This is included with the server product(s) and will install the SQL Server. When you run sybconfig (sybinit for System 10), you are creating the master device, the *master*, *model*, and *tempdb* databases and installing the system stored procedures, such as **sp_who**, creating an entry in the interfaces file for the server, creating a file that you can use to start the server (a RUN_<*servername*> file), installing the default character set and sort order as well as any additional character sets you need, and installing the default language and any additional languages you need.

After the sybconfig (sybinit for System 10) program has successfully completed, you will have installed the basic server. From there you will need to configure the server and create the server devices. After that, you will be ready to create user databases. Since the installation process is different for 4.9.x servers, which use the sybconfig program, and System 10 servers, which use the sybinit program, we cover the specifics of the installation process for each version of the SQL Server separately.

For the following discussions, comments about the sybconfig (sybinit for System 10) process are inserted in the actual sybconfig (sybinit for System 10) output. The comments are identified by /*<comment>*/.

3.2   sybconfig for SQL Server 4.9.x

You will need a number of pieces of data to answer the questions posed by sybconfig for 4.9.x SQL Server. They are listed below. We discuss many of these items individually before we review the output from the sybconfig program. Note that the output of sybconfig shown here may not match the output you will see when you run the sybconfig program on your specific platform, but the output here shows you what to expect as sybconfig moves through the installation process.

You must have the environment variable SYBASE set to point to the Sybase installation directory /dba/sybase. The sybconfig program uses the SYBASE variable to find the files needed to install the server, but it doesn't ask you what the path is to the Sybase installation (or home) directory. You can check this by executing the UNIX command echo $SYBASE.

You need to remember that sybconfig starts the newly installed server so it can install stored procedures and make several configuration changes. When you are done installing the server and move to the production directory structure and server startup scripts, you will need to stop and restart the server. Remember to stop the currently running server before you attempt to start the server from the production directory.

Table 3.3 discusses questions asked by sybconfig during SQL 4.9x installation.

Table 3.3   SQL Server 4.9.x sybconfig Questions

Question	Comment
Type of Master Device (Raw Partition or File system)	Use a raw partition for the master device. See Chapter 1 for discussion of raw partitions versus file systems.
Pathname for Master Device (Assuming Raw Partition)	Provide the complete path and file name of the file that controls the raw partition that will support the master device.
Size of Partition in Sectors (Assuming Raw Partition)	Specify the size of the master device raw partition in sectors. You can get this information from the output of the **dkinfo** command. Specify a whole number of megabytes for the number of sectors. Recall that #sectors * 512 bytes/sector gives total number of bytes. Note that 512 bytes/sector is platform specific, and you must check this parameter for your specific platform.
Server Name	Select the server name based on the naming standards you have set up for all the servers in your database system (see Chapter 1).
Server Query Port Number (1025)	Specify the query port number for the server by the standard environment you have set up for each of your servers (see Chapter 1).
Default Language	Specify a default language that is the same as the other servers in your database system. Be very careful before specifying a default language different from that of the other servers in your database system. Make sure you know the impacts this may have as you move data between servers and into and out of the system.
Default Character Set	Should be the same as the other servers in your database system. Make sure you know the impacts of having different character sets installed on different servers. Note that the selection of the default character set will have an impact on the default sort order that can be installed. This is the sort of information that you will get from reading the *Installation Guide* and related documentation.

Table 3.3   SQL Server 4.9.x sybconfig Questions (Continued)

Sort Order	The sort order is linked with the default character set. Note that the sort order is critical. Once the sort order has been set up and you load any data into the server you can't change the sort order without doing a logical dump and load of all the data in the entire server. If you change the sort order later, you can't load any of the database dumps you have made using SQL Server. Hence, you must choose the sort order with care. The sort order tells the server how to order the actual data out on disk. When you change the sort order, you must physically reorder the data on disk which will take lot of time for a large database. If you need to change sort order later on, review the situation with Sybase Technical Support and have a complete plan for recovering your databases before you make the change. The best advice is to check all the other servers in your database system. They should all have the same sort order and default character set. Your new server should match the others in your database system. The best way to determine exactly what character set and sort order are installed on a given server is to look at the server errorlog. Just after the server recovers after it is started, the errorlog shows the ID number for the default character set and the sort order. Make sure your new server displays the same ID values as the other servers in your database system.
Additional Languages	You can install additional languages later if needed.
Additional Character Sets	You can install additional character sets later if needed.
Serial Number	You will need the serial number of the SQL Server to run the **sybconfig** program. This serial number is not meaningful and you can use any number such as 99999. Note that the serial number appears in the output of **sp_configure**.

Here is an example of the output of sybconfig:

```
machine1% sybconfig

Select Sybase product to be installed:

  1 - SQL Server

  x - Exit
 ? 1
  Using 'us_english.iso_1' as the Sybase Locale

    Welcome To SQL Server Install

Please select type of install:

  1 - Initialize software
  2 - Install a new SQL Server
  3 - Check existing SQL Server for upgrade to Release 4.9
  4 - Upgrade an existing SQL Server to Release 4.9.1
  5 - Reconfigure existing SQL Server character set,
      sort order or languages

  h - Help
  r - Return to previous menu
  x - Exit to operating system
 ? 2

Select type of master device:

  1 - Raw disk partition
  2 - Regular Unix file

  r - Return to previous menu
  x - Exit to operating system
 ? 1
Enter full pathname of Raw disk partition
```

```
? /dev/rsd1b

Enter size of raw partition (/dev/rsd1b) in sectors:
? 61440
/* 61440 sectors (512 bytes per sector) = 30 Mb */
Enter Server name (default is SYBASE)
? DDSDBA1

Select the default language for this SQL Server

 1 - us_english
 2 - japanese
 3 - french
 4 - german

 h - Help
 r - Return to previous menu
 x - Exit to operating system
? 1

Select the default character set for this SQL Server

 1 - eucjis - Extended Unix Code for JIS-X0201 and JIS-X0208.
 2 - sjis - IBM/Microsoft Code for JIS-X0201 and JIS-X0208.
 3 - deckanji - DEC Kanji Code for JIS-X0208.
 4 - ascii_8 - ASCII, for use with unspecified 8-bit data.
 5 - cp437 - Code Page 437, (United States) character set.
 6 - cp850 - Code Page 850 (Multilingual) character set.
 7 - iso_1 - ISO 8859-1 (Latin-1) - Western European 8-bit
     character set.
 8 - mac - Macintosh default character set for Western
     European locales.
 9 - roman8 - Hewlett-Packard proprietary character set for
     European locales.

 h - Help
 r - Return to previous menu
 x - Exit to operating system
```

```
(Default is  7 - iso_1 - ISO 8859-1 (Latin-1) - Western
 European 8-bit character set.)
?


Select the sort order for this SQL Server

 1 - Binary sort order.
 2 - General purpose dictionary ordering.
 3 - Dictionary order, case insensitive.
 4 - Dictionary order, case insensitive with preference.
 5 - Dictionary order, case and accent insensitive.

 h - Help
 r - Return to previous menu
 x - Exit to operating system

(Default is  1 - Binary sort order.)
?


Select the additional languages you wish this SQL Server to
support:

 1 -   japanese
 2 -   french
 3 -   german

 h - Help
 c - Continue to next menu
 r - Return to previous menu
 x - Exit to operating system
? c


Select the additional character sets this SQL Server will
communicate with:

 1 -   eucjis
 2 -   sjis
 3 -   deckanji
 4 -   ascii_8
```

```
5 -   cp437
6 -   cp850
7 -   mac
8 -   roman8

h - Help
c - Continue to next menu
r - Return to previous menu
x - Exit to operating system
? c

Serial number:      999999
Master device:      /dev/rsd1b (Raw disk partition)
       size:        30 Megabytes = 15360 pages (bytes/page)
Server name:        DDSDBA1
Ports: query:       1025
       master:      1025
       console:     1026
Runserver file:     /dba/sybase/install/RUN_DDSDBA1
Do you want to proceed?
Enter 'y' to continue, 'n' to try again, 'q' to quit? y
WARNING: Creating a database device in /dev/rsd1b
overwrites any information now in /dev/rsd1b.
Do you want to continue? (Y/N)? y

Running buildmaster to initialize master device:
    /dev/rsd1b

Master device: /dev/rsd1b
writing configuration area
writing the MASTER database
writing the MODEL database
writing allocation pages for remaining 25 MB, (12800 pages)
25 MB
Buildmaster complete

00: 94/03/29 10:37:23.34 kernel: SQL Server/4.9.1/P/Sun4/OS
    4.1.2/1/OPT/Thu Aug 13 04:03:46 PDT 1992
00: 94/03/29 10:37:23.37 kernel: Logging SQL Server
```

```
          messages in file /dba/sybase/install/errorlog_DDSDBA1'.
00: 94/03/29 10:37:23.38 kernel: Using config area of disk
          for boot information
00: 94/03/29 10:37:23.41 kernel: Using config area from
          primary master device.
00: 94/03/29 10:37:23.47 kernel: Using 2048 file
          descriptors.
00: 94/03/29 10:37:23.47 kernel: Network and device
          connection limit is 2043.
00: 94/03/29 10:37:23.47 kernel: Dump/Load buffers
          configured with 8 pages.
00: 94/03/29 10:37:23.50 kernel: Initializing virtual
          device 0, "/dev/rsd1b"
00: 94/03/29 10:37:23.50 kernel: Virtual device 0 started
          using asynchronous i/o.
00: 94/03/29 10:37:23.52 kernel: network name machine1,
          type sun-ether, port 1026
00: 94/03/29 10:37:23.53 server: Number of buffers in
          buffer cache: 1416.
00: 94/03/29 10:37:23.53 server: Number of proc buffers
          allocated: 354.
00: 94/03/29 10:37:23.53 server: Number of blocks left for
          proc headers: 346.
00: 94/03/29 10:37:23.63 server: Opening Master Database...
00: 94/03/29 10:37:23.73 server: Loading SQL Server's
          default sort order and character set
00: 94/03/29 10:37:23.74 kernel: network name machine1,
          type sun-ether, port 1025
00: 94/03/29 10:37:23.76 server: Recovering database
          'master'
00: 94/03/29 10:37:23.86 server: server is unnamed
00: 94/03/29 10:37:23.93 server: Recovering database
          'model'.
00: 94/03/29 10:37:24.02 server: Clearing temp db
Waiting for the SQL Server connection ...
00: 94/03/29 10:37:25.70 server: Recovery complete.
00: 94/03/29 10:37:25.72 server: SQL Server's default sort
          order is:
00: 94/03/29 10:37:25.73 server: 'bin_iso_1' (ID = 50)
```

```
00: 94/03/29 10:37:25.73 server: on top of default
    character set:
00: 94/03/29 10:37:25.73 server: 'iso_1' (ID = 1).

Running installmaster (this may take a few minutes) ...

(1 row affected)
Installing sp_instmsg
(0 rows affected)
(1 row affected)
(1 row affected)
(1 row affected)
(1 row affected)
(1 row affected)
DBCC execution completed. If DBCC printed error messages,
see your System Administrator.
Installing sp_validlang
Installing sp_getmessage
Installing sp_addmessage
Installing sp_dropmessage
Installing sp_validaltlang
Installing sp_chklangparam
Installing sp_namecrack
Installing sp_addalias
Installing sp_addgroup
Installing sp_addlogin
Installing sp_addtype
Installing sp_addumpdevice
Installing sp_adduser
Installing sp_addremotelogin
Installing sp_addsegment
Installing sp_addserver
Installing sp_addlanguage
Installing sp_defaultlanguage
Installing sp_helplanguage
Installing sp_droplanguage
Installing sp_setlangalias
Installing sp_bindefault
Installing sp_bindrule
```

```
Installing sp_changedbowner
Installing sp_changegroup
Installing sp_checknames
Installing sp_start_xact
Installing sp_commit_xact
Installing sp_abort_xact
Installing sp_remove_xact
Installing sp_stat_xact
Installing sp_probe_xact
Installing sp_scan_xact
Installing sp_commonkey
Installing sp_configure
Installing sp_dboption
Installing sp_dbupgrade
Installing sp_defaultdb
Installing sp_depends
Installing sp_diskdefault
Installing sp_dropalias
Installing sp_dropdevice
Installing sp_dropdumpdevice
Installing sp_dropgroup
Installing sp_dropkey
Installing sp_droplogin
Installing sp_droptype
Installing sp_dropuser
Installing sp_dropremotelogin
Installing sp_dropsegment
Installing sp_dropserver
Installing sp_extendsegment
Installing sp_fixindex
Installing sp_foreignkey
Installing sp_helpdb
Installing sp_helpdevice
Installing sp_helpgroup
Installing sp_helplog
Installing sp_helpindex
Installing sp_helpjoins
Installing sp_helpkey
Installing sp_objectsegment
```

```
Installing sp_indsuspect
Installing sp_help
Installing sp_helprotect
Installing sp_helptext
Installing sp_helpuser
Installing sp_loaddbupgrade
Installing sp_lock
Installing sp_logdevice
Installing sp_lookup
Installing sp_helpremotelogin
Installing sp_helpsegment
Installing sp_helpsort
Installing sp_helpserver
Installing sp_markreport
Installing sp_monitor
Installing sp_password
Installing sp_placeobject
Installing sp_primarykey
Installing sp_recompile
Installing sp_remoteoption
Installing sp_rename
Installing sp_renamedb
Installing sp_serverinfo
Installing sp_serveroption
Installing sp_spaceused
Installing sp_unbindefault
Installing sp_unbindrule
Installing sp_who
(0 rows affected)
New login created.
(0 rows affected)
New user added.
New primary key added.
New primary key added.
New primary key added.
New primary key added.
New primary key added.
New primary key added.
New primary key added.
```

```
New primary key added.
New primary key added.
New primary key added.
New primary key added.
New primary key added.
New foreign key added.
New common key added.
No common keys exist between the two tables or views
supplied.
New common key added.
New common key added.
No common keys exist between the two tables or views
supplied.
New common key added.
No common keys exist between the two tables or views
supplied.
New common key added.
New common key added.
New common key added.
New common key added.
New common key added.
New common key added.
New common key added.
No common keys exist between the two tables or views
supplied.
New common key added.
New foreign key added.
New common key added.
New common key added.
No common keys exist between the two tables or views
supplied.
New common key added.
No common keys exist between the two tables or views
supplied.
New common key added.
New common key added.
New common key added.
Common keys dropped.
New common key added.
```

```
New primary key added.
New primary key added.
New primary key added.
New primary key added.
New primary key added.
New primary key added.
New primary key added.
New primary key added.
New primary key added.
New primary key added.
New primary key added.
New primary key added.
New primary key added.
New primary key added.
New foreign key added.
New common key added.
No common keys exist between the two tables or views
supplied.
New common key added.
New common key added.
No common keys exist between the two tables or views
supplied.
New common key added.
No common keys exist between the two tables or views
supplied.
New common key added.
New common key added.
New common key added.
New common key added.
New common key added.
New common key added.
New common key added.
No common keys exist between the two tables or views
supplied.
New common key added.
New foreign key added.
New common key added.
New common key added.
No common keys exist between the two tables or views
```

```
supplied.
New common key added.
No common keys exist between the two tables or views
supplied.
New common key added.
New common key added.
New common key added.
New primary key added.
New primary key added.
New primary key added.
New primary key added.
New primary key added.
Primary key for the table or view dropped.
New primary key added.
New common key added.
New common key added.
No common keys exist between the two tables or views
supplied.
New common key added.
No common keys exist between the two tables or views
supplied.
New common key added.
No common keys exist between the two tables or views
supplied.
New common key added.
New common key added.
New common key added.
New common key added.
New common key added.
(1 row affected)
Configuration option changed. Run the RECONFIGURE command
to install.
Loading of master database is complete.
Configuration option changed. Run the RECONFIGURE command
to install.
(return status = 0)
Loading of model database is complete.
Configuration option changed. Run the RECONFIGURE command
to install.
```

```
(return status = 0)
The current configuration is:
```

name	minimum	maximum	config_value	run_value
recovery interval	1	32767	0	5
allow updates	0	1	0	0
user connections	5	2147483647	0	25
memory	3850	2147483647	0	4096
open databases	5	2147483647	0	10
locks	5000	2147483647	0	5000
open objects	100	2147483647	0	500
procedure cache	1	99	0	20
fill factor	0	100	0	0
time slice	50	1000	0	100
database size	2	10000	0	2
tape retention	0	365	0	0
recovery flags	0	1	0	0
serial number	1	999999	999999	0
nested triggers	0	1	1	1
devices	4	256	0	10
remote access	0	1	0	0
remote logins	0	2147483647	0	0
remote sites	0	2147483647	0	0
remote connections	0	2147483647	0	0
pre-read packets	0	2147483647	0	0
upgrade version	0	2147483647	491	491
default sortorder id	0	255	50	50
default language	0	2147483647	0	0
language in cache	3	100	3	3
max online engines	1	32	1	1
min online engines	1	32	1	1
engine adjust interval	1	32	0	0
default character set id	0	255	1	1
stack size	20480	2147483647	0	28672

```
(30 rows affected, return status = 0)


SQL Server successfully installed.

Please select type of install:
```

```
1 - Initialize software
2 - Install a new SQL Server
3 - Check existing SQL Server for upgrade to Release 4.9
4 - Upgrade an existing SQL Server to Release 4.9.1
5 - Reconfigure existing SQL Server character set,
sort order or languages

h - Help
r - Return to previous menu
x - Exit to operating system
? x
machine1%
```

3.3　sybinit for SQL Server System 10

You will need a number of pieces of data to answer the questions posed by sybinit for System 10 SQL Server. Note that the output of sybinit shown here may not match the output you will see when you run the sybinit program on your specific platform, but the output here shows you what to expect as sybinit moves through the installation process.

There are several differences between SQL Server 4.9.x and System 10 that you need to understand before installing the System 10 version. Note that this discussion assumes you are installing from scratch, not upgrading a 4.9.x server to System 10 (see Chapter 13). The big difference as far as installing goes is the presence of three server devices that get created during the process of installing the System 10 server versus only one, the master device, for a 4.9.x installation.

For System 10, the sybinit program will create the master device and a device called sysprocsdev to support the *sybsystemprocs* database. The *sybsystemprocs* database stores most of the system stored procedures that were stored in the *master* database in the 4.9.x server. With the growth in the number of such stored procedures in System 10, the need arose to move most of them out of the *master* database. The alternative would have been to require anyone upgrading from 4.9.x to System 10 to enlarge the master device. However, many installations don't have much, if any, more room on their master device and enlarging the master device requires reinstalling the whole server (see Chapter 7). This would not be popular with the installed base, so the *sybsystemprocs* database was born.

The third server device that is created by the sybinit program for System 10 is the sybsecurity server device that supports the *sybsecurity* database. This database is needed to activate the server auditing functions, which are a new set of features for System 10. The auditing features allow the server to record various information regarding who is doing what and when to the server and the data in the server. Note that creating the sybsecurity server device and database are not required to install the server. However, the sybsecurity server device, like the sysprocsdev and the master device, should be on its own server device and should be mirrored and, as always, preferably all on separate controllers. This means that if you don't create a small (30-MB) partition early in the installation of the server, you would have to put the *sybsecurity* database on some server device that was already supporting other databases should you ever decide to activate auditing features. Since you should create the small server device and its mirror now as part of the installation, go ahead and install the auditing capabilities at the same time. This will make it much less painful for you when you do decide you need the auditing capabilities of System 10. Note that once you have installed the sybsecurity server device and database, you don't have to activate them so they won't affect the server performance.

sybinit will boot the newly installed SQL Server as part of the installation process. This is fine; you just need to remember that you already have a server running when you are finished with sybinit. When you proceed with the step of converting the server to run under UNIX user 'dba', you must first shut down the server that was booted as part of the sybinit process. You must remember that this applies to the Backup Server as well.

Recall that System 10 SQL Server uses a separate product, the Backup Server, to make database and transaction log dumps. The sybinit program installs the Backup Server as well. You can either install the Backup Server as part of the same sybinit session (as shown in the actual sybinit output below) or run a completely new sybinit session.

For System 10, you don't need a customer authorization string or a serial number to install the server. The customer authorization string is required when you load the server files from the Sybase product tape. The process of loading these files is covered in the *Installation Guide* and is platform specific.

Table 3.4 discusses questions asked by sybinit during SQL Server System 10 installation.

Table 3.4   SQL Server System 10 sybinit Questions and Recommendations

Question	Comment
Release directory	Specify the actual release directory. Should be the same as the Sybase installation directory (/dba/sybase).
Server name	Follow the server naming conventions you have established (see Chapter 1). Note that there are times when you don't want to give a new server its final production name. This would occur when you are installing a new server that will eventually replace an existing server. Since the existing server must continue in production until you can cut over to the new server, the new server should not be given the same name as the existing production server.
Configure server interfaces file entry	Specify the information needed for sybinit to create an interfaces file entry for the server. Note that this interfaces file entry will be made in a file in the installation directory, and you will need to add the server to your production interfaces file later on after the server installation is complete. Specify the port number of the server in accordance with the standards you have established for all the servers and server machines in your database system (see Chapter 1). Note that the server machine name is assumed to be the same as the machine you are running sybinit from; if not, you will need to change that entry within sybinit. You will be able to specify a Retry Count and a Retry Delay parameter as well as the basic machine name and port number. These affect what happens when a client connection to the server fails. Decide whether you need to change the default of 0 for one or both of these. In general, if your clients are failing to connect, there is a real problem and simply waiting a short time to reconnect doesn't help. These parameters are discussed more fully in the *Installation Guide*.
File for master device raw partition	Provide the complete path and file name of the file controlling the raw partition that will support the master device.
Size of master device in Megabytes	Specify the size of the master device in megabytes, not sectors (as with sybconfig for the 4.9.x SQL Server). Specify the largest whole number of megabytes that will fit on the raw partition (see Chapter 4).

Table 3.4   SQL Server System 10 sybinit Questions and Recommendations (Continued)

Question	Comment
File for sysprocsdev device raw partition	Provide the complete path and filename of the file controlling the raw partition that will support the sysprocsdev device. This device will support the *sybsystemprocs* database, which contains the system stored procedures. This device should be separate from the master device, preferably on a separate physical disk that is attached to a separate disk controller.
Size of sysprocsdev device in megabytes	Specify the size of the sysprocsdev device in megabytes. Specify the largest whole number of megabytes that will fit on the raw partition (see Chapter 4).
Errorlog location	Specify the errorlog location. You should accept the default which will put the errorlog in the install subdirectory of the Sybase installation directory. This means the errorlog would be /dba/sybase/install/errorlog. You need to realize that the sybinit process is going to start the newly installed SQL Server. The server must be started to install stored procedures and make several configuration changes. The errorlog that results from booting the server should be preserved along with all the installation files. Hence, accept the default, allow sybinit to generate errorlogs as it boots the new server, and when you have finished the server installation, move the errorlog to its final production location. Note that you need to periodically delete old server errorlogs from the production errorlog directory (/dba/<*servername*>/errorlog) to prevent the file system from filling up, which would kill the server. If you place the sybinit errorlog(s) in the production errorlog directory, you will soon delete them. These errorlogs are part of your documentation of the installation process and you should preserve them.
Backup server name	Specify the name for the Backup Server. Note that you are not installing the Backup Server at this point. Here sybinit is simply changing the name of the Backup Server in the system table *sysservers* from the default of SYB_BACKUP to the name you specify. You must install the Backup Server by using sybinit after you are done installing the server. You should be following your server naming conventions, so the Backup Server name would be <*servername*>_BCK.

Table 3.4   SQL Server System 10 sybinit Questions and Recommendations (Continued)

Question	Comment
Languages installed and default	Specify a default language that is the same as the other servers in your database system. Be very careful before specifying a default language different from that of the other servers in your database system. Make sure you know the impacts this may have as you move data between servers and into and out of the system.
Character sets installed and default	Specify a default character set that is the same as the other servers in your database system. Make sure you know the impacts of having different character sets installed on different servers. Note that the selection of the default character set will have an impact on the default sort order that can be installed. This is the sort of information that you will get from reading the *Installation Guide* and related documentation.
Sort order installed	The sort order is linked with the default character set. Note that the sort order is critical. Once the sort order has been set up and you load any data into the server, you can't change the sort order without doing a logical dump and load of all the data in the entire server. If you change the sort order later, you can't load any of the database dumps you have made previously by using SQL Server. Hence, choose the sort order with care. The sort order tells the server how to order the actual data out on disk. When you change the sort order, you must physically reorder the data on disk, which will take lot of time for a large database.
	If you need to change sort order later on, review the situation with Sybase Technical Support and have a complete plan for recovering your databases before you make the change. The best advice is to check all the other servers in your database system. They should all have the same sort order and default character set. Your new server should match the others in your database system.
	The best way to determine exactly what character set and sort order are installed on a given server is to look at the server errorlog. Just after the server recovers after it is started, the errorlog shows the ID number for the default character set and the sort order. Make sure your new server displays the same ID values as the other servers in your database system. This is another reason you need to be prepared to support a logical dump and load of the databases on your server (see Chapter 8).

Table 3.4   SQL Server System 10 sybinit Questions and Recommendations (Continued)

Question	Comment
File for sybsecurity device raw partition	Provide the complete path and filename of the file controlling the raw partition that will support the sybsecurity device. This device will support the *sybsecurity* database that allows you to use the auditing features of the System 10 SQL Server. Installing this device is optional; you can install the server without this feature. However, if you ever decide to install the auditing features later, you will then need to come up with a small (30-MB) disk raw partition and mirror. After you have the server set up and running, it may not be easy to find or create such a partition. Hence, it is simply easier for you to install the auditing features even if you don't activate them. This device should be separate from the master and sysprocsdev devices, preferably on a separate physical disk that is attached to a separate disk controller.
Size of sybsecurity device in megabytes	Specify the size of the sybsecurity device in megabytes. Specify the largest whole number of megabytes that will fit on the raw partition (see Chapter 4).
The following questions ask for information you must supply to sybinit to install the Backup Server for System 10. This can be done as part of the same sybinit session you have completed to install the server, or you can start a completely independent sybinit session. You must install the Backup Server before you can make any database or transaction log dumps of any database in the server.	
Backup server release directory	Specify the actual release directory. Should be the same as the Sybase installation directory (/dba/sybase).
Backup server name	Specify the Backup Server name and follow the server naming conventions you have established (see Chapter 1), which would be *<servername>*_BCK. Note that there are times when you don't want to give a new server its final production name. This would occur when you are installing a new server that will eventually replace an existing server. Because the existing server must continue in production until you can cut over to the new server, the new server should not be given the same name as the existing production server.
Backup server errorlog	Supply the location of the Backup Server errorlog; accept the default. See "Errorlog location" above.

Table 3.4   SQL Server System 10 sybinit Questions and Recommendations (Continued)

Question	Comment
Backup server interfaces file information	Specify the information needed for sybinit to create an interfaces file entry for the Backup Server. This interfaces file entry will be made in a file in the installation directory, and you will need to add the server to your production interfaces file later on after the server installation is complete. You will need to specify the port number of the Backup Server, which you should specify in accordance with the standards you have established for all the servers and server machines in your database system (see Chapter 1). Note that the server machine name is assumed to be the same as the machine from which you are running sybinit; if not, you will need to change that entry within sybinit.
Backup server language and character set	Should be the same as those you chose for the server itself.

Here is an example of the output from sybinit:

```
machine1% sybinit
The log file for this session is
'/dba/sybase/init/logs/log0401.001'.

SYBINIT

1. Release directory: /usr/local/sybase

2. Edit / View Interfaces File

3. Configure a Server product
4. Configure an Open Client/Server product


Ctrl-a Accept and Continue, Ctrl-x Exit Screen, ? Help.

Enter the number of your choice and press return: 1
Enter the pathname of the release directory to use (default is
'/usr/local/sybase'):
/dba/sybase
```

```
SYBINIT
1. Release directory:  /dba/sybase

2. Edit / View Interfaces File

3. Configure a Server product
4. Configure an Open Client/Server product


Ctrl-a Accept and Continue, Ctrl-x Exit Screen, ? Help.

Enter the number of your choice and press return: 3

CONFIGURE SERVER PRODUCTS

Products:

    Product          Date Installed   Date Configured
1. SQL Server          Apr 01 95 14:33   Apr 01 95 14:33
2. Backup Server   Apr 01 95 14:33 Apr 01 95 14:33


Ctrl-a Accept and Continue, Ctrl-x Exit Screen, ? Help.

Enter the number of your choice and press return: 1

NEW OR EXISTING SQL SERVER

1. Configure a new SQL Server
2. Configure an existing SQL Server
3. Upgrade an existing SQL Server


Ctrl-a Accept and Continue, Ctrl-x Exit Screen, ? Help.

Enter the number of your choice and press return: 1

ADD NEW SQL SERVER
```

```
1. SQL Server name: SYBASE
Ctrl-a Accept and Continue, Ctrl-x Exit Screen, ? Help.

Enter the number of your choice and press return: 1
Enter the name of the new SQL Server (default is 'SYBASE'):
DDSDBA1

ADD NEW SQL SERVER

1. SQL Server name: DDSDBA1


Ctrl-a Accept and Continue, Ctrl-x Exit Screen, ? Help.

Enter the number of your choice and press return:

SQL SERVER CONFIGURATION

1.  CONFIGURE SERVER'S INTERFACES FILE ENTRY      Incomplete
2.  MASTER DEVICE CONFIGURATION                   Incomplete
3.  SYBSYSTEMPROCS DATABASE CONFIGURATION         Incomplete
4.  SET ERRORLOG LOCATION                         Incomplete
5.  CONFIGURE DEFAULT BACKUP SERVER               Incomplete
6.  CONFIGURE LANGUAGES                           Incomplete
7.  CONFIGURE CHARACTER SETS                      Incomplete
8.  CONFIGURE SORT ORDER                          Incomplete
9.  ACTIVATE AUDITING                             Incomplete



Ctrl-a Accept and Continue, Ctrl-x Exit Screen, ? Help.

Enter the number of your choice and press return: 1

SERVER INTERFACES FILE ENTRY SCREEN

   Server name:  DDSDBA1

1.  Retry Count:  0
```

```
2.  Retry Delay:  0
3. Add a new listener service


Ctrl-a Accept and Continue, Ctrl-x Exit Screen, ? Help.

Enter the number of your choice and press return: 3

EDIT TCP SERVICE

1.  Hostname/Address: machine1
2.  Port:
3.  Name Alias:

4. Delete this service from the interfaces entry


Ctrl-a Accept and Continue, Ctrl-x Exit Screen, ? Help.

Enter the number of your choice and press return: 2
Enter the port number to use for this entry (default is ''):
1025

EDIT TCP SERVICE

1.  Hostname/Address: machine1
2.  Port: 1025
3.  Name Alias:

4.  Delete this service from the interfaces entry


Ctrl-a Accept and Continue, Ctrl-x Exit Screen, ? Help.

Enter the number of your choice and press return:
Is this information correct? y

SERVER INTERFACES FILE ENTRY SCREEN
```

```
      Server name:  DDSDBA1
1.  Retry Count:  0
2.  Retry Delay:  0

3.  Add a new listener service

Modify or delete a service

Listener services available:

   Protocol   Address      Port       Name Alias
4. tcp        machine1     1025


Ctrl-a Accept and Continue, Ctrl-x Exit Screen, ? Help.

Enter the number of your choice and press return:
Write the changes to the interfaces file now? y


SQL SERVER CONFIGURATION

1.   CONFIGURE SERVER'S INTERFACES FILE ENTRY     Complete
2.   MASTER DEVICE CONFIGURATION                  Incomplete
3.   SYBSYSTEMPROCS DATABASE CONFIGURATION        Incomplete
4.   SET ERRORLOG LOCATION                        Incomplete
5.   CONFIGURE DEFAULT BACKUP SERVER              Incomplete
6.   CONFIGURE LANGUAGES                          Incomplete
7.   CONFIGURE CHARACTER SETS                     Incomplete
8.   CONFIGURE SORT ORDER                         Incomplete
9.   ACTIVATE AUDITING                            Incomplete

Ctrl-a Accept and Continue, Ctrl-x Exit Screen, ? Help.

Enter the number of your choice and press return: 2

MASTER DEVICE CONFIGURATION

1. Master Device:
```

```
2. Size (Meg):  17.00



Ctrl-a Accept and Continue, Ctrl-x Exit Screen, ? Help.

Enter the number of your choice and press return: 1
Enter the pathname of the SQL Server's master device
(default is ''):
/dev/rsd4h

MASTER DEVICE CONFIGURATION

1. Master Device:  /dev/rsd4h

2. Size (Meg):  32.730469


Ctrl-a Accept and Continue, Ctrl-x Exit Screen, ? Help.

Enter the number of your choice and press return: 2
Enter the size of the SQL Server's master device in megabytes:
32

MASTER DEVICE CONFIGURATION

1. Master Device:  /dev/rsd4h

2. Size (Meg):  32


Ctrl-a Accept and Continue, Ctrl-x Exit Screen, ? Help.

Enter the number of your choice and press return:

SQL SERVER CONFIGURATION

1.  CONFIGURE SERVER'S INTERFACES FILE ENTRY     Complete
```

```
2.  MASTER DEVICE CONFIGURATION                    Complete
3.  SYBSYSTEMPROCS DATABASE CONFIGURATION          Incomplete
4.  SET ERRORLOG LOCATION                          Incomplete
5.  CONFIGURE DEFAULT BACKUP SERVER                Incomplete
6.  CONFIGURE LANGUAGES                            Incomplete
7.  CONFIGURE CHARACTER SETS                       Incomplete
8.  CONFIGURE SORT ORDER                           Incomplete
9.  ACTIVATE AUDITING                              Incomplete


Ctrl-a Accept and Continue, Ctrl-x Exit Screen, ? Help.

Enter the number of your choice and press return: 3

SYBSYSTEMPROCS DATABASE CONFIGURATION

1.  sybsystemprocs database size (Meg): 10

2.  sybsystemprocs logical device name: sysprocsdev

3.  create new device for the sybsystemprocs database: yes

4.  physical name of new device:

5.  size of the new device (Meg): 10


Ctrl-a Accept and Continue, Ctrl-x Exit Screen, ? Help.

Enter the number of your choice and press return: 4
Enter the physical device name for the sybsystemprocs database :
/dev/rsd5h

SYBSYSTEMPROCS DATABASE CONFIGURATION

1.  sybsystemprocs database size (Meg): 10

2.  sybsystemprocs logical device name: sysprocsdev
```

3. create new device for the sybsystemprocs database: yes
 4. physical name of new device: /dev/rsd5h

5. size of the new device (Meg): 38.964844

Ctrl-a Accept and Continue, Ctrl-x Exit Screen, ? Help.

Enter the number of your choice and press return: 5
Enter the size of the new device:
38

SYBSYSTEMPROCS DATABASE CONFIGURATION

1. sybsystemprocs database size (Meg): 10

2. sybsystemprocs logical device name: sysprocsdev

3. create new device for the sybsystemprocs database: yes

4. physical name of new device: /dev/rsd5h

5. size of the new device (Meg): 38

Ctrl-a Accept and Continue, Ctrl-x Exit Screen, ? Help.

Enter the number of your choice and press return:

SQL SERVER CONFIGURATION

1.	CONFIGURE SERVER'S INTERFACES FILE ENTRY	Complete
2.	MASTER DEVICE CONFIGURATION	Complete
3.	SYBSYSTEMPROCS DATABASE CONFIGURATION	Complete
4.	SET ERRORLOG LOCATION	Incomplete
5.	CONFIGURE DEFAULT BACKUP SERVER	Incomplete
6.	CONFIGURE LANGUAGES	Incomplete
7.	CONFIGURE CHARACTER SETS	Incomplete
8.	CONFIGURE SORT ORDER	Incomplete

```
9.   ACTIVATE AUDITING                              Incomplete
Ctrl-a Accept and Continue, Ctrl-x Exit Screen, ? Help.


Enter the number of your choice and press return: 4

SET ERRORLOG LOCATION

1. SQL Server errorlog: /dba/sybase/install/errorlog


Ctrl-a Accept and Continue, Ctrl-x Exit Screen, ? Help.

Enter the number of your choice and press return:

SQL SERVER CONFIGURATION

1.   CONFIGURE SERVER'S INTERFACES FILE ENTRY     Complete
2.   MASTER DEVICE CONFIGURATION                  Complete
3.   SYBSYSTEMPROCS DATABASE CONFIGURATION        Complete
4.   SET ERRORLOG LOCATION                        Complete
5.   CONFIGURE DEFAULT BACKUP SERVER              Incomplete
6.   CONFIGURE LANGUAGES                          Incomplete
7.   CONFIGURE CHARACTER SETS                     Incomplete
8.   CONFIGURE SORT ORDER                         Incomplete
9.   ACTIVATE AUDITING                            Incomplete


Ctrl-a Accept and Continue, Ctrl-x Exit Screen, ? Help.

Enter the number of your choice and press return: 5

SET THE SQL SERVER'S BACKUP SERVER

1. SQL Server Backup Server name: SYB_BACKUP


Ctrl-a Accept and Continue, Ctrl-x Exit Screen, ? Help.

Enter the number of your choice and press return: 1
```

Enter the name of the SQL Server's Backup Server (default is 'SYB_BACKUP'):
DDSDBA1_BCK

SET THE SQL SERVER'S BACKUP SERVER

1. SQL Server Backup Server name: DDSDBA1_BCK

Ctrl-a Accept and Continue, Ctrl-x Exit Screen, ? Help.

Enter the number of your choice and press return:

SQL SERVER CONFIGURATION

1. CONFIGURE SERVER'S INTERFACES FILE ENTRY   Complete
2. MASTER DEVICE CONFIGURATION   Complete
3. SYBSYSTEMPROCS DATABASE CONFIGURATION   Complete
4. SET ERRORLOG LOCATION   Complete
5. CONFIGURE DEFAULT BACKUP SERVER   Complete
6. CONFIGURE LANGUAGES   Incomplete
7. CONFIGURE CHARACTER SETS   Incomplete
8. CONFIGURE SORT ORDER   Incomplete
9. ACTIVATE AUDITING   Incomplete

Ctrl-a Accept and Continue, Ctrl-x Exit Screen, ? Help.

Enter the number of your choice and press return: 6

CONFIGURE LANGUAGES

  Current default language: us_english
  Current default character set: ISO 8859-1 (Latin-1) -
    Western European 8-bit character set.
  Current sort order: Binary ordering, for the ISO 8859/1
    or Latin-1 character set (iso_1).

Select the language you want to install, remove, or

designate as the default language.

Language	Installed?	Remove	Install	Make default
1. us_english	yes	no	no	yes
2. french	no	no	no	no
3. german	no	no	no	no

Ctrl-a Accept and Continue, Ctrl-x Exit Screen, ? Help.

Enter the number of your choice and press return:

SQL SERVER CONFIGURATION

1.	CONFIGURE SERVER'S INTERFACES FILE ENTRY	Complete
2.	MASTER DEVICE CONFIGURATION	Complete
3.	SYBSYSTEMPROCS DATABASE CONFIGURATION	Complete
4.	SET ERRORLOG LOCATION	Complete
5.	CONFIGURE DEFAULT BACKUP SERVER	Complete
6.	CONFIGURE LANGUAGES	Complete
7.	CONFIGURE CHARACTER SETS	Incomplete
8.	CONFIGURE SORT ORDER	Incomplete
9.	ACTIVATE AUDITING	Incomplete

Ctrl-a Accept and Continue, Ctrl-x Exit Screen, ? Help.

Enter the number of your choice and press return: 7

CONFIGURE CHARACTER SETS

   Current default language: us_english
   Current default character set: ISO 8859-1 (Latin-1) -
   Western European 8-bit character set.
   Current sort order: Binary ordering, for the ISO 8859/1
   or Latin-1 character set (iso_1).

Select the character set you want to install, remove, or
designate as the default character set.

```
Character set           Installed? Remove  Install  Make default
1. ASCII, for use with unsp  yes      no       no         no
2. Code Page 437, (United S   no      no       no         no
3. Code Page 850 (Multiling   no      no       no         no
4. ISO 8859-1 (Latin-1) - W   yes     no       no         yes
5. Macintosh default charac   no      no       no         no
6. Hewlett-Packard propriet   no      no       no         no
```

Ctrl-a Accept and Continue, Ctrl-x Exit Screen, ? Help.

Enter the number of your choice and press return:

SQL SERVER CONFIGURATION

```
1.   CONFIGURE SERVER'S INTERFACES FILE ENTRY     Complete
2.   MASTER DEVICE CONFIGURATION                  Complete
3.   SYBSYSTEMPROCS DATABASE CONFIGURATION        Complete
4.   SET ERRORLOG LOCATION                        Complete
5.   CONFIGURE DEFAULT BACKUP SERVER              Complete
6.   CONFIGURE LANGUAGES                          Complete
7.   CONFIGURE CHARACTER SETS                     Complete
8.   CONFIGURE SORT ORDER                         Incomplete
9.   ACTIVATE AUDITING                            Incomplete
```

Ctrl-a Accept and Continue, Ctrl-x Exit Screen, ? Help.

Enter the number of your choice and press return: 8

CONFIGURE SORT ORDER

```
Current default language: us_english
Current default character set:  ISO 8859-1 (Latin-1) -
Western European -bit character set.
Current sort order:  Binary ordering, for the ISO 8859/1
or Latin-1 character set (iso_1).
```

Select a sort order.

```
   Sort Order                                            Chosen
1. Binary ordering, for the ISO 8859/1 or Latin-1 character set (is   yes
2. General purpose dictionary ordering.
no
3. Spanish dictionary ordering.                              no
4. Spanish case and accent insensitive dictionary order.     no
5. Spanish case insensitive dictionary order.                no
6. Dictionary order, case insensitive, accent insensitive.   no
7. Dictionary order, case insensitive.                       no
8. Dictionary order, case insensitive with preference.       no
```

Ctrl-a Accept and Continue, Ctrl-x Exit Screen, ? Help.

Enter the number of your choice and press return:

SQL SERVER CONFIGURATION

```
1.   CONFIGURE SERVER'S INTERFACES FILE ENTRY      Complete
2.   MASTER DEVICE CONFIGURATION                    Complete
3.   SYBSYSTEMPROCS DATABASE CONFIGURATION          Complete
4.   SET ERRORLOG LOCATION                          Complete
5.   CONFIGURE DEFAULT BACKUP SERVER                Complete
6.   CONFIGURE LANGUAGES                            Complete
7.   CONFIGURE CHARACTER SETS                       Complete
8.   CONFIGURE SORT ORDER                           Complete
9.   ACTIVATE AUDITING                              Incomplete
```

Ctrl-a Accept and Continue, Ctrl-x Exit Screen, ? Help.

Enter the number of your choice and press return: 9

ACTIVATE AUDITING

1. Install auditing: no

2. sybsecurity database size (Meg): 5

3. sybsecurity logical device name: sybsecurity

4. create new device for the sybsecurity database: no

Ctrl-a Accept and Continue, Ctrl-x Exit Screen, ? Help.

Enter the number of your choice and press return: 1

ACTIVATE AUDITING

1. Install auditing: yes

2. sybsecurity database size (Meg): 5

3. sybsecurity logical device name: sybsecurity

4. create new device for the sybsecurity database: no

Ctrl-a Accept and Continue, Ctrl-x Exit Screen, ? Help.

Enter the number of your choice and press return: 2
Enter the size of the sybsecurity database in megabytes:
10

ACTIVATE AUDITING

1. Install auditing: yes

2. sybsecurity database size (Meg): 10

3. sybsecurity logical device name: sybsecurity

4. create new device for the sybsecurity database: no

Ctrl-a Accept and Continue, Ctrl-x Exit Screen, ? Help.

Enter the number of your choice and press return: 4

ACTIVATE AUDITING

1. Install auditing: yes

2. sybsecurity database size (Meg): 10

3. sybsecurity logical device name: sybsecurity

4. create new device for the sybsecurity database: yes

5. sybsecurity physical device name:

6. size of the new device (Meg):

Ctrl-a Accept and Continue, Ctrl-x Exit Screen, ? Help.

Enter the number of your choice and press return: 5
Enter the physical name of the device to use for the
 sybsecurity database
(default is ''):
/dev/rsd6h

ACTIVATE AUDITING

1. Install auditing: yes

2. sybsecurity database size (Meg): 10

3. sybsecurity logical device name: sybsecurity

4. create new device for the sybsecurity database: yes

5. sybsecurity physical device name: /dev/rsd6h

6. size of the new device (Meg): 38.964844

Ctrl-a Accept and Continue, Ctrl-x Exit Screen, ? Help.

Enter the number of your choice and press return: 6
Enter the size of the new device:
38

ACTIVATE AUDITING

1. Install auditing: yes

2. sybsecurity database size (Meg): 10

3. sybsecurity logical device name: sybsecurity

4. create new device for the sybsecurity database: yes

5. sybsecurity physical device name: /dev/rsd6h

6. size of the new device (Meg): 38

Ctrl-a Accept and Continue, Ctrl-x Exit Screen, ? Help.

Enter the number of your choice and press return:

SQL SERVER CONFIGURATION

1.	CONFIGURE SERVER'S INTERFACES FILE ENTRY	Complete
2.	MASTER DEVICE CONFIGURATION	Complete
3.	SYBSYSTEMPROCS DATABASE CONFIGURATION	Complete
4.	SET ERRORLOG LOCATION	Complete
5.	CONFIGURE DEFAULT BACKUP SERVER	Complete
6.	CONFIGURE LANGUAGES	Complete
7.	CONFIGURE CHARACTER SETS	Complete
8.	CONFIGURE SORT ORDER	Complete
9.	ACTIVATE AUDITING	Complete

```
Ctrl-a Accept and Continue, Ctrl-x Exit Screen, ? Help.
Enter the number of your choice and press return:
Execute the SQL Server Configuration now? y
Running task to create the master device.
Building the master device
............................Done
Task to create the master device succeeded.
Running task to update the SQL Server runserver file.
Task to update the SQL Server runserver file succeeded.
Running task to boot the SQL Server.
waiting for server 'DDSDBA1' to boot...
Task to boot the SQL Server succeeded.
Running task to create the sybsystemprocs database.
sybsystemprocs database created.
Task to create the sybsystemprocs database succeeded.
Running task to install system stored procedures.
.............................................................
.............................................................
..................................Done
Task to install system stored procedures succeeded.
Running task to set permissions for the 'model' database.
Done
Task to set permissions for the 'model' database succeeded.
Running task to set the Backup Server for the SQL Server.
Task to set the Backup Server for the SQL Server succeeded.
Running task to set the default character set and/or default
 sort order for the SQL Server.
Setting the default character set to iso_1
Sort order 'binary' has already been installed.
Character set 'iso_1' is already the default.
Sort order 'binary' is already the default.
Task to set the default character set and/or default sort
 order for the SQL Server succeeded.
Running task to set the default language.
Setting the default language to us_english
Language 'us_english' is already the default.
Task to set the default language succeeded.
Running task to install auditing capabilities.
.......Done
waiting for server 'DDSDBA1' to boot...
```

Auditing capability installed.
Task to install auditing capabilities succeeded.

Configuration completed successfully.
Press <return> to continue.

NEW OR EXISTING SQL SERVER

1. Configure a new SQL Server
2. Configure an existing SQL Server
3. Upgrade an existing SQL Server

Ctrl-a Accept and Continue, Ctrl-x Exit Screen, ? Help.

Enter the number of your choice and press return:

CONFIGURE SERVER PRODUCTS

Products:

	Product	Date Installed	Date Configured
1.	SQL Server	Apr 01 95 14:33	Apr 01 95 20:11
2.	Backup Server	Apr 01 95 14:33	Apr 01 95 14:33

Ctrl-a Accept and Continue, Ctrl-x Exit Screen, ? Help.

Enter the number of your choice and press return:

SYBINIT

1. Release directory: /dba/sybase

2. Edit / View Interfaces File

3. Configure a Server product
4. Configure an Open Client/Server product

```
Enter the number of your choice and press return:

Exiting.
The log file for this session is
 '/dba/sybase/init/logs/log0401.001'.

/* Now for the sybinit session to install the Backup Server
*/

machine1% sybinit
The log file for this session is
 '/dba/sybase/init/logs/log0401.005'.

SYBINIT

1. Release directory: /usr/local/sybase

2. Edit / View Interfaces File

3. Configure a Server product
4. Configure an Open Client/Server product


Ctrl-a Accept and Continue, Ctrl-x Exit Screen, ? Help.

Enter the number of your choice and press return: 1
Enter the pathname of the release directory to use
(default is '/usr/local/sybase'): /dba/sybase

SYBINIT

1. Release directory: /dba/sybase

2. Edit / View Interfaces File

3. Configure a Server product
4. Configure an Open Client/Server product
```

Ctrl-a Accept and Continue, Ctrl-x Exit Screen, ? Help.
Enter the number of your choice and press return: 3

CONFIGURE SERVER PRODUCTS

Products:

Product	Date Installed	Date Configured
1. SQL Server	Apr 01 95 14:33	Apr 01 95 20:11
2. Backup Server	Apr 01 95 14:33	Apr 01 95 14:33

Ctrl-a Accept and Continue, Ctrl-x Exit Screen, ? Help.

Enter the number of your choice and press return: 2

NEW OR EXISTING BACKUP SERVER

1. Configure a new Backup Server
2. Configure an existing Backup Server

Ctrl-a Accept and Continue, Ctrl-x Exit Screen, ? Help.

Enter the number of your choice and press return: 1

ADD NEW BACKUP SERVER

1. Backup Server name: SYB_BACKUP

Ctrl-a Accept and Continue, Ctrl-x Exit Screen, ? Help.

Enter the number of your choice and press return: 1
Enter the name of the new Backup Server (default is
 'SYB_BACKUP'): DDSDBA1_BCK

ADD NEW BACKUP SERVER

```
1. Backup Server name:  DDSDBA1_BCK
Ctrl-a Accept and Continue, Ctrl-x Exit Screen, ? Help.

Enter the number of your choice and press return:


BACKUP SERVER CONFIGURATION

1. Backup Server errorlog: /dba/sybase/install/backup.log
2. Enter / Modify Backup Server interfaces file information
3. Backup Server language: us_english
4. Backup Server character set: iso_1


Ctrl-a Accept and Continue, Ctrl-x Exit Screen, ? Help.

Enter the number of your choice and press return: 2


SERVER INTERFACES FILE ENTRY SCREEN

  Server name: DDSDBA1_BCK
1. Retry Count:  0
2. Retry Delay:  0

3. Add a new listener service


Ctrl-a Accept and Continue, Ctrl-x Exit Screen, ? Help.

Enter the number of your choice and press return: 3

EDIT TCP SERVICE

1. Hostname/Address: machine1
2. Port:
3. Name Alias:

4. Delete this service from the interfaces entry
```

Ctrl-a Accept and Continue, Ctrl-x Exit Screen, ? Help.

Enter the number of your choice and press return: 2
Enter the port number to use for this entry (default is ''):
1030

EDIT TCP SERVICE

1. Hostname/Address: machine1
2. Port: 1030
3. Name Alias:

4. Delete this service from the interfaces entry

Ctrl-a Accept and Continue, Ctrl-x Exit Screen, ? Help.

Enter the number of your choice and press return:
Is this information correct? y

SERVER INTERFACES FILE ENTRY SCREEN

  Server name: DDSDBA1_BCK
1. Retry Count: 0
2. Retry Delay: 0

3. Add a new listener service

Modify or delete a service

Listener services available:

  Protocol Address   Port   Name Alias
4. tcp   machine1   1030

Ctrl-a Accept and Continue, Ctrl-x Exit Screen, ? Help.

```
Enter the number of your choice and press return:
Write the changes to the interfaces file now? y



BACKUP SERVER CONFIGURATION

1. Backup Server errorlog: /dba/sybase/install/backup.log
2. Enter / Modify Backup Server interfaces file information
3. Backup Server language: us_english
4. Backup Server character set: iso_1


Ctrl-a Accept and Continue, Ctrl-x Exit Screen, ? Help.

Enter the number of your choice and press return:
Execute the Backup Server configuration now? y
Running task to update the Backup Server runserver file.
Task to update the Backup Server runserver file succeeded.
Running task to boot the Backup Server.
waiting for server 'DDSDBA1_BCK' to boot...
Task to boot the Backup Server succeeded.

Configuration completed successfully.
Press <return> to continue.

NEW OR EXISTING BACKUP SERVER

1. Configure a new Backup Server
2. Configure an existing Backup Server


Ctrl-a Accept and Continue, Ctrl-x Exit Screen, ? Help.

Enter the number of your choice and press return:

CONFIGURE SERVER PRODUCTS

Products:
```

```
      Product           Date Installed   Date Configured
   1.  SQL Server        Apr 01 95 14:33  Apr 01 95 20:11
   2.  Backup Server     Apr 01 95 14:33  Apr 01 95 07:04


Ctrl-a Accept and Continue, Ctrl-x Exit Screen, ? Help.

Enter the number of your choice and press return:

SYBINIT

1. Release directory:  /dba/sybase

2. Edit / View Interfaces File

3. Configure a Server product
4. Configure an Open Client/Server product


Ctrl-a Accept and Continue, Ctrl-x Exit Screen, ? Help.

Enter the number of your choice and press return:

Exiting.
The log file for this session is '/dba/sybase/init/logs/log0401.005'.
```

3.4   Post sybconfig (sybinit for System 10)

When you have successfully completed the sybconfig (sybinit for System 10) process, you have the basic server installed. You need to perform numerous steps before the server is ready to perform any useful work for your business. The steps listed below are needed for both 4.9.x and System 10 servers with only one exception. Review these steps and add or delete any steps as appropriate for your server. Table 3.5 lists the steps; we discuss them below.

Table 3.5   Post sybconfig (sybinit for System 10) Checklist

Dump *master* Database
Reset File Ownership
Change 'sa' Password
Configure Server Memory
Configure Number of Devices
Configure Dump Devices (4.9.x Only)
Shut Down Server
Move Files to Use RUN_<*servername*>
Verify Servermap
Create and Execute **disk init** Script
Create and Execute **disk mirror** Script
Create Server Configuration Script
Create and Execute Addservers Script
Create or Update Interfaces File
Bring in *syslogins* Data
Add Dump Users to *model* Database
Create User Databases
Dump *master* Database
Start Dumps of File Systems to Tape
Set Up Scripts for Production Environment

Dump master Database

Make a database dump of the *master* database immediately after completing the basic installation process. If you make a mistake on any of the following steps, you may need to recover the *master* database. Depending on the version of the server, you may need to install a server dump device before you can dump the *master* database. You may also need to change the ownership of files controlling the tape drive or the disk file system where you need to make the dump, so that the required file(s) are owned by the UNIX user who is making the dump of the *master* database. You should still be operating as UNIX user 'sybase' at this point.

Check to see what tape or disk dump devices you have installed before you try to dump any database or transaction log. Note that the System 10 SQL Server supports making dumps directly to a device (using Backup Server), that is, you do not have to specify a server logical dump device (you still can if you prefer, and to be backward compatible with dump scripts setup for 4.9.x). This means you can immediately dump the *master* database to a specific disk file after sybinit finishes. This is a major advantage of System 10 for the DBA because you can make each dump to a different filename without worrying about the dump being overwritten, as with 4.9.x and dumps made to disk files. For the 4.9.x SQL Server, you can only dump to a logical dump device.

When sybconfig runs, it creates several default dump devices. You can use these to make a dump of *master* but check them first by using **sp_helpdevice** to make sure they will dump the database to a disk file or tape device that actually exists on the server machine and has room to support the dump file. In general, you will have to add a dump device to the server before you can dump the *master* database. Also, you should dump the *master* database at several points during the full installation process. Remember that for the 4.9.x server it will only dump to the logical dump device. In the case of a dump made to a disk file, the server will always dump to the same file on disk, the file that is assigned to the logical dump device. You must ensure that each dump of the *master* database is copied to a separate disk file before the next dump is started.

Reset File Ownership

Reset ownership to UNIX user 'dba' of all files in /dba/sybase and all subdirectories, as well as the files controlling partitions that support the master device (and sysprocsdev and sybsecurity devices for System 10) and any dump devices or files.

Change 'sa' Password

If you want the new server to communicate with other servers in your database system, the 'sa' password should be the same on all servers. Review the specifics of your security and interserver communications needs to determine if this is absolutely required. In general, the server user 'sa' password should be the same on all servers.

Configure Server Memory

Configure the server to use as much of the server machine's available memory as possible. A good first cut is to assign 80 percent of the server machine's memory to the server. Note that you must leave 10 to 20 MB (verify this with the server machine SA for your specific hardware and operating system platform) for the operating system. The server must have sufficient memory assigned to it before you can make other configuration changes, such as increasing the number of devices and user connections. Both of these configuration changes require assigning more memory to support the increased number of devices and users connections. If the memory is not assigned before these configuration changes are made, the server will not start up and you will have to clear the configuration block of the server master device (see Chapter 8).

Configure Number of Devices

The server will be installed with the maximum number of devices (logical disk devices) set to 10 by default. You can see this and the other configuration parameters by executing **sp_configure** without any other arguments. You will need to increase this number to support the number of devices you will need for all the user databases you will create on the server.

Configure Dump Devices (4.9.x only)

If you are installing a 4.9.x server, you will need to add dump devices for tape drives and any disk files that you intend to dump to. Note that you may need to install at least one dump device before you can make a dump of the *master* database.

Shut Down Server

Since the installation process started the server, you need to shut down the server. Since the sybconfig (sybinit for System 10) process must be executed by UNIX user 'sybase,' that is who owns the server process and the files that control access to the devices supporting the server. You need to get the server and all needed files owned by UNIX user 'dba,' and that means shutting down the server before you change the files, and so on.

Move Files to Use RUN_<servername>

Now move files as needed to start the server as UNIX user 'dba' from /dba/server-name directory. Use the RUN_<servername> script as described in Chapter 1, with the server errorlog sent to proper directory, and so on. See Chapter 15 for discussion of these scripts. Once the files and file ownerships are all set correctly, reboot the server as UNIX user 'dba.' Note that the server must have an interfaces file in order to start up. See Chapter 11 for more details of how the interfaces file works. If you have been following the steps given here, you told sybconfig (sybinit for System 10) that the Sybase installation (or release or home) directory was /dba/sybase and that is where sybconfig (sybinit for System 10) created an interfaces file for the new server. If an interfaces file was already present, the entries for the new server were appended. You should have no problem when you reboot the server as UNIX user 'dba' because the server will continue to look to /dba/sybase for the interfaces file. If, for any reason, you are changing the way the server is started, you must make sure the appropriate interfaces file is in the directory where you tell the server to look for it.

Verify Servermap

With the server up and running, verify the servermap you created earlier to document where all the server devices that you are about to create will go. Record the size of each partition that will support a server device.

Create and Execute disk init Script

The script you create and execute will create the server logical disk devices needed to support creation of the user databases. This script will simply be a set of **disk init** commands with the server device names and sizes taken from your servermap. Remember to round down to the nearest whole number of megabytes before computing the size in 2K pages for each **disk init** command. See Chapter 4 for more discussion of the **disk init** command. Note that once you set up this script, you shouldn't just run it all at once. The script is a vital piece of documentation in case you need to rebuild the server, but the **disk init** process is very important and even one typo can screw up all the other **disk init**s that follow. You should create the script, then cut and paste each **disk init** command and execute them one at a time on the server. This way, you can catch any errors as they occur. Recall that any **disk init** error will lock up the *vdevno*. It is much easier to catch such errors if you are doing one **disk init** at a time. You can then edit your script with the corrections and move on, restarting the server if needed to reuse the *vdevno*.

As discussed in Chapter 7, you must not execute a **disk init** for the master device, and you must remove the master device from the default pool of disk space.

Create and Execute disk mirror Script

Now you should create and execute a script to create all the disk mirrors you need. As with the **disk init**s you should create this script based on what is on your server-map, then execute each **disk mirror** command one at a time.

Create Server Configuration Script

As you make changes to the server configuration, you should be recording these changes in a configuration script. This script would contain, for example, the server commands needed to assign server machine memory to the server and to increase the maximum number of devices allowed. This script makes it very easy to rebuild the server if needed. You should also dump the server configuration frequently during installation and configuration by executing the **sp_configure** command. The output will allow you to build the configuration script if you don't do so as you go along.

Create and Execute Addservers Script

The addservers script will contain all the server commands to add the local and remote servers to the new server. This script will probably be very similar to a script that should be on your other server machines. The remote servers for the new server are probably all the same servers that existing servers need to talk to. All existing servers that need to communicate with the new server will also need to have the new server added to their *sysservers* table, as well as to their own addservers script.

Create or Update Interfaces File

You need to review the entire database system and determine which users and which other servers need to have information about the new server added to their interfaces file(s). You probably need to set up (if you haven't already) an interfaces file that contains the information about all the other servers in your system on the new server machine. Depending on the nature of the new server, you may or may not want to add the new server to the interfaces file that all your users have access to. An easy way to handle this is to make sure a copy of your current server version of the interfaces file for your database system is copied to the installation directory (/dba/sybase) before you install the new server. This way, the new server is appended to the existing interfaces file, which already contains the information about all the other servers. See Chapter 1 for more details about client and server versions of interfaces files.

Bring in syslogins Data

Now that the new server is up and running, you should add any and all users to the new server. Depending on the intended use of the new server, you may want to add only a subset of the users of your overall database system. You can generate a script to find each entry in the *syslogins* table in the *master* database of one of your existing servers and generate a script to execute **sp_addlogin** for each such user.

You can also simply use the bcp utility to dump all the entries in the *syslogins* table to a disk file, copy the file to the new server machine, and bulkcopy the file into the *syslogins* table of the new server. This is much faster if you need to move all the users from one server to another. However, you must edit the file before you load it into the new server. The new and existing server will both have an entry for *suid* = 1, which is the server user 'sa.' The *syslogins* table has a unique index on *suid* and will abort the bcp if it contains a row for *suid* = 1. You could work around this by deleting all the entries from *syslogins* of the new server, but you must not do this—you should never leave a server without the 'sa' login. Examine *syslogins* of the new server. Then, edit the disk file and delete the row for *suid* = 1 for the 'sa' login. Now you can load the disk file without problem. Note that this is appropriate only when you want to have all the users from an existing server added to the new server. Also, it is better to add all these users to the new server now, so that the *suid* for each user will be the same for the new server as on the existing server. This is very important if you are intending to load a database dump from the existing server to the new server because the dump will contain user information for the database and object permissions within the database that are all based on the *suid* values.

To add some users to the new server that are not on existing server, add them after loading all existing users. This will minimize *suid* problems later. If you have been setting up your database systems carefully, all the users should have the same *suid* on all servers. This will save you a lot of time chasing down permissions problems later.

Add Dump Users to model Database

Any user who needs to be able to dump a database must be added to the database and granted permission to dump the database. In general, you will have a group of users that make the database dumps for your database system. For a 4.9.x server, you will save lots of time if you add each of these users to the *model* database so that they will appear as users in every user database that is created later on in the server. Don't forget to add these same users to the *master* database as well.

First, create a group in the *model* database for users that need to be able to dump a database, add each such user to the *model* database and to the new group, and then grant permission to **dump database** to the new group. You should document this process as a script in case you need to rebuild the server later. For a System 10 server you should simply grant the **oper_role** to each of these server logins. That will allow them to dump any database in the server.

Create User Databases

Now that you have the server running, the server configured for memory and number of devices, the server disk devices created (initialized and made known to the server by executing **disk init**) and the users that need to dump databases added to the *model* database, you can create the user databases. You should prepare a script that creates all of the user databases that you know about at this time. This script, as with the others discussed above, will allow you to rebuild the server quickly when needed. This script also saves time whenever you need to set up any of the user databases on another server.

Dump master Database

You must dump the *master* database again after creating the user databases. You may well need to create more databases later on, but for now, dump the *master* database after you have created the initial set of user databases. You should be dumping the *master* database regularly from this point on anyway.

Start Dumps of File Systems to Tape

Now start dumps to tape of file systems, capturing files and any logdumps and database dumps that are being made to disk files. If you are copying dump scripts from existing systems, check them and make any changes needed to reflect the disk or tape devices on the new server machine that are different from those on the machine where the existing script was running.

Set Up Scripts for Production Environment

You now set up any and all scripts needed to regularly dump databases, transaction logs, perform **dbcc** runs, **update statistics,** and so on. See Chapter 1 for a listing of such scripts, and Chapter 15 for examples of such scripts.

3.5   sybconfig (sybinit for System 10) Errors

You will find that many things can go wrong with the sybconfig (sybinit for System 10) process. For many of the common problems, you can go to another window or UNIX session, correct the problem that sybconfig or sybinit is complaining about, and then proceed with the installation process. We list some of the most common problems in Table 3.6 and discuss how to fix them.

File Permissions
$SYBASE Not Set Correctly
Device File Permissions
Server Won't Boot
Installation Errorlog Files

File Permissions

The most common problem is simply file permissions. The sybconfig (sybinit for System 10) process needs to read and create many files in several different directories as well as accessing the devices needed to create server devices (master device etc.). If any of these files have incorrect permissions for the UNIX user 'sybase,' then the installation will fail. Note that you will see these errors in the sybconfig or sybinit process itself, the log file for the installation (which is listed at the beginning and end of the sybinit session), and in the errorlog of the server that is booted as part of the installation for problems with device access. Note that for sybconfig, the installation errorlog is mentioned deep within the output from sybconfig. The installation in our example sybconfig output shown previously was /dba/sybase/install-/errorlog_DDSDBA1.

You must ensure that the UNIX user 'sybase' has all the access needed. This is why you are better off to simply change the ownership to UNIX user 'sybase' of all the files in and below the installation directory, that is, /dba/sybase and all subdirectories. And, you must change the ownership of the files that control the raw partitions that will support the master device (and sysprocsdev, sybsecurity for System 10) to UNIX user 'sybase.'

$SYBASE Not Set Correctly

If the environment variable SYBASE is not set correctly, the installation process will not get very far. Make sure the variable SYBASE is set to the installation directory, /dba/sybase. Note that sybinit specifically asks you to specify the release directory (same as installation or home directory) for the sybinit process.

Device File Permissions

We have discussed device file permissions repeatedly, but we will cover it again because it comes up so often. You must change the ownership of the files that control the raw partitions that will support the master device (and sysprocsdev, sybsecurity for System 10) to UNIX user 'sybase.'

You should not be fooled by some of the errors you will see that are really caused by device file permission problems. For example, the server errorlog may say something like "insufficient space on device," when in reality the problem is file permissions. Whenever you get an error during the installation process, you should check exactly what device(s) you are asking sybconfig or sybinit to use and check the ownership on the files that control those devices.

Finally, review all the files involved for correct ownership and permissions after you complete the installation process as UNIX user 'sybase' and move to the files and startup scripts owned by UNIX user 'dba.' You may have problems starting the server as UNIX user 'dba' if you don't get all the file and device ownership and permissions changed to UNIX user 'dba.'

Server Won't Boot

The server may not boot during or after the installation process. As always, the problem is often related to file ownership and permission problems. However, the server may not boot for all the same reasons any server may not boot. These include memory problems, disk failures, network problems, and so on. Check the errorlog for the server to determine what is going wrong. Note that you may not get much help from sybconfig or sybinit, as they may simply say "waiting for server to boot" and hang up at this point. You need to find the errorlog for the server and figure out what is going on.

If you don't see the problem and its solution right away, you can kill the installation process and find the RUN_<*servername*> file that the installation process has created. You then kill the start server process, try to fix the problem, and then try starting the server manually, using the start server file created by the installation process. This saves you from having to run through the whole installation process each time you try to fix the problem. When the server will finally boot, kill it and return to the installation process.

You must understand what the server errorlog is telling you (see Chapter 11). Whether you are in the midst of the installation or well past that point, if the server won't boot, examine the server errorlog very carefully.

After installation is complete and you have moved to the startup scripts that you will use for the server in production, check the errorlog to make sure the server that you are running is indeed the version you think you are running. The installation process runs the server binary that came off the product tape, so you are pretty likely to be running the correct version of the server during installation. But once you get past installation, you may have several versions (EBFs, etc.) of the server in the same directory (/dba/<*servername*>/bin); you need to check the errorlog to make sure you are booting the correct version. Sometimes problems that prevent the server from booting are caused by trying to boot an older version of the server.

Installation Errorlog Files

There are several log files for sybconfig (sybinit for System 10) that you may need to examine to diagnose problems. First, there is the sybconfig or sybinit process itself that will display various messages on the screen as the installation process moves along. Second, the sybconfig or sybinit session generates a log file itself. The file name is displayed at the beginning and end of each sybinit session and deep within the output for sybconfig. Third, look at the server errorlog. During the installation process, the server errorlog will be in one of the subdirectories of the installation directory (/dba/sybase/install). After the installation process, the server errorlog will be in /dba/<*servername*>/errorlog. Finally, check the hardware errorlog for the server machine. Here you will find errors relating to the server machine and operating system hardware. Any and all of these errorlogs will help you find and fix problems during and after installation.

Chapter 4

Physical Server Design

You must understand the way the SQL Server is installed on the UNIX server machine. This process impacts how you add space to databases and create new databases in the future. While various aspects of the relationships between server, disks, disk controllers, and so on, have been mentioned elsewhere, we cover them in an orderly fashion here.

You may think you as a DBA don't need to understand the details of physical disks and partitions as seen by the operating system and how they relate the SQL Server devices that you work with. As your database system grows, you will be supporting servers that take over entire server machines and use almost all the disk space on the machine. You will need to understand these issues in order to keep up with the accelerating space demands of these large databases. You will also need to see the relationship between physical disks and segments to improve and maintain the server performance relative to the largest databases on each server. We discuss the following:

4.1	Physical Disks
4.2	Raw Partitions vs. File Systems
4.3	SQL Server Logical Disk Devices
4.4	Disk Partitioning
4.5	Disk Controllers
4.6	Initializing Server Devices
4.7	Database Segments
4.8	Mirroring Server Devices
4.9	How to Layout the Devices and Segments of a Server
4.10	Summary

4.1   Physical Disks

The disks of the server machine are where all the parts of the SQL Server are located, from the binaries that make up the server to the data within the databases. The term "disk" refers to the physical hard disk drive (also called a spindle) that is attached to a controller that is part of the server machine (see Figure 4.1). These physical disks are known to the server machine operating system by names like sd0 and sd4.

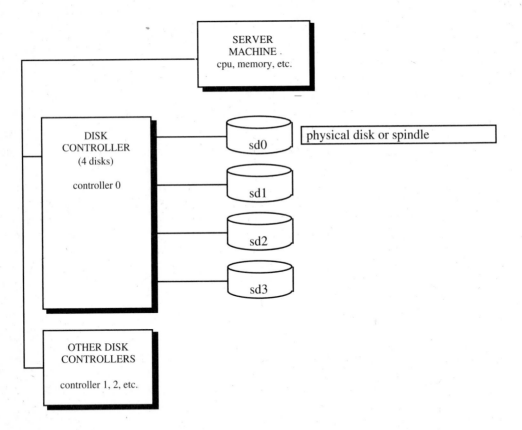

Figure 4.1   Server machine disk controllers and disks- -

The server machine divides each physical disk into partitions. The number of partitions allowed varies among operating systems; for SunOS the number of partitions is eight, and the partitions are labeled 'a' through 'h' (see Figure 4.2).

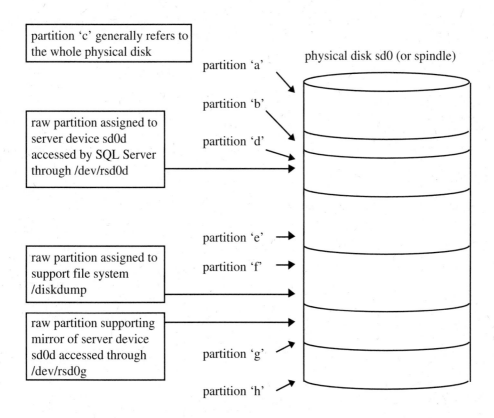

partition 'c' generally refers to the whole physical disk

physical disk sd0 (or spindle)

partition 'a'

partition 'b'

raw partition assigned to server device sd0d accessed by SQL Server through /dev/rsd0d

partition 'd'

partition 'e'

raw partition assigned to support file system /diskdump

partition 'f'

raw partition supporting mirror of server device sd0d accessed through /dev/rsd0g

partition 'g'

partition 'h'

Figure 4.2   Physical disk partitions (for SunOS) -

The server machine accesses each partition of each physical disk through files that are located in the server machine file system /dev, with a typical example being /dev/rsd0d for the 'd' partition of the physical disk known to the server machine as sd0. The "r" indicates that the partition is to be accessed in character mode as a raw partition. The character mode of accessing a partition means that the data is written to disk immediately with no buffering, which is what you want for all SQL Server devices. For each partition there is a companion file (in this case, /dev/sd0d), which is for accessing the partition in block mode, which you must not use for a server device. The block mode of accessing a partition means that the data is buffered before being written to disk. If the server machine or the disk had a problem before the buffer was flushed to disk, you could lose data. The files /dev/sd0d and /dev/rsd0d are known as "special" files that control the access mode to the 'd' partition of the physical disk sd0. Note that these special files are in /dev for all eight possible partitions for each physical disk on the server machine. You don't have to use all the partitions possible for any disk, and the size of each partition on a disk is configurable.

4.2   Raw Partitions vs. File Systems

Each partition of each physical disk on the server machine can contain file systems or can be used as a raw partition. SQL Server uses disks to store the databases and their data and can use either file system files or raw partitions for storage. File systems are controlled by the operating system and are where all the files needed for the operating system are stored. Since they are controlled by the operating system, file systems are buffered to improve speed. The operating system will buffer the writes to a file system on disk and make a group of writes all at once. You need to understand the implications of this to the integrity of your data. If you use an operating system file system as a server logical disk device, you may improve performance; however, since the writes to disk are buffered, you are risking the integrity of the data within your server. The SQL server relies on *committing* transactions in order to maintain data integrity. See Chapter 8 "SQL Server Recovery" for a detailed discussion of how the server assumes that a committed transaction has been written to disk and the problems it would cause if the writes to disk were actually in an operating system buffer.

When the server issues a disk write, it assumes that the disk write is executed immediately without any buffering, which is the case when you use a raw partition of the physical disk for a server logical disk device. If you are using an operating system file system and the disk writes are buffered, the server will believe it has written a transaction to disk, which means the transaction is committed, even though the write is only sent to memory. If a failure occurs between the time the server believes the disk write was completed and the time the operating system buffer is flushed out to disk, the parts of any transaction that were in the buffer are lost. When the server recovers (if it can recover with pieces of transactions lost), it will believe the transaction was indeed written to disk when in fact it was not, and the affected databases on the server will be inconsistent.

For this reason, you should not use operating system file systems for server logical disk devices. There is an exception to this rule: If you don't care about a particular database and you just want improved performance, then you can try a file system logical device. This technique is often used for *tempdb,* where the data is never recovered by the server, so losing it is not a concern (see Chapter 9).

Note that raw partitions are ignored by the operating system other than to check user permissions on the partition(s) as processes access them.

4.3   SQL Server Logical Disk Devices

You need to be clear on the terms. The term "disk" can be confusing. A physical disk is also called a spindle. A physical disk can contain several SQL Server logical disk devices (subsequently referred to simply as server devices, or just devices), or operating system file systems, and either of these (but not both) can occupy a single partition on the physical disk. The SQL Server will refer to a physical disk partition as a logical device. We use the phrase "server logical disk device" to make it clear that we are referring to the device known to the SQL Server, and that such a device is indeed a logical device in that it only refers to whatever you have assigned it to. This is in contrast to a physical disk, or device that refers to the actual disk drive or to a partition of such a physical disk. Note that, in general, the term "server device" refers to a server device that is assigned to a portion of a physical disk. Tape drives and operating system files used for dumping databases and transaction log dumps are referred to as "server dump devices."

Physical disks are not known to SQL Server; instead, a section of a partition of a physical disk is defined to the SQL Server as a logical disk device, see Figure 4.3. Once this is done, that section of the partition of the physical disk can be used by the server for creating databases, and so on. Note that the server does not have any knowledge of the size of the partition on the physical disk, only the size of the logical disk device that you defined to the server. Note that the size of the server logical disk device that you define to the server is defined as a number of 2K pages (a data page contains 2048 bytes and is called a "2K page"; this number is platform specific), and you can assign any number of 2K pages to the server logical disk device that will fit within the partition you have selected. However, you can only have one SQL Server logical disk device for a given partition of a physical disk. So, you must do one of two things. Either define the server logical disk device to be as large as possible on the partition you are working with, or, after deciding how big a server logical disk device you need, change the sizes of the partition of the physical disk to such a size that will just allow the size of the server logical disk device you want.

147

You can define the server logical disk device to be smaller than the partition will allow, but this is a waste of space since you can't assign another server logical disk device to a partition once it has been assigned to a server logical disk device. Further, you can't assign an operating system file system to a partition that is assigned to a server logical disk device.

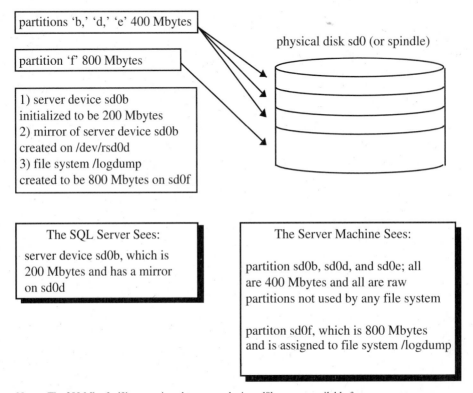

Notes: The 200 Mb of sd0b not assigned to server device sd0b are not available for any use.
Not all partitions of a disk must be assigned any space, i.e. sd0a, h

Figure 4.3   Server devices -

4.4   Disk Partitioning

You also need to understand the partitions that are allowed for the operating systems that are running on the server machines in your database system. For this discussion we review the specifics of the SunOS 4.1.3 disk partitioning. You must review this information with the server machine SA for your server machines to make sure you have accurate information for your system. You may think that the partitioning of disks is up to the server machine SA, but the SA may not have any insight into what SQL Server needs. You must ensure that the partitioning that is done, regardless of who is responsible, is optimal for the SQL Server. The following discussion is relevant to UNIX operating systems supplied by many vendors. We discuss:

SunOS Disk Partitions
Partition Sizes
Assignment of Disk Space to Partitions
Cylinder 0
Standard Disk Partitioning
Assignment of Whole Physical Disks to One Use

SunOS Disk Partitions

The SunOS operating system allows a physical disk to have up to eight partitions, named 'a' through 'h.' Each of these partitions, except for partition 'c,' can be assigned some portion of the space on the physical disk (spindle). The operating system will allow you to set up overlapping partitions, but you should not do this. Overlapping partitions can cause disaster when one of the partitions is used for a server logical disk device. As data is written to one of the partitions and fills the partition to the point that data is now written to the disk where the partitions overlap, data that was on the second partition is overwritten. If the second device is a server logical disk device, it will be destroyed as the data spills over from the first partition.

Partition Sizes

You can assign almost any size portion of the physical disk to any of the partitions. You can even assign the entire physical disk to one partition, although you generally shouldn't do this, because you want multiple partitions to support multiple server logical disk devices or their mirrors. When you install the physical disk, the operating system will assign all the space on the disk to partition 'c.' You should leave this the way it is, because it gives you a good way to verify the size of the whole physical disk. You see this by running the UNIX command dkinfo, which outputs the size of each partition. By leaving the 'c' partition as it is, you have documentation of the size of the physical disk. There are situations when you do need to assign the entire physical disk to one partition for use as a file system. For example, your server will need a file system to use as a location for database dumps made to disk. Since these database dumps will be large, you may need to assign the entire physical disk to the one file system to be used for the database dumps.

Assignment of Disk Space to Partitions

The assignment of a portion, or all, of the physical disk to a partition is done by using the format command. You should work with your server machine SA person to accomplish this task. Unless you are expert in the use of the format command and unless your group (that is, DBA) is assigned to do this work, you should leave it to the SA. The improper use of the format command can very quickly destroy your server. Note that although you can assign almost any part of the disk to a partition, that doesn't mean you should. The format command will allow you to create overlapping partitions, which you must not do because the data written to one partition can overwrite the adjacent partition. Further, you can assign cylinder 0 to a partition, but again, you must be very careful about doing this. Make sure you do not assign cylinder 0 of any disk to a partition that will support server devices or their mirrors. The standard disk partitioning scheme discussed later will prevent you from making this mistake.

Cylinder 0

The physical disk has vital information regarding the size, rotation speed, and so on, of the disk stored on the first or 0 cylinder of the disk. Cylinder 0 can be part of a partition that supports an operating system file system. You must never allow cylinder 0 to be part of any raw partition that is assigned to a server logical disk device. If you do, as soon as the server performs the **disk init** and starts writing to the raw partition, the data in cylinder 0 will be overwritten and lost. The worst part of this error is that there are no symptoms until it is too late. The data contained in cylinder 0 is not accessed by the operating system until the server machine is booted. Up until the next server machine reboot, the server will operate normally and you will be able to write critical business data to the device. When you next reboot the server machine, the operating system will look for the data that was in cylinder 0 to identify the disk. When the data is not found, the operating system will not recognize the entire disk at all. The server device that was using cylinder 0 is lost, and any other server devices on the disk are unavailable until the disk is available again. The only way to recover the disk is to get the proper data for the disk and write it back to cylinder 0, but that process destroys the data that was stored in the server device assigned to that partition. Note that this data is not readily available unless you have an identical disk somewhere in your database system. If this is the case, it is relatively easy for the server machine SA person to retrieve this data from an identical disk and write it out to the disk that had cylinder 0 overwritten. If this data is not available on your system, you must obtain it from the manufacturer of the disk. While this can be done, it means the disk and the server that relies on that disk may be unavailable for a significant amount of time.

If the server device that included cylinder 0 contained user databases, those databases can be rebuilt on the same server device (after repartitioning to avoid cylinder 0 and doing **disk init** on the new, smaller partition) if you have room and the latest database dump can be loaded from tape or disk. However, you lose all data since the last database dump and any subsequent transaction log dumps that you have. If the disk contained the server master device, the entire server is lost. You must repartition in such manner that cylinder 0 is no longer part of the server device. Then, reinstall the master device (that is, the server itself) and load a dump of the *master* database, assuming that the new master device, which now does not include cylinder 0, is big enough for the dump of *master*. If the dump of *master* is current enough to include all changes made to the system tables (that is, to include all databases and server devices) then you should be able to recover all the databases that were on the server. If the master dump is not current, you will have to make any needed changes manually, if in fact you can remember what those changes were. This again is an argument for dumping the system tables regularly. See Chapter 15 "Scripts" for details of the dump_systables script.

Of course, a functioning mirror of the master device would prevent this problem. Note that overwriting the data in cylinder 0 is a problem only if cylinder 0 is part of a partition that is assigned to a server device. Cylinder 0 may be part of a file system, and that will not cause any problems.

Standard Disk Partitioning

Now that you understand why cylinder 0 is so important, you should set up a simple disk partitioning standard to avoid the whole problem, as shown in Figure 4.4.

You should assign cylinder 0 to partition 'a' for all physical disks that will have partitions assigned to server logical disk devices and make it a rule that you and the other DBAs never assign anything to partition 'a.' This does reduce the number of partitions by one, but you still have plenty of them left. This standard is very easy to communicate to the server machine SA person since it is the same partitioning for all the physical disks that support server logical disk devices throughout your database system. You will find it much easier to check that cylinder 0 is not being used by any server device if it is consistently assigned to partition 'a' and your servers never use partition 'a.' Again, you can set up file systems on partitions that contain cylinder 0.

As discussed above, partition 'c' should be left alone to document the overall size of the disk.

This leaves partitions 'b,' 'd,' 'e,' 'f,' 'g,' and 'h' to be assigned to the remaining space of each physical disk as you desire. However, you should further simplify the process by having a standard partitioning for these partitions as well. You will need to have a small partition somewhere in the server for the master device and another device of the same small size to support the mirror of the master device. While the master device rarely needs to be larger than 10 Mb, it is good to allow plenty of room for expansion, since it is impossible to increase the size of the master device later and it is also impossible to alter the *master* database from the master device to another device (see Chapter 7 for details). You should create a 30-Mb partition on every whole physical disk to support the master device, its mirror, and other small databases that you may have. You may think this wastes the partition on disks other than those supporting the master device. However, you will need these small devices to support other small databases when you upgrade to System 10 (see Chapter 14 for details). You should keep the partitioning scheme simple by making the 'h' partition of all the disks that support server logical disk devices 30 Mb.

This leaves partitions 'b,' 'd,' 'e,' 'f,' and 'g.' You should again keep the scheme simple by taking the remaining space on the disk, after assigning cylinder 0 to partition 'a,' assigning 30 Mb to partition 'h,' and assigning one-fifth of the space to each of the remaining partitions. This leaves you with a simple partitioning scheme that you can apply to all the server disks in your database systems. Your SA person(s) will appreciate a scheme that is this simple to remember and set up. Your standard partitioning scheme will reduce errors and make installing disks a quicker process.

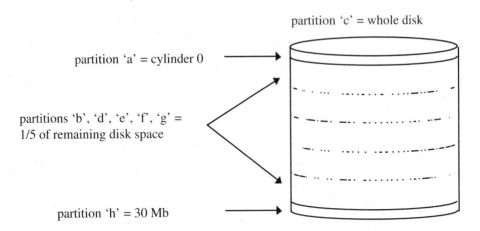

Figure 4.4   Standard partitioning for physical disks supporting
server devices or mirrors -

Assignment of Whole Physical Disks to One Use

Once you have set up the previously described partitioning convention, you should
also adhere to the following rule: Assign whole physical disks to support either
server logical disk devices or file systems, but not both. The partitions of a physical
disk should be assigned to either server devices or file systems, see Figure 4.5.

The convention makes it much easier for you to direct the server machine SA person.
You agree with the SA person as to which physical disks of the server machine are
for server devices and direct the SA person to apply your standard partitioning to all
those disks. You then direct the SA person to use the remaining physical disks for the
needs of the operating system and the file systems that you specify for holding the
files needed for the server. This allows the SA person to partition the file system
disks with complete freedom while not worrying about the server devices. You know
that you can check the partitions on the physical disks for the server and not worry
about any file system partitions. You can use any partitions on the disks specified for
the server without fear of overwriting a file system partition. All of this reduces the
need for you as DBA and the SA person to wait for each other before doing routine
server device tasks. You can also simplify the mirroring process by using whole
physical disks for server logical disk devices and their mirrors. You will find it much
easier to simply mirror all the partitions used for server devices to the same partitions

on another whole physical disk used to support the server. It is also easier to assess the impact of a disk failure if the entire disk is assigned to the server (as either server devices or their mirrors) or to file systems.

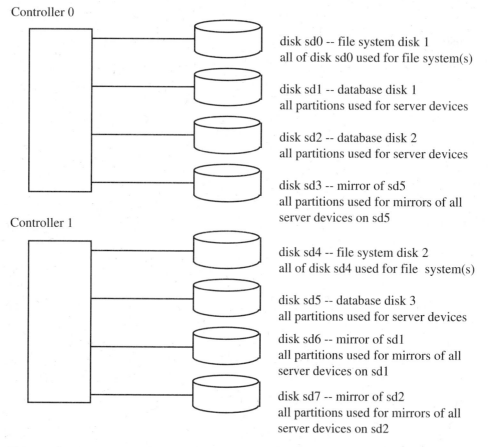

Controller 0

disk sd0 -- file system disk 1
all of disk sd0 used for file system(s)

disk sd1 -- database disk 1
all partitions used for server devices

disk sd2 -- database disk 2
all partitions used for server devices

disk sd3 -- mirror of sd5
all partitions used for mirrors of all server devices on sd5

Controller 1

disk sd4 -- file system disk 2
all of disk sd4 used for file system(s)

disk sd5 -- database disk 3
all partitions used for server devices

disk sd6 -- mirror of sd1
all partitions used for mirrors of all server devices on sd1

disk sd7 -- mirror of sd2
all partitions used for mirrors of all server devices on sd2

This example is for a server machine with eight disks. Note that each physical disk is used only for one purpose: file system(s), server devices or mirrors of server devices.

Figure 4.5   Using whole physical disks for server devices, mirrors or file systems - - - - - -

4.5   Disk Controllers

Now that you have the disks of the server machine divided into two groups, one for supporting server logical disk devices (or their mirrors) and the other for supporting operating system file systems, you need to understand the issues surrounding disk controllers. Disk controllers are the devices in the server machine that interface the physical disks to the server machine itself. We discuss the following disk controller issues:

Disks and Controllers
Tape Drives and Controllers
Spreading Disks across Controllers
Standard for Assigning Disks to Controllers

Disks and Controllers

You can attach many physical disks to a single disk controller, but you will find that throughput performance goes down after a certain number of disks are attached. You must review this with your server machine SA person to get the maximum number of disks that you can attach to a single controller before performance drops off. For SunOS, the maximum number of physical disks that can be attached to one controller without adversely affecting performance is four. This number may vary with operating systems and hardware platforms. Note that this number is important when you add disk space to a server, because you will need to get another controller for each set of disks you add.

Further, you must be aware that there are different types of disk controllers, such as fast SCSI and slow SCSI. You need to know what kind of disks and disk controllers you have on each system and be aware of these distinctions when trying to add more disks to the server. For example, you may be able to add slow SCSI disks to a fast SCSI disk controller but not the other way around, although you are probably wasting the performance of the fast SCSI controller.

You can see which disks are attached to which controller by executing the operating system command format. You must be logged into the server machine as UNIX user 'root' to execute this command, another reason you must have su privilege on all the server machines in your system (see Chapter 1). The output of the format command will list each physical disk on the server machine along with the controller name and number. You must be careful with the format command; don't use it if you don't know how, because mistakes can erase an entire physical disk.

Tape Drives and Controllers

You also need to realize that the tape drives on each server machine are attached to a disk controller, too. You can attach tape drives to the same controller that is support-ing the maximum number of disks, but you should have a separate controller for the tape drives (see Figure 4.6). This prevents the controllers that support disks from being slowed down whenever you need to use the tape drive(s).

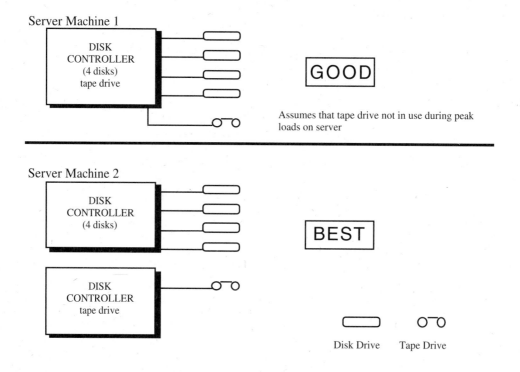

Figure 4.6   Tape drives and disk controllers -

Spreading Disks across Controllers

You need to realize that which disks are attached to which controllers is also an important issue. You want to have the physical disks that support server logical disk devices spread over as many controllers as possible. This means that you don't attach all the server disks to one set of controllers and all the file system disks to another set (see Figure 4.7). You want to balance the number of server disks and file system disks on all the controllers. You need to do this for two reasons, both of which involve only the disks that support server devices. You will need to spread the file system disks over the controllers simply to make room to spread the server disks.

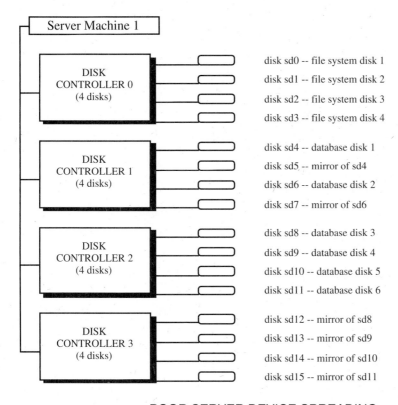

disk sd0 -- file system disk 1
disk sd1 -- file system disk 2
disk sd2 -- file system disk 3
disk sd3 -- file system disk 4

disk sd4 -- database disk 1
disk sd5 -- mirror of sd4
disk sd6 -- database disk 2
disk sd7 -- mirror of sd6

disk sd8 -- database disk 3
disk sd9 -- database disk 4
disk sd10 -- database disk 5
disk sd11 -- database disk 6

disk sd12 -- mirror of sd8
disk sd13 -- mirror of sd9
disk sd14 -- mirror of sd10
disk sd15 -- mirror of sd11

POOR SERVER DEVICE SPREADING

Having all file system disks on one controller reduces the number of controllers available for spreading server devices. Having server devices and their mirrors on physical disks attached to the same controller means a single controller failure will make the databases on those server devices completly unavailable even though they are mirrored. Spread server devices and mirrors evenly over the controllers available.

Figure 4.7   Poor server device spreading over controllers -

First, you need to spread out the server devices for database integrity. You need to have mirrors set up for the databases on your server; we discuss mirroring below. When the server writes to disk, it needs to write to the primary disk and also to the disk that is the mirror. If the primary and mirror disk are attached to the same controller and the controller fails, both disks may get corrupted. You must locate these two disks on separate controllers so that a controller failure will not affect both disks.

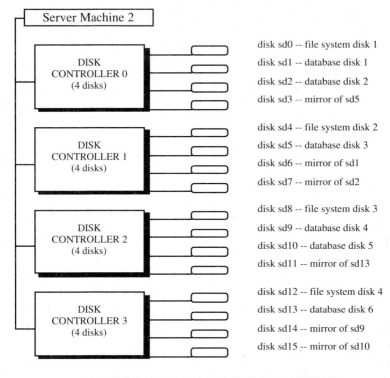

OPTIMUM SERVER DEVICE SPREADING

Note: Total of 16 disks, one-quarter assigned to file systems, the remaining 12 disks split evenly among supporting database server devices and their mirrors.

Figure 4.8   Optimum server device spreading over controllers -

Second, you need to spread out server devices for performance reasons. As your databases grow, you will need to spread the objects within the database over several disks by using segments, which we discuss below. A good example of this is locating the indexes for the most heavily accessed tables on a separate segment from the tables themselves. This means the server can retrieve information about an index from one server device while a request for information from the table itself is being retrieved from another server device. You need to have these two server devices attached to separate controllers or you won't see the very performance benefits you wanted in the first place (see Figure 4.8).

Standard for Assigning Disks to Controllers

You can simplify this process of deciding which disks get attached to which controller by deciding what fraction of the total number of physical disks on the server machine will support file systems, then spreading those disks evenly over the number of controllers on the server machine. Then, all the other disks are attached to the controllers, within the maximum number of physical disks per controller, and you are all set.

Further, you should assign the file system and server device disks in the same order on each controller. If you have one-quarter of all the disks dedicated to file systems, you should have the first disk on each controller supporting file systems. This simple convention makes it very simple to determine which disks do what. This information is vital for both DBA and SA when a disk error occurs. You need to know as quickly as possible what parts of the server or server machine are affected by failures. Also, you need to know what is on a disk when you need to find more file system space. You will be able to do this much faster if the first disk on each controller is a file system disk, instead of having to look at each physical disk to determine what is out there.

Note also that you will need to be aware of the balance of file system and server device disks when you need to add disks to the server machine. You should get a new controller and a set of disks at one time. You will find that as you need more disks for either file systems or server devices, you will need disks for the other kind as well.

4.6   Initializing Server Devices

Now that you have arranged the partitions of the physical disks and spread the server disks over the available controllers, you need to be aware of some details in the process of initializing a portion of a physical disk so that it is available to the SQL Server. We discuss these server device initialization topics:

The **disk init** Server Command
device_name
physical_name
virtual_device_number (*vdevno*)
number_of_blocks
Final Notes on **disk init**

The disk init *Server Command*

You need to understand the process by which a disk partition or an operating system file becomes a server device. This process will initialize the server device, and this must be done before the server device is even known to the server. This process uses the **disk init** server command. Note that you need to do this for either type of server device, that is, a server device that is assigned to a raw partition or to a file in the operating system file system. You perform this with the **disk init** command; the syntax is shown below, and we then discuss each of the parameters you must supply to the command (see Figure 4.9).

```
disk init
name = "device_name",
physname = "physicalname",
vdevno = virtual_device_number,
size = number_of_blocks
```

Where:

- The ***device_name*** is what the server logical disk device will be called.

- The ***physicalname*** is the name of the raw partition or the operating system file system file that the server device will be assigned to. Note that the ***physicalname*** is what the operating system recognizes. The **disk init** command is simply establishing a connection between a device that the server knows about and a piece of a physical disk that the operating system knows about.

- The ***virtual_device_number*** is a number that is unique to each server device.

- The ***number_of_blocks*** refers to the size, in 2K pages, that the server device will be. As discussed earlier, the size of the server device can be as large as the raw partition it is being assigned to.

device_name

The **_device_name_** is what the server device will be called within the server. This is the name that you will use in the server commands **create database**, **alter database**, and so on. You must establish and follow a server device naming convention. The simplest convention is the best. Use the operating system command format to display all the physical disks attached to the server machine. You must be logged into the server machine as UNIX user 'root' to run the format command. Note that this is one of the reasons you as DBA must have su permission on all the server machines. The output of the format command will show you what the operating system calls each of the physical disks. These are the names that you must use, along with the partition name, when creating server logical disk devices. A typical output of the format command will tell you that the physical disks have names like sd0, sd1 through sd6, for example. When you decide to use the raw partition 'd' of physical disk sd1, you must use sd1d for the **_device_name_**. This convention must be applied to all the server devices in your database system. Note that you use the name of the disk as specified by the output of the format command, even though the 'special file' that the server will use to access the raw partition is called /dev/rsd1d.

If you are using operating system files as server devices, you don't need a server device naming convention that includes the partition name. In fact, you won't have the problems described above at all because the server will report errors for the device by the file name of that device, and the file name includes the full path of the file, so it will be clear which physical disk the file (server device) is on.

;-)   Your server crashes, the errorlog shows write errors to server device "baddog1", but you don't remember which physical disk contains the raw partition (or the file in the file system) that is assigned to "baddog1." Since the server has crashed, you can't run **sp_helpdevice** to see what the physical disk partition is. You're stuck. You shouldn't attempt a restart of the server until you can diagnose the disk problems or you risk further server corruption. Your only choice is to run hardware diagnostics on all the disks on the server machine, which is a big waste of time. You must have a simple server device naming convention so you know immediately which physical disk is supporting which server device.

physical_name

The **_physical_name_** refers to a portion of a physical disk as known to the operating system. For a raw partition, the **_physical_name_** is the full path of the file that is accessed in order to access the raw partition. Recall that a partition of a physical disk can be accessed in two ways, block or character. A SQL Server device that accesses a raw partition uses only one (the character access version) of the two operating system files available to control the disk device. This means that the file used is rsd1b for the 'b' partition of the server machine physical disk called sd1, and this file is located in the /dev file system. Note that the "r" in rsd1b tells you this is the character version. Note also that you must check with the server machine SA to be sure what these files are called for your specific hardware platform. You would then specify /dev/rsd1b for **physical_name**. If you are using a file for a server device, you would specify the complete path of the file, <path>/<**device_name**> for **physical_name**. You should indicate what file system the server device file is in as part of the **physical_name**.

virtual_device_number (vdevno)

The **virtual_device_number** is somewhat arcane, but you must understand why it exists and how it can block your attempts to create devices. Each server device consists of some number of 2K pages. These pages are numbered sequentially from 0 to N - 1, where N is the total number of pages in the device. However, there must be some way to give the pages in multiple server devices a unique page number. This is where *vdevno* comes in. It is used in combination with the page number in each server device to create a unique page number within the entire server. This means that *vdevno* is very important. Clearly, the server will require that each time you execute **disk init** you supply a *vdevno* that is not currently in use. You can see which *vdevno* values are already in use by executing the server command **sp_helpdevice**. Note that you will have trouble with *vdevno* under the following circumstances.

Table 4.1   Virtual Device Number Problems

Problem	Recommendation
vdevno is already being used	Sometimes, you will find that the simplest solutions are indeed the best. Check that the *vdevno* you used in the **disk init** command isn't already being used by an existing server device. Check the output of the **sp_helpdevice** server command (without any arguments) to see the *vdevno*s already being used. Note that selecting all the rows from the system table *sysdevices* will not show you the *vdevno*s in use. The *vdevno* values are not stored in *sysdevices* rather they are computed for the output of **sp_helpdevice**.

Table 4.1   Virtual Device Number Problems (Continued)

Problem	Recommendation
Earlier **disk init** failed	If an earlier attempt to execute **disk init** with a particular *vdevno* value failed for any reason (size specified was larger than the raw partition, for example), you can't use that same *vdevno* value again until the server is rebooted.
Dropped a server device	If you have dropped a server device from the server (using the stored procedure **sp_dropdevice**—note that a server command creates server devices but a stored procedure drops them) since the last server restart, you can't use that *vdevno* of the server device that was dropped until the server is rebooted.
devices value in **sp_configure**	The maximum number of server devices that is allowed is part of the server configuration. You can see what the maximum number is by executing the server command **sp_configure** and looking for the value of **devices**. This value is 10 by default when the server is installed. Note that a value of 10 for **devices** means you can only create server devices with *vdevno* values of 0 through 9. When you try to execute **disk init** with a *vdevno* of 10, it will fail. Note that this a very common reason that **disk init** fails. Note further that the error you will see when **disk init** fails does not tell you it is due to a lack of allowable *vdevno* values. Instead, you will get an error that the specified physical device doesn't have room to create the server device. When you see such an error, check the *vdevno* values in use and the maximum allowable value of **devices**. If you need to increase the number of **devices**, you do that by using **sp_configure**; you must reboot the server to have this configuration change take effect. You need to be aware that increasing the maximum allowed number of server devices does use some of the server machine's available memory, so you don't want to set **devices** to a number higher than you really need. Also, remember that **devices** set to 10 means the maximum *vdevno* allowed is $10 - 1 = 9$, and that the master device always uses *vdevno* = 0. Also, when you have a **disk init** fail, remember that you can't use that *vdevno* again until you reboot the server. Note that the maximum number of devices as specified by **devices** does not include server dump devices. You do not need to worry about **devices** or *vdevno* when adding server dump devices.

;-) You need to be careful with this process. You can easily become very confused. Your first **disk init** fails because you specified a size that was too large for the disk partition, but now you try again with that problem fixed and you fail again this time because you tried to reuse the same *vdevno*. You try to use *vdevno* + 1 but that fails because you happened to exceed the maximum allowable *vdevno*, which is confusing since it is N–1 where N = the value of **devices** in the output of **sp_configure**. You now become befuddled trying to see if the size you specified is too large (still) since the error messages you get tell you there isn't enough room on the physical disk, or if the *vdevno* is in use (which it isn't) or why you can't use *vdevno* = 10 when **devices** = 10. Relax, and figure it out. Don't just keep trying **disk init** over and over.

;-) Another *vdevno* mess. By being a little too clever, the DBA can really mess things up. For performance reasons, all of *tempdb*, including the 2 Mb that are created on the master device at installation time, were moved to a separate logical server device on a separate physical disk. (Don't do this—please!). This may have been great for performance, but when the DBA then fiddled with some other **sp_configure** server parameters, the server would not start, probably due to increasing one of the server configuration parameters so that it required more memory than was physically available. To cure this, the DBA ran buildmaster–r, which resets all the server configuration parameters to their default values. The server would start, but the DBA couldn't do anything. Why? For reasons that were never fully explained, when *tempdb* was moved the new server logical device was defined by **disk init** with a value of *vdevno* = 20. This, like so many DBA maneuvers, doesn't appear to be a blunder until much later. Since buildmaster–r had been run, the maximum number of devices was reset to 10, which means the highest allowable *vdevno* = 9. So, the server would start but it would not recognize the server logical device that contained *tempdb*. This situation isn't deadly, but for the DBA on pager duty when it all comes unraveled, it can be a very tiring experience. The cure was to use isql and simply use **sp_configure** to change the maximum number of devices and restart the server. Note that you couldn't do anything in this case that required *tempdb* until you got the maximum number of devices increased. Commands like **sp_helpdevice** use *tempdb* and won't run if *tempdb* is unavailable. This is yet another example of how DBA actions ripple through your entire database system.

number_of_blocks

The **number_of_blocks** refers to the size of the server device specified in 2K pages. You need to be careful of the various terms, blocks, 2K pages, allocation units that refer to the amount of disk space the server acquires at one time (equal to 256 2K pages), and so on. For **disk init**, a block is a 2K page. You are assigning a server device to a raw partition on a physical disk. The size of the partition in question can be seen by executing the operating system command dkinfo <*diskname*>. Note that you supply the name of the physical disk as it is known to the operating system, such as dkinfo sd1. The output will show the number of sectors and cylinders for all of the partitions of the physical disk. See Chapter 3 for an example of the output of the dkinfo command.

The number of sectors for a partition is what you care about. The size of the partition in bytes is computed by multiplying the number of sectors by 512 bytes/sector. You then compute the number of megabytes in the partition by dividing the number of bytes by 1024 * 1024 (= 1 Mb). The size of the partition will probably not be a whole number of megabytes. Now, you need to round this number down to the nearest whole number of megabytes and convert that number of megabytes into the number of 2K pages to use for the **disk init** command. You need to understand how the server goes out and gets disk space when it is executing a **create database** or **alter database** command.

When the server goes out to a server device to create or alter a database, it looks for space on the disk in 0.5 Mb chunks, called allocation units, which are 256 2K pages or 0.5 Mb. You normally don't care about this because the **create database** and **alter database** server commands only allow you to specify a whole number of megabytes for the size of the database or the amount you are adding to the database. You will care, however, in the following scenario.

One of your fellow DBAs decides to create or add to a database but didn't check that the space requested was available on the server device(s) specified. The server goes to each server device to allocate the space requested. For any server device that doesn't have the full amount of space requested, the server allocates as much as it can, in 0.5 Mb chunks. If the server device was created with a **disk init** command whose size parameter specified something other than a whole number of megabytes, specifically, xx.yy Mb, where xx is some number of megabytes and yy is greater than

0.5 Mb, the server will allocate as many whole megabytes as it can and an additional 0.5 Mb. This may never be a problem for you. When you need to recreate this database, either as a rebuild after disaster or on another server as part of a migration, you may not be able to load the dump of this database without creating corruption. The new database that you create by using the **create database** and **alter database** server commands must be done using sizes in whole megabytes. Since the load of a database is just a physical copy of the data pages in the order they appear in the database, when they are loaded they must appear in the same order in the new database after loading. Since you can't recreate the 0.5 Mb on the new database, you can't be sure that the load won't create corruption. For this reason, always run **disk init** on server devices with a size that is the largest whole number of megabytes that will fit in the space that is actually available.

If you are assigning a server device to an operating system file, first examine the overall size of the file system where the file will be and determine what, if any, space in that file system will be needed by other files, then determine the size available for the server device, then convert that into the number of 2K pages available for the **disk init** command. The size of the file system can be obtained from the output of the operating system command df. Determining the amount of space available for your server device versus any other files that need to be in the file system is more complex. You may need to have a file system dedicated to each server device that will be supported by a disk file; then your **disk init** should assign all of the file system space (the largest whole number of megabytes) to the server device.

;-)

Some disk trivia. The reason a 2 K page keeps appearing as a basic unit of server storage space is that this is the unit of data that is moved in a single I/O action. Hence, you move a 2 K chunk of data each time you read from or write to disk. Since this is the size of the chunk that is moved for each I/O, it might as well be the basic size of all operations within the server.

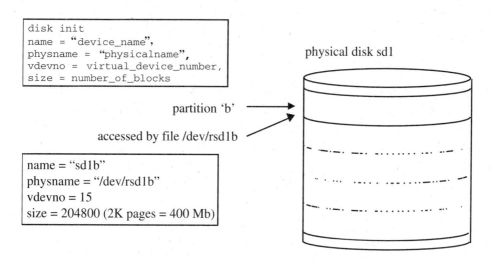

```
disk init
name = "device_name",
physname = "physicalname",
vdevno = virtual_device_number,
size = number_of_blocks
```

physical disk sd1

partition 'b'

accessed by file /dev/rsd1b

name = "sd1b"
physname = "/dev/rsd1b"
vdevno = 15
size = 204800 (2K pages = 400 Mb)

name consists of physical disk name and partition name.
physname is the full path to the file that controls block access to the physical disk raw partition.
UNIX user 'dba' must own the file specified by physname.
vdevno must be less than configuration value "devices" in output of `sp_configure`.
vdevno must not already be in use.
size is largest whole number of Mb that fit in partition size.
partition size determined from output of dkinfo sd1 for partition 'b.'

Figure 4.9   Initializing server logical disk devices -

Final Notes on disk init

Several final notes on the **disk init** command that you need to know.

You do not use **disk init** for creating the master device that will support the *master* database. The master device is created when you run buildmaster, which is supplied with the SQL Server, or, more normally, when you run sybconfig (sybinit for System 10), which is the normal way to install a SQL Server.

Further, you must not execute **disk init** specifying a partition that is already being used for the master device. If you do this you will destroy the server. Worse still, the server will continue to run until you need to do something with it. You must check very carefully anytime you are doing a **disk init** to verify where the master device is to be sure you are not affecting it. Similarly, you must not execute **disk init** on a partition that is already being used for any server device. In theory, the server will not allow you to do this, but you should not depend on the server; you should verify that you are using the correct partition. Also, you must not **disk init** to any partition that will be used for the mirror of a server device. A mirror of a server device is always created on a raw partition using the **disk mirror** command. All of this can be prevented by creating and using an accurate servermap.

;-)

> You are new on the job. You are asked to install SQL Server. What could be easier? You take the specifications for the server devices and away you go. You don't check the server device naming convention in use at the site. Actually they don't enforce a server device naming convention and that is the problem. You go ahead and **disk init** the list of devices you were told to. All is well until you dump the *master* database to disk as you always should after installing the server. You get errors. You run **dbcc** and get errors. You panic. You look bad. After the panic fades you decide to check things. You find the master device was on one of the partitions that you did a **disk init** on. The list of server devices included a device on the partition that had the master device. This is confusing but you should have checked. The only solution now is to reinstall. Not a good first impression. Always check where the master device is for the server you are working on and for any and all servers that may be on the same server machine. Don't assume anything, especially about a new environment.

When you execute the **disk init** command, the server device created is not automatically assigned to the pool of default disk space. Default disk space is where database objects are created when no server device is specified. Normally, you don't want to have any of your server devices be default devices since you must place all databases (at least) on specific server devices to control server performance and data integrity. If you do want a server device to be a default disk, remember that you must do this as a separate step, using the stored procedure **sp_diskdefault**.

To execute the **disk init** command successfully, you must have the permissions to access the special files that control the raw partitions of the physical disks. For example, if you are creating server devices as UNIX user 'dba' (see Chapter 1 for why you don't want to be UNIX user 'sybase'), then UNIX user 'dba' must own the device files /dev/rsd1b in order to create a server device that is assigned to the 'b' raw partition of the physical disk sd1.

4.7   Database Segments

Once you have the server devices spread over the controllers, and the file system disks filling out the maximum number of disks attached to one controller, you need to understand segments, which are very misunderstood. They can be confusing and complicated, but they do serve a purpose that makes them worthwhile. You may think that segments means nothing more than putting the transaction log for a database on a separate server device. You are wrong. Segments are the way in which a DBA can control the placement of database objects, including the transaction log. The DBA needs to control the placement to improve server performance. You must understand what segments can do to help you and also how they can hurt you. Once you have set up segments for your databases, you must maintain them. You will find that the advantages of segments can easily be lost by one DBA on your team who doesn't understand them and alters a database by adding space on a new device and assigning multiple segments to the new device.

We discuss the following topics:

Why Segments Exist
The Transaction Log Segment
Large Object on a Separate Segment
Segments and the **create database** Server Command
Segments and the **alter database** Server Command
Creating a User-defined Segment
Segments and Capacity Planning
Addition of Space to a User-defined Segment
Final Notes on Segments

Why Segments Exist

You can best appreciate why segments exist by considering a server that didn't have any. You create a database and fill it with data. The transaction log records are on disk, along with the database tables and other objects, all mixed up together. As the database fills up the space available on the server device, you create another server device on another disk partition and alter the database to put further growth on the new server device. Whenever you recover the server, which is every time you restart the server, you cause the server to look at the contents of the transaction log. Since it is spread out all over the server device(s), this is a long process. If the transaction log records were all in one place, it would save time on recovery. You want to tell the server to put all the transaction log records and only such records in one place. Hence the need for segments.

The Transaction Log Segment

The most common use for segments is placing the transaction log (the log segment) on a server device separate from the rest of the database. This is required by SQL Server before you can dump the transaction log and keep a copy of it. See Chapter 8 for discussion of why you want to dump a copy of the transaction log.

Large Object on a Separate Segment

Now imagine a large table on your hypothetical server. This table is heavily accessed and has several indexes on it. You could improve server performance if you could place this table on a separate server device. You could do more by placing the table on a partition of a disk that was on a different controller from other databases. This way, your server could send requests regarding the table to a whole separate I/O chain while handling all other requests through some other controller and disk(s). You also would benefit in that the space allocated for the table would be controlled. When all objects vie for the same disk space, you never know how much space is free as other objects become bigger or smaller. By placing the table on its own segment, you have guaranteed that only pieces of the table will be in that segment and no other database objects can use that space. Here you need another segment for a given table. You would want to do the same thing for an index for a large table. This is especially good if many queries to the table use an index that "covers" the query, which means the index entries contain the data the query needs. You only need to access the index, not the actual table, to answer these queries. If you place such an index on a segment that is on a partition that is separate from those used for the table and the rest of the database, the server can get better I/O throughput because some requests go to the controller and disk that hold the table whereas others go to the controller and disk that hold the index.

To place a table (or an index) on a specific segment, you simply include the **on <segmentname>** clause in the **create table** server command. The same syntax applies to the **create index** command.

This discussion of your hypothetical server makes it clear why you want to have segments at your disposal. Segments are the only way you can control what is placed where on the disks. This control allows you to get better throughput and controls which objects can compete for which parts of the server's disk space.

Segments and the create database Server Command

You need to understand how segments are created and how to manage them. Whenever you execute the **create database** or **alter database** server commands you are creating segments. When you execute

```
create database <dbname>

on <server_device_name> = <size_in_Mb>
```

the server allocates the space to the database and assigns the segments called *system*, *default* and *logsegment* to the server device. The *system* segment means that system tables, and so on, are placed here; the *logsegment* means all the transaction log records will be stored here; the *default* segment means all other objects will be placed on this device. Note that we have three segments of the database on the same device, and this means you have objects that belong to the *system*, *default*, and *logsegment* segments all stored together on the same server device; see Figure 4.10. You can see this by executing **sp_helpdb <dbname>**, which outputs information about the database, including a list of all the server devices that contain portions of the database and the segments assigned to each device. In order to see the segments and the server devices you must first be in the database by executing the **use <dbname>** command. Note that this means objects created in any of these three segments can completely fill the disk space of the server device. Note also that segments are assigned to a device. This means that for any database all of the portions of a server device that are assigned to that database will have the same segment assignments.

You need to understand this and it is confusing. A single server device can support multiple databases, but the segments of any database are assigned on a device basis. Another implication of this you need to realize is that if you want to put objects in a separate segment, you will need to use a server device that does not already support any parts of the database. See Chapter 10 for discussion of the implications this has for capacity planning.

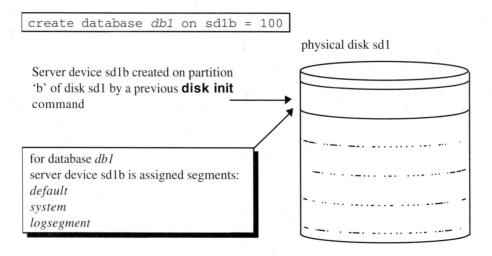

```
create database db1 on sd1b = 100
```

physical disk sd1

Server device sd1b created on partition 'b' of disk sd1 by a previous **disk init** command

for database db1
server device sd1b is assigned segments:
default
system
logsegment

Figure 4.10   Segments assigned automatically (by default) -

For your production databases, except *master*, you need to place the *logsegment* on a separate server device. Note that the *master* database can't be extended beyond the master device, and therefore the *master* database can't have its transaction log (*logsegment*) separated to another device. The *master* database always has the segments *system*, *default*, and *logsegment* assigned to all the disk space assigned to the *master* database. Normally you will do this when you first create the database by using the syntax

```
create database <dbname>

on <server_device_1> = <size1> ,

log on <server_device_2> = <size2>
```

This will automatically set up server_device_2 with the *logsegment* assignment only, see Figure 4.11.

Note that server_device_1 still gets the segment assignments of *system* and *default*. If you don't create the transaction log on a separate device, as shown in Figure 4.11, the transaction log will be mixed in with the *system* and *default* segments. You can move the transaction log later to a separate device using **sp_logdevice** as described in the System Administration Guide. For the remainder of the discussion we assume you have created the database with the transaction log on a separate device.

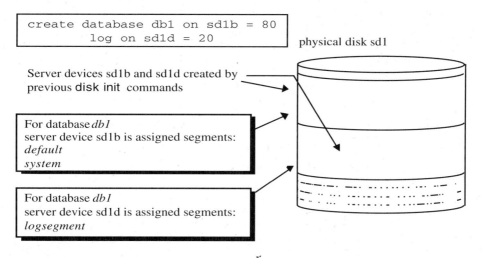

```
create database db1 on sd1b = 80
        log on sd1d = 20
```
physical disk sd1

Server devices sd1b and sd1d created by previous **disk init** commands

For database *db1* server device sd1b is assigned segments: *default* *system*

For database *db1* server device sd1d is assigned segments: *logsegment*

logsegment should be on a device on a separate physical disk attached to a separate controller

Figure 4.11   Log segment on separate server device -

Segments and the alter database *Server Command*

You have now created the database on server_device_1 with the transaction log (*logsegment*) on server_device_2; server_device_1 has the segments *system* and *default,* and server_device_2 has only the *logsegment.* You need to understand what happens when you alter the database. When you alter a database to add space on a server device that already supports part of the database, the new space will be given the same segment assignments that already exist on that server device. We have two possible situations for the database you have set up so far. If you alter the database on server_device_1, the new space will get the same segment assignments that already exist for this database on server_device_1, namely, *default* and *system*. If you alter the database on server_device_2, the new space will get the segment assignment of *logsegment* only.

When you alter a database to a server device that is not currently supporting the database, the new device will get the segment assignments *default* and *system*. Note that the new device would also get the segment assignment *logsegment* if the *logsegment* was not already assigned to be the lone segment on a separate server device. You alter the database to server_device_3 and it gets the segment assignments *default* and *system*.

Creating a User-defined Segment

You have things under control up to this point. Now you need to set up a segment that is not *default* or *system* or *logsegment*; we call these segments user-defined segments. In order to set up a user-defined segment, you must first decide if your user-defined segment needs to be on its own device, separate from the others. While it probably doesn't make much sense to add another segment without putting it on its own device, we cover the process here so you'll know how. In your database so far, you could add a segment called *myseg0* to server_device_1 by using the server command

```
sp_addsegment <segment_name>, <server_device>
```

which for this case would be

```
sp_addsegment myseg0, server_device_1
```

The output of **sp_helpdb <*dbname*>** would show that device server_device_1 now has the segment assignments of *system*, *default*, and *myseg0*.

You now want to do the more interesting case of adding a new user-defined segment that will have its own device. You don't want to have any other segments assigned to this server device. First, you must alter the database to this device,

```
alter database <dbname>

on <server_device_3> size = <size3>
```

You recall that since server_device_3 has not been supporting any part of database *dbname* before this point, the segment assignments will be the standard set of *system* and *default* see Figure 4.12. Again, this standard set of segment assignments would include *logsegment* if you had not already made server_device_2 the log device, that is, only the *logsegment* is assigned to that device. Now you will add your segment to this device using **sp_addsegment myseg1, server_device_3**. You can run **sp_helpdb <dbname>** and see that server_device_3 now has three segments assigned to it, *system*, *default,* and *myseg1*.

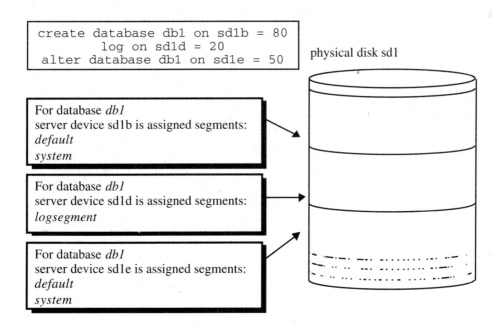

```
create database db1 on sd1b = 80
          log on sd1d = 20
   alter database db1 on sd1e = 50
```
physical disk sd1

For database *db1*
server device sd1b is assigned segments:
default
system

For database *db1*
server device sd1d is assigned segments:
logsegment

For database *db1*
server device sd1e is assigned segments:
default
system

logsegment should be on a device on a separate physical disk attached to a separate controller

Figure 4.12 Altering database to new server device- -

You need to realize that you are not done at this point. If you don't finish the job, the whole reason you created *myseg1* is in jeopardy. Your new segment, *myseg1* is on a separate device, but the segment assignments of *system* and *default* are still there as well. As you create objects within the database *dbname* that are stored in the segment *default* or *system*, they can be placed on any of the server devices that support the *system* or *default* segments. This means that such objects could be placed on server_device_3.

You don't want this to happen for two reasons. First, you wanted segment *myseg1* on a separate server device, preferably on a controller that does not support the server devices for the other segments of database *dbname*, to improve performance. You wanted to separate the I/O for *myseg1* from the I/O for the other segments of the database. By allowing objects of the *system* and *default* segments to live on server_device_3, you have lost control. Any requests that access objects of the *system* and/or *default* segments that live on server_device_3 will conflict with the I/O for the objects in *myseg1*. You probably wanted *myseg1* separated from the other segments because the objects you put in *myseg1* are accessed often. You don't want anything to interfere with that process.

Second, you assigned some amount of disk space to *myseg1*. By allowing objects of other segments to use the disk space you thought you were assigning to *myseg1*, you don't know how much space is being used for *myseg1* or the other segments. You could find that *myseg1* runs out of space as objects in *system* and *default* segments are really filling the disk space.

In order to prevent this problem, you need to drop the *default* and *system* segments from the server device named server_device_3 by using the **sp_dropsegment** server command. For this case, they would look like this:

```
sp_dropsegment system, server_device_3

sp_dropsegment "default", server_device_3
```

(see Figure 4.13). You will have to put " " around *default* because it is a reserved word within SQL Server.

Note that in the rare case that server_device_3 was the only server device that supports *system* or *default* segments for the database, you can't drop these segments from the device. You shouldn't run into this since server_device_3 should be a server device that will support a segment that is separate from the server devices that already support *system* and *default* segments. The order in which you add (or extend) and drop segments is important. You need to understand that when you create a table or other database object, you either specify a segment in the create statement or you don't. However, when you don't specify a segment, the server assumes the segment is *default*. You need to realize that anytime you create a database object, you are specifying a segment where the object will be located. That is why you can't drop all segments from a server device, which means you must first add a user-defined segment to the desired device and then drop the segments you don't want.

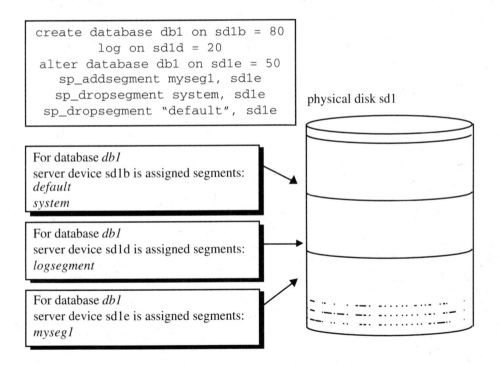

```
create database db1 on sd1b = 80
        log on sd1d = 20
alter database db1 on sd1e = 50
    sp_addsegment myseg1, sd1e
    sp_dropsegment system, sd1e
  sp_dropsegment "default", sd1e
```

physical disk sd1

For database *db1*
server device sd1b is assigned segments:
default
system

For database *db1*
server device sd1d is assigned segments:
logsegment

For database *db1*
server device sd1e is assigned segments:
myseg1

logsegment and *myseg1* should be on a device on a separate physical disk attached to a separate controller

Figure 4.13   Creating user-defined segment -

Segments and Capacity Planning

You have now seen how to set up a user-defined segment. You are done for the moment, but the next problem is how to add space to the segment *myseg1*. This is where you can lose control again. You must realize that you may have done every-thing correctly, but one of your fellow DBAs can add space to the database, render-ing your carefully constructed segments useless. You can alter the database *dbname* on server_device_3 and all will be fine. You recall that if you alter a database on a server device that already supports the database, the added space will carry the same segment assignments that the server device had for this database before the **alter database** command was executed. This makes sense since segment assignments apply to all portions of the database on any one server device.

However, if you need to add space to any segment other than *system* and *default* and you need to add this space on a server device that does not already support the data-base, you must be careful. You can execute

```
alter database <dbname> on server_device_4
```

but the server automatically assigns segments *system* and *default* (and *logsegment* if the log segment for database *dbname* is not assigned as the only segment on one or more of the server devices supporting the database) to the disk space that belongs to database *dbname* on server_device_4. If you are trying to add space to the *system* or *default* segments of database *dbname*, you are done.

However, if you are adding space to the segment *logsegment*, you must use the **sp_extendsegment** server command to add this new space to the existing server devices that support the segment *logsegment*. Note that for the *logsegment* segment only, when you execute **sp_extendsegment logsegment, <*server_device*>** the server automatically adds the *logsegment* segment to the new server device and drops the other segments that were assigned to the new server device (that is, the *sys-tem* and *default* segments). You will see that **sp_extendsegment** is copying the seg-ment assignments that already exist for the other server devices that support the *logsegment* segment, namely, that the *logsegment* segment is the only segment that those devices support for the database *dbname*. If you are adding space to any user-defined segment, you must follow the process detailed previously. You must first **alter database** to server_device_4, add the user-defined segment to the new server device, and drop the segments *system* and *default* from the new server device.

;-)

During one of your few off-hours, one of your colleagues needs to add space to the largest production database in the entire system. Later, when you stumble on this fact (nobody documented the event), you notice that the new space was put on a server device that had not been supporting the database before. More interesting still is the fact that the space on this new (to this database anyway) server device has been assigned the segments *system* (OK), *default* (OK) and *data* (huh?). You know that this database has had a user-defined segment called *data* for some time. But, that segment was created specifically to isolate the biggest tables of the database onto a server device that was separate from the rest of the database and even on a separate physical disk and controller. This was done to improve performance, but now that part of the space that belongs to the *data* segment is on this new server device, which is not on the same controller or physical disk as the rest of the *data* segment, and the fact that the *data* segment is now comingled with the *default* and *system* segments means the whole point of separating the *data* segment is at risk for two reasons.

First, objects on the *data* segment may or may not be on the separate (from the rest of the database) disk as you intended. As the server needs to access this segment, it may need to go to this new server device, where it will have to compete for disk access with everything else on the new server device.

Second, since the segments are commingled, objects that are created in the *system* or *default* segments may be placed on this new server device along with parts of objects from the *data* segment. Again, as the server needs to access objects in this part of the *system* or *default* segments, it will be competing with access to the objects that are in the part of the *data* segment that is on the same device.

Finally, there isn't a good way to fix this problem once it happens. You would have to identify each object in the segment *data* that uses the new server device, and move that object to space on the correct devices for the *data* segment. This could be done by dropping tables, and so on, after using bcp to bulk copy out the data to a file. After clearing the *data* segment on the new server device, you would then drop the *data* segment from the new device. This process is tedious and error-prone; it shouldn't be necessary. You must realize the administrative headaches you are taking on when you set up user-defined segments. They are useful but they come at a price.

Addition of Space to a User-defined Segment

From all of this you should also notice the impact segments have on capacity planning, (see Chapter 10) and on your ability to add space to a database as needed. For each segment of a database that needs to be separated from the other segments of the database, you need a separate device (see Figure 4.23). In the example here, we needed a device for the *default* and *system* segments (both are assigned to the same server device), a device for the *logsegment* segment, and a device for the user-defined segment *myseg1*. Further, if any of these devices run out of space, you must add space on yet another server device, since segments for any one database apply to all of a server device. So, when you run out of space on any of the three server devices mentioned, you would need to have space on another device ready to use. As all three devices fill up. you would need three more, for a total of six server devices for one database. Couple this with mirroring, which mirrors a whole device, and you are suddenly looking at a lot of disks to support and allow expansion of user-defined segments.

Final Notes on Segments

Finally, some notes on segments and server devices; we discuss:

Multiple segments for multiple databases on a server device
system and *default* segments on same device
Many meanings of 'default'
Data and log devices
Restrictions on log device
Log segment not on separate device
Must add device to server before adding segments
Can't drop all segments
Segments part of a single database

Multiple segments for multiple databases on a server device

You must understand a subtlety of segments. We have repeatedly discussed the need for a given segment to be on a separate server device from the other segments (note that the *system* and *default* segments are often assigned to the same device). This implies that each segment must be completely alone on the server device. This is correct, but only for each database. A server device can have the *logsegment* segment of *database1,* the *default* and/or *system* segments of *database2,* and the user-defined segment *myseg1* of *database3.* All of these can be set up on a single server device as long as each one belongs to a separate database, as shown in Figure 4.14.

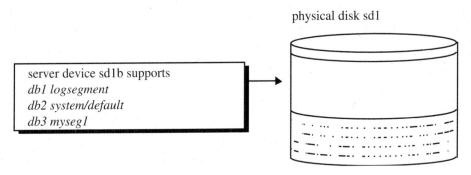

physical disk sd1

server device sd1b supports
db1 logsegment
db2 system/default
db3 myseg1

Figure 4.14 Segments of multiple databases on same device- -

system and *default* segments on same device

Note that the *default* and *system* segments are often collocated on the same server device(s). You can separate these segments if you wish, but you will be better off putting the individual objects (tables and indexes most commonly) on their own dedicated segments6 as needed and leave the *system* and *default* segments alone.

Many meanings of 'default'

Don't confuse the *default* segment with a server device that is part of the pool of default disk space. Further, realize that when you execute **create database,** the devices you specify will be assigned the segments *system* and *default* by default. That is, these segment assignments are made automatically, and if you don't want the segments assigned that way, you must manually add new segments and drop those that you don't want. Be careful when you see or think about the term "default" and make sure you know what you mean by the term.

Data and log devices

The SQL Server documentation often refers to server devices as "data" devices or as "log" devices. Here the data device(s) are those server devices that support all the segments of a database other than the *logsegment* segment.

Restrictions on log device

Once you have placed the *logsegment* segment on a server device that supports only the *logsegment* segment, you can't add any other segments to that server device for that database. Once a server device is a *logsegment* device, it will remain that way unless you move the *logsegment* segment to another server device by using **sp_logdevice**. Further, once the *logsegment* segment is on its own server device, you can't add or extend the *logsegment* to all the server devices supporting the database. Recall that when you add or extend the *logsegment* segment to a server device, the *logsegment* segment becomes the only segment for that server device for that database. You can't extend the *logsegment* segment to all the server devices supporting the database; doing so would make all the server devices exclusively *logsegment* devices, and there would be no room for database objects that normally go in the *system*, *default*, and user-defined segments.

Log segment not on separate device

You can set up a database so that the *logsegment* segment is commingled with the *system* and *default* segments. This is only done when you do not need to dump (and recover) the transaction log. You can't dump the transaction log for a database that doesn't place the *logsegment* segment on a separate server device.

Must add device to server before adding segments

You can't add or extend segments for a database to a server device that isn't already assigned to the database. You must alter the database to include space on the new device (which will assign a set of segments to the new device, that is, *system* and *default*) before you can do anything with the segment assignments.

Can't drop all segments

You can't drop the *system*, *default*, or *logsegment* segments from all of the server devices supporting a database. At least one server device must support each of these segments. The database must have room for each of these segments. Similarly, you can't drop a server device that is the only device supporting any of these segments of the database. For a user-defined segment, you must first drop the segment from the database before you can drop the last server device supporting that segment. For server devices that are not the only one supporting any of the segments of the database, you can drop all the segments from the server device. This makes the server device completely unusable by the server.

Segments part of a single database

Always remember that segments only apply within a single database. Always remember that any segment assigned to a server device applies to all the space on that device that is assigned to the database.

4.8 Mirroring Server Devices

Now that you have all of your database segments under control, you can worry about mirroring, which simply assigns another raw partition or file system to a server device; any writes to the server device are also written to the mirror. In case of a failure of the server device, the server can continue by using the mirror. Note that we are not discussing the area of hardware or operating system mirroring, only the mirroring of SQL Server server devices within the server itself. We discuss the following topics:

Mirroring Defined
Why Mirroring is Needed
Mirroring the Master Device
Mirroring Transaction Log(s) of User Databases
Mirroring and Replacing a Failed Disk Drive
Mirroring during Server Upgrade
Mirroring during Server Machine Upgrade
Mirroring All Server Devices
Creating Mirrors
Primary Device, Mirror Device, and Logical Server Device
Dropping One Side of a Mirrored Device
Dropping Secondary Device
Dropping Primary Device
Remirroring
Primary and Secondary Devices Different Sizes
Adding Database Space and Mirrored Devices
Mirroring Devices versus Databases
Administering Mirrored Devices

Mirroring Defined

SQL Server mirroring maintains a copy of the server device on another server device. The original server device is called the primary and the mirror is called the secondary or mirror device, see Figure 4.15. SQL Server will write any changes to the database to both the primary server device and the mirror device. When SQL Server detects an error on the primary server device, it will fail over to the secondary server device and processing will continue without interruption. If the server detects errors on the mirror device, it will simply drop the mirror and continue processing, using just the primary device.

You may want to use RAID devices to provide this same capability for your most critical databases. The subject of RAID, the various levels, how to determine the needs of your system, how to decide between a vendor's disk and generic disks for the RAID array, and so on, are not covered in this book.

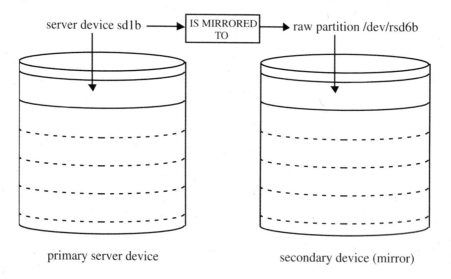

server device sd1b ⟶ IS MIRRORED TO ⟶ raw partition /dev/rsd6b

primary server device   secondary device (mirror)

The primary server device (sd1b) and the secondary device or mirror (/dev/rsd6b) together form the mirror pair, which is still known to the server only as the server logical disk device sd1b.

Figure 4.15   Mirroring of a server disk device -

Why Mirroring Is Needed

The reasons to mirror your server devices and thereby your databases are several. The most obvious reason is to prevent downtime. More accurately, mirroring allows you to control, not eliminate, downtime caused by physical disk problems. If a server device is not mirrored and the underlying physical disk crashes, those databases that rely on the server device(s) on that physical disk will fail. Depending on which databases are involved, the SQL Server may not be able to continue (master device, device that contains the transaction log for a critical database, and so on). In both cases the databases in question are immediately out of service. With mirroring, the SQL Server detects the errors with the server device and stops using it. The server device is dropped by the SQL Server and the server automatically switches over to the mirror device. You must still shut down the server and the server machine to replace the drive, but you get to choose when the downtime occurs.

Mirroring the Master Device

You should mirror the master device. Doing so will provide a mirror of the *master* database, the first 2 Mb of *tempdb,* and the *model* database. Having a mirror of the master device is critical for two reasons. First, if anything goes wrong with the master device, you lose the *master* database, which means the entire server and all the databases are completely shut down. If the master device is mirrored, your server can move through these problems and continue processing. Second, if you lose the master device, your server is dead and recovery is much more complicated. When you lose the master device, if you don't have a mirror, you may need to recover the server by first rebuilding the *master* database, reapply any server configuration changes necessary to fully recover the server (for a 4.9.x server you need to add the dump device before you can load dumps), load a dump of *master,* and then fix any other problems to recover the server fully. With a mirror of the master device, the most tedious part of recovering the server is already at hand, namely, recovering the *master* database. *You must mirror the master device.* Since the master device is typically the smallest device on the server, you have no excuse not to provide a mirror.

Mirroring Transaction Log(s) of User Databases

You should mirror the device(s) that support the transaction log for each and every user database that is critical. Here we mean "critical" in the sense that you need to ensure that in the event of problems you can recover the database as completely as possible. Depending on the nature of your business, you must decide how much data you can afford to lose. Note that if you have a problem and you must drop back to your last database dump and the subsequent series of transaction log dumps to recover, you are still losing the database changes that have occurred since the last transaction log dump. By setting up a mirror of the transaction log for this database, you provide insurance that you can get a copy of the transaction log that is current, even if the transaction log on the primary device is lost. Without the mirror, if you lose the transaction log, you have no way to recover the database to a state more recent than the last transaction log dump (see Chapter 8 for details of this process). Note that in order to mirror the transaction log for any database, you must mirror the primary server device where the transaction log is located.

Mirroring and Replacing a Failed Disk Drive

Mirroring is also very useful when you do need to replace a physical disk drive. Even if you choose not to mirror all of the server devices, you should be prepared to mirror any disk drive that supports the server. This means you need to be ready to mirror all of the server devices that are on any given physical disk. When you have a disk failure, it is much easier for you, and a lot faster, if you simply mirror all the server devices on the disk to another physical disk on the server, see Figure 4.16.

For some disk drive problems, the drive is still accessible even though it is beginning to fail. In this case, mirroring allows you to save all the data in all the server devices on the disk drive before a hard failure occurs. Sometimes the disk failure that forces you to replace the disk will have damaged some portion of the disk and one or more of the server devices that are assigned to the disk. However, for all the other server devices, you can mirror off to another disk, drop the server devices that are on the damaged disk, and replace the drive. Then, you simply mirror back from your spare drive to the replacement drive. This is much faster and less error-prone than rebuilding databases from dumps. Further, if the process is done properly, you will not lose any data from the databases that you mirror off the damaged drive. In order to do this, you need to have a disk drive or drives on the server machine that can handle the overall storage and number of partitions needed to mirror all of the server devices on any given disk that is supporting the server.

If you mirror all the server devices on your server, you don't need to do even this much to replace a bad drive. You simply drop the devices on the failed disk from their respective mirror pairs, shut down the server machine, and replace the drive. After you have the server machine back online, you remirror the affected server drives.

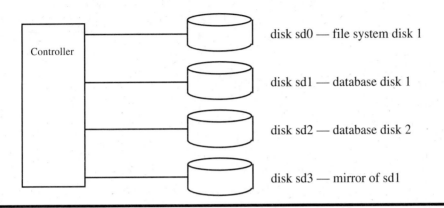

SERVER BEFORE SERVER DEVICE SD2B FAILS

Controller

disk sd0 — file system disk 1

disk sd1 — database disk 1

disk sd2 — database disk 2

disk sd3 — mirror of sd1

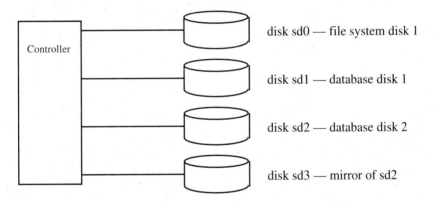

SERVER AFTER SERVER DEVICE SD2B FAILS

Controller

disk sd0 — file system disk 1

disk sd1 — database disk 1

disk sd2 — database disk 2

disk sd3 — mirror of sd2

This example assumes disks sd1, sd2, and sd3 have identical partitioning to allow mirroring of all server devices on sd1 to sd3 and sd2 to sd3. After failure of server device sd2b, drop mirrors on sd3 and mirror from all but failed server device on sd2 to sd3. Drop primary devices of these mirror pairs (i.e., drop the server devices on sd2). Shut down server machine, replace disk sd2, remirror from devices on sd3 to sd2. Only need to recreate and load databases that were supported by the failed device on sd2.

Figure 4.16   Mirroring to simplify replacing a failed disk -

;-) It is December 25. You are home. Your son is opening his Brio set. You have been looking forward to this probably more than he has. You reviewed the server errorlogs earlier in the morning, since you are on call through the holiday. You noticed that one of your many production servers had a device write error and it failed over to the mirror. You notify your management; they agree that since the production system is processing normally, there is no need to replace the disk drive immediately. You don't get paged, and you don't need to page the server machine SA person who is home with his/her family. The users worldwide that depend on the production server throughout the holidays don't even know anything happened. You replace the drive the next week after mirroring off any other server devices that were on the physical drive that failed. Note that if you had assigned whole physical disks to server devices and whole physical disks to be mirrors of those devices, you wouldn't even need this step— you could simply drop the mirrors on the failed or failing disk and replace it. At times like these, the disk space needed to support mirrors seems very cheap. After your son goes to bed, you get your Brio layout whipped into shape. Er, your son's layout....

Mirroring during Server Upgrade

Mirroring is also very useful during a major upgrade. Mirroring all the server devices, including the master device, and then dropping (using the **disk unmirror** comand) but not removing the mirrors prior to starting the upgrade process, makes the previous version of the server available. See Figure 4.17.

If the upgrade were to run into problems, you can fail back to the previous version of the server with all the data intact in all the user databases. Basically, you start the upgrade—and if you need to—revoke the UNIX level permissions to the operating system files that control access to the physical disk partitions that support the server and reestablish the mirrors for these devices. Doing this for the server devices that were being upgraded and restarting the server forces the server to fail over to the mirrors, which are really the previous version of the server. Note that this implies you have enough disk space and enough partitions to mirror every server device at once. See Chapter 13 for more details of upgrading using this mirroring technique.

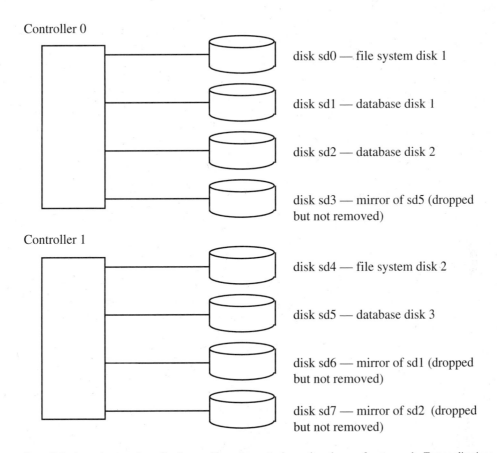

Controller 0

disk sd0 — file system disk 1

disk sd1 — database disk 1

disk sd2 — database disk 2

disk sd3 — mirror of sd5 (dropped but not removed)

Controller 1

disk sd4 — file system disk 2

disk sd5 — database disk 3

disk sd6 — mirror of sd1 (dropped but not removed)

disk sd7 — mirror of sd2 (dropped but not removed)

Stop all database changes, drop all mirrors with `mode=retain` option, then perform upgrade. Test applications against new server version. If necessary, fail back to the mirrors that had been dropped just before the upgrade began. These mirrors contain the previous version of the server the way it was just before the upgrade. Don't allow any changes to production data until convinced upgrade was successful.

Figure 4.17   Mirroring to simplify a server version upgrade -

Mirroring during Server Machine Upgrade

Another time that mirroring is very useful is during a server machine hardware upgrade. While your server may be operating normally, you may need to either add a large amount of disk space to accommodate database growth or replace some or all of the existing disk drives with larger, faster drives. In either case, you can add some of the new disk drives, mirror the existing server devices to the new drives, drop the old server devices, and remove the old drives. Then you can add the rest of the new drives and by mirroring spread the server devices around on the new drives as you wish, see Figure 4.18. Note that this approach, as with the others mentioned above, saves a lot of time and hassle for you the DBA, is less error-prone, and results in a server that is completely up-to-date (that is, no data loss due to rebuilding from dumps that may not be completely up-to-date).

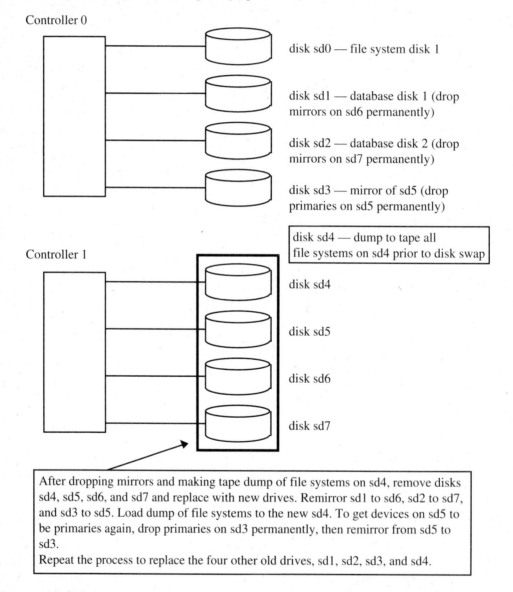

Controller 0

disk sd0 — file system disk 1

disk sd1 — database disk 1 (drop mirrors on sd6 permanently)

disk sd2 — database disk 2 (drop mirrors on sd7 permanently)

disk sd3 — mirror of sd5 (drop primaries on sd5 permanently)

disk sd4 — dump to tape all file systems on sd4 prior to disk swap

Controller 1

disk sd4

disk sd5

disk sd6

disk sd7

After dropping mirrors and making tape dump of file systems on sd4, remove disks sd4, sd5, sd6, and sd7 and replace with new drives. Remirror sd1 to sd6, sd2 to sd7, and sd3 to sd5. Load dump of file systems to the new sd4. To get devices on sd5 to be primaries again, drop primaries on sd3 permanently, then remirror from sd5 to sd3.
Repeat the process to replace the four other old drives, sd1, sd2, sd3, and sd4.

Figure 4.18   Mirroring to simplify major server machine disk upgrade- - - - - - - - - - - - - - - - -

Mirroring All Server Devices

Choosing what you will mirror and what you won't is very important. As you will see later, you will save yourself a lot of time and disk management mistakes if you simply mirror all of the devices in the server. However, you need to understand the issues involved so you can decide on the mirroring plan that is best for your server.

You will note a theme throughout these examples of the benefits of mirroring, namely, that you should mirror all of your server devices. This may seem extravagant in terms of disk space and disk controllers, but you need to weigh such costs against the cost to your business of lost data, downtime while you manually fix the problems that mirroring can automatically take care of, and the additional hassles you must deal with, keeping track of which server devices are mirrored and which aren't.

Creating Mirrors

Now that you are aware of the reasons to mirror server devices and which server devices are most important to mirror, we cover the mechanics of mirroring a server device. You should have noticed a recurring theme throughout this section, namely, that you mirror devices, not databases. You must understand this concept. You create a logical server device that associates a server device with a raw partition of a physical disk or a file in a file system by using the **disk init** server command. You then create a mirror of the server device. Note that you can't create a mirror of a server device on a partition that is already supporting a server device. This also means you must not use **disk init** on the partition that you want to use as the mirror of a server device. Finally, if you do want to mirror to a partition that is already supporting a server device you must first drop that server device. It doesn't matter how many databases have space on the server device; they all get mirrored. Further, it doesn't matter how a given database is segmented or spread across multiple server devices; a mirror only mirrors a single server device, a mirror does not mirror a database or a segment. You must ensure that you are mirroring all the server devices you need to be mirroring to protect the databases or database segments you need to. You set up mirroring of a server logical disk device by using the server command:

```
disk mirror
name = "device_name",
mirror = "physicalname",
writes = { serial | noserial }
```

Let's discuss the various components of the command:

device_name
physicalname
writes
Primary and secondary devices on same controller
Primary and secondary devices on separate controllers
disk mirror example

device_name

The *device_name* is the name of the server disk device that you wish to mirror. Again, this *device_name* is the name of the device that is known to the SQL Server, not the name of the device known to the UNIX operating system. The server device that you use as the *device_name* becomes the primary server device.

physicalname

The **mirror** is the device that will mirror the primary device; the *physicalname* is the full path of the operating system file that controls the access to the raw partition that will be the mirror.

Note that you must not create the mirror device by using **disk init**. Further, if you need to mirror to a raw partition that is currently in use as a server device, you must clean off anything on the server device and drop the server device before using it as a mirror device. The mirror device is the secondary device relative to the primary server device.

writes

The **writes** parameter specifies how you want the mirror to function. The default is **writes = serial**, which means the server writes database changes to the primary server device, waits for that write to complete, then writes to the secondary or mirror device. The **writes = serial** option is the most secure.

Primary and secondary devices on same controller

If both the primary and secondary devices are assigned to partitions on physical disks that are attached to the same controller, it is possible for a controller error to corrupt the write to both devices; this is why you should have a device and its mirror on separate physical disks attached to separate controllers. You also want the device and its mirror on disks on separate controllers to allow the server to function if any one controller were to fail altogether. This should be part of your standard server device configuration (see Chapter 1).

Primary and secondary devices on separate controllers

If your primary and secondary devices are on separate controllers, you don't need to use **writes = serial** and can use the faster **writes = noserial** option. Note that the default is **writes = serial**, so you must specify the **noserial** option to get the faster mirroring. For the examples that follow, we assume you are using the standard server device naming conventions discussed in Chapter 1.

disk mirror example

For example: You already have created a server device (using **disk init**) called sd1b and you want to mirror this server device to a raw partition 'b' which is part of the physical disk called sd6. This raw partition is controlled by the UNIX operating system file /dev/rsd6b, and the physical disks sd1 and sd6 are attached to separate disk controllers (if not, you should consider the **writes = serial** option). You specify the mirror as follows:

```
disk mirror
name = "sd1b",
mirror = "/dev/rsd6b",
writes = noserial
```

Primary Device, Mirror Device and Logical Server Device

The primary server device taken together with the mirror device (also called the secondary device) form one logical server device, which we also call the mirror pair (see Figure 4.19). It is important that you understand this relationship. The primary device is a server device that you created with **disk init** and is therefore known to the

server. However, the mirror device is not a server device by itself, and you don't create the mirror with the **disk init** command. In fact, you never identify the mirror
device to the server other than through the use of the **disk mirror** command.

Note that UNIX user 'dba' must own the files that control access to both the primary
server device (/dev/rsd1b) and the secondary mirror device (/dev/rsd6b).

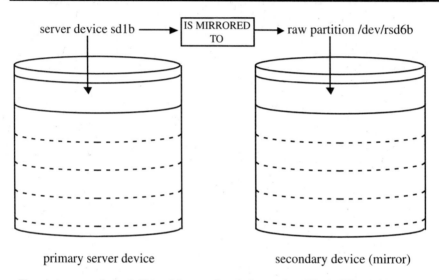

The primary server device (sd1b) and the secondary device or mirror (/dev/rsd6b) together
form the mirror pair, which is still known to the server only as the server logical disk device sd1b.

Figure 4.19   The mirror pair -

Notice that when you need to drop a mirror you use the **disk unmirror** command that
only references the server logical device. Notice, too, that you can drop either side of
the mirror relationship, either the primary (the server device) or the secondary (the
mirror which is really a raw partition), but, whichever side of the mirror relationship
you drop, you specify the same server logical device. This can confuse you especially when a crisis hits. If you need to drop either side of the mirror pair, use the
server command:

```
disk unmirror
name = "device_name",
```

```
side = { primary | secondary },
mode = { retain | remove }
```

Here again you must be clear on the terms. Table 4.2 lists and discusses the various components of the command.

Table 4.2   The **disk unmirror** Command Components

Component	Description/Recommendation
device_name	Is identical to that used to define the mirror.
side parameter	Specifies which side of the mirror pair you want to drop. You can drop either the primary or secondary side of the mirror. For example, if you need to replace a disk drive, the choice of which side of the mirror pair needs to be dropped is clear: The side of the mirror pair that is on the disk to be removed from the server machine is the side of the mirror pair that you need to drop.
mode parameter	Allows for another level of complexity and confusion regarding mirroring. If you unmirror or drop one side of a mirror pair, you can specify **mode = retain** or **mode = remove**. The **retain** option tells SQL Server not to read from or write to the device specified by the **side = <device>**, but the server does not free the device for other uses. The device is still there and can be brought back on line by using the server command **disk remirror** (see below). Note that if you use the **mode = remove** option, the specified side of the mirrored device is dropped permanently and you cannot use the **disk remirror** command to restore the mirror of the server device. Of course, you can use the **disk mirror** command to create a new mirror of the server device. You must realize what it takes to mirror or remirror a server device: The server must make a complete copy of the server device data even if no changes have occurred between the primary and mirror.

Dropping One Side of a Mirrored Device

When you need to drop either side of a mirrored device, you need to be very careful that you understand what all the terms mean. Here you need to be very clear on what the "*device_name*" refers to. The *device_name* is the logical device name by which the SQL Server knows about the mirror pair. If you drop either side of the mirror pair with either **mode = retain** or **mode = remove**, the server still refers to the remaining device as *device_name*. Consider the example of defining a mirror pair discussed earlier. The syntax to drop the primary side of the mirror pair, which is the actual server device that the mirror pair was originally named for, would look like this:

```
disk unmirror
name = "sd1b",
side = primary,
mode = retain
```

And, if you wanted to drop the secondary side of the mirror pair, which is actually a raw partition that the server has no prior knowledge of, the syntax would look like this:

```
disk unmirror
name = "sd1b",
side = secondary,
mode = retain
```

Dropping Secondary Device

In both examples we chose to retain the side of the mirror that was dropped. Now you need to realize what has happened in each case. First, consider the second case where you dropped the secondary side of the mirror pair. In that case, before you dropped anything, you had a mirror pair called sd1b that consisted of a primary side, which was the server device called sd1b, and the secondary device, which is the raw partition controlled by the operating system file /dev/rsd6b; see Figure 4.20.

By dropping the secondary side of the mirror pair and specifying **mode = retain**, you still have the server device called sd1b and you still have the raw partition /dev/rsd6b. That partition contains a copy of the server device sd1b, a copy that was up-to-date until the time the **disk unmirror** command was executed, but which will not be updated any further. If you specified the **mode = remove** option, you would simply be back where you started, with the server device called sd1b referring to raw partition /dev/rsd1b and nothing else. Whichever mode you specify, you are left with the server device called sd1b which is a server device of the size you specified when you created the server device by using the **disk init** command; this server device sd1b is associated with the 'b' partition of the physical disk sd1 controlled by the UNIX operating system file /dev/rsd1b. Note that this is precisely the process the server goes through when it detects an error on the secondary side of the mirror pair and drops the mirror or secondary device with the **mode = retain** option. You will not be impressed by this lengthy explanation at this point.

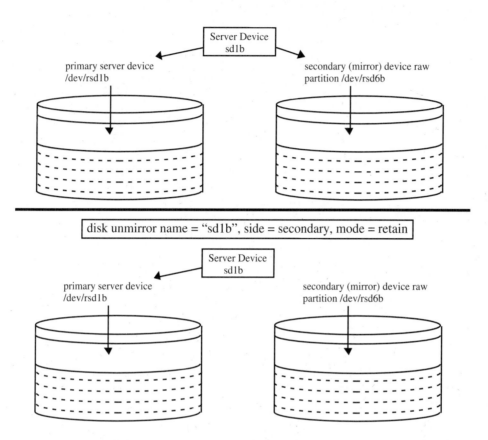

The secondary device will continue to have a copy of data on /dev/rsd1b but will only reflect the data as of the time the disk unmirror command was executed. If the mode = remove option was used, the data in /dev/rsd6b would be lost permanently.

Figure 4.20 Dropping secondary (mirror) device of a mirror pair -

Note that if you were to now execute the server command—

```
disk remirror name = "sd1b"
```

—the situation would be returned to exactly the way it was before the **disk unmirror** command was executed; that is, the primary server device would be /dev/rsd1b and the secondary or mirror device would be /dev/rsd6b.

Dropping Primary Device

Now consider the first case, where you dropped the primary side of the mirror pair. In that case, before you dropped anything, you had the same mirror pair as before. However, note that the primary side of the mirror pair, the server device called sd1b, really points to the raw partition 'b' on the physical disk called sd1 and controlled by the UNIX operating system file /dev/rsd1b; the secondary device, which is the raw partition, is controlled by the operating system file /dev/rsd6b, as shown in Figure 4.21.

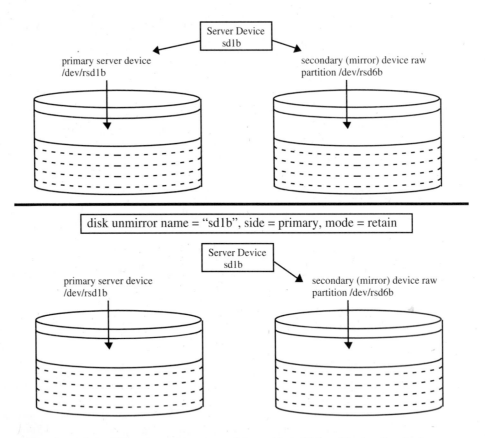

disk unmirror name = "sd1b", side = primary, mode = retain

The primary device will continue to have a copy of data on /dev/rsd6b but will only reflect the data as of the time the disk unmirror command was executed. If the mode = remove option was used, the data in /dev/rsd1b would be lost permanently.

Figure 4.21   Dropping primary server device of a mirror pair -

By dropping the primary side of the mirror pair and specifying **mode = retain,** you still have the server device called sd1b, but it now is assigned to only the secondary side of the mirror pair, a raw partition on another physical disk. Note that the 'b' partition of the physical disk called sd6 has never been identified to the server through **disk init**.

You need to be clear on what is happening when you drop the primary side of the mirror pair. When you execute the **disk unmirror** command, the SQL Server automatically converts the secondary side of the mirror pair into a normal server device just as if you had created that server device with **disk init**. The server simply takes the actual size of the primary device and uses that to size the secondary device, which is now the only active server device in the mirror pair. This can be confusing. Note that this is precisely the process the server goes through when it detects an error on the primary side of the mirror pair and fails over to the secondary device, making it the primary and making it a normal server device.

Note that if you were to now execute the server command—

```
disk remirror
name = "sd1b"
```

— the situation would be returned to exactly the way it was before the **disk unmirror** command was executed; that is, the primary server device would be /dev/rsd1b and the secondary or mirror device would be /dev/rsd6b.

Remirroring

To restore the device of the mirrored device pair that you have previously dropped, use the **disk remirror** command, which looks like this:

```
disk remirror
name = "device_name"
```

As before, **_device_name_** is identical to that used to define the mirror. Notice that the remirror command doesn't care whether you dropped the primary or secondary side of the mirror pair; it simply brings whichever device was dropped back online and will bring the device back up-to-date relative to the device of the mirror pair that was not dropped. Note that the **disk remirror** command will not work if you used the **mode = remove** option of the **drop mirror** command.

You should notice here that dropping the primary device from a mirror pair (/dev/rsd1b) causes the secondary device (/dev/rsd6b) to become the primary. If you dropped the primary device with the **mode = remove** option and you now execute—

```
disk mirror
name = "sd6b",
mirror = "/dev/rsd1b",
write = serial
```

— then you will have the same raw partitions in a mirrored pair as before. However, the raw partition that is primary and secondary has been reversed; that is, the primary device will be /dev/rsd6b, the secondary or mirror device will be /dev/rsd1b, and the mirrored pair will be known to the server as server device sd6b.

Following our example: You started out with server device sd1b, which was assigned to /dev/rsd1b and mirrored to /dev/rsd6b. Then, you dropped the primary side of the mirror pair, which leaves server device sd1b assigned to /dev/rsd6b with the size that was used originally in the **disk init** command that created sd1b. Now, since you executed the **disk unmirror** command with the **mode = retain** option, you can reinstate the mirror relationship at a later time. If one side of the mirror device failed and the server dropped that side of the mirror pair, and you later find the failure was not serious enough to warrant replacing the disk, you would then want to remirror. Using the **disk remirror** command is only slightly easier than performing the original **disk mirror** because the server still has to completely copy from the primary device (whichever the primary device is after one side of the mirror pair is dropped) to the mirror device, but it is easier in that you don't have to remember what the mirror device is.

Primary and Secondary Devices Different Sizes

There is an implication in all this that you need to remember. If you have a small device, say 100 Mb (sd1b) and you mirror this small device to a larger device of, say 200 Mb (/dev/rsd6b), and then for whatever reason you drop the primary side of the mirror pair, you will have a server device of 100 Mb on the secondary device of the mirror pair; see Figure 4.22.

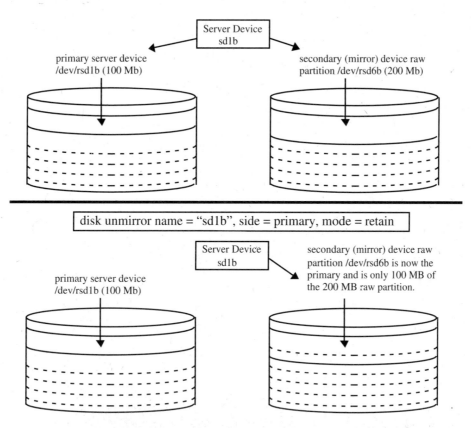

Figure 4.22   Mirroring from small to large partitions -

Note that mirroring uses the entire secondary device, usually the whole raw partition assigned, but after dropping the primary, the secondary device becomes a server device with the size of the former primary server device. In this case, it would appear that you had executed **disk init** on /dev/rsd6b with a size of 100 Mb, even though the partition could support 200 Mb. Hence, you have wasted a lot of space. This is the reason you need to have a standard disk partitioning scheme that ensures your disks have partitions that are very similar. All the physical disks on the server machine that you are using to support the SQL Server may not be the same size. To make mirroring as easy as possible, you should segregate the SQL Server disks into groups that are the same size; after applying the standard partitioning to all the SQL Server disks, you can use the disks of the same size in the mirror pairs that you need. Further, you should assign whole physical disks to primary server devices and whole physical disks to be used for the mirrors of these primary server devices. Since the physical disks involved in the mirror pairs are the same size, the standard disk partitioning scheme will result in the partitions of the disks being identical. This means you can mirror, drop either side, and remirror without wasting any disk space at all.

Notice that this means you can mirror from a smaller partition to a larger partition, drop the primary (server device on the smaller partition), which causes the secondary to become a server device on the larger partition, and then remirror to the smaller partition. The ability to mirror from a larger partition to a smaller partition is based solely on the actual size of the server device, not on the size of the partition that supports the device.

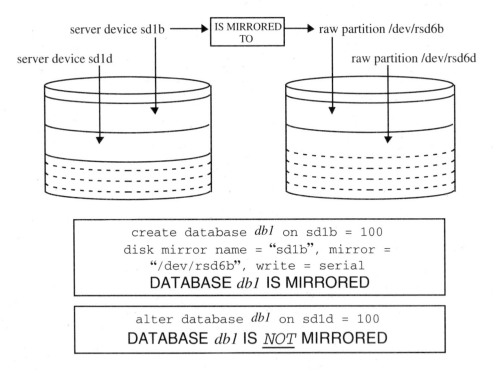

Figure 4.23   Devices are mirrored—databases may not be -

Adding Database Space and Mirrored Devices

Finally, once you have set up the mirrors of your server devices, note that adding space to a database becomes more complex, as illustrated in Figure 4.23.

As long as you are adding space on a server device that is already supporting the database that needs more space, which implies the mirroring is already set up correctly, then adding space proceeds without any concern for the mirror, because again, the mirror copies the entire primary server device. When you need to add space to a database, or more accurately, to a segment of the database, and all the server devices supporting that database segment are already full, you must alter the database onto a new device, a device that has not been supporting the database or the database segment previously. Clearly, you can alter the database to the new device, but if you don't check the mirroring, you may be extending the database to a device that is no longer mirrored. This is a hidden danger in mirroring. Again, mirroring is done on a server device basis, not on a database or database segment basis. It is easy for one of your fellow DBAs, either through haste or laziness, to alter the database to a new device and not go the extra distance to check that the new device is mirrored also.

Mirroring Devices versus Databases

Recall that you can't mirror a database directly, because a database will, in general, span several server devices and you can only mirror server devices. You should consider another approach that, when applied as a standard, makes managing the mirrors of your database server devices much easier. Once you have determined which disks of the server machine will support the SQL Server, then decide which whole physical disks will be primary server devices, create the server devices for all the databases on your server, and then create mirrors for all the server devices on the remaining whole physical devices assigned to support the secondary side of the mirror pairs. You will note that you are mirroring every server device in the whole server. This may seem extravagant, but it is much easier to maintain than having some server devices mirrored and others not.

;-)

It is the end of your business cycle, be it the end of year or end of month, and the load on your server(s) is heavier than ever. One of your fellow DBAs had to add space to one of the production databases. No problem, what could be simpler? You didn't check, and they didn't check, and it turns out that the new device they used for the new database space isn't mirrored. Your users report their applications crashing after getting errors that indicate corruption in the database. No problem, the database is mirrored, just check the mirrors, see which one failed over to the secondary device, and processing should continue. You start checking and find that the corruption occurred on the one portion of the entire database that wasn't mirrored. You are lost. You must restore the entire database to recover this one portion, because there is no way to recover just a segment or an individual object from the database dumps. You spend hours rebuilding the database—all because you didn't have all of it mirrored. You could have prevented this by mirroring all the server devices on the entire server. That way, no matter where you (or anyone else) added space, the server device would already be mirrored. With this sort of setup, to cause such a disaster, your fellow DBA would have to drop the mirror of the device before altering the database or would have to perform a **disk init** of a whole new server device on a disk partition not normally part of the SQL Server. This is a lot more work and is therefore unlikely. It is very easy for the DBA to simply alter a database to an existing server device that isn't mirrored and cause disaster.

Administering Mirrored Devices

Once you have set up the mirroring for your server, you are not finished, and not just because you need to add space in the future. You must monitor the mirrors to make sure they are functioning. The server will print error messages to the server errorlog when a failure of either side of a mirror pair occurs. You must monitor the errorlog for these failures. Whenever you restart the server, you must go through the errorlog that shows the server starting up. This is where you would see the master device being opened and the mirror of the master device being accessed as well. You must also check the *status* of any other mirrors that you have set up. The procedure **p_mirror** is useful for this, and you should check it regularly, along with dumping the server system tables (see Chapter 15 for details). The output you get from **p_mirror** or from **sp_helpdevice** or from simply selecting from the *sysdevices* table in the *master* database will show you the *status* of each server device. Note that a failed mirror will have a *status* value that is different from the *status* values for the other server devices. This makes it easy for you to spot any problems with mirrors.

;-)

It is the Friday before you have a week off for training. You get called at home. One of your fellow DBAs tells you one of the production servers won't restart, and it is your problem. You had asked the server machine SA to repartition one of the file systems so that it filled the entire physical disk to allow storage of more transaction log dumps. You had checked all the server devices that the server was using by running **p_devspace** and had checked all the existing file systems by running df at the UNIX command line. What had happened? The DBA who set up the server had decided, for reasons that are not clear, to place the master device on a partition on a physical disk that was used for file systems. The master device was the only server device on that disk, and when you checked **p_devspace**, you failed to check what physical disk the master device was on. You assumed that all the server devices were on physical disks separate from the physical disks used for file systems, but you didn't check. The server machine SA had then extended the file system so that it took over the entire physical disk, which erased the master device. You think, well, you screwed up, but that's why we have a mirror of the master device, and you'll just restart the server with the master mirror. You start looking at the old errorlogs and notice that for the last month whenever the server was restarted the master device mirror had failed, but no one was checking this. So, you have no mirror of the master device. You find a dump of the *master* database on disk and have to recreate the partition for the master device, load the dump of *master,* and then recover the server. Note that your initial screwup would have been a minor and forgettable event if the mirror had been functioning. You must mirror *master,* and you must check the mirror every time the server starts, and check it periodically between restarts. Further, you must regularly dump the *master* database, and you must dump the server system tables frequently so you have all the information you need in the event you need to rebuild the server.

;-)

Better living through mirroring. Mirroring saves personal lives. It's all done with mirrors.

4.9   How to Layout the Devices and Segments of a Server

The process of sizing the server for the database(s) needed to support your applications is detailed in Chapter 10, "Capacity Planning." The process centers around how many independent segments (that is, segments that are the only segment assigned to a server device) are required for the largest database of the server. Once this number of segments is determined, you know that you need the same number of server devices (and a few more for master device, and so on) at a minimum. Ideally, each of these segments would be on a physical disk attached to a separate controller. This tells you the number of controllers you need (you may need more, of course). From here you need to allocate the number of disks on each controller to support the size of each segment. Knowing how many physical disks can be attached to each controller before I/O performance is impacted allows you to populate the controllers with disks. Now you need to allocate disks to support mirrors of server devices and see if you have enough room left over to support the other database(s) and file systems required. Figure 4.24 illustrates the process.

In this example are a database *db1* that requires the standard segments of *system*, *default*, *logsegment,* and two user-defined segments: *ncindexes* for the nonclustered indexes and *bigtable* to support one huge table that is heavily accessed. For maximum performance, the user-defined segments *ncindexes* and *bigtable* must be supported by physical disks that are attached to controllers separate from those controlling the disks for *system/default* segments or the *logsegment*. This means the server machine must have four controllers at a minimum. This requirement for segments on separate controllers dictates the basic configuration of the server machine. At this point, you populate the controllers with the maximum number of disks allowed without impacting I/O performance (four for Sun machines). After allocating one-quarter of the total number of physical disks for file system (four disks) and splitting the remaining 12 disks in half for server devices and their mirrors, you have the basic server layout. Note that this layout assumes you have enough disk space on the physical disks for each controller to support the segments of *db1*. You must realize that if one of the segments of *db1* grows beyond the disk space available on the current controller, you would need to add another controller to support more disk space for that segment. If you simply add space to the segment on another controller, then the I/O for that segment would contend with the I/O for the other segment of *db1* that is already supported by the controller.

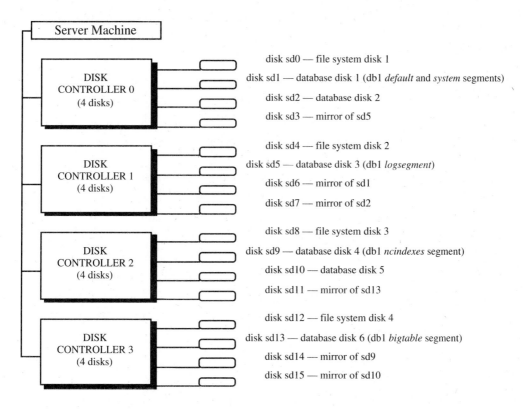

disk sd0 — file system disk 1

disk sd1 — database disk 1 (db1 *default* and *system* segments)

disk sd2 — database disk 2

disk sd3 — mirror of sd5

disk sd4 — file system disk 2

disk sd5 — database disk 3 (db1 *logsegment*)

disk sd6 — mirror of sd1

disk sd7 — mirror of sd2

disk sd8 — file system disk 3

disk sd9 — database disk 4 (db1 *ncindexes* segment)

disk sd10 — database disk 5

disk sd11 — mirror of sd13

disk sd12 — file system disk 4

disk sd13 — database disk 6 (db1 *bigtable* segment)

disk sd14 — mirror of sd9

disk sd15 — mirror of sd10

Database db1 has *system/default, logsegment,* and two user-defined segments: *ncindexes* and *bigtable*.
Note: Total of 16 disks, one-quarter assigned to file systems, the remaining 12 disks split evenly among supporting database server devices and their mirrors.

Figure 4.24   Example server device, mirror and segmentation layout - - - - - - - - - - - - - - - -

For example, if segment *ncindexes* needed more disk space and the disks sd9 and sd10 (the only database disks on controller 2) were already full with *ncindexes* and other databases, then you need to add space to *ncindexes* on disks on another controller. However, if you add the needed space on disks on controller 0 or 1 or 3, you will have I/O for objects in the *ncindexes* segment contending with I/O for objects in the existing segment of *db1*. If you added space to *ncindexes* on sd2 (controller 0), then I/O for *ncindexes* segment would contend with I/O for *default/system* segments. This means capacity planning to improve performance is more complex for databases that require multiple, user-defined segments. You can't simply look at total free disk space; you must be aware that you really need free space on the correct controller to be able to add space to a given segment. This also means you need to justify having many user-defined segments very thoughtfully since you will need to spend more time managing them.

4.10 Summary

The process of installing and maintaining a server requires that you as the DBA have a good understanding of what many DBAs think of as server machine SA functions. You can ignore these SA functions but you will not be able to control your server's environment very well. As your server(s) grow in size and complexity, the need to be able to understand and manage segments on server devices becomes critical. In order to provide your users with the best uptime possible, you must take the time to understand the issues behind the process of partitioning physical disks, segments, and mirroring. Understanding these issues also provides motivation for establishing and enforcing various standards for your server environment, such as disk partitioning, using whole physical disks for server devices (or their mirrors) or file systems (but not both), mirroring the master device and mirroring all of the database segments if possible.

Chapter 5

Documenting a Server

As we saw in Chapter 1, you cannot expect one person to keep track of multiple databases on many production and development servers without standardized documentation. You must have a reliable method for keeping track of what you have on each server. You must be able to provide your customers with reliable access to their data. You must keep ahead of the demand for database space. The only way to do these tasks in a responsible manner is to document what databases you have on each disk of each server, how big they are, and how much room you have left to use. The resulting document for each server in your database system is called a servermap, as shown in Table 5.2.

You must first find out exactly what you already have on each server. This includes each server and its associated server machine, and the overall "network" of servers that make up your company's database system. Your documentation of your database system is the first step in applying the standard configuration you have defined (see Chapter 1). It is also an excellent way to bring new people up to speed on the structure and workings of your system. You will need this documentation not only for training DBAs, but for application developers, data administrators, general users, and management as well. You cannot justify the installation of a new server without such supporting documentation, nor can you efficiently train a new DBA without it. Finally, you should not consider planning the installation of Replication Server without such documentation.

We will discuss the steps needed to generate and use the servermap for an existing SQL Server, followed by the slightly different process required for a new server installation. Once you have the servermap(s) for your database system, we will discuss documenting the server configuration. Finally, we cover the steps needed to document the overall database system, including a summary of all the server machines and the topology of your database system.

5.1	The Servermap and Why You Need It
5.2	Generating Servermap for Existing SQL Server
5.3	Generating Servermap for New SQL Server
5.4	Server Configuration
5.5	Database Usage and Relative Importance
5.6	Server Health
5.7	Server Machine Configuration
5.8	The Database System

5.1 The Servermap and Why You Need It

Imagine yourself trying to remember how full device sd5d is on server 10. What will you do when you need to check the disk space available for all your systems? Imagine yourself running **p_devspace** (see Chapter 15 "Scripts" for discussion of this stored procedure for displaying the free space on all server devices) for every server and **sp_helpdb** for each and every database on every server. There is no way to do this in a consistent and reliable manner other than to document it. Further, the other DBAs on the team are going to need to know the status of the servers. This documentation is also vital to planning your database space allocations in the future. Whether it is as simple as where to add more space on the existing disks, how many disks to order now, or deciding when to install a new server machine, you must first create the servermap.

The servermap you will create takes the form of a spreadsheet showing all the disks on the server machine and what is allocated to each partition of each disk. This includes all the disks attached to the given server machine, not just those disks that house SQL Server devices, because they are all important in the process of capacity planning. Your servermap should include the overall size of each disk, the overall size of each partition and the database, segment name, and segment size for each segment that occupies space on each partition.

The servermap will also be necessary when you need to train a new DBA. In the environment you will be administering, you must have a team of DBAs. At any given time you should be planning for at least one of the team members to leave.

One of the first things you will have to show the new person is what servers you have, what databases are on which server, and so on. The servermap provides a consistent way for you to meet all of these requirements.

You should automate the process of compiling and maintaining the servermap; however, such efforts are very difficult at the present time. While you can easily automate the SQL involved in getting the server information, as well as the operating system commands for information about the server machine's disks, there isn't a good way to automate the process of combining both sets of data into a servermap. Until a sophisticated database documentation tool becomes available, you should get all the information in front of you and write it out. That way, you know how to get it in the future from the various utilities that you will find on any server you encounter. Depending on a custom application is fine until you come upon another system that doesn't have the tool, or until you upgrade to a version of the server that the custom tool doesn't support. Your ability to document and administer multiple servers that are at various release levels on various server machines is the whole point of this exercise.

There are two basic paths that you as the DBA will be forced to follow when approaching a server for the first time. The first, and the most likely, is that the server already exists. This means someone made a lot of decisions before you were even being interviewed. The second, and the most enjoyable, is installing the server on a new machine dedicated to running SQL Server. In the latter case you get to determine how much disk space will be installed and how to partition and use this space. We will cover both paths, starting with the case of an existing server.

;-)   Real DBAs will agree that the second path is a lot more fun—pretenders view both paths as just a way to make a living.

;-)   Note, regarding the decisions made by your predecessor(s): Since they didn't do things the way you would, they made "bad decisions."

5.2 Generating Servermap for Existing SQL Server

The process you need to follow to generate the servermap for an existing server consists of dumping various system tables from the server and dumping the output of various operating system commands for the server machine. We discuss the sequence of steps listed in Table 5.1.

Table 5.1   Generating Servermap for Existing Server

Generate Data from Server
Generate Data from Server Machine
Generate the Servermap
Make Database Entries in Servermap
Use the Servermap

;-)

You've been hired, you've spent the signing bonus (What? You didn't get one? OOPS! Forget I said anything!!) and now you've shown up. The other members of the DBA team have said their welcomes ("Look, Fresh Meat!") and now they give you the system password and your pager ("Hell, the users hardly ever page at night!"). Now what? First, find out what word processor they have on their system. Ideally, you already know how to run it. If not, learn how real fast. Then load your resume and update it every few months. Now relax, and have a look around. After all, things are only going to get worse from here!

Generate Data from Server

You need to gather the various data from the server regarding the existing databases and devices:

sp_helpdevice
sp_helpdb
p_devspace
sp_helpdb <*database name*> for each database listed by **sp_helpdb**

(See Chapter 15 for scripts that will assist with this process.)

sp_helpdevice output

The output of **sp_helpdevice** lists all the devices that are known to the server. This will include disk devices and tape dump devices. Note that disk devices will be of two types. The first type will be server logical devices that house the databases on the server. The second type will be disk dump devices, which are server logical devices that point to operating system files. These disk dump devices are used to dump databases and/or transaction logs to disk instead of to tape.

For this step in the process, you will make entries in your servermap for the first type of disk device. You will not make entries in your servermap for the tape dump devices (tape drives). The information about these tape dump devices will be used later when you are documenting the configuration of your server machine. The **sp_helpdevice** output will also tell you the raw partitions that are currently being used as mirrors of server logical disk devices. The raw partitions that correspond to the mirrors will be entries in your servermap.

sp_helpdb output

The output of **sp_helpdb** will tell you all the databases that exist on the server. Each database in this output will appear as one or more entries in your servermap.

p_devspace output

The stored procedure **p_devspace** is not part of the standard product set. (See Chapter 15 for a description and the text of this stored procedure for displaying the free space on all server devices.) The output from this procedure will tell you all the logical devices known to the server. You will notice that this output is a subset of the output you get from **sp_helpdevice**. However, the output from **p_devspace** is useful because it shows you only the devices that can support parts of databases. Each device shown in this output should have entries in the servermap that show the device being used by, or available for use by, a database. None of these devices should be shown in the servermap as the mirror of a logical device or as part of any file system on the server machine. This output also shows you the free space available on each of the devices. Note that this may not be relevant to discussions of how much space is available for a given segment of a specific database. This output also shows you the total disk space assigned to the server and how much of that space is already allocated. See Chapter 6 for more details.

sp_helpdb output (again)

The previous run of **sp_helpdb** (without specifying a database) gave a listing of all the databases on the server. You need to generate output for **sp_helpdb** for each and every database listed in the previous output of **sp_helpdb**. You need to be in each database before running **sp_helpdb** and must execute

```
sp_helpdb <database name>
```

to get the proper information for this step. For this step, the output of each run of **sp_helpdb** will tell you where all the pieces of a database are. Recall that each database can have multiple segments and those segments may be on separate device or they may share devices. This output is the servermap but in a very "user-hostile" form. Do this for each and every database on the server, including *master, model,* and *tempdb.*

;-)

> This user-hostile form of the servermap is the form you would give to any smart-ass users that think they know about the server...I mean YOUR server.

Generate Data from Server Machine

You need to gather various data about the disk partitions and file systems of the server machine. See Chapter 3 "Installation of SQL Server from Scratch" for sample output for each of the commands listed below. The process for gathering data is summarized below.

format listing of all disks on server machine
dkinfo for all disks on the server machine
df for the server machine

format listing of all disks on server machine

This output will tell you all the disks on the server machine. This is necessary because the server will only report on those devices that have been made known to it. The output of the df command will report only on those devices in use for operating system file structures. You may find that there are partitions or even an entire disk that is not being used by anyone at all. It is important to find all the disks on the server machine to ensure that you are using your resources efficiently. Each disk on the server machine becomes a column heading in the servermap.

You should have your SA person run this command. You can run format yourself, but make very sure you know what you are doing. If you do something wrong with format, you can destroy the entire server.

dkinfo for all disks on the server machine

Dump the output of dkinfo for each disk listed in the format output. The output of dkinfo for each disk shows the size of all the partitions on the disk. You will use this output to compute the size of each partition, which you will then enter in the server-map. You will also use this output later to check for any partitioning errors that need to be rectified.

The size of each partition is shown as both sectors and cylinders. Basically, there are 512 bytes per sector. This is what you use to convert sectors to megabytes for entries in the servermap. You also use this conversion to determine the number of 2Kpages available on the raw partition when you set up the **disk init** commands. Note that there is not a similar relationship for cylinders. The size of a cylinder varies between disks, and although the cylinders come up in the details of adding disk space, you don't need to worry about cylinders while creating the servermap. The number of bytes-per-sector can vary. You should check with the server machine SA to get the number of bytes-per-sector for the disks on your machine.

df for the server machine

The output of df for the server machine shows you the partitions that are being used for operating system file structures. You will use this output to make an entry in your servermap for each operating system file structure on the server machine. The output also shows the file structures that are being automounted, but these are not relevant to the servermap. You can tell which file structures are being automounted by the remote machine name that precedes the directory name in the df output.

Generate the Servermap

You now generate the servermap using the data gathered in the previous steps. See Table 5.2.

Table 5.2   Typical Servermap

	controller 0				controller 1			
	sd0	sd1	sd2	sd3	sd4	sd5	sd6	sd7
a	N/A	**KEEP OUT**	**KEEP OUT**	**KEEP OUT**	**KEEP OUT**	**KEEP OUT**	**KEEP OUT**	**KEEP OUT**
b	*800 Mb*	*474 Mb*	*474 Mb*	*474 Mb*	*800 Mb*	*474 Mb*	*474 Mb*	*474 Mb*
	/ 800	raw	db4 log 50	sd5b mirror	/logdump 800	db4 100	sd1b mirror	sd2b mirror
c	*2.4 Gb*	*2.4 Gb*	*2.4 Gb*	*2.4 Gb*	*2.4Gb*	*2.4 Gb*	*2.4 Gb*	*2.4 Gb*
d	*800 Mb*	*474 Mb*	*474 Mb*	*474 Mb*	*1200 Mb*	*474 Mb*	*474 Mb*	*474 Mb*
	/dba 800	dbl 400	dbl ncin- dexes 100	sd5d mirror	/diskdump 1200	dbl log 200	sdld mirror	sd2d mirror
e	N/A	*474 Mb*	*474 Mb*	*474 Mb*	*400 Mb*	*474 Mb*	*474 Mb*	*474 Mb*
		dbl 400	db3 50	sd5e mirror	raw	db3 log 20	sdle mirror	sd2e mirror
f	*800 Mb*	*474 Mb*	*474 Mb*	*474 Mb*	N/A	*474 Mb*	*474 Mb*	*474 Mb*
	swap 800	dbl 400	raw	sd5f mirror		tempdb 200	sdlf mirror	sd2f mirror
g	N/A	*474 Mb*	*474 Mb*	*474 Mb*	N/A	*474 Mb*	*474 Mb*	*474 Mb*
		db2 log 100	tempdb log 100	sd5g mirror			sdlg mirror	sd2g mirror
h	N/A	30 Mb	30 Mb	30 Mb	N/A	30 Mb	30 Mb	30 Mb
		master 10	sybsecu- rity 10**	sd5h mirror		sybstem- procs 10**	sd1h mirror	sd2h mirror
		model 2						
		tempdb 2						
				MIRROR OF SD5			MIRROR OF SD1	MIRROR OF SD2
Note: See Figure 1.4, "Spreading Disks Across Controllers," Chapter 1 **for System 10 server only								

The following topics are discussed in this section:

Servermap is a spreadsheet
Row entries in first column for partitions
The 'c' partition
Column for each disk on server
Entry for each partition of each disk
Check for all partitions accounted for

The fonts used in the sample servermap are listed in Table 5.3.

Table 5.3   Fonts Used in Servermap

overall size of disk, in Gb, italics, bold, underlined; _**2.4 Gb**_
partition not used; N/A
partition 'a', bold; KEEP OUT
partition size, in megabytes, italics; _391 Mb_
database segment name and size, Mb assumed; master 5
mirrors, sd1e mirror
raw partition, file system or other; 100 Mb raw
file system names, size, Mb assumed; /usr 84

Servermap is a spreadsheet

You can start by using the spreadsheet program of your choice and laying out the server. You should make this information accessible to all members of the DBA team by using a standard spreadsheet and storing the servermaps in a central location. You must ensure that all members of the DBA team have this spreadsheet available to them and that they can access the servermaps. When you're starting out, there isn't anything wrong with a clean sheet of paper. The point here is that you should not spend the next week designing a spreadsheet that computes the covariance of database free space versus time. You simply need to ensure that the structure of the server is documented.

Row entries in first column for partitions

Make the row entries in the left-most column a listing of all the raw partitions available for each disk. For UNIX this will be 'a' through 'h'. Note that partition 'c' is special, see below. The 'a' partition can be used like other partitions, but you should dedicate partition 'a' to cylinder 0 of the disk.

Cylinder 0 can be used as part of a partition supporting an operating system file structure but cannot be used by a database server device or its mirror. Unless cylinder 0 is part of a partition supporting an operating system file system, you must make sure it is not used by a server device or a mirror of a server device. You do this either by partitioning 'a' to have one cylinder (this one cylinder being the 0 cylinder) and then not using partition 'a' or by simply making sure that none of the partitions include cylinder 0. Note that you must also be sure none of the partitions overlap, because this can cause data corruption as data written to one partition starts to overwrite data in the adjacent (overlapping) partition. Cylinder 0 contains data vital to the operation of the disk. If this cylinder is written to by the server, you will lose the disk and you will have to grovel to get the SA person to help you. Note that there is no guarantee that the SA person can recover this data quickly, since it varies between disk manufacturers and may or may not be available online at your site. You will save a great deal of yelling and screaming in the future if you simply assign cylinder 0 to partition 'a' and make it a rule that partition 'a' is never to be used to support a server device or its mirror.

The 'c' partition

The 'c' partition refers to the entire disk. Unless you need to use the entire disk as one single partition for a file system structure, don't use the 'c' partition. However, since it refers to the whole disk, the size of the 'c' partition and the corresponding entry in the servermap provide a convenient place to document the size of the whole disk. Format these entries with the bold, underlined, and italic version of the chosen font. Note that SunOS does allow you to use the 'c' partition as a subset of the entire disk. Unless you have a very specific reason for making the 'c' partition smaller than the entire disk, don't do it. This will cause confusion as compared to servers in your system that are not running on SunOS.

Column for each disk on server

Create a column for each device listed in the output of the format command. Label each column with a subset of the logical device name that the server will use. Subset here means the portion of the logical device name common to all the partitions on the disk. In general, the logical device name known to the server should be similar to the name of the device known to the operating system. For example, the operating system knows the disk to be sd3, so the server logical devices should have names like sd3d, referring to the 'd' partition. You should use sd3 as the column heading for this disk.

Entry for each partition of each disk

For each partition of each disk make an entry in the servermap to document the total size of the partition in megabytes. This is computed for each partition, using the number of sectors shown in the output of the dkinfo command. Convert to bytes by multiplying by 512 (bytes/sector), then convert to megabytes by dividing by 1024 squared (1024 * 1024 = 1 Mb). Format these entries with the italic version of your chosen font to make them stand out from the entries for database/file system space. Round these entries down to the nearest whole number of megabytes. Server logical devices should be initialized to the largest whole number of megabytes that will fit on the partition (see Chapter 6).

Check for all partitions accounted for

Check that all partitions of all the disks on the server machine have been accounted for. Note any partitions that are not being used by either a file system or by the SQL Server. Any such partitions should be reviewed with the server machine SA, who will tell you what the partition(s) will be used for. Make entries in your servermap to reflect these uses. Any other partitions are for you to use. If you intend to use them for server databases, then go ahead and initialize (**disk init**) them now and make entries in the servermap to document these partitions as belonging to the server. Any partitions that you plan to use but have not initialized should be labeled as "raw" along with the size of the partition in megabytes. For example, Replication Server requires the use of a raw partition to build the stable queue (see Chapter 2).

Make Database Entries In Servermap

You now make entries in the servermap for all segments of each database on the server. This process is summarized below:

Make entries for all segments of all databases
Make entries for mirrors
Make entries for file systems
Account for all server logical devices

Make entries for all segments of all databases

Now, using the output of **sp_helpdb** for each database, figure out the sizes of all the pieces of each database and which device they are on. The output of

```
sp_helpdb <database name>
```

when used within a given database, lists the disk space allocations for a database in alphabetical order of the device name. This will tell you, for example, that database1 has 20 Mb of the default segment on device sd1h. The output may list several disk allocations for the same segment of the database and that's fine—just sum them all up and determine that db1 has 60 Mb of the default segment on device sd1h.

You now make an entry in your servermap spreadsheet at the intersection of the row for partition h for all disks, and the column for disk device sd1. The entry should be something like "db1 60 Mb". Note that the default and system segments are both assigned to the same parts of a database. There is no need to break these segments out on the servermap. You should make a single entry for the total space taken by both these segments for a given database on a given partition. For segments other than the default/system segments, include the segment name in the servermap entry. Do this for all the databases listed in the output of **sp_helpdb** without specifying a database.

Make entries for mirrors

Next, examine the output of the **sp_helpdevice** command. Look for all devices that are mirrored. The output for a device that is mirrored will look like **mirror = <raw_device_file>**. Recall that a mirror takes up an entire raw partition and is known to the server as a raw device file. Each device mirror should be entered in your servermap. If device sd1h is mirrored to rsd2g, then make an entry in the servermap for sd2g like 'sd1h mirror.' This is very important since the server won't tell you about the mirrors with **p_devspace,** and so on, and you don't want to be using a partition for anything else once it is being used for a mirror. Note that SQL Server mirrors an entire device to an entire device. You don't include any database name in the servermap entry for a mirror, since it may be a mirror of many parts of many databases. See Chapter 15 for a stored procedure to check all of the server devices and any associated mirrors, **p_mirror**.

Make entries for file systems

Make the same kind of entries in the servermap for the output of the df command. Each line of the df output will list the size in Kb (Kb = kilobytes = 1024 bytes) of each file system and the name of the partition it is on. Convert the Kb to Mb (Mb = megabytes = 1024 * 1024 bytes). The servermap entry should consist of the file system name as shown in the df output and the size in megabytes.

Account for all server logical devices

You should now look at the dump of **sp_helpdb** for each database. Make sure that all of the devices listed are shown in your servermap for each database. There shouldn't be any devices that don't appear in both the servermap and the output of **sp_helpdb** for any database.

Use the Servermap

With the servermap complete, you now need to make use of it. This process is potentially endless. However, there are a number of things that you should check on a regular basis. These checks are listed and discussed below:

Determine server setup
Identify largest database
Evaluate database location versus size and importance
Examine *master* database/device
Check mirroring of all databases
Examine log segments
Examine user-defined segments

;-)
> Your servermap for an existing server tells you how your fellow DBA team members (or your predecessor, depending on the stress level of the environment) have done their job(s). This may seem harsh, because it is. But, you will be held accountable and now is the time to figure out what they did and how you're going to do it better.

Determine server setup

Now that you have the servermap for an existing server, you must examine it and determine what has been done. When the end of your business cycle (quarter, calendar year, fiscal year, etc.) comes around, you need to know if you can trust your fellow DBAs to have set up and modified the server in a reasonable manner. If you find that they haven't been tracking the issues listed below, discuss it now. The end of the business cycle is not the time to debate which databases should have separate index segments.

Identify largest database

You should note which database(s) are the largest, how big they are in total, and how they are spread over the disks. Lots of small allocations of space for one database are a sign of poor administration. This makes recovery and mirroring more complex than necessary. As a database grows, the rate tends to accelerate. As you are required to increase the size of the database, the absolute amount of space added each time should increase as well. Databases that are spread over many devices may need to be rebuilt on fewer devices to improve performance. Make sure you understand why the databases are spread over many devices. Unless there is a good reason, there probably never was a reason for doing this and the problems will only get worse.

Evaluate database location versus size and importance

The location of databases based on size and business importance is also revealing. You should group the smaller and less critical databases onto a few partitions. This is especially true for small databases that aren't growing rapidly. These relatively static databases should be collected onto a few partitions. These partitions can be mirrored ensuring that all the segments of these databases are mirrored without needing as many partitions.

You don't need to dump the transaction log for static databases. These can easily be restored from the previous dump without any data loss. You must make sure that these databases are indeed static, or that the loss of data that would be added or changed during the interval between database dumps is acceptable. If these static tables are copies of other tables located elsewhere in your database system, you must ensure that the original table is being cared for properly with transaction dumps and whatever is needed. For all databases, ask yourself how you would recover the data for the server in question. If your answer assumes that the data will be recovered from some other source, make sure you understand how that source is maintaining the data.

You must also check large databases and, of course, those that are critical to the business. For these databases, you must understand whether they are growing and how fast. This will have a big impact on your capacity planning. As these databases grow, you must plan where you will add the required space. You must ensure that you will have enough space on enough devices (controllers) to support the growth of the various segments and their associated mirrors. If any of these databases are growing quickly, you should be planning for their transition to a server of their own.

Examine *master* database/device

The partition for the master device should be small and should not have anything else on it, other than *model* and a small part of *tempdb*. The *master* database should not be used for user databases for several reasons, so it should not need to grow very much (see Chapter 7). Given that, and the fact that any server logical device completely occupies a given raw partition, you should not place the master device on a raw partition larger than the sum of the *master* database and *model* and the first 2 Mb of *tempdb*. This applies to the partition used for the mirror of the master device as well.

Check mirroring of all databases

Not all the databases have to be mirrored, especially those that are relatively static or are copies of data maintained elsewhere in your system. However, remember that if any database on the server is unavailable, all the applications that use that database are dead. While some of the databases may not seem critical to you, if they are not mirrored and they encounter a problem, your users will be stopped just as much as if a critical database were lost. Mirroring databases will prevent downtime as well as allowing you to recover data from the secondary if the primary becomes corrupted. See Chapter 15 for a stored procedure, **p_mirror,** to check all of the server devices and any associated mirrors.

Examine log segments

Look at the location and size of the log segments for the largest and most important databases. All databases should have the log segment on a separate physical device (spindle) from the data segments. Ideally, the log segment should be on a disk that is connected to a disk controller separate from that of the data segments. Small, non-critical databases are an exception to this rule; for these databases the log segment can be put on a separate partition on the same physical disk (spindle) as the rest of the database. Databases used for archiving applications are another exception to this rule and usually don't want to have the log segment on a separate device. The size of the log segment for each database is also important. The larger the log segment, the more the transactions that can be open and progressing before the log fills—but this can also delay recovery (see Chapter 4).

Examine user-defined segments

Examine the location and size of any user-defined segments. Any segment other than *system*, *default,* or *logsegment* is a user-defined segment. Each of these should be on a separate device (or devices) from the associated data segments. This also applies to any segment set up for a table or small set of tables. Segments are discussed elsewhere, see Chapter 4, but recall that for a given database, all segments of that database on a given device share all the segments assigned to that device. You create a user-defined segment to segregate database objects. In order to keep these objects segregated from the rest of the database, the segment you set up must be the only segment on the device. You would prefer having such segments on separate physical devices (spindles) as well. Frequently, you will put the most heavily used indexes of a large table on a user-defined segment and then put this segment on a separate physical device, ideally, a device on a different controller, to get better I/O performance.

Further, don't just check for the location of the segments of just one database over the disks. You also need to be aware of the placement of any other segments that are heavily accessed. It may not do any good to move one heavily used index of *database1* to a device separate from the rest of its database, if you put another heavily used object or database on the same device or on another device on the same physical disk (spindle).

5.3   Generating Servermap for New SQL Server

The process you need to follow to generate the servermap for a new server installation is much the same as that for an existing server. However, you will find that with a new installation the process is iterative. You will need to go through many of the same steps as for an existing server when you are actually sizing and configuring the server and the server machine. When you have created the databases and other objects needed to move the server into production or turn it over to the users, in the case of a development server, you must repeat several parts of the process to complete the documentation. We discuss the sequence of steps listed in Table 5.4.

Table 5.4   Generating Servermap for New Server

Install Server Machine
Generate Data from Server Machine
Generate the Servermap
Install and Configure SQL Server
Create Databases
Make Database Entries in Servermap
Use the Servermap

;-)

You may have been hired to do this installation, but more likely you've been a member of the team ("you slimy weasel, get the hell out of my cubicle!"—this is the 3-month point) for a while, and you get tasked with a new SQL Server installation. What now? Make sure that your resume is warm and fax a copy or two to the headhunters that have been calling every two weeks ("It's hard to find experienced Sybase DBAs..."). Then, relax—and try to figure out where the hell to start.

Install Server Machine

With a new installation, you must determine how much database space is needed to support the users and their applications that have caused this new installation to come about. See Chapter 10 for a discussion of capacity planning. With this information you will determine what server machine, server, and how much total disk space are required to go into production.

Generate Data from Server Machine

See "Generating Servermap for Existing SQL Server" earlier in this chapter. Once the server machine is installed and is operating, you need to decide what the partitioning of all the disks needs to be, which again takes you back to capacity planning. With your specifications defined, have the server machine SA partition the disks. Then you can generate the type of data needed to lay out the servermap. At this point, of course, the servermap will be a blank except for the file system(s) already existing to support the OS on the server machine. Still, you will have all the partitions and their sizes laid out to support the installation of the server itself.

Generate the Servermap

See "Generating Servermap for Existing SQL Server."

Generating the servermap is the same as described for an existing server. Again, you won't have any servermap entries for databases, but you will be ready to support the installation of the server.

Install and Configure SQL Server

You now install the server, using the partitions for master you have laid out in the servermap. You should follow the *Sybase SQL Server Installation Guide* faithfully. While you think you know it all already, there are many checks and hints in the documentation that will prevent you from getting into trouble. Also, in the multiple server environment you will be responsible for more servers than you can keep track of in your head. By following and filling out the worksheets in the *Installation Guide*, you provide a record of your actions during the installation. This is vital when you must recover from problems with the master device. It also makes your job of training and documenting much easier if you keep the installation worksheets. See Chapter 3 for an example of server installation.

Create Databases

You now create the databases needed on the server. See Chapter 10 for details of how to determine what the user needs are and how to set up databases to meet those needs.

Make Database Entries in Servermap

See "Generating Servermap for Existing SQL Server."

Making database entries is the same as for an existing server. Once you have created the databases on the new server, you have an existing (new) server.

Use the Servermap

See "Generating Servermap for Existing SQL Server."

Using the servermap is the same as for an existing server. Again, at this point you have an existing server.

5.4   Server Configuration

The servermap is the heart of your documentation of the server. There are other parts as well. You will need to be aware of how the SQL Server is configured internally. The following discussion relates to both an existing server and a new installation. In both cases, you will need to know what the situation is for each of the areas listed in Table 5.5. There is no way to document all the issues that will be raised as you survey your existing or new server. The point here is to provide a set of observations that will allow the DBA to see what the server configuration is now, how it evolved, and what the implications are.

Once you have documented the server with a complete servermap, you must also examine the configuration of the server. As with the servermap, there are many things that should be checked and monitored. We will discuss those that should be checked regularly. These checks are listed in Table 5.5 and discussed below.

Table 5.5   Server Configuration Checklist

1.	Check server version and EBF or rollup level.
2.	Dump **sp_configure.**
3.	Determine maximum number of devices.
4.	Compare maximum number of open databases.
5.	Check memory allocation.
6.	Evaluate user needs.
7.	Evaluate group needs.
8.	Look at object protection.
9.	Check aliases to 'dbo'.
10.	Check users of *master* database.
11.	Check statistics pages.
12.	Check database ownership.
13.	Check object ownership.
14.	Examine remote login privileges.
15.	Review **allow updates** option.
16.	Verify that master device is not a default disk.
17.	Verify mirroring of *master* database.
18.	Check users of *model* database.
19.	Evaluate dump device capacity.
20.	Check device initialization scheme.
21.	Evaluate database and transaction log dumping plans.

1. *Check server version and EBF or rollup level.*

The server version and EBF or rollup level is vital to documenting the server configuration. This information is vital for system planning and for times when you need the help of Sybase Technical Support. This information is readily available in the server errorlog. See the section titled "Startup of Server in Errorlog" later in this chapter, and Chapter 11 "Operational Details of SQL Server" for more information on the server errorlog.

2. *Dump* **sp_configure.**

The configuration of the server is easy to see by dumping the output of **sp_configure**. The output of **sp_configure** will tell you a lot about the way the server is being used. The number of **user connections** will tell you how many users you will be supporting. Compare this to the output of **sp_who** at various time during your business cycle and time of day. The ratio between the two tells you how many users use the server all the time, as well as the maximum load you may need to support. Note that many applications require multiple user connections for each user who is using the application. Consider this when comparing the output of **sp_who** and the number of user connections the server is configured for.

3. *Determine maximum number of devices.*

The maximum number of devices (**devices**) is important to your capacity planning efforts. Note that this refers to disk devices only; dump devices are not included. Compare this number with the contents of *sysdevices* to compare the largest *vdevno* currently in use and the maximum currently set. You may need to boost **devices** before you can add any more devices by using **disk init**. Note that making this configuration change requires restarting the server, so you should know ahead of time that it needs doing. You should set the maximum number of devices to be 10 higher than the actual number of devices the server currently has. The master device is always device 0 ($vdevno = 0$). If **devices** is set to 10, you can have devices 0 through 9.

4. *Compare maximum number of open databases.*

You should compare the maximum number of databases that can be open (**open databases**) with the actual number of databases currently on the server (use **sp_helpdb**). If **open databases** is less than the number of databases on the server, then you have databases that aren't used very often. This should be corrected. Users should need to access all the databases at some point in the business cycle, or the unused databases should be dropped. You should set the maximum number of databases that can be open to be five more than the number of databases on the server.

5. Check memory allocation.

The amount of memory and the percentage of memory allocated to procedure cache are important for performance and tuning of the overall server. Simply compare the amount of memory the server has to the amount of memory available on the server machine. This should conform to the standard you have established for your system.

Determine if anything other than the SQL Server is running on the server machine. If there are other demands on the server machine, determine what they are and why they are there. Determine the usage patterns of these other processes. If they demand a large part of the server machine power at the same points in the business cycle as the SQL Server, you will have severe performance problems. As described in Chapter 1, the SQL Server should be the only application running on the server machine.

Server memory is also affected by the number of user connections allowed, the number of locks allowed, the number of devices, and so on. As any of these configuration parameters changes, so does the amount of server machine memory that is used by the server for each of these needs.

6. Evaluate user needs.

You need to know how users are added to the server(s). Although this may be an entirely separate process (see Chapter 1), you can get a good idea of what is going on by simply getting the row count of *syslogins* for a given server. If you see thousands of users in syslogins but the server is configured for a maximum number of connections that is much lower, you need to know if all of these users will ever need to access the server. Determine how many of these users will need to access the server during periods of peak demand during the business cycle. You should also determine what (if any) mechanism exists to purge users that no longer have a valid need for access to the server.

Along with examining the users on the server, you must understand how the user passwords are generated and controlled. User passwords must be kept in sync across the servers in your system, if users are to be able to perform remote procedure calls between servers (see Chapter 1).

7. Evaluate group needs.

Now look at the output of **sp_helpgroup** for each database, or at least the largest ones. This tells you if there is a plan for granting access to databases and objects within databases. A long list of groups for a given database implies little or no user permission management. You shouldn't need to have lots of different groups to control permissions to the objects in the database. You need to determine how this is managed along with adding users, as we discussed previously. You will need to maintain all these groups as you add and drop users and objects. You must understand how users are added to the different groups to get the permissions they need. Or, you need to understand who in your organization will specify to you what groups a given user falls into. Whatever the system you have is, check to see if it appears to be consistent across databases and across servers in your system. There should be a standard set of user groups and permissions for your servers (see Chapter 1).

8. Look at object protection.

Along with users and groups you should take a look at permissions on objects. Certainly you can't look at all of them. Use the output of **sp_helprotect** for several tables in the largest databases, or more correctly, those databases that are most important to your business. If you see lots of permissions granted, especially to lots of individual users, you need to understand why and how you will maintain this. Ideally, permissions should be granted to a small number of groups.

9. Check aliases to 'dbo'.

As you are examining the way users, groups, and permissions are established and maintained, you must check who has been aliased to 'dbo' in each database. This is especially important for the databases that are critical to your business. You need to know why these users need this access, and you must be confident that they will be responsible for any actions they take with this increased authority.

10. Check users of master database.

While you may not be able to examine every database in your system at first, you should check the *master* database on each server to ensure that there are no users of master other than the server user 'sa' and those server logins that will need to dump the *master* database.

11. Check statistics pages.

You need to check that the statistics pages for all indexes exist. Certainly the DBA must ensure that these statistics pages are regularly updated by **update statistics**, but at the very least you should check that such pages have been established. These pages are used by the query optimizer and can seriously degrade performance if they are out of date or don't exist at all. These conditions can arise from seemingly innocuous events. Each time a table is truncated (before bulk loading data into the table with bcp, for example), the index statistics pages are dropped. If **update statistics** is not run against all such tables, there are no statistics for the optimizer to use. This is a common cause of sudden table scans for queries that performed well the day before. It also makes the DBA look bad so check for this problem (see Chapter 11 for details of how to detect this condition).

While you can't detect how recently **update statistics** has been run for all the indexes in the database, you must understand what the mechanism is to perform this routine maintenance. The process that gets this done regularly should be a part of your standard environment for the server (see Chapter 1). These comments apply to the running of **sp_recompile** as well. In fact, you should think of **update statistics** and **sp_recompile** as a single event. In most instances, you shouldn't do one without the other.

12. Check database ownership.

Check that all the databases on all of your servers are owned by the server user 'sa.' This is important because ownership affects how users and their passwords are checked when remote procedure calls are made between servers. If the ownership of all the databases is not standardized, users may not be able to communicate with other servers. You also need to know that only the server user 'sa' can perform certain database commands. While you can selectively alias users to 'dbo' as need be, you should have the original owner be server user 'sa.' Use **sp_changedbowner** to correct any problems you find.

13. *Check object ownership.*

To facilitate maintenance, the server user 'sa' should also own all the objects in the database, even though server user 'sa' operates outside the permissions manager of SQL Server. If the object is not owned by 'sa,' then the **set user** command must be used before the objects owned by another server user 'sa' can be seen by 'sa.' If 'sa' tries to look at objects not owned by 'sa,' then the server will report that the object does not exist. In addition, users who own objects can't be aliased to 'dbo' (should that need arise later on) because a user must first be dropped from a database and then aliased to 'dbo,' and a user who owns objects in a database cannot be dropped from that database.

14. *Examine remote login privileges.*

You need to examine the contents of *sysservers* and *sysremotelogins* for each server in your system. The former tells you all the other servers that the current (local) server can contact. You need to know if this list of servers is complete and accurate. There is no reason to allow a possible security hole to exist if no one needs to communicate between the servers. You need to check that for each server named there is a similar entry for the local server in the *sysservers* table of the remote server. *sysremotelogins* describes how remote user logins will be handled. Be very careful if you see that password checking has been disabled. This means users from a remote server can gain entry to the local server without a password on the local server. Depending on the way remote users are aliased on the local server, they may also gain permission on the local server.

15. *Review* allow updates *option.*

You should check the configuration option **allow updates**. It should be turned off (0) to prevent any ad hoc changes being made to the server system tables. If this option is turned on (1), find out why. If possible, find out how long this option has been on and keep in mind that users may have been making changes for some time. Recall that a stored procedure that updates system tables and was created during the time the **allow updates** configuration variable was turned on will still be able to update system tables after the **allow updates** variable it turned off.

16. Verify that master device is not a default disk.

The master device for the server should not be a "default disk." A default disk is any disk that can be used (by default) for new or existing objects that need more disk space. The master device is a default disk (by default) when the SQL Server is first installed. The output of

```
sp_helpdevice master
```

will contain the phrase "default device" if the master device is part of this pool of default disk space. Use

```
sp_diskdefault master, defaultoff
```

to remove the master device from the default disk pool (see Chapter 7).

17. Verify mirroring of master database.

The *master* database should be mirrored. If not, you must understand why it is not mirrored and what the implications are for recovery. Further, if you are new to the server, you must dump *master* and *model* to disk as soon as possible. Do NOT put this off! This should be one of the first things you do, along with dumping the system tables to disk (see Server Machine Configuration, below).

18. Check users of model database.

You must check the users defined in the *model* database. Each time you create a database or recreate a database as part of recovery, all the users of the *model* database become users of the database created. Make sure you know who is being added as a user to these new databases. Also, for each database on the server, make sure the user(s) that will dump the database are included as users and that these users have been granted permission to execute **dump database**.

19. Evaluate dump device capacity.

You should check that the largest database dump does not exceed the capacity of the dump device. If you are dumping databases to disk (to operating system files), you must check the capacity of the file system that will house these dumps. Make sure there is enough space to store all the dumps that will be generated before the file system is backed up to tape, and make sure the dumping of the file systems to tape is happening regularly and very soon after the dumps to disk are complete.

If you are dumping databases to tape, you must check the capacity of the tape drive. As your databases grow, the dumps can become quite large. While the tape drive on your server may be a 10-Gb drive, you must ensure that you (or your tape operators or your cron job scripts) are using the correct tape drive device driver. The tape drive on a UNIX system will often have device drivers to support multiple capacities such as 2, 5, 10 Gb. Make sure the correct driver is being used for your dumps. Note that using the proper tape device driver is also important if you plan to load the tape dump on another server machine. The tape drive on the remote server machine must support the same capacity as the host drive. All of this applies to transaction log dumps as well.

20. Check device initialization scheme.

The servermap you construct shows the size of each partition on all the disks attached to the server machine. It is good practice to create server logical devices that fill the entire partition. You should check that this is the case. If not, the server-map entries should be augmented with the size of the server device. There is no point in documenting the size of the partition if you can't use all of that space for the server device. Further, server disk devices should be initialized as some number of whole megabytes. Check that this is the case. While this is hard to correct without dumping the databases on the device, dropping the databases on the device, dropping the device, recreating the device with a whole number of megabytes, recreating the databases, and reloading from dumps, it is another sign of sloppy work by the previous or fellow DBA(s). See Chapter 4 for a discussion of proper server disk device initialization.

21. Evaluate database and transaction log dumping plans.

Make sure you understand the dumping plan and how it is integrated into the recovery plan. You need to know how often database and transaction log dumps are done, and whether to disk or to tape, who checks that these dumps succeeded, who fixes problems when they occur, what the business impacts are of failed dumps, what the constraints are on running such dumps when necessary during times of peak server usage, and how all this is connected with the running of **dbcc** checks on the databases.

5.5 Database Usage and Relative Importance

With the server and its configuration documented, you now need to document who is using the server for what purposes. Find out from whomever you can what each database is used for. This tells you the importance of each database, which has an impact on the need for mirroring and the use of separate segments. Also, find out what the relative load on each database is. This means the number of users and the applications that run against each database. You will decide where to put indexes and tables, based on how many users are trying to use them at once.

This information doesn't relate directly to any one entry in your servermap. Rather, you must understand this information to intelligently place and alter databases and objects on the server. When you are forced to recover from a disaster, it is vital that you understand, before the crisis hits, what the order of importance is for the servers and their databases. For the overall design of your system, you must know which databases need to have standby servers and how up-to-date these standbys must be.

Check that the dump and recovery plans agree with the order of importance you determine for each server. You must ensure that critical databases are dumped regularly along with transaction logs.

5.6 Server Health

You have been documenting the structure of a server. Now you have to examine the health of the server itself. This process is summarized in Table 5.6 and discussed below.

Table 5.6   Server Health Checklist

1.	Determine free disk space.
2.	Check databases marked suspect.
3.	Check size of errorlog.
4.	Evaluate time between shutdowns.
5.	Examine errorlog for startup of server.
6.	Examine **dbcc** output.

1. Determine free disk space.

Now that you have an accurate servermap, you should determine how much disk space is available on each device. And, how does this affect the databases, especially the largest ones? You must verify that there is a reasonable amount of free space for each database. If not, you must begin the process of acquiring more disks. Make sure you have free space before you enter a period of heavy server use (see Chapter 10 for a discussion of capacity planning in general). You must not be fooled by the output of **p_devspace**. While the server may have lots of free space overall, this free space must be on the correct devices to make it usable for the databases that may need it most.

2. Check databases marked suspect.

Check the output of **sp_helpdb** and verify that none of the databases have "marked suspect" or "don't recover" listed in the *status* section of the output. A database with *status* "marked suspect" is one that didn't recover the last time the server was restarted. A database with *status* "don't recover" is one that was created with the **for load** option and will not be available until the database is successfully loaded from dump. For both of these, you must understand why they are in this state and what is needed to return them to service.

3. Check size of errorlog.

The server errorlog contains the minute-by-minute status of the server. You should check this errorlog at least daily. When first documenting a server, you should check for several things. Determine how long the server has been running. Verify that each time the server is restarted the errorlog is copied away to file system archive per your standard environment (see Chapter 1). Check that the errorlog(s) are not about to fill the server machine file system. If this happens, the server will crash. If the server has been running for a long time, you may need to shut down and reboot the server machine. Discuss this with the server machine SA to determine if this is necessary.

4. Evaluate time between shutdowns.

Check the current errorlog and as many of the previous errorlogs as exist on the server machine to get an idea of how long, on average, the server runs between shutdowns. Determine how many of these shutdowns are requested versus crashes. Check for any errors in all the errorlogs. If the same errors keep occurring, determine if these errors are being tracked and if there is an open case with Sybase Technical Support. Lots of 1105 errors (database segment full) indicate that some part of a database (or databases) is filling on a regular basis. This should be cured either by enlarging the database segment(s) in question or altering the use of the database to prevent this situation. Check for stack traces in the errorlog(s). The presence of a stack trace generally signals a more serious problem.

5. *Examine errorlog for startup of server.*

Examine the very beginning of the errorlog where the server is starting up, initializing the disk devices and mirrors, and recovering the databases. Verify the SQL Server version (4.8.x, 4.9.x, etc.) and EBF or rollup level. Check that this is what it should be. Verify that the version and EBF or rollup level is consistent with other servers in the system. For example, you may not be able to load dumps of one server into another if the versions are different. Examine this information for all the previous errorlogs. This will tell you if the server has been upgraded lately and if the EBF level has been changing rapidly. Look for the master device being opened and the mirror of the master device being started. Note that this is a good way to verify what physical device the master device is on. For each device, check that there are no errors and that the mirror (if any) is activated. Examine the database recovery messages to verify that no errors occurred. Also, note the time it takes to recover each database; this will be useful later for estimating the time it takes for a normal recovery.

6. *Examine* dbcc *output.*

Examine the output of the most recent **dbcc** runs for all the databases on the server. If **dbcc** checks have not been run recently, find out why. You should run **dbcc** checks on any databases that aren't routinely checked. This will ensure that all the databases are free from corruption at this point. Databases that don't change very quickly or contain data that is maintained elsewhere may not have **dbcc** checks run very often, but all the databases should be checked at this time. Cure any problems you find as soon as practical. Document the corruption that is present and fix it soon. This also provides a basis for comparison to determine if corruption occurs in the same places over time. Further, the **dbcc** runs you do now provide a basis for planning how to do **dbcc** checks routinely. You must understand how the **dbcc** checks are run in the environment. Determine if they are cron jobs or if they are done manually, how often they are done, who checks the output, and who fixes the problems uncovered.

5.7   Server Machine Configuration

In the preceding steps you were documenting the structure and health of the server. Now you must examine the server machine that supports all of the server activity. The steps in this process are listed in Table 5.7 and discussed below.

Table 5.7   Server Machine Configuration

1.	Check that server starts with -r option.
2.	Dump system tables.
3.	Check 'dba' ownership of server disk partitions.
4.	Look at partition use.
5.	Check disk partitioning.
6.	Check server machine errorlog(s).

1.   Check that server starts with -r option.

The server machine will have the executables necessary to start the server. You must check the command that starts the server (in the RUN_<*servername*> script) and ensure that the -r option is used. The -r option tells the server where the master device mirror is located as the server starts up. This option should be used any time the master device is mirrored, and the master device should always be mirrored.

2.   Dump system tables.

You should be dumping the server system tables to disk regularly (see Chapter 1). Check that this is being done and that the current version of the disk file looks complete. If you are examining a server for the first time, make sure this process is being done and make a hard copy of the disk file as soon as possible.

3. Check 'dba' ownership of server disk partitions.

The server machine UNIX user 'dba' must own all the raw disk partitions that will be used by the server. You should check that this is the case. While those partitions already in use by the server must have been owned by server machine UNIX user 'dba,' any partitions that have yet to be initialized or were formerly being used as file system partitions must have the permissions changed. Check this now before trying to initialize these partitions.

4. Look at partition use.

While not part of the process, look at the server machine file /etc/fstab to see what devices are "ignored" by the OS. This is not foolproof. I have yet to see a machine setup where the /etc/fstab file really included all the partitions that were not being used for operating system files. As a final double-check, you should show the server-map to the server machine SAs. Ask them to verify that they have no interest in any of the partitions that you are using, or plan to use, for database partitions.

5. Check disk partitioning.

Partitioning the disks on the server machine is the responsibility of the server machine SA. However, since it is vital that the partitioning be correct, you must check it yourself, or at least verify that the server machine SA has checked it recently. As you are part of a team of DBAs and you will need to be able to become root on the server machine for various reasons (see Chapter 1), any of your fellow DBAs can partition disks on the server machine, and they can do a sloppy job of it. You must check that there are no overlapping partitions and that cylinder 0 of each disk is not a part of any partition that is used by a SQL Server disk device. The process of checking all of the partitions on the server is very tedious. If you don't get to them all, make sure you check the partitions of the server master device and its mirror.

6. Check server machine errorlog(s).

You must check the server machine errorlogs to see if the hardware or operating system software is generating any errors. Such errors may or may not be related to errors seen by the server. The location and structure of these errorlogs is platform specific.

;-)

You have been ordered to take over a production server that has been installed and configured by one of your experienced coworkers. You realize that your coworker neglected to make any database dumps to disk or tape! While trying to make a tape dump of the entire server, you discover problems with the server machine tape drive which require rebooting the server machine. As the server machine reboots, it refuses to recognize two of the disks. Similarly, the server itself refuses to start because those two disks contain the master device and its mirror! The server machine SA finds that "someone" had repartitioned these two disks such that the server disk devices in partition 'a' included cylinder 0. Hence, the server overwrote the disk data of cylinder 0, which contains the disk label. This didn't hurt anything until the server machine was rebooted, at which time it requires the disk label to know what the disk is. Without the master or its mirror and without any dump of anything, there was no way to recover the server. It had to be reinstalled from scratch. Fortunately, the production data that was lost was available from another source. Don't assume that a server that has been stable for months is a healthy server. Verify the health of the server yourself!

5.8   The Database System

Now you are almost done. After having done all this for one server, you need to repeat the process for each and every server that you and the team are responsible for. When you have that complete, you need to document the overall database system you and your fellow DBAs are supporting. The steps to do this are listed in Table 5.8 and discussed below.

Table 5.8   Documenting the Database System

1.	Map the server network.
2.	List configuration of all server machines.
3.	List applications versus server and database(s).
4.	Compare with standard configuration.

1. Map the server network.

You need to document how all the servers interact to form a network of servers. Start with a map—yes, a map, as in geography. The scale of the map (building, city, county) will be dictated by the scope of your business. Are all the servers in one building? Probably not, as your business grows and adds servers at remote offices. Lay out a map showing the geographical location of all the servers. This can be as simple as listing the names of the servers around town or around the world, near their location on the map. This is very helpful for training, discussions of network problems, capacity planning when new servers are added in remote locations, discussions of distributed data applications, and so on.

2. List configuration of all server machines.

With a map of all the servers, generate a listing of all the server machines and their hardware and operating system configurations. You need to document what the server machine configuration is. This documentation does not have to be detailed. The data needed for this is described below. It is generally more useful to keep the information about server machine configurations in one place, as opposed to adding this information to the servermap for each server. You should include any machines used by the DBA group that don't support a server. This would include machines used to run cron jobs, and the like.

The listing for each server should include the server name, the server type (SQL Server, Open Server), the server version (4.9.x. or 10.0.x and EBF, or rollup level) the processor, amount of memory, number and type of controllers (i.e., x IPI and y SCSI), the operating system, including version and the capacity and format of any tape drives (i.e., 5-Gb 8mm tape drive). This listing is necessary for training and especially useful when calling Sybase Technical Support. For example, which of your servers are System 10 and which are running Solaris on a SPARCStation® 1000? How would your newest DBA trainee find this out, other than asking you and writing it all down?

3. List applications versus server and database(s).

You need another listing that shows all the applications the DBA team supports and which machine(s) these applications run on. This listing should include what the application does, the formal application name and any commonly used nicknames, the server(s) that it runs against, and the databases within each server that the application accesses.

4. Compare with standard configuration.

Finally, with all this documentation complete, compare the servermap and the server configuration with your standard configuration to bring each server into line.

Chapter 6

Physical Database Implementation

Now that you have your server disks segregated into a set of physical disks for server devices and a set for file systems, and your server devices have been set up on the raw partitions of the physical disks, and you have the appropriate mirrors established, you need to understand the issues surrounding placing the databases on the server devices of the server. Note that we have divided the subject into two parts, with Chapter 4 focusing, with a server-wide focus, on the issues of disks, devices, segments and mirrors. Here we discuss the same issues, but with the focus on the impact these issues have on each database and all databases on the server.

We discuss the following topics:

6.1	Transaction Log on Separate Server Device
6.2	Transaction Log Not on Separate Device
6.3	Sizing the Transaction Log
6.4	Placing a Database on Disks and Controllers
6.5	Placing Databases on Disks and Controllers
6.6	Mirroring Priorities
6.7	Why You Should Be Hesitant to Add Database Space

6.1   Transaction Log on Separate Server Device

You must pay attention to the transaction log of each database on the server. The transaction log is one of the vital elements of the Sybase SQL Server that ensures data integrity and recovery from database, server, or server machine failures. You need to understand the following issues to provide your users with the optimum balance of data security, recoverability, and speed. As discussed in Chapter 4 regarding segments, you don't have to place the transaction log (also known as the log segment or just the log) on a server device separate from those server devices that support the other segments of a database, but you almost always want to. We discuss why this is the general rule and why you will sometimes break this rule.

The most important reason to place the transaction log or *logsegment* on a separate server device is to be able to dump the transaction log independently of the database. See Chapter 8 for more discussion of the process of recovering databases. If you don't place the transaction log on a separate server device, you can't dump the log without dumping the entire database. Dumping the database takes much longer and for larger databases often requires dumping to tape because your server may not have enough file system disk space to allow dumping databases to disk. Dumping to tape is also slower than dumping to disk. Longer dump times slow the system down for longer periods of time, which reduces the time the system is available for business use. The fact that dumping the complete database is slower will prevent you from dumping as often as you should. Further, if you dump the database, which also dumps the transaction log along with the rest of the database, the transaction log is not truncated. When you dump the transaction log separately, all the committed transactions in the transaction log are automatically dropped, a process called truncating the transaction log.

You must be able to dump the transaction log in order to recover the database as completely as possible. There are two levels to this recovery: The first assumes you must rebuild the database from dumps already completed, and the second assumes the server itself is still functioning and can access the *sysdatabases* system table in the *master* database.

All of the above means you should, in almost all cases, place the transaction log (*logsegment*) of each database on a separate server device. As explained previously, you should place the transaction log (same as *logsegment*) on a separate server device that is part of a separate physical disk, and the physical disk should be one that is attached to a disk controller different from those that control the other physical disks of the database.

6.2   Transaction Log Not on Separate Device

Now that you have this general rule about placing the transaction log on a separate server device for every database, you need to know about the exception to the rule.

For certain databases you do not want the transaction log separated from the data segments, that is, from the rest of the database. Such a database could not be recovered to a state more current than the last full database dump. A database that is used to archive some portion of a production database would fit this description.

You will set up such a database for an application that will do a great deal of processing on a very infrequent basis, perhaps at the end of each month to reduce all the orders for your business to summary statistics of interest to decision support users. This type of database requires a very large transaction log for a very brief time while it process large quantities of data. After the periodic processing is complete, the database can easily be dumped. The processing is usually started by either the individual responsible for the periodic processing or is scheduled to run automatically via a cron job at the UNIX level. This means it is easy for the database to be dumped completely immediately after the processing is complete; in fact, the dumping should be part of the same script or scripts that perform the processing. Such a database would not be impacted by recovery based on database dumps only and therefore does not require that the transaction log be on a separate server device to support dumping the transaction log separately from the database.

Between these periods of intense processing, the database may be virtually static because it is used mostly on a read-only basis to support report generation. During these periods, there is no need for a large transaction log. This type of database is an example of a database that does not need a separate transaction log segment. During the periods of intense processing, the user(s) of the database will require a very large transaction log. If a separate transaction log of sufficient space were created, it would be empty for most of the time and unavailable to the database for any other use. Therefore, you should consider creating such a database with the segment *logsegment* applied to each and every server device that supports the database. You accomplish this by executing the **create database** command without the **log on** clause. This set of circumstances may not come up often, but you should be aware of this option.

6.3   Sizing the Transaction Log

You will often wonder what the appropriate transaction log size is for any given database. Note that the discussion that follows covers the impact of the transaction log filling. See Chapter 8 "SQL Server Recovery" and Chapter 14 "Transitioning to System 10" for discussion of thresholds that can prevent the transaction log from filling up. We discuss the following:

Impact of Large Transaction Log
Default Transaction Log Sizing
How Transaction Log is Truncated
Can't Dump a Full Transaction Log
Dumping a Full Transaction Log
Dumping Transaction Log Doesn't Free Up Space
Transaction Log Size
Initial Transaction Log Sizing
Transaction Log Never Big Enough

Impact of Large Transaction Log

In fact, the proper size will vary from day to day and perhaps even more frequently than that. You don't want the transaction log to fill because the server must be able to make entries in the transaction log for all the activity in the database to ensure recoverability. If the log fills up, the database becomes useless until at least some space in the log is freed up by a transaction log dump. However, once the transaction log has filled completely, you can't reduce its size (truncate) by dumping the log because even the dumping of the log requires making an entry in the transaction log. This is how the server keeps track of the order in which transaction logs were made (see Chapter 8).

So, if the log fills completely you must dump the transaction log with the **no_log** option, but you must not use the **no_log** option unless you have verified that the transaction log is really full; see Chapter 11 for a procedure to do this. This means that the transaction log has been truncated, but a copy of the deleted transaction log records was not made. Thus, you can't recover the database by using transaction logs beyond the point of the previous transaction log dump, because the server can't log the transaction log dump and therefore doesn't have a complete record of all activity in the database. Since there is a gap in the set of transaction log dumps, the server won't allow you to dump the transaction log anymore until you do a complete database dump.

You need to understand the implications this situation has for your ability to recover the database. When the log fills completely, the database is effectively lost to your users. You must dump the transaction log with the **no_log** option, which takes time and creates more downtime for the database. Note that the larger the transaction log is, the longer it takes to perform the dump (with **no_log** option) before you can have the database available again. Now, since you can't continue to make transaction log dumps, you should make a complete database dump or risk losing the database changes made from the time of the failure onward. So, you should make a full database dump, which creates further downtime. Overall, you don't want to let the transaction log fill for any database that is accessed by applications that are critical to your business. Your first inclination will be to make the transaction log so big that it can never fill up. You would be making a big mistake.

Default Transaction Log Sizing

You need to think about why users may need more log space one day and why they don't need so much the next. As with all database space, you can't retrieve it once it has been assigned to the database without a complete logical rebuild of the database (see Chapter 8 for more details). You are certainly aware of the general rule that the transaction log should be 20 percent of the overall database space; that rule is fine for many databases. Still, as your databases become large, do you really need 2 Gb of transaction log for a 10-Gb database? You can only answer that by knowing what goes on in the database. For small databases the 20 percent rule may be fine, but beyond that you may be wasting a lot of server disk space.

You need to determine what the transaction volume for the database is and how large the typical transaction is and compare this with how often you are going to dump the transaction log. Based on these numbers, you can figure out how big your transaction log must be to support all the transactions that would be in the transaction log at any one time. Note that such a scientific analysis is not something you have the time or the tools to carry out; after all, this is one database in one server among many in your database system.

A more practical approach is to size the transaction log when you initially create the database, with the help of the application designers if possible. Then, let the application go into production and see what happens. You don't want to increase the transaction log in the futile effort of preventing the transaction log from ever filling up. See below for a description of how any one transaction in the log can cause the log to fill no matter how big it is. You probably don't want any transaction log to exceed 100 Mb without a very good reason. If you need more space than that for the transaction log of a single database, you must be able to explain what the database is doing with that much space day after day. You also need to explain what is going on with the size of the transaction log dumps as well. See Chapter 9 for more details of the implications of large transaction log dumps.

How Transaction Log Is Truncated

You need to understand the way the transaction log works and how it relates to the issue of the log filling up. Before database changes are made, the server records those changes for each database in the transaction log for that database. The records in the transaction log represent each step in each transaction that is being applied to the database. Each transaction has a beginning, intermediate steps, and either a commit or a rollback. Whether the transaction commits or rolls back, the transaction is complete as far as the database is concerned. Since all changes to the database are recorded in the log, the log will continue to grow.

You can reduce the size of the transaction log only by truncating the log, which occurs when you dump the transaction log. Dumping the transaction log makes a copy of the transaction log records for committed transactions on the dump device you specify and then deletes the records of all the committed transactions. This usually reduces the size of the log each time you dump it. However, there is a catch that is not immediately obvious, a catch that can be deadly and confusing. When you dump the transaction log, the server starts looking at the transactions in the log to determine which transactions can be deleted to reduce the size of the log. The server scans through the log, looking for the beginning of the first transaction that has not completed. When it finds the beginning of the first transaction that has not (at the time of the **dump transaction**) yet completed with either a commit or a rollback, the server stops deleting records from the transaction log. This means the server will only delete the completed transactions from the transaction log up to the beginning of the first incomplete transaction.

Can't Dump a Full Transaction Log

You may encounter the following situation. Once the transaction log for a particular database is full, you cannot make any more entries in the transaction log for that database. Since you cannot turn off transaction logging for a database, the database is no longer available for inserts or updates; selects will still operate because a select is not logged. When the transaction log fills and the SQL Server attempts to write to the transaction log, the write fails, generating an 1105 error. (System 10 thresholds can prevent this, see Chapter 14 "Transitioning to System 10"). The 1105 error in the server errorlog indicates a database segment is full, not necessarily the log segment. See Chapter 11 for details of how to verify which segment caused an 1105 and what to do about it. For this discussion, we assume the 1105 error was caused by the transaction log being full and that dumping the transaction log did not free up any space.

Once the transaction log is full and dumping the transaction log does not reduce its size, the server will not be able to make any further transaction log dumps. This may not seem logical, but consider the way the server will use the transaction log(s) and database dump when recovering the database. To recover a database, you will first load the most recent database dump and then apply the subsequent transaction log dumps in the order they were made. The server looks at the timestamp on each transaction log to make sure the correct order of the transaction logs is preserved as they are applied to the database. In order to mark the time of each transaction log dump, the server makes an entry in the transaction log itself, indicating when the transaction log dump was started. So, if the transaction log is full, the server can't write into the transaction log to record the time of the dump.

Dumping a Full Transaction Log

You have only one option at this point and that is to dump the transaction log with the **no_log** option. This option has implications for your ability to recover the database so use it only when you have to and only after you understand the implications (see Chapter 8). When you use the **no_log** option, the server does not attempt to make any entries in the transaction log; since it can't record the time of the transaction log dump, there is no point in making an actual dump of the log entries either, because the server would not allow you to apply it to the database anyway. With the **no_log** option, the server simply deletes all the completed transactions up to the beginning of the first transaction it finds that is still open.

Dumping Transaction Log Doesn't Free Up Space

Now we can continue the discussion of the 1105 error. Once you have the 1105 error and you have verified that the transaction log is indeed full (see Chapter 11 for a procedure to verify this), you must use

```
dump transaction <databasename> with no_log
```

However, you will see situations where even this does not reduce the size of the transaction log. How can this be? Recall that the server only deletes the transaction log entries for completed transactions up to the point of the beginning of the first transaction that has not completed.

But, what if the very first entry in the transaction log is the beginning of an open transaction? This means even the **no_log** option will not reduce the size of the transaction log. The only way to cure this situation is to kill the server process that owns the open transaction. If you can identify the offending server process ID (*spid*), you can kill the *spid* from within the server; doing so should remove the transaction log entries for that transaction. However, there is no direct way for you to identify which server process is responsible. You can make reasonable deductions to determine which *spids* might be the cause and kill all of them, but if this doesn't work pretty quickly, you might just as well shut down and restart the server. Restarting the server will allow you to dump the transaction log after the database has recovered.

Transaction Log Size

Finally, with all this background, you can see why this is relevant to database physical design. We need to discuss the appropriate size of the transaction log for the database. You will be tempted to make the transaction log huge in the thought that you can somehow prevent the transaction log from ever filling up. You would be making a reasonable assumption, but you would be wrong. As we just explained, you can make the transaction log bigger and bigger, but one open transaction can still force the log to fill completely, no matter how large the transaction log is. Certainly, the larger the transaction log, the longer it will take to fill up, but you must realize an important impact of this. When the transaction log does finally fill and you must use

```
dump transaction <databasename> with no_log
```

option; the larger the transaction log, the longer it will take to dump the transaction log. Since a full transaction log basically shuts down the database, which can shut down your business (again, selects will operate, but any updates will fail), a larger transaction log that will delay the crisis of a full transaction log will actually make the crisis worse because the **dump transaction** will take that much longer. You can't completely avoid filling the transaction log just by making it bigger.

Initial Transaction Log Sizing

With all that said, you need to make a reasonable guess as to the initial size of the transaction log, say, 20 percent of the database size and then see how it goes. If this transaction log fills up repeatedly and you can explain why the applications that run against the database have a good reason for creating enough transactions at one time to fill the transaction log, then you should expand it by using the **alter database** command. You need to be careful, though. This 20 percent rule-of-thumb can get you into trouble.

Take a real world example. A production database is 5 Gb and the transaction log is 200 Mb, which is only 4 percent of the overall database size. If the transaction log ever fills up, it takes about 30 minutes to dump the transaction log to disk. Can your business afford to be without this database (for updates and inserts) for more than 30 minutes? Further, can you provide any reasonable explanation as to why your users have a need to fill more than 200 Mb of transaction log while running the applications that depend on this database? Probably, most of the data in this database is not new but old and getting older all the time. Hence, your users are probably only working with a small percentage of this database at any one time, and if you look at this much smaller subset of the database as the actual database size, the size of the transaction log at 200 Mb seems much more reasonable. The 20 percent rule-of-thumb is probably useful until the size of the transaction log goes beyond 100 Mb. For a transaction log larger than 100 Mb you need to make sure you and your users understand how long it will take to dump the transaction log if it ever gets full. We have discussed the impacts of dumping a full transaction log, but you can still have very long dump times for a large transaction log that is not completely full. If you normally dump the transaction log periodically and for some reason you miss several of those transaction log dumps, the next transaction log dump will take much longer because the transaction log continues to fill up as the normal dump times go by without a successful dump of the transaction log.

Transaction Log Never Big Enough

You must educate your users and your management about the facts: The transaction log can't be turned off for any database; no matter how large it is, it can still fill up if only one user opens a transaction and never executes a commit or rollback; and it takes longer to dump the transaction log the larger it becomes. Your users will always want a larger transaction log to prevent database downtime due to a full transaction log, but those same users will not want to suffer the greater database downtime that occurs when you need to dump a larger transaction log.

6.4   Placing a Database on Disks and Controllers

Once you have the basic physical design decisions settled for a database that will exist in the server, you need to consider how to place the various segments of the database on the available server devices. We have already covered most of this elsewhere, but we summarize the problems and the solutions here. Note that this process is where your servermap really pays for itself.

You should place the transaction log (*logsegment*) on a server device that is separate from the server devices that support any other segments of the database. This server device should be dedicated to the *logsegment,* which means only the *logsegment* of the database is on that server device. You should place the *logsegment* on a server device supported by a physical disk that is attached to different controllers from those that support the other segments of the database. You should examine the objects in the database. If there are any large objects such as a large table or the index on a large table, separate segments should be created for these objects, and these segments should be placed on separate server devices, preferably on physical disks attached to different controllers than the other server devices supporting the database. You want to spread these user-defined segments evenly over several server devices to maximize the I/O throughput for the most heavily accessed objects (see Chapter 9).

You may now understand the issues regarding the size of the transaction log, but you also need to realize what matters as far as placing the database transaction log on server devices, that is, disks. For many other portions of a database, you want to use multiple server devices on different disk controllers. This isn't the case for the transaction log. Since all activity in the transaction log occurs at the very end of the transaction log and since you have no control over this behavior, it doesn't help to have the transaction log spread over multiple server devices or controllers. Hence, once you have settled on the size of the transaction log, you should place it on one server device. Recall that you do want to place the transaction log on a server device that is not supporting any other segment(s) of the database. Further, you should mirror the transaction log to further ensure recovery and to reduce downtime for your database.

6.5   Placing Databases on Disks and Controllers

Now, consider the problems of placing several databases over the available server devices and controllers. To satisfy the needs of each database, spread the various segments over several server devices on physical disks attached to different controllers. However, you must integrate the needs of several, if not many, databases on one server. Although you would prefer to have a whole set of server devices and controllers for each database, that isn't practical. You have to place all the databases you have on the limited set of server devices you have, attached to a limited set of controllers. As we mentioned earlier, this is where you will really appreciate your servermap. And if you haven't created a servermap, now you will see why you should have done so.

The first database(s) you will place are *master*, *model*, and the first portion of *tempdb,* which you put on the master device when you installed the server. Next, look at your databases and decide which one will be under the heaviest I/O load. Note that this may not be the largest database. Note also that we use the term "decide" because you really can't figure out what the I/O problems will be until the entire server with all the databases and all the users is up and running. You can make an educated guess, but any determination can only be done after the server is in full service. For the database that you decide needs the most I/O throughput, you should look at the objects that are planned for the database. Tables that are large or frequently accessed may need to be placed on a user-defined data segment separate from the rest of the database. Similarly, you may need a separate user-defined segment to contain the largest or most frequently accessed indexes for these tables. Segments created for either large tables or indexes may be better off if placed or spread over server devices attached to different controllers from those for the other segments of the database.

With the first user database placed on the server, next fit all the other databases into the space available. This is an iterative process. You should fit the largest databases in early, but you must also give those databases that need the most I/O throughput high priority because they will need the most flexibility as far as number of server devices and controllers. You also must consider the future. It may be tempting to simply place the databases so that you fill each physical disk in turn, leaving as many disks as possible free for the future. This is not a good move. When you place the database(s) that need the most I/O performance, you should have a good reason for creating each user-defined segment and a good reason for its location.

Now, as each of these segments expands, you want to allow them to grow so that they don't have to span server devices in a way that upsets your initial plans. If a database needs a user-defined segment that must be isolated from the other segments of the database to avoid an I/O bottleneck, then you don't want to add space to that segment on a server device on another controller supporting another segment of the same database. You need to look at each segment of your most important databases and make sure it has room to grow on the same physical disk(s) attached to the same controller that they are already on. This means you do not fill every server device on every physical disk. Rather, you should spread your databases and their segments over the server devices and controllers as much as possible, leaving room for each segment to grow on the disks on each controller.

You also make it easier to add space later if you leave an obvious place for such space to be added. Whether a given database segment is spread over server devices on one or several physical disks, you should leave some room on at least one of the server devices on each physical disk so it will be easy to add space to the segment without upsetting the way the segment is spread over the physical disks and controllers. If you don't plan for adding space from the beginning, the first time you need more space you may be forced to add that space on a server device that conflicts with your performance objectives. You also need to make it as easy as possible to add the space properly; you will be relying on other members of your DBA team to add space as needed, and they will not all be as aware as you are of the impacts of a hasty addition of space. Finally, adding space to the segment on the same physical disk that already supports the segment makes it easier to maintain the mirrors of the segment. As part of your standard environment, you should allocate entire physical disks to support server devices and other entire physical disks to support the mirrors of those server devices.

You will run into conflicts as you place each database among the steadily decreasing supply of server devices and controllers. The conflict will come when you have a very heavily used segment of one database placed on a physical disk and you need to place a heavily used segment of another database on the same physical disk or on a physical disk attached to the same controller. There will not be a right answer, and the optimal solution will change over time as the database segments grow and spread from disk to disk. When you have performance problems, you should reexamine the layout of your server and make changes as needed.

6.6   Mirroring Priorities

We have discussed various aspects of physical database design, and mirroring has been covered in detail previously. However, this is a good place to discuss the mirroring priorities you should consider when placing databases on the server devices, physical disks, and controllers available to the server.

If you have the disks (and if you don't, you should get them), you should be using all of each physical disk to either support only server devices (using the standard disk partitioning described earlier) or mirrors of server devices. It is easiest to maintain the mirrors of server devices if all the physical disks that support the server are partitioned identically; then, you simply mirror all the server devices (partitions) of one whole disk to another whole disk.

If you don't choose to go this way, you need to mirror some things more than others. First you must always mirror the *master* database, which of course means you must mirror the master device. Because the server mirrors a server device to a raw partition, you must mirror the master device. A mirror of the master device will allow the server to operate continuously if the master device (*master* database) fails. Since the *master* database is the heart and soul of your server, any problems with the *master* database bring down the whole server. You should always mirror the *master* device of each of your servers.

After the *master* database, you should mirror the transaction log of the most critical database(s) on the server. The database dumps that you have, along with the transaction log dumps, allow you to recover the database to the point in time of the most recent transaction log dump. If you can still get at the transaction log on disk, you can recover the database to the state it was in at the moment of the failure. If there is any problem with the disk that supports the transaction log, you can still recover the transaction log from the mirror device. Mirroring the transaction log ensures that you can recover the database and all the transactions that had been committed against it even though a disk failure has occurred. Note that it is more important to mirror the transaction log than the database itself. If any of the disks that support the database fail and the database is not mirrored, you can reload the database from database dumps and transaction logs, and since you can recover the up-to-date transaction log from disk, you can recover the database completely. If you mirror the database itself, but not the transaction log, and the disk supporting the transaction log fails, you have no way to recover the database beyond the most recent transaction log dump.

You will need to spend your time checking that the mirrors of the transaction logs are working. This can become tedious when you add space to one of the databases and the new space must be on a server device that was not previously mirrored. This is why, from a management perspective, it is a whole lot easier to simply mirror all the server devices (partitions) in the server and to mirror all server devices on one physical disk to another whole physical disk. This ensures that no matter where you add space, the data is mirrored.

One exception to this scheme is *tempdb*. Since *tempdb* is never recovered, there is no need to mirror *tempdb* or the transaction log of *tempdb*. Still, if *tempdb* is not mirrored and the disk that supports *tempdb*, or its log, fails, *tempdb* fails and the entire server is effectively shut down. For *tempdb* you want to mirror both the database and the transaction log to ensure that your server will not be brought down by a single disk failure. You will trade this off against the overhead involved with mirroring, because mirroring means writing the same data to two different disks all the time. If *tempdb* for your server is very heavily loaded, you may want to drop mirroring for *tempdb*. Understand that you are trading performance against system availability.

6.7   Why You Should Be Hesitant to Add Database Space

Now that you are aware of the many complexities regarding database placement on server devices, you need to be aware of the reasons you as DBA don't want to add space to any database on the server without careful consideration. The actual act of adding database space is so easy, it is difficult to appreciate the negative impact that a hasty addition can have. If you need to add database or transaction log space on server devices that are currently supporting the database or transaction log in question, you are probably fine. Recall that you may not want to add space to the transaction log for the reasons discussed earlier; that is, one open transaction can fill a very large transaction log, and the larger the transaction log, the longer it takes to dump once it is full. If the transaction log fills completely and must be dumped with **no_log** option, the database is not available for changes while the transaction log is dumped; the larger the transaction log, the longer the database will be unavailable.

Whenever you add space to any database on your server, you must check that all the server devices that should be mirrored are mirrored. Make sure the space you are adding is on a device that is mirrored already, or set up the mirror, or be sure you don't need that device mirrored. Again, it is best to simply mirror everything; that way, you don't have to wonder if your fellow DBAs will understand which server devices need mirrors and which server devices don't.

Finally, understand that while a server device may have lots of free space, there may not be any free space that you can use. When you add space to a database or its transaction log, you must add space to that segment, not just to the database. If you need to add space to the transaction log, you can't add that space on any server device that is already supporting the other segments(s) for that database—the transaction log must be on a server device that doesn't support any other database segments. If you need to add space to a user-defined segment, the same logic applies. Unlike the case with the transaction log, you can have a server device supporting a user-defined segment and some other segment. You probably set up the user-defined segment to isolate, for performance, certain database objects (large tables and their nonclustered indexes) from the rest of the database. You should not add any other segment of the database to the server devices that support the user-defined segment. If you do mix the segments on such a server device, you may lose all the performance gain you had, as users contend for the two types of database objects on the server device. Just because a server device has free space, it may not have any free space that you can use. Further, you don't want any user objects on the master device, and that means any free space on the master device is not really available for use. If you created the master device to be much larger than the *master* database, it will have lots of free space. Be aware of this when you look at how much free space you have in the whole server. You should not count any free space on the master device in your total of free space on the server. Be careful to examine the total free space on the server to make sure it is on the right server devices to support the growth of the various segments of the databases that are growing the fastest.

For all these reasons, treat the simple act of adding database space very carefully. Adding database space has many long-ranging impacts.

Chapter 7

The master Database Is Special

We have discussed various aspects of database physical design, and now you need to know about some issues that are specific to the *master* database. The *master* database and the master device are unique.

We discuss various aspects of the *master* database. And because the *master* database and the master device are so intimately related, we discuss the master device as well, as listed below.

7.1	The *master* Database and Master Device
7.2	Sizing the Master Device
7.3	The *logsegment* of the *master* Database
7.4	Master Device Name and Mirroring
7.5	Master Device and **disk init**
7.6	Master Device and Default Server Disk Devices
7.7	Loading a Database Dump of the *master* Database
7.8	Moving the Master Device to a Larger Partition
7.9	Clearing Server Configuration in *master* Database

7.1 The *master* Database and Master Device

The *master* database is the database that stores all the information relating to the SQL Server, such as the names and structures of all the databases in the server, all the server user logins, and so on. The *master* database is where the system tables for the server level are stored. There is only one *master* database per server. The *master* database is the heart and soul of the server, and you must not mess with it. If you scramble the *master* database, or the master device, you scramble the whole server.

Your recovery plans must make recovery of the *master* database (and master device) the number one priority, because losing the *master* database or master device destroys the entire server.

The *master* database always exists on the server device called the master device. The master device is a server device that is created only through installation by using sybconfig (sybinit for System 10) or by executing buildmaster, a task that sybconfig does internally. You should not be creating master devices without a very good reason and without being very careful. The master device is never created by using **disk init** the way other server devices are. Further, the *master* database can't be extended beyond the master device. This means that if the *master* database fills the master device, you can't execute the **alter database** command to extend the *master* database to another server device. And that means that if the master device fills up, you must reinstall the contents of the master device on another larger device—a complete reinstallation of the server. You don't want to face this unpleasant duty. You must not let the master device fill up. Note that you could mirror the master device to a larger partition, drop the primary side of the mirrored server device pair, and then manually update the size of the master device in the system table *sysdevices* as detailed in Section 7.8, "Moving the Master Device to a Larger Partition."

Hence, you must realize two things. First, the *master* database can't grow beyond the size of the master device. When you create the master device through sybconfig (sybinit for System 10) at installation or manually after installation by using buildmaster, you determine the maximum size of the *master* database when you specify the size of the master device. Second, you must not cause the *master* database to grow unnecessarily. This is why you don't want any user objects in the *master* database or any user databases on the master device. You must make sure the master device is not in the pool of default server disk devices (see Section 7.6, "Master Device and Default Server Disk Devices"). Only the *master* database, the *model* database, and the first 2 Mb of *tempdb* should be allowed on the master device.

7.2   Sizing the Master Device

Now that you understand the relationship between the *master* database and the master device, how big should the master device be? You shouldn't need more than 30 Mb for the master device. For a standard installation where the master device supports 2 Mb of the *model* database and 2 Mb of *tempdb,* you still have 26 Mb of space for the *master* database. Note that some applications may require installing stored procedures in the *master* database. If there are lots of these stored procedures, you may need a larger than normal *master* database. This situation usually comes up when dealing with a third-party application that you are installing. You should ask the vendor how much room is required by these stored procedures and use that in planning the size of the *master* database and the master device. Similarly, for the *model* database, you may need to create a number of users or lots of database objects that you need to have in all the user databases created after this point. In that case, the *model* database may be larger than normal. Unless you have some special need to have a large *model* database or have a need to fill the *master* database with lots of data, 30 Mb should be more than you will ever need.

You may not see the other side of the relationship between the master device and the *master* database. Since the *master* database doesn't need much more than 30 Mb and since you can only have one server device assigned to one disk partition, there is no purpose in placing the *master* database on a master device that is any larger than 30 Mb. This means you should create a 30-Mb partition on a physical disk and use that partition for the master device. From this you see the need for another 30-Mb partition to support the mirror of the *master* database. Recall from Chapter 1 that the recommended standard for partitioning all the physical disks on your server machine that will be assigned to server devices and their mirrors includes a 30-Mb partition. All too often a server will be set up wherein all the physical disks are partitioned into several equal partitions. This seems logical until the master device is set up. These equal partitions are often several hundred megabytes each, and using one of these for the master device ends up wasting several hundred megabytes that are controlled but not used by the master device, as well as even more waste by the large partition used for the master mirror.

;-)

> You check your server to see how much free space you have. You see there are several hundred megabytes free. You think all is well and you put off purchasing more disks. You don't notice that most of that free space is on the master device. You shouldn't be using this space for anything other than the *master* database (and *model* and part of *tempdb*). When you actually need to use the space you thought you had, you realize what has been going on. Suddenly, you don't have much, if any, free space at all.

7.3   The *logsegment* of the *master* Database

Another unique quality of the *master* database is that the *logsegment* can't be separated from the rest of the database. This means you can't place the *logsegment* on a separate server device as you can and should with almost all other databases in the server. You won't think this is a big deal, but it is. Recall that if the *logsegment* is not on a separate server device—a server device that is dedicated to supporting only the log segment of that database—you can't dump the transaction log separately. Dumping the database is the only form of dump you can make for such a database. But, recall also that while dumping the database does make a copy of the transaction log, as well as the rest of the database, it doesn't truncate the transaction log. This means that even though you dump the master database regularly, as you must, the size of the transaction log for the master database continues to grow. Certainly, you should not be performing any heavy processing in the *master* database, and therefore the transaction log should grow slowly. Still, the fact that the transaction log is growing at all means it will fill up eventually, and it always fills up at the most inappropriate time. The only way for you to reduce the size of the transaction log of the *master* database is to dump the transaction log with the **truncate_only** option. So, along with a regular dump of the *master* database, you must dump the transaction log with **truncate_only** after each database dump. Although dumping the transaction log with **truncate_only** may seem contradictory to the fact that you can't dump the transaction log separately, it isn't. The **truncate_only** option means that the size of the transaction log is reduced but a copy of the transaction log is not made.

7.4   Master Device Name and Mirroring

Another odd characteristic of the master device comes up regarding mirroring. Once you have set up the master device and before you have created the mirror of the master device, the output of **sp_helpdevice** for the master device will look very odd. The output will tell you that the *device_name* is "master" as you would expect, but the *physical device* is "d_master," which is not the case at all, because you would expect the physical device name to be the name of the disk partition that supports the master device. Further, as soon as you create the mirror of the master device, this oddity disappears and the physical name becomes the actual device name, as it should have been all along. If you don't mirror the master device, you can't tell which server device is the master device from the information in *sysdevices* or the output of **sp_helpdevice**. You can find out the server device that is the master device from examining the errorlog, however. See Chapter 11 for details of examining the server errorlog. Note that this peculiar behavior of the unmirrored master device comes up during the upgrade process (see Chapter 13). During the upgrade process, you may need to change the physical name of the master device entry in *sysdevices* to reflect the actual physical name of the server device. Shown below is the output of the **sp_helpdevice** command for the master device before mirroring, the output of the **disk mirror** command, and the output of **sp_helpdevice** for the master device after the mirroring is complete.

```
1> sp_helpdevice master
2> go
    device_name              physical_name
    description
    status cntrltype device_number low         high
 ----------------------------- ----------------------------
        ----------------------------------------------------
----------------------------------------------------------
 -
        ------ --------- ------------- ----------- ---------
 master                   d_master
 special,defaultdisk,physicaldisk,32.00MB
     3      0        0        0       16383

(1 row affected, return status = 0)
1> disk mirror
2> name="master",
3> mirror = '/dev/rsd8h',
4> writes=serial
5> go
Creating the physical file for the mirror...
Starting Dynamic Mirroring of 16384 pages for logical device
'master'.
        512 pages mirrored...
       1024 pages mirrored...
       1536 pages mirrored...
       2048 pages mirrored...
       2560 pages mirrored...
       3072 pages mirrored...
       3584 pages mirrored...
```

```
        4096 pages mirrored...
        4608 pages mirrored...
        5120 pages mirrored...
        5632 pages mirrored...
        6144 pages mirrored...
        6656 pages mirrored...
        7168 pages mirrored...
```
The remaining 9216 pages are currently unallocated and will
be mirrored as they are allocated.
```
1> sp_helpdevice master
2> go
  device_name                physical_name
  description
        status cntrltype device_number low          high
  ------------------------------- --------------------------
        ------------------------------------------------------
  ------------------------------------------------------------
  -
        ------ -------- ------------ ---------- ---------
 master                     /dev/rsd4h
          special, MIRROR ENABLED, mirror = '/dev/rsd8h',
serial writes, reads mirrored, default disk, physical disk,
32.00 MB
          739          0            0          0        16383

(1 row affected, return status = 0)
```

7.5   Master Device and disk init

Another special situation you must watch out for relates to the physical name of the
master device, as described in the previous section. If the master device is not mirrored, the output of **sp_helpdevice** will show that the *device_name* is "master," as
you expect, but the *physical_device* is "d_master" and not the actual path of the disk
partition that supports the master device. Now, this odd behavior of the SQL Server
causes another problem to arise. When you install the SQL Server by using sybconfig (sybinit for System 10), the master device is created as part of the installation. As
part of setting up the server, you will need to execute **disk init** against each physical
disk partition that will be used to support a server device. You must be careful, how-

ever, that you do not execute a **disk init** against the physical disk partition that supports the master device. You would expect that the server would prevent this error from occurring, and normally you would be right. For any other server device, if you execute **disk init** and specify a partition that is already supporting a server device for that server, the server will generate an error. But this process is based on the server looking in *sysdevices* and seeing that the partition is already in use.

For the master device, the server thinks the partition supporting the master device is "d_master" and therefore, if you execute a **disk init** and specify the path of the partition that really does support the master device, the server will allow it to happen. Worse still, the server will continue to function. This sort of error is deadly and very embarrassing. When you dump the *master* database as part of the installation process, you will get errors, and if you do **dbcc** checks on the *master* database, you will get 605 errors. At this point, the *master* database is dead and the only recourse is to load a dump of *master* or reinstall the server.

You must be very careful whenever you execute **disk init**. Make very sure that you have checked the server errorlog and verified that you know what disk partition is supporting the master device and verify that you are not trying to run **disk init** on that partition. Also, check any script that you set up to perform multiple **disk init** commands. You can manually update the *sysdevices* table to reflect the path of the partition supporting the master device, but the real solution is to mirror the master device so the server will catch and prevent this error. You should be mirroring the master device anyway, so it doesn't hurt to mirror it right away.

7.6 Master Device and Default Server Disk Devices

When you first install the SQL Server by using sybconfig (sybinit for System 10), the master device is installed and assigned to the default pool of server disk space. Note that the term "default" here is different from the *default* segment. When any server disk device is assigned to the pool of default server disk devices, and any database is created or altered without a specific server disk device being specified, the additional database space will be created on a server disk device in the pool of default server disk devices. The disk devices are chosen from the default pool in alphabetical order as each disk fills up. This means that any segmentation you have set up for data integrity or performance reasons could be jeopardized by the default pool. You must make sure that any server devices that are assigned to the default pool of disk space are not involved in supporting segments of the important databases on the server. Better yet, you should not assign any disk devices to the default pool at all. This requires that any creating or altering of databases be done to specific server disk devices. This is how it should be done anyway, because it forces the DBA to review the performance impacts of creating or altering the database.

Note that the master device is the only device that is automatically assigned to the default pool of disk space. You must manually assign any other server disk devices to the default pool by using the **sp_diskdefault** server command. Further, you must not allow the master device to remain assigned to the default pool. You must use the **sp_diskdefault** command to remove the master device from the pool. You can see if any device is assigned to the default pool by executing the **sp_helpdevice** server command.

Shown below is the output of the **sp_helpdevice** and the **sp_diskdefault** commands to remove the master device from the default pool of disk space.

```
1> sp_helpdevice master
2> go
 device_name                physical_name
   description
         status cntrltype device_number low         high
 --------------------------- ---------------------------
         -------------------------------------------------
 -------------------------------------------------------
 -
         ------ --------- ------------- ----------- ---------
 master                  d_master
 special,defaultdisk,physicaldisk,32.00MB
      3          0         0        0          16383

1> sp_diskdefault master, defaultoff
2> go
(return status = 0)
1> sp_helpdevice master
2> go
 device_name                physical_name
   description
```

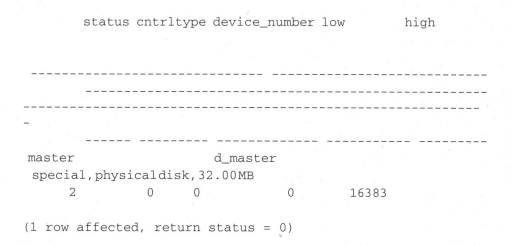

```
        status cntrltype device_number low        high


        ---------------------------- ----------------------------
                ----------------------------------------------------
        ----------------------------------------------------------
        -
                ------ --------- ------------ ---------- ---------
master                          d_master
 special,physicaldisk,32.00MB
        2       0    0            0          16383

(1 row affected, return status = 0)
```

7.7 Loading a Database Dump of the *master* Database

Loading a database dump of the *master* database is part of the recovery process (see Chapter 8). When you need to do this, you will need to put the server into single-user mode. Note that you can't change the database options for the *master* database; that means you can't put the *master* database into single-user mode the way you can for any other database. To put the server into single-user mode, you have to add the -m option to the execution of the server binary in the RUN_<*servername*> script in the /dba/<*servername*> directory. Then, you must restart the server to put it into single-user mode. Now you can load the *master* database from the dump. Note that when the server has finished loading the dump of the *master* database, it will shut down the server. Also, you need to realize that the server loads the database dump of *master,* which overwrites anything that was in the *master* database, but that is all that the server does. The server does not try to recover any of the other databases or even open the other server devices. Normal server recovery doesn't happen until you start the server again.

7.8 Moving Master Device to the Larger Partition

If you must move the master device to a larger partition, be aware of some details that could confuse you. This need can come up because you have filled the master device (don't let this happen) or you plan ahead for a larger master device when you upgrade you server hardware or migrate to a new machine. You should have 30 Mb for your master device, so any time you can make the move to give the master device this much room, you should be ready to do so.

The problem comes in the actual move of the *master* database. Assuming that you have either added the new disks to the existing machine or you are moving to new disks on a whole new machine, you will want to move the current *master* database with all the information it contains about the current server into the *master* database you have created on the new larger master device.

If you are simply adding new disks to the existing server machine, you can mirror the existing master device (on the old, smaller partition) to the new master device (on the new, larger partition) and then drop the primary side of the mirror of the master device. This gives you the *master* database on the new, larger master device. If you are installing the server from scratch, the installation process will create the master device for you; you will then want to load a dump of the *master* database. This also gives you the *master* database on the new, larger master device.

However, in neither case do you get what you expect. You wanted to get the current *master* database onto a new larger master device so you would have room to increase the size of the *master* database as needed. Whether through mirroring the master device or loading a dump of the *master* database, the new *master* database (on the new, larger master device) carries along with it the old (current) information in the *sysdevices* system table. This information will reflect the old (current) smaller size of the master device, and the server will believe the size of the master device to still be the smaller size. You must update the information for the size of the master device manually so that the server can use the extra space actually available on the new master device.

WARNING:

- Updating system tables is not supported by Sybase—there is no guarantee that the system table schema will be maintained between releases, which means manual updates that work for one version may not work on another.

- Do not perform such updates without first consulting Sybase Technical Support.

- Make sure you have dumps of everything you might need to rebuild the server in case the manual updates destroy something.

- After updating system tables, you should restart the server to copy the changes into memory.

This procedure must be done with caution, and you must review the specifics of your server situation with Sybase Technical Support before proceeding. The output of the actual process is shown below. As with any updates made to a system table, this change must be done within a transaction to prevent updating other devices. See Chapter 11 for more details about manually updating system tables.

You should dump the *master* database to a disk file and drop the mirror of the master device before starting this procedure. Note that you must be certain that the partition that the master device is on is indeed the larger size you think it is.

In this example, the new master device is 15360 2K pages, which is 30 Mb, which means the low datapage will be 0 and the high datapage will be 15360 - 1 = 15359; data page 0 through data page 15359 is 15360 pages.

```
1> sp_configure "allow", 1
2> go
Configuration option changed. Run the RECONFIGURE command to
install.
(return status = 0)
1> reconfigure with override
2> go
1> select * from sysdevices where name='master'
2> go
 low       high      status cntrltype name
    phyname
    mirrorname
 ----------- ----------- ------ --------- ------------------
         ------------------------------------------------
         ------------------------------------------------
        0      7904     2         0 master
    /dev/rsd1h
    NULL
```

```
(1 row affected)

1> begin tran psycho
2> go
1> update sysdevices set high=15359 where name='master'
2> go
(1 row affected)
1> select * from sysdevices where name='master'
2> go
 low        high       status cntrltype name
    phyname
    mirrorname
 ----------- ----------- ------ --------- ------------------
        ------------------------------------------------
        ------------------------------------------------
        0     15359     2        0 master
    /dev/rsd1h
    NULL

(1 row affected)
1> commit tran psycho
2> go
1> sp_helpdevice master
2> go
 device_name              physical_name
   description
        status cntrltype device_number low       high
 --------------------------- --------------------------
        ------------------------------------------------
 ------------------------------------------------
 -
        ------ --------- ------------- ----------- ---------
 master                    /dev/rsd1h
          special
, physical disk, 30.00 MB
        2         0            0          0     15359

(1 row affected, return status = 0)
1> sp_configure "allow", 0
2> go
```

```
Configuration option changed. Run the RECONFIGURE command to
install.
(return status = 0)
1> reconfigure
2> go
```

You must remirror the master device to a partition that is the same size as the new, larger master device.

7.9   Clearing Server Configuration in *master* Database

The entire configuration of the server is stored in system tables in the *master* database. When you make changes to the server configuration by using the **sp_configure** command, you may increase a configuration parameter so much that the server can't start up with the memory available on the server machine. One example of this would be increasing the number of user connections, each of which takes a certain amount of server machine memory. Once you have increased a configuration parameter too far and you **shutdown** and try to restart the server, the restart will fail. At this point, you can't get into the server to fix the problem, because the server isn't running. You must reset the server configuration to the default values by using buildmaster with the -r option. You must be very careful about using the buildmaster command. If you don't get it right, it may overwrite the existing *master* database, wiping out all information regarding the existing server. You should work with Sybase Technical Support before attempting to use the buildmaster command.

WARNING:

• Do *not* use buildmaster without first consulting Sybase Technical Support.

• Make sure you have dumps of everything you might need to rebuild the server in case you destroy something.

You also need to realize that running buildmaster -r will reset all of the server configuration parameters to the default values, not just the one (or more) configuration parameter you increased too far. This means that all the other server configuration information is lost. This is why it is vital that you regularly dump the system tables of the server to disk files. See Chapter 15 for a script that should be run as a cron job to accomplish this. After you run buildmaster -r, you will need the rest of the server configuration information stored in the disk file(s) to restore the server configuration.

Chapter 8

SQL Server Recovery

The process of recovery for the SQL Server is another topic that is largely ignored. It isn't exciting to most people and it usually only comes up when things have gone bad in a big way. You need to understand more about the recovery process and what the implications are for the way you operate your database system.

You can do yourself a great deal of good simply by making use of the references that are available to you. With the advent of online documentation for Sybase products, you now have an incredible way to search through thousands of pages of documentation looking for what you need, and more often, finding related information that will help you understand the products better. Specifically, SyBooks™ is available on CD-ROM for the System 10 document set for SQL Server, Open Server, and the Troubleshooting Guide. While these are the System 10 versions of these documents, the vast majority of the information is relevant to the 4.9.x version of SQL Server. Similarly, there is another CD available called AnswerBase™, which is a compilation of many technical notes and installation guides that cover many of the technical issues you are likely to encounter. Obtain and use these references.

;-)

> You must read the *SQL Server Troubleshooting Guide*. It isn't thrilling, but it will remove most of the 'thrills' of the real disasters that are waiting for you and your users. Learn how to recover from these disasters now.

8.1	Recovery Planning Revolves Around the Cost of Downtime
8.2	The Database Is Nothing without the Transaction Log
8.3	Recovery Is Transaction Based
8.4	Standby Server Strategies
8.5	*master* Database Not for Users

8.1 Recovery Planning Revolves Around the Cost of Downtime

No matter how much you understand about database dumps, **dbcc** runs, or mirroring, the real point behind recovery is minimizing downtime for your business. Also, decide how much effort you need to put into preparing for recovery of your database system. If your business needs to access the databases 24 hours a day every day, you must plan well ahead and you can justify the resources it will take to be as ready as possible when the inevitable disaster hits.

Everything that follows revolves around this concept of the cost of downtime. If you can have exclusive access to the server(s) every weekend, then you have time to do maintenance on the server and the server machine such as running **dbcc** checks, and so on. This allows you to set up a recovery plan that is very different from one set up for a system that can't ever be down. In the latter case, you may be required to set up and maintain a standby server that is a complete duplicate of the primary system. This represents a great deal of time and money all tied up in a server and server machine that simply sit and wait. But, compare the cost of this duplicate hardware to the cost of downtime. You must determine how long you think it would take to rebuild the primary server and server machine, and what the cost to your business would be from that much downtime. Perhaps the duplicate server isn't so expensive after all.

8.2   The Database is Nothing without the Transaction Log

It is important that you understand the basic process of recovery that the SQL Server goes through. With an understanding of this process, you can better plan your recovery and understand some of the background behind the procedures that the manuals tell you to do. This explanation will cover the basic recovery process, which links the database and its transaction log. From this you will see why the transaction log is absolutely vital and why you must protect it carefully. Note that the following discussion is about one database and its transaction log, the recovery process, and what the checkpoint process has to do with it all. However, you should remember that this same process applies, and is constantly under way, for each and every database in your system. The entire process of recovering a SQL Server database is very complex and involves many subtleties. Here you need only understand why the transaction log is the most important piece of the database.

From reading the manuals and using the SQL Server you would think that the database (here we mean everything but the transaction log) and the transaction log are completely separate entities, as shown in Figure 8.1.

SQL Server

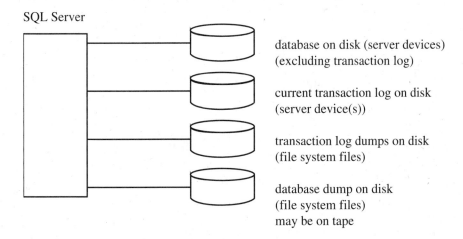

database on disk (server devices)
(excluding transaction log)

current transaction log on disk
(server device(s))

transaction log dumps on disk
(file system files)

database dump on disk
(file system files)
may be on tape

Figure 8.1   The database on disk and the dumps -

You would think that if the disk that supports the transaction log fails, well, that's OK because you still have the actual database out on other disks so you have one set of the business data that the database represents. Conversely, you would think that if the disks that support the database fail, well, that's OK, too, because from the database dump and the set of transaction logs (including the current transaction log that has not been dumped), you can recreate the database and again have a set of business data that the database represents. This view is not unreasonable, and various things contribute to it; for example, the fact that a committed transaction is immediately written to disk implies that the database is being kept up-to-date with all committed transactions. Also, it seems that if you have a problem with the transaction log, the database itself is OK; after all, it appears that the database itself is only updated when a transaction is committed, so you would be asking what sense it would make to write a partial transaction to the database. This is one reasonable view, but it is wrong on several subtle, but vital points. We review the process that the server goes through and see how the database and the transaction log are affected as well as reviewing what the checkpoint process really does. We discuss these topics:

What the Server Goes Through
How Database and Transaction Log Are Affected
What the Checkpoint Process Does

What the Server Goes Through

We start with the observation that any access of the database or the transaction log takes place in data cache, that is, server machine memory. Any read or write to a data page of the database actually takes place in memory after the page has been loaded from disk if necessary. As a transaction begins and reads from or writes to data pages of the database, the needed pages are loaded from disk if they are not in cache. Once a page is in cache, it is not automatically written back out to disk, even if changes are made to the page. The server writes pages out of cache only if it needs to load a page that is not currently in cache and there is no more room in cache. At that point the server looks for the page in cache that has gone the longest without any changes. The "oldest" page is then written to disk, and the required page is loaded into cache in place of the page that was just written out. The algorithm for determining which page in cache should be written out to disk is called LRU or the Least Recently Used algorithm.

How Database and Transaction Log Are Affected

This is great, but take a look at Figure 8.2 and notice what the case implies.

	SQL SERVER DATA CACHE (RAM)		
DATABASE ON DISK	**DATA PAGES IN CACHE**	**TRANSACTION LOG IN CACHE**	**TRANSACTION LOG ON DISK**
data page 1 ⟶	data page 1 **	updates to data page 1	
data page 2	data page 2 **	updates to data page 2	
data page 3	data page 3 **	updates to data page 3	
data page 4	data page 4 **	updates to data page 4	
data page 5	data page 5 **	updates to data page 5	
data page 6	data page 6 **	updates to data page 6	
data page 7	data page 7 **	updates to data page 7	
data page 8	data page 8 **	updates to data page 8	
data page 9	data page 9 **	updates to data page 9	
data page 10 ⟶	data page 10 **	updates to data page 10	
data page 11			
data page 12			
data page 13			
data page 14			
data page 15			
data page 16			
data page 17			
data page 18			
data page 19			
data page 20			
Data pages loaded into cache until cache is full	** Data pages modified in cache but not written to disk	Changes to data pages recorded in transaction log	Nothing recorded in transaction log on disk until transaction is committed

Figure 8.2   Server loading database data pages into data cache - - - - - - - - - - - - - - - - - -

Suppose the server has room in cache for only 10 data pages at one time (the DBA should add memory!!) and the database consists of 20 data pages as in Figure 8.2. We are ignoring indexes and the transaction log pages for the moment, both of which also must be in cache to be changed. Assume the transaction that we are following is an update of all rows in the database. As the transaction moves along it will load a page of the database into cache, update the rows in that page and then load the next data page. Note that as each row of a page in cache is modified, the data in the row before and after the modification is written to the log, which is also in cache, as in Figure 8.2. This works fine until the 11th page of the database is needed, at which time the first page (the oldest page) would be written back to disk to make room for the 11th page to be loaded in to cache, as shown in Figure 8.3.

At the instant that the first page is written back to disk, the database itself (again, the database here excludes the transaction log) is not in a consistent state. The update transaction has not committed, but the changes due to a part of the transaction have been written back to the database on disk. (Note that when this happens, the portion of the transaction log that contains the changes to this page are also written to disk.) If the transaction log were lost, the changes made in the first page would still be part of the database; without the transaction log, there would be no way to tell which changes in the database on disk are parts of committed transactions or parts of transactions that were under way.

Further, as each update to a database page is made in cache, the update is recorded in the transaction log but only in cache. Until the transaction commits, the portion of the transaction log that describes all the changes made by the transaction is not written to disk. If the transaction log is lost, there will be no record of what the transaction did. Recall that, at the same time, there is no guarantee that none of the database pages that were changed in cache have not been written out to disk to make room for other pages. You can wind up with pieces of the transaction out on disk in the database and no way to decode which changes on disk should be there and which should be changed back. And, without the transaction log, which stores the data in a row before and after the change, there is no way to tell how to change a database page on disk back to the way it was before the transaction started. This means that after all 20 data pages of the database have been loaded and updated, but before the transaction commits, all the changes recorded in the transaction log for these updates are in cache, while some (half in this case) of the modified database and transaction log data pages are already out on disk; Figure 8.4 illustrates the case.

SQL SERVER DATA CACHE (RAM)			
DATABASE ON DISK	**DATA PAGES IN CACHE**	**TRANSACTION LOG IN CACHE**	**TRANSACTION LOG ON DISK**
data page 1 ** ◄	data page 11 **	updates to data page 1	updates to data page 1
data page 2	data page 2 **	updates to data page 2	
data page 3	data page 3 **	updates to data page 3	
data page 4	data page 4 **	updates to data page 4	
data page 5	data page 5 **	updates to data page 5	
data page 6	data page 6 **	updates to data page 6	
data page 7	data page 7 **	updates to data page 7	
data page 8	data page 8 **	updates to data page 8	
data page 9	data page 9 **	updates to data page 9	
data page 10	data page 10 **	updates to data page 10	
data page 11		updates to data page 11	
data page 12			
data page 13			
data page 14			
data page 15			
data page 16			
data page 17			
data page 18			
data page 19			
data page 20			
Cache is full; oldest data page is written to disk -- ** data page contains changes but transaction has not been committed	Data page 1 in cache is written to disk and data page 11 loaded into cache	Changes to data pages recorded in transaction log	All transaction log records written to disk when transaction is committed

Figure 8.3   Oldest cached data page written to disk -

| | SQL SERVER DATA CACHE (RAM) | | |
DATABASE ON DISK	DATA PAGES IN CACHE	TRANSACTION LOG IN CACHE	TRANSACTION LOG ON DISK
data page 1 **	data page 11 **		updates to data page 1
data page 2 **	data page 12 **		updates to data page 2
data page 3 **	data page 13 **		updates to data page 3
data page 4 **	data page 14 **		updates to data page 4
data page 5 **	data page 15 **		updates to data page 5
data page 6 **	data page 16 **		updates to data page 6
data page 7 **	data page 17 **		updates to data page 7
data page 8 **	data page 18 **		updates to data page 8
data page 9 **	data page 19 **		updates to data page 9
data page 10 **	data page 20 **		updates to data page 10
data page 11		updates to data page 11	
data page 12		updates to data page 12	
data page 13		updates to data page 13	
data page 14		updates to data page 14	
data page 15		updates to data page 15	
data page 16		updates to data page 16	
data page 17		updates to data page 17	
data page 18		updates to data page 18	
data page 19		updates to data page 19	
data page 20		updates to data page 20	
Cache is full; oldest data page is written to disk -- ** data page contains changes but transaction has not been committed	Data page 11 through 20 loaded into cache	Changes to data pages recorded in transaction log	All transaction log records written to disk when transaction is committed

Figure 8.4   All database changes made to satisfy query -

The fact that the transaction log records for a particular transaction are not flushed to disk until the transaction is committed should clarify for you why the transaction log should be stored on a server device that is supported by a raw partition. When the server commits the transaction, it writes out the relevant portion of the transaction log to disk; the server believes it has been written to disk immediately. If you use a UNIX file system, then the writes to disk are buffered and the server has no idea if the write has actually been made or not. Since the server assumes the write of the transaction log records occurs immediately, you can really mess up the recovery of a database if the server machine were to crash (all data in any buffers would be lost) before the buffered writes made it to disk.

This behavior of writing database pages out to disk before transaction commits can't be avoided unless the server were to require that enough memory always be available to store all the pages of the database, including data and index pages. Hence, the server can't require that all needed pages be in cache. If this were possible, the server could load all the pages affected by the update transaction, make all the updates to the rows of all the pages, and then, as part of committing the transaction, write all the changed pages to disk for both the database and the transaction log. This would result in both the database and the transaction log containing all the changes made by the transaction. Until the transaction committed, the database would not be changed. However, this is not the way it works, for two reasons. First, as mentioned already, this would require that all the pages affected by any transaction be loaded into cache which would prevent many real-world transactions. Second, waiting for the transaction to commit before writing any of the transaction's changes is bad for performance because all the pages would need to be written at once. It is faster for the server to simply leave the changed pages in cache until they become old and are moved out to make room for new pages.

Note that while the transaction is running, the pages that are being updated are locked by the server so that no other user can access them. From the point of view of the other users, the changes to the database caused by the transaction are not made available to them until the entire transaction commits.

What the Checkpoint Process Does

Now that you understand what the server is doing when a transaction is running, you need to understand what the checkpoint process and the server command **checkpoint** do and how it affects the pages in cache and on disk. You now know that there are changes to database pages that remain in cache and may not be written to disk for some time. You can also see that if the server were to fail and need to recover the database, it would have to read the transaction log to see which database pages had been changed as part of a transaction. The server would also have to determine from the transaction log whether the transaction committed, rolled back, or simply failed to commit; then, either let the database page changes stand or change them back to the way they were before the transaction started. Depending on how many changes have been made through multiple transactions, there may be many database pages that would need to be changed to bring the database on disk into line with what was happening at the time of the server failure. Bringing the database on disk into line means you make the database on disk reflect the changes resulting from the committed transactions and you make sure that any changes that made it to disk for transactions that didn't commit are changed back. This is why the transaction log contains both the row data before and after each change to each row of a database page.

Since there may be many such changes to check and possibly reverse, it might take the server a long time to perform all these changes. This time period is called the recovery interval. You can reduce the time the server takes to recover a database by reducing the number of changes that the server must check. When checkpoint runs, it flushes out to disk all the database pages in cache that have been changed since the last checkpoint. After the checkpoint process runs, the database on disk agrees with all the database pages in cache, see Figure 8.5.

Note that the checkpoint process writes a record in the transaction log to record that fact that, at this instant, the database on disk and the data pages in the data cache are in sync. This means that from this time back, the changes recorded in the transaction log have already been written to the database on disk. The server must check the transaction log only from the most recent checkpoint forward when recovering the database. Of course, if the server needs to roll back a transaction that began before the last checkpoint, then the server will need to read the transaction log farther back than the last checkpoint to reverse all the database changes made by that transaction.

SQL SERVER DATA CACHE (RAM)			
DATABASE ON DISK	**DATA PAGES IN CACHE**	**TRANSACTION LOG IN CACHE**	**TRANSACTION LOG ON DISK**
data page 1 **	data page 11 **	updates to data page 1	updates to data page 1
data page 2 **	data page 12 **	updates to data page 2	updates to data page 2
data page 3 **	data page 13 **	updates to data page 3	updates to data page 3
data page 4 **	data page 14 **	updates to data page 4	updates to data page 4
data page 5 **	data page 15 **	updates to data page 5	updates to data page 5
data page 6 **	data page 6 **	updates to data page 6	updates to data page 6
data page 7 **	data page 7 **	updates to data page 7	updates to data page 7
data page 8 **	data page 8 **	updates to data page 8	updates to data page 8
data page 9 **	data page 9 **	updates to data page 9	updates to data page 9
data page 10 **	data page 10 **	updates to data page 10	updates to data page 10
data page 11 **		updates to data page 11	updates to data page 11
data page 12 **		updates to data page 12	updates to data page 12
data page 13 **		updates to data page 13	updates to data page 13
data page 14 **		updates to data page 14	updates to data page 14
data page 15 **		updates to data page 15	updates to data page 15
data page 16			
data page 17			
data page 18			
data page 19			
data page 20			
Cache is full; oldest data page is written to disk -- ** data page contains changes but transaction has not been committed	Data page 11 through 15 loaded into cache	Changes to data pages recorded in transaction log	Checkpoint flushes all changed ('dirty') data pages to disk whether committed or not

Figure 8.5   All data pages with changes written to disk

There are two ways in which checkpoints are executed. You need to be clear on both.

The server itself will automatically check the transaction log for each database approximately once per minute to see how much has been recorded in the transaction log for committed transactions. The server then figures out how long it would take to recover all these changes; that is, how long it would take to repeat all the changes recorded in the transaction log since the last checkpoint in order to recreate all the changes due to committed transactions. If the server computes a recovery time greater than the recovery interval that is specified for the server (**recovery_interval** is part of **sp_configure** output and is configurable), then the server will execute a **checkpoint** to flush all the changed database pages (only those changes made since the last **checkpoint**) from cache to disk. Note that again this flushes all the changed database pages, not just the changed pages due to committed transactions.

The other way the checkpoint process gets executed is manually by you. It is a good idea for you to issue a **checkpoint** command just before you shut down the server with the **nowait** option to reduce the recovery time as much as possible. Note that the **shutdown** command without the **nowait** option runs a **checkpoint** command in every database automatically. Also, the **dump database** command performs a **checkpoint** command in the database, so that the dump represents all the changes that had been made to the database at the instant the dump was made. Again, note that the dump of a database also contains database page changes that may or may not be due to committed transactions; when the database is loaded, the only way the server can figure out which changes should stay and which should be reversed is to read the transaction log. This is why the **dump database** command also dumps the transaction log along with the database.

Now that you have been convinced that the database really isn't an accurate representation of the state of your business data without the transaction log, consider what happens when the transaction log is not available. If something goes wrong with the server device that supports the transaction log, the server can't recover the database the next time the server is started. As the server tries to recover the database it will be unable to read all of the transaction log and will mark the database as "suspect" and you won't be able to execute **use <dbname>** or otherwise access the database. The term "suspect" is very appropriate. As you now appreciate, the database may be completely accessible with no corruption that any **dbcc** check could find, but without the transaction log, the server can't tell you which pieces of the database reflect a change to your business data or just a possible change that was part of an incomplete transaction. Hence, the database is indeed suspect. Now, you can manually update the system table *sysdatabases* and tell the server that the database is no longer suspect. The server may have no problem running after you do this, but you must realize what you are doing. If you tell the server that a database that was marked suspect is no longer suspect, you are telling the server that any database page changes that are out on disk are now valid business data. You must confer with your users before taking such a drastic step. You should also consult Sybase Technical Support. Just because you can convince the server that the database is suddenly OK, doesn't mean it is. Again, this is further evidence of the need to keep the transaction log on a separate server device, on a separate physical disk, and attached to a different controller, separate and different from the server devices that support the rest of the database. It is also further evidence of why the transaction log of the database should be mirrored. Although you should mirror all the server devices, if you can't, then you should mirror the transaction logs as a second priority after mirroring the master device.

Because the transaction log is so vital, you must be aware of another recovery situation involving the transaction log. Note that all recovery situations involve the transaction log. If one or more of the server devices supporting the database fails and you aren't mirroring that server device, you will need to drop and recreate the database and reload from database and transaction log dumps. However, to recreate (recover) the database, including all the transactions that were in the transaction log at the time of the failure, you need to dump the current contents of the transaction log. If you can't do this through the normal means of **dump transaction** because the database is not accessible, try dumping the transaction log with the **dump transaction <dbname> with no_truncate**. This will use data stored in the *master* database to directly access the current transaction log out on disk and dump it to a file that can later be applied to the database after the full sequence of normal transaction log dumps have been applied. Note that you must have the server running and the *master* database must still be usable for this approach to work; see Figure 8.6.

Once the current contents of the transaction log have been dumped, you can drop the database and begin recreating it. Because the server has had a failure, you may not be able to restart the server. You must make your attempt at dumping the current contents of the transaction log before you shut down the server, assuming the failure didn't bring the server down.

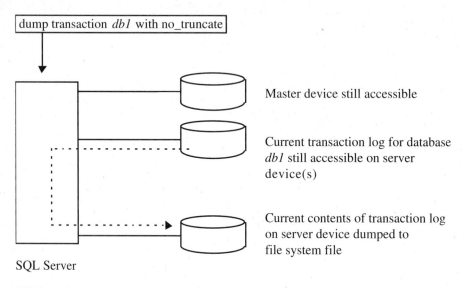

dump transaction *db1* with no_truncate

Master device still accessible

Current transaction log for database *db1* still accessible on server device(s)

Current contents of transaction log on server device dumped to file system file

SQL Server

SQL Server has some problem and you need to drop and recreate database *db1*. In order to recover *db1* to the state it was in at the time of the problem, you need the current contents of the transaction log. Server must still be running, master device and server device(s) that support *dbl* transaction log not damaged.

Figure 8.6   Dumping current contents of transaction log -

You can prevent this situation by mirroring the transaction log server devices. That way, you won't need to dump the current contents of the transaction log because the server will simply fail over to the secondary server device (the mirror) for the transaction log; the server should move along normally from there. However, consider the situation where even though the transaction log is mirrored, one of the server devices for the database itself fails. You must still drop and recreate the database and load it. Dropping the database will get rid of both server devices (the primary and its mirror) of the mirrored transaction log. So, you must remember that even though the transaction log is mirrored, when a server device other than those supporting the transaction log fails, you must still dump the current contents of the transaction log before you start trying to repair the server.

Given the need to dump the current contents of the transaction log when a server device fails for the database and the need to have the *master* database perform such a transaction log dump, you should now understand even better why you mirror the master device (recall that you mirror server devices, not databases) and why you should mirror the transaction logs next. You should, if possible, mirror all of your server devices (see Chapter 1).

Finally, we started with the premise that it would be reasonable to think that the database (excluding the transaction log) formed one set of consistent data that represents your business. And that the current transaction log, along with all the transaction logs since the last database dump along with the last database dump, form a second set of consistent data that represents your business. As it turns out, only the second half of this theory is correct. You will be better able to deal with the various recovery situations you will encounter now that you understand what is going on.

You should now understand that the database is nothing without the current transaction log. Without the current transaction log, the only way to bring the database back in a consistent state is to go back to the last database dump, load it, and apply all the transaction log dumps that you have. You now realize that this won't bring the database back to the state it was in when the failure occurred. Further, you should realize that when you don't have the current contents of the transaction log that is out on disk, you have lost not only the transactions that were in progress at the time of the failure, but also the committed transactions for which the database changes had not yet been flushed out to disk, as illustrated in Figure 8.7.

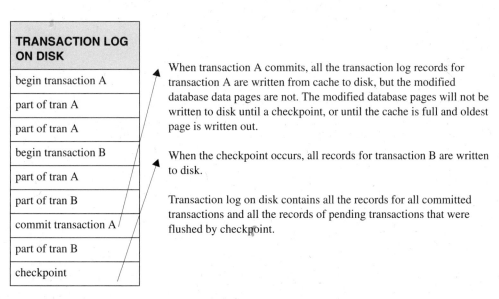

TRANSACTION LOG ON DISK
begin transaction A
part of tran A
part of tran A
begin transaction B
part of tran A
part of tran B
commit transaction A
part of tran B
checkpoint

When transaction A commits, all the transaction log records for transaction A are written from cache to disk, but the modified database data pages are not. The modified database pages will not be written to disk until a checkpoint, or until the cache is full and oldest page is written out.

When the checkpoint occurs, all records for transaction B are written to disk.

Transaction log on disk contains all the records for all committed transactions and all the records of pending transactions that were flushed by checkpoint.

Figure 8.7   Transaction log records on disk -

All of this explains why you must protect the master device and the transaction log of each database. Even though you have database and transaction log dumps, you can only rebuild from these up to the point of the last transaction log dump. Depending on the nature of your business and the applications you are supporting, the loss of the transactions that are in the current transaction log may represent a very large cost to your business.

8.3 Recovery Is Transaction Based

As a DBA you think of recovery in terms of the server and the error messages you see during the recovery process. Remember that the server recovers in terms of transactions, not in terms of business data. If the applications that run on the server do not package their transactions in line with the business, then even though you recover all the committed transactions, you may not have saved the business. You can't check all the applications to see what they are doing in any given transaction, but you must keep this in mind when the users ask you if the server has recovered. It may have, but that doesn't mean the database is guaranteed to be in a state that represents a valid business condition. For example, if an accounting application updated the deposits and account balances in separate transactions, even though you recover the server completely, you can't tell which accounts had deposits or balance updates pending against them. The server simply rolls back all pending transactions that didn't commit. The server does not tell you if the associated balance update for each deposit was completed.

This is clearly an application design and logical database design problem, but you must know about it to lobby for care during application design and modification. This sort of problem is why you want to prevent downtime altogether—because these sorts of transaction problems would never happen if the server never went down. The application going down might still cause them. Further, they are an argument for tight security on the primary OLTP server. Any user who can get into the server can potentially, without malice, update the database in a way that is not consistent with the business; again, the server will recover without complaint.

8.4 Standby Server Strategies

While you normally think of recovery in terms of database and transaction log dumps, it really means everything involved in reestablishing a working and consistent set of data that users can access to support your business. One way to minimize the downtime caused by a server failure is to set up a standby server. A standby server can be used to support the business while the primary is repaired. We discuss below the many issues involved with setting up such a server. We assume that a standby server will be running on its own dedicated server machine and that the primary server in question is the OLTP server.

First, you need to go back to determining the cost to your business of server downtime. Until you have that set of information, you can't really address the issues surrounding the creation of a standby server. You also need to determine whether the standby server needs to be a long-term or a short-term replacement for the primary server. In order to provide a standby server that is a long-term replacement for the primary server, the standby server should be as close to a complete duplicate of both the server and the server machine as possible. This requirement includes the server machine hardware type, operating system version, number of processors, number of physical disks and controllers, amount of memory and network connections, mirroring of server devices, dump devices for backups, cron jobs, logins, and so on. You also need to determine which of the primary databases will be supported by the standby server. For a long-term replacement, the standby must duplicate all the databases on the primary server.

For a short-term standby server, you can build up a smaller or less powerful server and server machine that would support only those databases that would be needed to get the business through a short period of time while the primary server is repaired. If you do not provide a standby server that is a duplicate of the primary, you need to be aware that server performance will probably be inferior and your ability to provide complete recoverability may be limited as well, for example, if you don't have enough disk space to dump databases quickly to disk. Note that a standby server is expensive in terms of purchase but also in terms of personnel. You must have sufficient staff to install and maintain the standby system. For a standby server to do you any good, it must be ready when needed. This means some of your personnel will need to work on the standby server regularly, even though it doesn't provide any service most of the time.

You need to decide if it is worth it to your business to have a standby server that is a complete duplicate. No matter what standby server scheme you go with, there will be some amount of downtime while you fail over from the primary to the standby server. You need to weigh the cost of this downtime against the cost of the various possible standby server configurations. You may find that for the cost of a long-term standby server you could keep enough spare parts on hand to virtually rebuild the primary server machine. In that case, you need to determine how long a complete rebuild of the primary server would take and compare that with the time it would take to fail over.

Once you are ready to build a standby server, determine how you will keep it in sync with the primary server. The point of having a standby server is to reduce overall server downtime by coming back up on the standby faster than if you waited for the primary to be repaired. To realize this benefit, you must maintain the standby server in a state that is as close to that of the primary as possible.

You can take the regular database dumps from the primary and load them into the same databases on the standby. This is typically what is done to refresh a decision support server. This means that in the worst case the standby is behind the primary by the database dump interval. If you dump the databases on the primary once each day, then the standby will be about one day behind the primary before the standby loads the next set of primary database dumps. When the time comes to fail over to the standby, you would need to apply, in the worst case, a whole day's worth (a whole database dump interval) of transaction logs to the standby server databases after copying all these transaction log dumps between the server machines. This process will take time that may be too long. Note also that this assumes the primary server machine is still available to supply the transaction log dumps. This may not be the case, and that means you should be copying the transaction logs from the primary server machine to the standby server machine as soon as they are dumped on the primary.

If the time to apply all the transaction logs is unacceptable, then you need to use an approach that keeps the standby more in sync all the time. This means that as you copy the transaction log dumps from the primary server machine, you apply them to the databases on the standby server (that is, by using **load transaction <*dbname*>**). This way you are maintaining the standby databases so that they are only behind the primary by the transaction log dump interval, as shown in Figure 8.8. This assumes that you apply the transaction logs to the standby server databases as soon as they are copied between the machines.

Depending on how much you need to minimize the time needed to fail over, you may decide to load the transaction logs to the standby server databases less frequently, perhaps every few hours. Again, you need to determine what the cost and benefit is of each stage of the failover process to decide the optimal approach for your business. Note that this process can be labor intensive. If there is any problem loading a transaction log to one of the standby server databases that can't be cured by recopying the transaction log dump from the primary, then you have no choice but to do the following: Wait for the next primary database dump; load that into the standby database; apply whatever transaction log dumps have occurred since the database dump on the primary; and then resume applying the transaction log dumps from the primary as they occur. Once you have had a failure of the process of loading a transaction log, it is unlikely that you can cure it by simply retrying the transaction log load. Hence, you must wait for the next primary database dump before synchronizing the standby database any closer to the primary than the point the standby database was in when the loading of the transaction log failed. No matter how often you load the transaction logs into the standby server databases, you must copy them from the primary server machine to the standby server machine as soon as each transaction log dump on the primary server machine completes. When the primary server machine fails, it is too late to remember that you need the transaction log dumps to bring up the standby server.

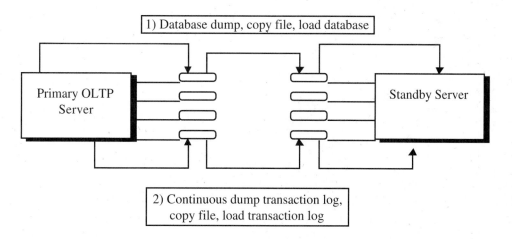

Figure 8.8   Keeping standby server in sync using transaction logs - - - - - - - - - - - - - - - - -

When you do need to fail over with this approach, you still need to dump the current transaction log of the primary database and apply it to the standby database so that the standby is completely up-to-date with all the committed transactions that the primary database had. You may think the standby server is at a disadvantage because it is, at worst, one transaction log dump interval behind the primary. But consider this. If there were no standby server at all and the primary suffered a failure, you would still need to dump the current transaction log on the primary to apply to the database after dropping, recreating, and reloading. Hence, the standby server is no farther behind than the primary would be, since the primary could not be recovered beyond the last transaction log dump without dumping the current contents of the transaction log. And, the standby has an advantage in that it doesn't need to drop, create, and reload the database. The standby database only needs to copy and apply the dump of the current contents of the transaction log that was made on the primary server and then it is ready for use. Note that if the dump of the current contents of the transaction log on the primary database fails, the standby can't get completely up-to-date, but then, neither can the primary database after dropping, recreating, and reloading because it won't have that dump either.

There are some details that are required for this process to work. For two reasons, the standby server must not be accessible to the users. First, any changes in the standby databases would prevent the loading of transaction logs; and second, the presence of any users will prevent the loading of transaction logs, even if no changes have been made in the database.

In order for this process to work, you need to be continuously copying the transaction logs from the primary server machine to the standby server machine. Further, if the process fails on the standby server, you will probably need to get the next primary database dump as well. All of this is faster and much easier for you to maintain if it can be done with dumps on disk. This means the primary and the standby both need to have enough disk space to support database and transaction log dumps. Note that you may need to support transaction log dumps that span several database dump intervals in case one of the database dumps is bad. This and the need to keep the current primary database dump on disk for all the databases on the primary can add up to a lot of disk space (see Chapter 10). Also, while you want to dump database and transaction log to disk on the primary mainly because it is faster, you want the same disk space capacity for the standby to support copying the dumps from the primary to the standby. After failing over to the standby, you will need the disk space for the same reasons as the primary does now, that is, to speed up the dumps. Note that for System 10 this scheme is even better, since you can speed up the dumps by dumping to multiple disk files (striping).

In order to fail over to the standby server and be ready to support the users as quickly and as smoothly as possible, you must maintain the standby so that it is a duplicate of the primary in all respects. Since the databases on the standby are first loaded with a database dump from the primary and then updated with transaction log dumps from the primary, the standby databases will have all the same changes made to the primary databases. But, this doesn't cover any changes made to the primary *master* database. For System 10 servers, this is also a problem for the *sybsystemprocs* and *sybsecurity* databases. This means that the standby server will not have any server logins that were added to the primary. You must synchronize the server logins manually when you first create the standby server by using the bcp utility to dump the data from the *syslogins* table of the *master* database on the primary server. You must use the -c option of bcp to get a human-readable output file. You need the file because you must manually edit out the first row of the bcp output file, which represents the 'sa' login. You must edit this line of data out of the bcp output because the standby server already has an entry for the 'sa' login and will not allow you to bulk copy using bcp in a file that tries to insert a duplicate entry in *syslogins*. If your system uses the two-phase commit process, you also need to have the server user 'probe' in *syslogins*. As with the 'sa' login, you need to edit the data for the 'probe' user out of the bcp output file if the 'probe' user is already in the *syslogins* table on the standby server.

When the time comes to fail over, you must again sync up the *syslogins* table between the standby and primary servers. You will need to delete all the rows of the standby server's *syslogins* table, except for the 'sa' login (and the 'probe' login, if needed) to make room for loading the bcp file from the primary server. You must not truncate the *syslogins* table on the primary. If you did that, there would be no logins at all and you couldn't access the server again to load the bcp file or do much of anything else.

There are many details of the failover process that you need to work out in advance. If you don't have a detailed plan of how to fail over, you will waste time figuring it out during the crisis. The whole point of having a standby server is to reduce server downtime; any delays caused by a lack of planning simply reduce the value of having a standby server. You will need to plan how to get all the users accessing the standby server once it is ready to go. This will require that a new interfaces file be distributed or the users will need to change their local DSQUERY environment variable to point to the standby server instead of to the primary server. If you plan on doing the latter, that is, having the users change their local DSQUERY, you must be sure that the interfaces file they currently have already has an entry for the standby server.

Once again you can see the benefit of smaller databases. Here smaller databases mean that less disk space is required to store database dumps, which allows for more transaction logs to be kept for a longer time. Smaller databases also mean the dumps and loads will happen faster. Further, smaller databases will allow **dbcc** runs to be done more quickly and hence more often, which improves the chances that all the database dumps and all the transaction log dumps are clean. In turn, the clean dumps improve the chances that this whole process will run smoothly, providing your users with an up-to-date standby server and minimizing the time it would take you to fail over to the standby. All of this leads you back to archiving to keep the databases as small as possible.

You also need to plan ahead for some very basic standby server maintenance tasks. Up to this point, we have been keeping the primary and standby server in sync as far as the data in the databases is concerned. You also need to consider how you will keep the databases in sync when you add space to a database on the primary. You must add the same amount of space on the standby database, or the next load may not work. While the transaction log loads to the standby database may keep working, they will fail as soon as they need to access space that is beyond the boundaries of the standby database. Also, the next time you need to load a database dump into the standby database that attempt will certainly fail. While you can get away with adding more space to the standby database than was added to the primary database, you must not do this for three reasons.

First, the next time you need to add database space on the standby server, you may need to add space to a different segment (see Chapter 4) to match the database segment that was extended on the primary. However, since you added more space on the

standby than on the primary last time, now the segmentation of the standby is different from the primary. While a transaction log or database load may still succeed with
different segmentation, you will have big problems later if database objects from one
segment on the primary database get loaded into a different segment on the standby.

Second, when the time comes to fail over to the standby, you want the standby to be
the same as the primary. The segmentation of the primary was set up for a reason (if
not a good reason), and you must duplicate this segmentation on the standby databases, or the performance of the standby server may not match the primary.

Third, it is much easier for you to add space to the standby database if you can simply use the exact same command that you used on the primary database. You should,
as part of creating the standby server, set up the exact same controllers, physical
disk, and partitions as on the primary. Then, as part of creating the databases on the
standby server, you should simply use the exact same scripts that were used to create
the databases on the primary server. If you don't have such scripts, use the
p_dbcreate script described in Chapter 15 to generate the script from the existing
primary databases. As long as you follow this procedure, then each time you add
space on the primary database, you can simply execute the very same command on
the standby database and both databases will continue to have the same segmentation, as shown in Figure 8.9.

Finally, if you determine you don't need a dedicated standby server, you can set up a
server that normally is a decision support server or a server dedicated to running
dbcc checks. Then, when needed, you could load the databases of such a server with
the latest primary database dumps, if needed, and apply whatever transaction log
dumps are necessary to bring the standby databases in sync with the primary databases. As with a dedicated standby server, you should maintain the same segmentation and disk layout as on the primary so that this server can function as the primary
if needed.

Replication Server can be used to replicate transactions from the primary to the
standby (see Chapter 2). However, applying transaction logs replicates all the transactions at once and may be a simpler solution for maintaining a standby server.

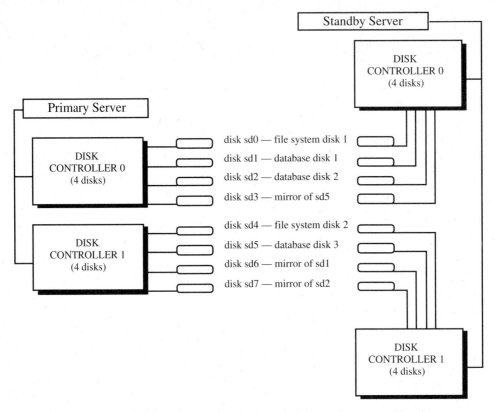

Primary and standby server both have same number of disks, each disk on both servers partitioned identically and assigned the same server devices or file systems. This means any commands to create or alter a database can be used on both primary and standby server without any modification.

Figure 8.9   Primary and standby server disk layout- -

8.5   *master* Database Is Not for Users

You must not allow any user-created database objects in the *master* database. You must not put anything into the *master* database, either. Recovering the *master* database is faster and simpler the less there is in it. Further, if you need to restore the *master* database, you will end up running buildmaster with some options and doing so will wipe out any user-created objects in the master database. If you had created any objects in master, they would be lost and you would have to maintain a script to recreate them. You could load a dump of *master,* but that is a fair amount of work.

Also, depending on why you ran buildmaster, you may not want to load a dump of *master* because it contains system table information about devices and other things that you may not want to load.

If you need stored procedures or other database objects for DBA use, you should create a dedicated database for this purpose and create all the objects in that database. See Chapter 1 for a description of the *dbadb* database. That way, you can make a database dump of the *dbadb* and restore all your database objects quickly and completely. This also provides a quick and safe way to transfer the contents of *dbadb* to another server through a simple database dump and load. If you had created these same database objects in *master,* you would have to manually extract their definition and recreate each one in the *master* database of the new server.

For System 10, you could put your own procedures and database objects into the *sybsystemprocs* database, but as with the *master* database, when rebuilding after a failure, the *sybsystemprocs* database will be rebuilt and all of your own database objects will be wiped out. It is simpler to keep all such objects in a database of your own creation and make database dumps of that.

8.6   The Use of dbcc

You are certainly aware of the need to run **dbcc** checks on all the databases in the server on a regular basis. However, there is more to it than that. We review many points that you should be aware of even if you are religious about running **dbcc** checks. The syntax of the various **dbcc** commands and the details of what they do is documented very well in the *Sybase SQL Server System Administration Guide* and the *SQL Server Troubleshooting Guide.* Therefore, we do not cover this material again here.

Running **dbcc** checks represents a form of server downtime, since you have to put a database into single-user mode to get accurate results. If you don't put the database into single-user mode, you may get spurious **dbcc** errors caused by the other users in the server running transactions that are making changes in the database while the **dbcc** is in progress. Further, the *master* database should be included in your **dbcc** runs, but since you can't set any database options for the *master* database (see Chapter 7), you can't put the *master* database into single-user mode. The only way to get accurate results for **dbcc** runs on the *master* database is to put the whole server into single-user mode which is done using the -m option in the dataserver command, which requires restarting the server. All of this takes time away from the users and therefore is server downtime.

Since the time taken to run **dbcc** checks on the databases on your production OLTP server represents server downtime, it competes with your users and the needs of your business. As the business demands the server be available more and more hours of each day, week, month, and so on, and as the size of the databases grows, as it inevitably does, you quickly find yourself not having the time, or not being permitted to take the time away from the users, to run the complete set of **dbcc** runs as you should. Soon you are aren't running all the recommended **dbcc** checks on all the databases, and then you start running **dbcc** only against certain tables. Eventually, you aren't ever running all the **dbcc** checks against all the databases—this is a bad way to go.

At some point, you can't afford to take the risk of not finding database corruptions and it is time to consider your options. You must return to running **dbcc** checks on all the databases regularly. You should go back and consider the cost to your business of server downtime, and the cost to your career when you have to explain why you weren't running all the recommended **dbcc** checks. You have two options.

The first option—and this just keeps coming up—is to reduce the size of the databases by archiving as much as possible of the data out of the on-line production server databases and into archive databases. This is covered in detail as part of Chapter 9.

The second option is to simply move the entire **dbcc** process off the online servers and onto a dedicated DBCC server on a dedicated server machine. This way, you are free to run any and all **dbcc** or other processes without interfering with the production server. You then need to recreate the production databases on the DBCC server and load a recent database dump into each, as illustrated in Figure 8.10. Then you can start running the whole set of **dbcc** runs. When the **dbcc** runs are done, check for errors as you normally would. Unlike a normal **dbcc** situation though, you need to plan how to fix any corruptions that **dbcc** finds, because you still have to fix these errors on the production database on the production server machine. At least you have narrowed the location of any corruption to a specific table, and that means you can minimize the server downtime that it takes to fix the problem.

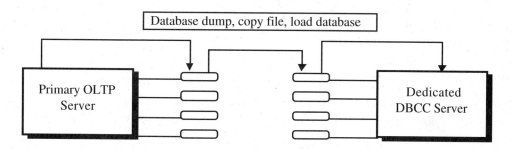

Figure 8.10 Loading DBCC server from primary server -

Still, don't forget that you must run **dbcc** checks for all the databases in the primary server, including the *master* and *model* databases (and *sybsystemprocs* and *sybsecurity* for System 10). You can't load a dump of the primary *master* database into the DBCC server because the controllers, physical disks, and partitions aren't going to be the same—a DBCC server can't really justify being a complete duplicate of the production server. Hence, you can't run **dbcc** checks for *master* and *model* databases anywhere other than the primary SQL Server. You can run without the single-user mode and see if you get any **dbcc** errors for *master* and *model*. If you don't, then that's it. If you do, then restart the primary server in single-user mode and rerun the **dbcc** checks. Note that while all this is server downtime, the time needed to run **dbcc** checks against the *master* and *model* databases is very short. Still, you must not neglect the **dbcc** runs against the *master* and *model* databases. Any problems with the *master* database must be detected as soon as possible.

Using a dedicated DBCC server is fine, but that means a corruption may go undetected for a longer period of time. Suppose **dbcc** of *db1* (8 Gb) takes 30 hours to run after requiring 7 hours to load on the DBCC server. You may not find an error for 37 hours, during which you have made another database dump. The latest dump now contains the corruption, as do all previous dumps made since the last clean **dbcc** run. This means you may have multiple database dumps and many transaction log dumps that contain the corruption. You could go all the way back to the latest database dump made before the last clean **dbcc** run, and you can load transaction log dumps all the way up to the present time.

Note that a database dump doesn't affect the sequence of transaction log dumps: You can load a sequence of transaction log dumps that move right through the time of a database dump. Of course, depending on the **dbcc** errors found, you may not be able to bring the database back, because there may be corruption in the transaction log dumps as well. If any failures occur during the process of loading transaction logs, that's it, and you can't recover the database any further than the point of the transaction load failure. If you have another server with the data (a standby or DBCC server), you can check the database there; if it doesn't have the corruption, you can dump from that server and use that dump, if needed, for recovery. If you have a copy of the database object where the corruption has occurred on another server and it doesn't contain the corruption, you can drop the corrupted database object and recreate it from the other server, which can be much faster than dealing with the whole database.

The DBCC server should have same segmentation as the primary server. Since you are going to load database dumps and run **dbcc** checks, any differences in the way the DBCC server database is set up regarding the size or ordering of the chunks of disk space and the segments assigned to each chunk will result in **dbcc** errors. This really boils down to reproducing the right parts of *sysusages* between the primary and DBCC servers. See Chapter 11 for details of what *sysusages* means. Further, as with the decision support server and the standby server, you will need to add space to the database on the DBCC server whenever you add space to the database on the primary server. While the DBCC server probably will not have the exact same disks and controllers as the primary server, you do need to have the same segmentation as the primary. This means you need to have the same number of server devices, they need to be the same size or larger than those of the primary, and the DBCC server needs the same number of partitions of the same or larger size as the primary. You should ensure that the DBCC server has the same server devices grouped together on the same physical disks as the primary, because you will add space to the primary databases on the available server devices until they fill up; then you will need to add space on a new server device (new to the database, anyway). It will be much easier for you to add the same space on the DBCC server if the same number of disks are partitioned the same way as the primary server; see Figure 8.11. Then, when you run out of space on a server device on the primary server, you will also run out of space on the DBCC server. This makes it easier to remember to add the space on the DBCC server in the correct way (extending segments to new server devices, etc.) because you will do the same things as you did on the primary server.

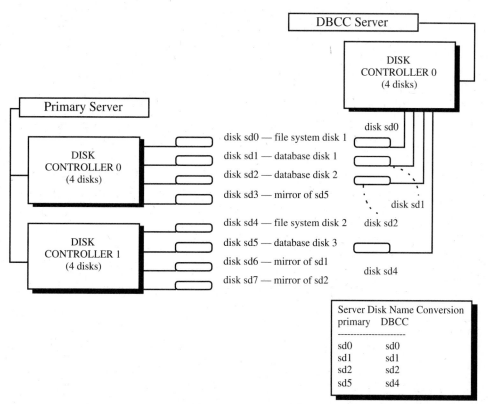

disk sd0 — file system disk 1
disk sd1 — database disk 1
disk sd2 — database disk 2
disk sd3 — mirror of sd5

disk sd4 — file system disk 2
disk sd5 — database disk 3
disk sd6 — mirror of sd1
disk sd7 — mirror of sd2

disk sd0
disk sd1
disk sd2
disk sd4

| Server Disk Name Conversion | |
primary	DBCC
sd0	sd0
sd1	sd1
sd2	sd2
sd5	sd4

Primary and DBCC server both have same number of database disks, each disk on both servers partitioned identically and assigned the same server devices or file systems. Any commands to create or alter a database on primary need only be edited to change the disk names before executing on DBCC server.

Figure 8.11   Primary and DBCC server disk layout -

Once you have the same number of same size server devices on the DBCC server as on the primary server, you can run the **p_dbcreate** script, described in Chapter 15, on the primary. The script will output the commands needed to completely recreate the databases on the primary server, which means the output commands reflect the names of the server devices on the primary server. You need to edit this output to reflect the names of the appropriate names of the server devices on the DBCC server. Since you have set up the same size and quantity of server devices as are on the primary server, you only need to edit the server device names, not the amount of database space created on each, and you will have a set of commands that will recreate the databases on the DBCC server.

Recall that as you add databases to the primary server you must also add them to the DBCC server and update any procedures or scripts that move the primary database dumps to the DBCC server machine, load the databases on the DBCC server, and run the **dbcc** checks to include the new databases as well.

Similar to the reporting and standby servers is the need for enough disk space to hold the database dumps from the primary databases. This allows you to automate the process of loading the databases on the DBCC server and running the **dbcc** checks because you don't have to rely on a tape operator to move dump tapes between server machines. As soon as the dumps complete, you can copy the latest set of database dumps from the primary server machine, and load into the DBCC server databases, and begin the **dbcc** checks again.

By not archiving and running with larger and larger databases, you are exposing yourself to more and more risk simply because of the time delay you encounter when trying to detect corruptions in a large database.

;-)

A good example of the insidious kind of corruption that would only be caught by **dbcc** checks: Everything seems fine on the primary server. You load a recent dump onto the DBCC server and begin the **dbcc** checks. Suddenly you are looking at 605 errors in the **dbcc** output. Note that a 605 error means data on disk doesn't match data in cache (see the *SQL Server Troubleshooting Guide* for more details). You panic because it has been a very long time since you last ran a complete set of **dbcc** checks because it takes 30 hours to run all the checks on the largest database and nobody is really concerned. Now you wonder how long this corruption has existed and how many of your database dumps are corrupt as well. If you had to rebuild from a database dump, how far back would you have to go and how far forward could you go with transaction log dumps before encountering the same corruption? You jump to conclusions and shut down the primary server to user access while you run **dbcc** checks on the database object that had the 605 errors on the DBCC server. The **dbcc** checks on the primary server report only minor corruptions and not a single 605 error. The users are relieved but annoyed that they lost lots of server time for a nonexistent problem. What happened?

Turns out the corruption was that a data page in the primary server was full of data but was not linked properly to the other data pages for the database object in question. An interesting detail about the way the **dump database** command works is that it only dumps the pages of the database that are linked properly, so the database dumps had been running without any errors but were not dumping this one page. So, until the dump was loaded into the DBCC server, there did not appear to be any problem. The **dbcc** runs on the DBCC server, however, went looking for the page that was (still) on the primary server database but was not on the DBCC server database that was loaded from the dump and that caused the 605 error. This also explains why the same **dbcc** runs report only minor errors when run against the primary server database.

The point is that you need to run the **dbcc** checks regularly so that you can tell yourself and your users how long you might need to go back to get a clean dump. This also points out the need to periodically verify the database and transaction log dumps that may appear to be dumping without problems but may be useless when the time comes to really rebuild the database. The proper way to have handled this situation would have been to detect the 605 error much sooner after the corruption in the primary database happened. Then you would have known when the last clean dump had been made, so you could describe the worst case damage to your users. Then you would have scheduled the downtime necessary to check the primary database, which would reveal the true and minor corruption. Then you would schedule the downtime needed to run **dbcc** checks that would fix the page linkage problem. Panic was not required and was not productive. The sudden downtime on the production server could have been completely avoided.

Once again the theme of archiving comes up. If the databases are kept smaller, then **dbcc** checks can be run more often, which reduces the period of time when a corruption can appear and yet go undetected. This in turn reduces the worst case loss of data resulting from being forced to revert to the last clean database dump. You should look at the cost to your business of server downtime and of losing some period of business data and compare that with the costs of archiving and running **dbcc** checks more often. You will find the cost of any amount of lost data to be quite staggering and probably beyond measure. If nothing else, you must make your users aware of the situation so that all involved can share the risk.

If possible, you should have a service-level agreement with the users that defines what risks they are willing to take and when. You should include things like how to handle a transaction log problem during the business hours, for example, does the DBA dump the database or not? Other examples would include when to run **dbcc** checks and how quickly DBA should move to correct any corruption found.

;-)

> Get any agreement to share risk in writing. Specify the worst case length of time that the server might be unavailable and the worst case loss of data that might result from not archiving and not running **dbcc** checks more often. Keep a copy away from your work site. Perhaps have the text printed on tee-shirts to be worn to the regular meetings you have with the users and your management. Don't get mad, just be prepared to get even.

8.7 Mirroring

The benefits of mirroring server devices have been discussed already. We repeat some of the discussion here for emphasis. You don't have to mirror all the server devices, but you should. You should mirror all the server devices so that database space added to any server device will still be mirrored.

Through the detailed discussion of the way the database and its transaction log interact, it should be clear that if you don't mirror all the server devices, you should mirror server devices in the following priority.

First, the master device must be mirrored: Any problems with the master device will bring the whole server to a halt. Further, anytime you have a problem for any of the other databases on the server you will need information stored in the *master* database to recover the user database, another reason the master device should be mirrored. Note that for System 10 you should also mirror the server devices that support the *sybsystemprocs* and *sybsecurity* databases.

Second, you should mirror the server device or devices that support the transaction log of the most critical database. As described above, you need the transaction log to make sense out of the database itself. You should prioritize the databases on the server and mirror the transaction log server devices in that order until you run out of devices to use as mirrors. Again, you really should mirror all of the server devices.

Third, after the master device and the transaction logs of all the user databases, you should mirror the server devices that support the most critical database. This will simply prevent server downtime. Even though the transaction log is already mirrored, if there is a failure of one of the server devices supporting the database itself, the database will no longer be available and you will have server downtime. You should mirror the user databases in the same priority order that you established for mirroring transaction log server devices.

Finally, you may think *tempdb* is exempt from all this, but you would be wrong. You certainly don't need to mirror *tempdb* for recovery purposes, because no one ever tries to recover the contents of *tempdb*. However, since preventing server downtime is really what the recovery process is all about, you should mirror *tempdb* as well. Unless your applications never use *tempdb*, which is unlikely, the whole server will come down if *tempdb* has a problem. Therefore, you should mirror *tempdb*.

Note that mirroring is a form of standby server that offers instantaneous failover. You don't have to mirror within the SQL Server; you can mirror at the operating system level also, if available for your hardware platform. Mirroring prevents most of the disasters that result in server downtime. Actually, the failures that will be helped by mirroring still need to be fixed, but with mirroring you can determine when you suffer the downtime rather than having the server simply crash and force the repair immediately. Note that mirroring doesn't help if the server machine crashes.

Even if you don't mirror everything during normal operations, you should be prepared to mirror the server devices on any one physical disk to another set of partitions somewhere on the server. This is why all of your physical disks that are supporting server devices should be partitioned the same way—so that you can mirror from any partition on one physical disk to the same size partition on another disk (see Chapter 1). When you have a disk failure, it is usually localized to one specific place on the disk, which means only one server device will be lost. Using mirroring, and being properly prepared to do so, you can simply mirror all the unaffected server devices on the disk that failed to other physical disk partitions on the server machine and then replace the bad disk. This means you only have to drop, recreate, reload, and apply transaction log dumps for the databases that used the server device that failed. All the other databases are unaffected and can be mirrored back to the server devices that will be created on the replacement disk. This saves a great deal of time, all for the cost of reasonable partitioning and perhaps a little extra disk capacity.

Mirroring can save you a great deal of server downtime because it allows you to choose when the downtime occurs for a failed server device. But, in order to gain this benefit, you must ensure that the mirrors are all working. If a mirror fails and you don't notice, you are in worse shape than if you don't have a mirror at all. Once the mirror fails and you don't notice, you are running as if there were never a mirror at all but you think the server device is mirrored. You must check that all the mirrors are functioning properly. See Chapter 15 for the script **p_mirror** that will help you check all the mirrors on the server.

8.8 Archiving

The topic of archiving to move older data out of the online production databases is discussed in detail in Chapter 9. There, it was discussed as a performance and tuning tool, while here the emphasis is on recovery. Archiving simply means reducing and then controlling the size of the databases on your production servers. This technique is very powerful, because it means all of your recovery procedures will run faster and recover more quickly. The time to run **dbcc** checks is greatly reduced, as is the time to dump or load a database. This allows you to run **dbcc** checks more often on the current production data, thus detecting corruptions sooner, which means in the worst case you won't have to go back as far to find a clean database dump to rebuild from.

With archiving you create archive databases and you regularly move the older production data into the archive databases, as illustrated in Figure 8.12. At the end of each archiving interval, you can take the completed archive databases, load them into a decision support server or a DBCC server, and run the complete **dbcc** set on them without interrupting the production server. You can correct any corruptions found and then make a clean dump of the archive database. Now you know that you have a clean dump of all this data up to the time the latest archive interval starts. Further, the current databases are smaller and the **dbcc** checks for them run much faster because they are not worried about checking the same old data over and over.

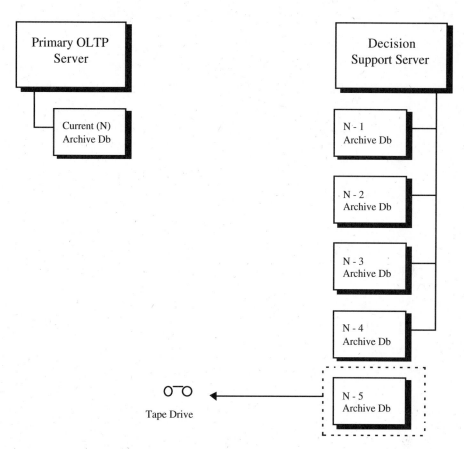

The primary server may contain an archive database for the current archive period. Any records older than a specified length of time are moved into the current archive database. At the end of the archive period, the current archive database is moved to the decision support server, and a new current archive database is created on the primary server.

The decision support server contains the previous archive period databases (4 in this case). As each archive period is completed, the oldest archive database is moved off the decision support server so that it is only available from tape. This makes room to bring over the current archive database from the primary server. Alternatively, the primary server could retain all data until the end of the current archive period and then move all records to an archive database on the decision support server.

Figure 8.12   Archive databases on primary and decision support server- - - - - - - - - - - - - -

8.9 More Server Devices Are Better

This material is discussed in detail in Chapter 9. Many times the question comes up of why it is better or worse to have more or fewer server devices supported by any one physical disk. This translates into a question of how best to partition the physical disk. There are three reasons why you want to use more, not fewer, partitions, one of which will benefit you from a recovery point of view.

A. This relates more to preventing server downtime and enhancing server recovery but that too is a form of improved server performance. When a physical disk goes bad, usually only a piece of it does. The rest of the disk may be fine. The fewer partitions and server devices you have on a single physical disk the more of your database that is lost for any single disk problem. If you have 6 server devices on 6 physical disk partitions and the disk develops a bad block in one partition, only the one server device is lost. With only one server device for the whole physical disk, all of the database(s) on that server device are lost even if only one block of the disk goes bad.

B. More partitions of a physical disk, with a server device assigned to each partition, makes it more meaningful and therefore more useful to identify which server device is being used the most. This assists you in tracking down server performance problems.

C. Internally the SQL Server maintains a queue of access requests for each server device. The fewer the number of server devices for a given number of server device access requests, the more that pile up waiting in the internal queue for each server device. More server devices helps to minimize any waiting that would go on due to these internal queues.

8.10 Recovery Notes

Here we offer various tips that will help you plan your recovery process.

When you bulkcopy (using bcp) out the contents of the system table *syslogins*, you must use the -c option. You must be able to edit out the 'sa' and 'probe' login information if present. Note that the 'probe' login is needed to support two-phase commit; see Chapter 2 "Replication Server" for discussion of two-phase commit. When you are dumping the *syslogins* information and you are going to load it into another server's master database, you must not have any entries in the bcp file that are duplicates of what is already in *syslogins;* otherwise, you will be attempting to insert duplicate rows and the bcp load will fail. You must check the *syslogins* table that you are loading to see which server logins are there already. The 'sa' login must be there, but the 'probe' user may or may not be present. Whichever combination is there, you must edit them out of the bcp file before you try to load the *syslogins* table. Do not truncate the *syslogins* table. If you do, the server user 'sa' login will not be there, nor will there be any other server logins, and you won't be able to bulk copy in the data or do anything else with the server.

When recovering from problems, you must have a current dump of various system tables and you must have this data before the server goes down. See Chapter 15 for a script that can be used as a cron job to make dumps of these system tables on a regular basis. You should also make sure the file system dump is running right after the cron job that dumps the system tables to ensure that the most recent dump of the system tables is captured to tape as soon as possible.

You should make sure the RUN_*<servername>* script that is created by the sybconfig (sybinit for System 10) is backed up as part of the file system dump of the server machine and is current, because it and the server errorlog are the only places to find the actual device pathname for the master device when it isn't mirrored. You will need this information for various recovery procedures.

Planning for recovery must begin early. You should dump *master* right after installation (sybconfig, sybinit for System 10) and perform **dbcc** checks on *master* as well. You must make sure the **dbcc** checks are clean before dumping *master.* Repeat this several times during the installation. See Chapter 3 or Chapter 13 for upgrading.

When you need to recreate a database either on the same server or on another server and you plan to load a dump of the database, you need to recreate the segmentation of the database exactly to ensure that the database dump will load the correct database objects and data into the proper database segments. See Chapter 11 for a full discussion of the *sysusages* system table and the **p_dbcreate** stored procedure that will create the commands needed to recreate the database.

8.11 Database Dumps

Database and transaction log dumps are the heart of any of your recovery plans. You will need to consider the points discussed below in deciding how to make the dumps you need in order to recover the databases in the server. Several of the items discussed below apply to both database and transaction log dumps. Although SQL Server doesn't require the server to be offline while making database dumps, the server performance is reduced while dumps are running. You should measure the performance of your critical applications while dumping the database(s) during peak business load and determine whether you can dump the database(s) while the business is operating. In most cases you will find that the application performance is reduced enough that your users will not want database dumps done while they are using their application(s). Therefore, consideration of the time the server spends making database dumps as server downtime should lead you to consider archiving.

Decide whether to make a given database dump or transaction log dump to a disk file or to tape. Then, determine if you wish to place multiple dumps on a single tape. Note that SQL Server 4.9.x doesn't support multiple dumps to one tape, whereas SQL Server System 10 with the Backup Server does. See Chapter 15 for a UNIX shell script that will support placing multiple dumps on a single tape.

Transaction log dumps should be made frequently to allow recovery as close to up-to-the-minute as possible; that means running the dumps during the time the server is online. Dump these transaction logs to disk files because that is faster than dumping to tape and will interfere less with server performance. Database dumps can be made to either tape or disk, depending on your needs. If you have the disk space on the server machine, it is better to dump to disk, since that is faster and therefore minimizes the time when server performance is slowed by the **dump database** running. Clearly, a database dump to tape is captured permanently, whereas any dump to disk is at risk if the server machine or the disk supporting the file system has a failure. Once you start dumping anything to disk, you must ensure that all the file systems that contain transaction log or database dumps are captured by a UNIX-level file system dump to tape. Ideally, this file system dump to tape would begin soon after the database dumps to disk completely to minimize the window during which the database dumps are only on disk. It is best to simply dump all the file systems on the server machine to tape regularly to ensure that all dumps to disk are captured no matter where they are located.

Note that you will now have to perform a two-step process to restore any dump that is on a file system dump tape. You will first have to restore the file itself to a file system and then load the dump into the database. This will take more time than if you loaded a dump made directly to tape.

You should have some process to verify that the dumps you are making are good. Again, for dumps made to disk and then to tape, the process of verifying the dumps will take longer. A good way to verify the dumps is to regularly load the most recent database dump into another server and apply some of the transaction logs. Note that if you are maintaining a decision support server (see Chapter 9) or using a dedicated DBCC server (discussed previously), you are already loading database dumps and applying transaction logs routinely to keep these servers in sync with the primary production server. This process will automatically verify all the dumps that are loaded.

As discussed in great detail above, you must protect the current transaction log, but that doesn't do any good if the database dump and all other transaction log dumps aren't available or contain any corruption. This, of course, ties in with running **dbcc** checks frequently and correcting the corruptions that are found as soon as possible. Remember that unless you have a whole set of transaction logs that are clean and a good, clean database dump, you can't recover the database; see Chapter 6 for discussion of the transaction log.

Along with dumping all the databases on a regular basis, you must always dump the *master* database as well. Because the *master* database can't have its transaction log on a separate server device, you can't dump the transaction log separately. This means you can't truncate the transaction log for the *master* database the way you can for other databases. You must use the

```
dump transaction master with truncate_only
```

command to truncate the transaction log of the *master* database, and you must execute this command immediately after the dump of *master* is complete (see Chapter 7 for details).

You should also dump the *model* database. If you need to recreate the *model* database, you do that by using sybinit (sybconfig for System 10) to recreate the *master* database, which automatically creates the *model* database. Then, you can load a dump of model to restore any and all database objects you have created in model. See the *Sybase SQL Server Troubleshooting Guide* for the various procedures you need to use depending on the circumstances of the loss of the model database.

If one of the segments of a database fills up, you will get an 1105 error. If the database segment that fills up is the transaction log, see Chapter 6 for details of dealing with the situation. However, from a recovery point of view, you have a greater problem. Once the transaction log has filled to the point of generating the 1105 error, there isn't even enough room left in the transaction log to log the **dump transaction** command. The only choice is to use

```
dump transaction <databasename> with no_log
```

which will not make a transaction log entry that a dump was done. This means you don't get a copy of the current contents of the transaction log, so you can't recover beyond the last successful transaction log dump. Further, once the problem is cleared and the database can be used again, you still can't recover beyond the last good transaction log dump. Since the **dump transaction** with **no_log** doesn't get logged into the transaction log, the server has no idea that the dump ever occurred. This breaks the chain of transaction logs since the last full database dump. The server won't even let you dump the transaction log any more because of the nonlogged dump you had to do to clear the transaction log. At this point you have a troublesome decision to make. You can continue processing, waiting for the next regularly scheduled full database dump and knowing that while you wait, any database changes can't be recovered in the event of a server failure. Or, you can stop the business while you make a full database dump immediately. This is not a technical decision, but a business decision. You must communicate the risks to the users and decide with them what to do.

You can prevent this 1105 dilemma in System 10 by using thresholds (see Chapter 14). A threshold on the transaction log prevents it from filling up to the point that a **dump transaction** with **no_log** is required. Instead, the threshold will suspend or abort (configurable) all the user transactions as the transaction log runs out of room but before it is completely filled up. This way, you are given a chance to clear the log or even to add more space to the log before the user transactions are allowed to continue. This should prevent the situation described above.

As with most of life, these failures generally occur during times of peak server load, which usually also represent times of peak business activity. It is during such times that the business needs access to the server the most, yet can least afford to lose any of the data the business is so desperate to put into the server.

Finally, a note about loading database dumps. Since the whole point of dumping the database is to be able to load the dump when you need to recover the database, you need to realize that the process of loading the database dump involves checking each and every data page of the database. Even if there are only 10 Mb of data in the database dump but the database is 100 Mb overall, when that dump is loaded into the database, the server will examine and initialize all 90 Mb of data pages that are empty after it loads the 10 Mb of actual data. You need to be aware of this, since it will mean that the time to recover a database from a database dump is based on the overall size of the database, not on the size of the database dump. Of course, when the database dump is made, the less data in the database, the less time the dump will take.

8.12 Transaction Log Dumps

Note that several points in "Database Dumps" apply to transaction logs as well. You should review the previous section as well as the material below.

The most important reason to place the transaction log or log segment on a separate server device is to be able to dump the transaction log independently of the database. If you don't place the transaction log on a separate server device, you can't dump the log without dumping the entire database. Dumping the database takes much longer and for larger databases often requires dumping to tape; the server machine may not have enough file system disk space to allow dumping databases to disk since the maximum file system size is 2 Gb. System 10 Backup Server can dump (stripe) to multiple disk files, thus supporting database dumps to disk larger than 2 Gb. Dumping to tape is also slower than dumping to disk. Longer dump times slow the system down for longer periods of time, which reduces the time the system is available for business use. The fact that dumping the complete database is slower will prevent you from dumping as often as you should. Further, if you dump the database, which does also dump the transaction log along with the rest of the database, the transaction log is not truncated. When you dump the transaction log separately, all the committed transactions in the transaction log are automatically dropped, which truncates the transaction log.

You must be able to dump the transaction log in order to recover the database as completely as possible. There are two levels to this recovery: The first assumes you must rebuild the database from dumps already completed; the second assumes the server itself is still functioning and can access the *sysdatabases* system table in the *master* database.

In the event of a server failure that prevents you from accessing the *master* database, you must rebuild the server and databases from dumps. You will load the most recent database dump for each database, but the database can only be recovered to the state it was in at the time of the most recent full database dump. To recover the database to a state more recent than the last database dump, you must have the transaction log dumps that were made between the last database dump and the server failure.

In the event you can still access the *sysdatabases* table in the *master* database, which usually means the server suffered a disk failure on a disk that supported one or more databases but did not support the *master* database, you can use the **dump transaction** command with the **no_truncate** option to dump the entire contents of the transaction log. By applying this transaction log dump, you can bring the database back to the state it was in right up to the time of the failure. Both of these situations rely on the transaction log dumps being made, which is only possible if the transaction log is on a server device that does not support any other segment of the database.

Dumping the transaction log is an incremental process. Each transaction log dump makes a copy of the transaction log as it was at the time of the dump and then deletes the inactive portion of the log; that is, the completed transactions are dropped. This means that a transaction log dump, unlike a database dump, does not have to dump the same information over and over. This and the fact that a transaction log dump does not dump the actual database makes a transaction log dump much faster and smaller. Because the transaction log dump is smaller, you can dump transaction logs to disk, which makes them faster still. Thus, you can (and must) dump the transaction log while users are running on the system, and you will be minimizing the performance slowdown caused by dumping. You can (and must) dump the transaction log often, so that you can recover the database to a more current state than database dumps alone would provide.

Since we are discussing transaction log dumps, recall that in order to make a transaction log dump in the first place, not only does the transaction log need to be on a separate server device, but the database options **select into/bulkcopy** and **truncate log on checkpoint** must not be enabled. If **select into/bulkcopy** is enabled, as soon as any nonlogged activity takes place (such as a 'fast' bcp in), the server will refuse to dump the transaction log since the continuity of the transaction log has been broken. Similarly, if the **truncate log on checkpoint** option is enabled, each time the checkpoint process executes it will simply delete the committed transactions from the transaction log without making a copy of them, which again breaks the continuity of the transaction log. The server will not dump the transaction log unless the log represents a complete picture of all the activity in the database since the last full database dump.

Note that the *master* database can't be extended beyond the master device; therefore, the *master* database can't have its transaction log separated to another device. The *master* database always has the segments *system*, *default,* and *logsegment* assigned to all the disk space assigned to the *master* database. This means you can't recover the *master* database to a state that is any more current than the last database dump. This is why you must dump the *master* database anytime you make changes to it. See Chapter 7 for details.

8.13 Logical Dumps and DataTools SQL BackTrack

Up to this point we have been discussing database, transaction log, and file system dumps. All of these are physical dumps; that is, the data out on disk is copied to another disk file or to tape directly. Physical dumps are faster but can't necessarily be loaded to other hardware platforms or other SQL Server versions.

A logical dump refers to a dump of the server database objects in such a way that you get a dump of the server commands necessary to recreate the database objects as well as dumping the data associated with the objects. A logical dump can be read by humans to see what the commands are to recreate an object, and the commands in the logical dump can be edited as well. A logical dump of your server can be taken to another SQL Server version or to another hardware and operating system platform. Because a logical dump contains the commands to create each server object, you can extract just the data or command associated with one or more objects that you need to recreate on an existing or new server.

As you will read in Chapter 10, if you don't make logical dumps, you should be prepared to load any of your databases at any time to a server that isn't supporting a production application. Then, you can extract a database object, its definition, or its data to recreate that object on the production system where it was lost.

You are always admonished to create and maintain scripts to recreate all the objects in the servers in your database system. You are further chided to also bulkcopy (using bcp) out the table data for each and every table in your system. For a database system of any size, this advice is useless. The concept of the DBA having time to regularly bulkcopy out all the data in all the tables, manually edit scripts to recreate each new object, capture all changes to existing objects, as well as having the disk space to store all this, is far removed from reality. Even one mistake in such a set of scripts would result in a rebuilt server that might not even run, let alone have all the objects in the right places with all the right data.

As your database system grows, the concept of anyone manually managing a set of scripts to recreate the servers, the databases, the stored procedures, the triggers, the segmentation, and so on, is absurd. You need an automated way to capture all this information quickly and reliably. You as the DBA should have far better things to do than worry about scripts like this, and a logical database dump of all the databases on your system is just what you need.

You need to have a logical dump of your servers for several reasons:

- You will need to have the commands required to rebuild a server, a database, or any of the objects in a database in order to recover from various disaster situations. If you have a logical dump of your system, you can extract the needed commands and data for the object that was corrupted. This is also very useful when

you want to change the segmentation of a database to improve server performance. While you will need to drop and recreate the database, it is very useful to
have all the commands for all the objects at hand so you can edit them to place
each on the appropriate new segment.

- Having the commands is the only way to create selected database objects on
  another server. Otherwise, you must examine the existing object and write your
  own commands to recreate the object in the other server.

- When you need to migrate from one server machine to a new server machine from
  a different vendor, your physical dumps made through SQL Server are worthless
  because they are hardware dependent.

- You will need a logical dump to migrate database objects between SQL Server
  versions, that is, you can't move a physical database dump from a 4.9.x server to a
  System 10 server.

- Your users will frequently delete a piece of a database object, such as ten rows of
  a million-row table, and then want them restored. Without a logical dump, the
  only way to do this is to find space somewhere to recreate the whole database,
  load from physical database dump, and then extract the ten rows they need.

- A logical dump gives you the complete set of scripts to recreate everything from
  the server, the disk inits, the configuration of the server, the databases, their segmentation across server devices, and all the database objects to the data in those
  objects. Once you have an automated way to produce logical dumps for all your
  servers you don't have to worry about maintaining scripts to recreate your servers.

- A logical dump serves to document the server; the documentation can be very
  useful when the time comes to make changes.

You can make logical dumps of your servers and databases manually by writing
scripts that will select all the information needed from each of the system and user
tables. You then need to bulkcopy out the data for each table, and you will need to
keep track of all the relationships needed to rebuild any object, such as the order in
which you create the rules and the datatypes. Assuming you could keep all this
straight, how would other people find all this and extract what they need from it?
Consider also that when you go to recreate something, you must worry about the

order in which you recreate all the dependent objects. For example, if you try to recreate a database manually, you must worry about the order in which you create everything, because each object may require that other objects be in place before the current object can be created. All of this requires a great deal of manual intervention and is very error-prone.

Unless your databases are very small, you should automate the process of making logical dumps and integrate this into the rest of your normal dump procedure. The product SQL BackTrack from DataTools will do this and a lot more. SQL BackTrack works with the SQL Server to provide logical dumps of any part of your server, from the whole thing down to an individual database object. SQL BackTrack also dumps the data for tables, as well as making the logical dump of the table's definition. Further, SQL BackTrack can make physical dumps of a database, and enables you to extract the logical definition of a database object from the physical dump. The product is very flexible. For example, you can retrieve the logical dump of a table from either the logical or physical dump of the database and then specify at the command line that you want the table recreated on a different segment of the database. SQL BackTrack also allows you to make incremental physical backups of a database similar to the file system dumps made at the UNIX level. This can reduce server downtime by reducing the time it takes to do your regular database dumps.

SQL BackTrack also simplifies the whole process. Compare making a logical dump of a database manually—which would require dumping the system tables by using bcp, selecting all the information needed to reproduce all the tables, rules, user-defined datatypes, stored procedures, and triggers, and then bulkcopying out all the data for all the tables—to a single command line for SQL BackTrack that will handle the whole thing. When it comes time to load all or a portion of the logical dump, the same comparison holds, namely, that done manually you would have to remember the order in which to create everything and where all the bcp files were, compared to the single command line for SQL BackTrack.

;-)

> The database is 5.6 Gb spread across many server devices. The users approach. Like frightened gazelles thundering across the Serengeti, they raise the clouds of dust on the horizon that signal yet another user-induced panic on the plains. Breathlessly, they explain how no one did anything, but ten rows of a table just disappeared, and they gotta have that data right now. The users start to mill around your cubicle, snorting and stomping their hooves. Turns out that table only has ten rows, but you have to load the entire database dump to get the data. You just don't have time or the disk space to store, update and catalog a bcp dump of all 800 tables in the server. So, you stop running **dbcc** checks on the dedicated DBCC server so you can load last night's database dump, but first you have to clear enough space on the DBCC server by dropping databases, then you have to create the 5.6 Gb database and wait while it loads. The users are getting ugly—much baring of teeth and meaningless threats.
>
> Finally you can bulkcopy out the ten rows of data and give it to the users. It only took most of your day, and you will have to do it all over again the next time someone (officially, no one) deletes data from your production system. The user herd thunders off. You begin sweeping up the gazelle droppings and pull out that purchase request for that third-party product that makes logical dumps of entire servers automatically. Time to go see the king of the jungle for some approvals. Sure hope The Great One is awake in the corner office....

8.14 Recovery Matrix

Each of these problems will occur sometime. You must be prepared to deal with them. You should think about how you will recover in each of these instances. For each type of failure, we address the recovery process needed to restore the server. Note that there are many solutions to each problem. If a standby server is available, you can fail over to the standby server and extract data needed to rebuild the primary. The same applies if you have a decision support or DBCC server that can fill in as a standby server while the primary server is repaired. We also assume you have the normal set of database dump and transaction log dumps that are known to be clean.

;-)

Don't you just love the phrase "known clean dumps"? It's sorta like "guaranteed for life" or "I'll always love you." Just exactly how do you ever know for sure? More to the point, who has time to really verify each and every dump, let alone do what the manuals require by running all **dbcc** checks and fixing any corruption found before each and every database or transaction log dump? Sure, your users will understand why their system will be down 30 hours to run full **dbcc** checks on all 8 Gb of database before dumping the transaction log, and you have to dump the transaction log every 15 minutes to provide recovery that is close to the current state of the database.

For each failure listed in Table 8.1, we discuss what you need to do to recover. Unless you are sure you understand the failure and how to recover, you should contact Sybase Technical Support before proceeding.

Table 8.1   SQL Server Recovery Matrix

Server Restart
1105 Error
Transaction Log Dumps Fail
Loss of One or More Transaction Log Dumps
Normal **dbcc** Finds Corruption
Loss of User Database
Loss of Server Device
Loss of Mirror of Server Device
Loss of Physical Disk
Loss of Server Machine
Loss of *master* or Master Device
Loss of Database Object and/or Data from Database Object
Loss of Data or Database Object from Previous Server Version

Server Restart

As the server restarts it goes through the recovery process for each database on the server. The server must have access to the current transaction log to fully recover a database.

1105 Error

If the 1105 error is due to a database segment other than the transaction log being full, then you need to add space to the segment that is full. If the 1105 error is due to the transaction log being full, see Chapter 6 for discussion of dealing with a full transaction log.

If the 1105 error occurs in *tempdb* because the transaction log is full, simply execute

```
dump transaction tempdb with no_log
```

Normally, you would be worried that this would break the sequence of transaction log dumps and affect recovery, but you never try to recover *tempdb,* so it doesn't matter. If the transaction log dump doesn't work, restart the server, which clears *tempdb* completely.

Transaction Log Dumps Fail

You should be regularly dumping the transaction logs of the production databases on the server. This allows you to recover the database closer to its state when a failure occurred and truncates the transaction log more often, which prevents it from filling up. If this process of regularly dumping the transaction log fails, the transaction log starts to fill. If you lose the transaction log, you won't be able to recover the database close to its state at the time of the failure because the last transaction log dump was longer and longer ago as this problem persists.

Loss of One or More Transaction Log Dumps

If you are regularly using the transaction log dumps to keep another server in sync with the primary server, you will know immediately that you have a problem, because the load of the transaction log will fail. Either the transaction log you were loading has a corruption of some kind or the next transaction log in the sequence is missing. If the load of the transaction log fails with an error message indicating the dump is "out of sequence," then you need to find that missing transaction log dump. If you can't, then you are indeed missing one of the transaction log dumps and you can't recover the primary server database beyond the last available transaction log dump in the sequence. You have to make a full database dump before you can resume dumping the transaction log. Any changes made to the database before the next full database dump can't be recovered in the event of a server problem.

Normal dbcc *Finds Corruption*

You will need to run the appropriate **dbcc** command or commands to fix the corruption, which will require putting the database (or the whole server to run **dbcc** checks in *master*) into single-user mode. This will require forcing all the users out of the database or the server for the *master* database.

If your attempts to fix the corruption fail, you may have to reload the database from dumps. If that fails, then you have lost the database (see below).

Loss of User Database

If you can still get at the *master* database and if the server device that supports the transaction log for the database is still accessible, you must use the **dump transaction** command with the **no_truncate** option to dump the current contents of the transaction log to disk. Next, you will need to drop and recreate the database. You can use the information that you have in the dumps of the system tables that you have been making regularly to see how the database was segmented, that is, how much database space on which server devices and in what order. After recreating the database, load the most recent database dump and apply the transaction log dumps since the last database dump, including the dump made of the current contents of the transaction log.

Loss of Server Device

If the other server devices on the same physical disk are still accessible, you should mirror them off to other partitions on other physical disks. Then, drop the primary side of the server devices that you just mirrored (see Chapter 4). Now you can replace the physical disk. Once the new disk is installed, you need to drop, recreate, load from the most recent database dump, and apply all the transaction logs since the last database dump for the database on the server device affected.

If you do have to replace the physical disk, see below.

Loss of Mirror of Server Device

You don't have any immediate problem. You should try to determine why the mirror failed and whether it was the primary or secondary side of the mirrored server device. You may try to remirror the server device; if that works, you're all set. Check with the server machine SA person to make sure there aren't any errors in the server machine hardware error log before you remirror.

If you need to replace a physical disk, follow the steps below. Note that having the server device mirrored means you choose when the server downtime occurs to fix a failed server device.

Loss of Physical Disk

If you aren't mirroring all the server devices on the physical disk that is lost, you will have lost the server devices on that physical disk. You need to determine which server devices are affected from looking at the dumps you have on disk of the system tables or from your servermap. If the server has not crashed and if you can still get to the *master* database, dump the current contents of the transaction log to disk using the **dump transaction** command with the **no_truncate** option. You should do this for all databases that are affected by the disk loss. Then, the server and the server machine can be shut down and the physical disk replaced. Once the server machine is back up and the server is running, you can use the information in the dumps you have of the system tables in the *master* database to recreate the server devices that were on the disk that failed. Once that is done, you will need to drop all the databases that used a server device on the failed disk, recreate each database with the same segmentation that it had before the failure, and load the most recent database dumps. Then, apply the transaction logs since the last full database dump for each database, including the dump of the contents of the transaction log just before you brought down the server to replace the disk.

If you are mirroring all the server devices, you don't have an immediate problem. When you are ready to replace the bad disk, simply unmirror each server device that has either its primary or mirror on the physical disk that failed. Depending on whether the primary or mirror of the server device was on the physical disk that failed, you would unmirror the primary or secondary respectively and use the **mode = remove** option (see Chapter 4). Once the proper **disk unmirror** commands have been completed, you can shut down the server, the server machine, replace the disk, and restart the server machine and server. Then, you recreate the partitions as they were on the failed disk and mirror the server devices affected by the disk failure back to the appropriate partitions on the new disk.

Note that this is the whole point of mirroring: It allows you to decide when to take the server downtime.

If the master device was on the physical disk that went bad and you don't have a mirror on another physical disk, then you have lost the master device (and the *master* database) and that is the same as losing the whole server (see below).

Loss of Server Machine

The server recovery needed for this disaster is highly dependent on what exactly happened to cause the server machine to fail. If the server machine is restored and there is no known damage to the disks that support the server, you can restart and see if the server recovers. Depending on the errors you see as the server recovers, you may need to rebuild the master device, one or more user databases, or the whole server.

If the server has been wiped out, you will need to reinstall the server from scratch (see Chapter 3). Once the server is installed, you can use the scripts you have for **disk init,** and so on, to create the server devices and the databases that were on the server before the crash. Since you have recent dumps of the system tables for the server, you can examine them as soon as the server machine is repaired (or restore them from file system dumps) and verify that you have created the same server devices on the same partitions, and so on. Then, you can use a recent dump of the *master* database to restore the *syslogins* table. Now, you can load the database dumps to restore the database of the server. Note that you do need to have access to the information in the *master* database system tables; that is why you must be dumping this data regularly.

If you have a logical dump of the server, you can use that to recreate all the server devices, and so on. This again is a reason to make regular logical dumps of your server; see description of SQL BackTrack above.

Loss of master or Master Device

This is the same as losing the whole server.

If only the master device is damaged, you can recreate it by running buildmaster. Make sure the server is not running when you do this. You will also need to specify the size of the master device to the buildmaster command. Recall that you can obtain the size of the master device from the RUN_*<servername>* script created by sybconfig (sybinit for System 10) or the server errorlog. Be careful that you specify the size of the master device in the proper units for buildmaster. You must review all the possible options in the *Sybase SQL Server Troubleshooting Guide* to see what you need to do for each of the possible failure scenarios.

Once the master device or the *master* database is rebuilt, you can load a database dump of *master*. This should restore all the information about the server that was in the *master* database previously, and the server should now recognize all the server devices and databases that were on it before the failure. If any changes were made to the server that would have changed system tables in the *master* database since the last dump of *master*, you must recreate those changes exactly or you may have problems. This is why you must dump *master* regularly.

If other parts of the server are damaged as well, you will need to repair those next.

Loss of Database Object and/or Data from Database Object

If you have any other server that has a copy of the database, you can retrieve the database object from that server. Examples of such a server would include a standby server, a decision support server, or a DBCC server. If the database object is not available this way, you must load a database dump that does contain the object somewhere on your system and retrieve the object from there. See Chapter 10 for a discussion about the need to have enough disk space on a server machine somewhere in your database system to support recreating and loading old database dumps to retrieve old database objects.

The situation can be greatly simplified if you are making regular logical database dumps. Since the SQL Server does not directly support making logical dumps, you should investigate a third-party product such as SQL BackTrack from DataTools (see Section 8.13). With a logical dump that contains the object you need, you can simply retrieve the data or the commands needed to recreate the database object directly.

Loss of Data or Database Object from Previous Server Version

Assume that you upgraded the server from 4.9.x to System 10 and now someone needs to retrieve data that was on the 4.9.x server but was updated or otherwise deleted from the server before the upgrade. You must somehow determine which 4.9.x dump has the data the user needs and then recreate the database on a 4.9.x SQL Server and load the database. See Chapter 10 for a discussion about the need to have a previous version SQL Server somewhere in your database system. Once you have the 4.9.x database loaded, you can retrieve what the user needs. If the user now needs the data or database object loaded into the System 10 server, remember that there are changes between the server that may complicate this recreation (see Chapter 14).

;-)

If you realize that you haven't made the dumps that you should have and you haven't verified the dumps as you know you should and you never checked to see if all the segments of the biggest production server in your company really are mirrored and the server is lying in pieces in a pool of blood and you can hear the footsteps of management coming down the hall followed by the herds of neglected users, you can always resort to the following:

step 1) update resume (with nowait)

step 2) go (to next job)

Chapter 9

Performance and Tuning

A lot has been written about the subject of performance and tuning, and, like the weather, you wonder if anyone is really doing anything about it. While there are many theories, and they look good on paper, many of them simply don't apply to the real-world production systems that you deal with every day. We discuss many real-world issues that can affect your server performance.

You can read an entire book on the subject, and you should see Chapter 16. Further, the class on SQL Server Performance and Tuning offered by Sybase is excellent. You should attend such a class before you make any serious attempt at determining or improving your server's performance. Here we discuss issues that are specific to the SQL Server that will help you do what you can and detect the rest for what it is:

9.1   Theory Is Nice

The theory is that you can identify a very few number of transactions that the application runs against the server and that you can then identify the indexes required. Beyond this the theory tells you to worry about joins and how to denormalize some of the tables to reduce the number of joins the server needs to do.

You will benefit from going through the process, but you need to know what you can do about the application that your business runs on every day and that has been around for years. You are not going to simply step in tomorrow and denormalize the million-row tables that are the very basis of your business. You probably don't have the downtime or the disk space to create many new indexes on your largest tables, either. The application is not static, and you can't completely control who is able to run exactly what queries as they try out changes to the applications.

A good example of the theory of database performance and tuning that is specific to the SQL Server is update in place. The theory is great, namely, that if you do everything just right you can perform updates in place. This saves the server a lot of work as opposed to the normal update that performs a delete followed by an insert, which may require shuffling the data pages around as well.

As good as the predicted performance gain may be, look again at all the requirements that you must meet before the server will perform an update in place. Some of these requirements are that the update must not affect any index on the table, that the update does no joins, and that the table does not have an update trigger. Now, you need to wonder how many mission-critical applications are going to depend on tables that meet all these restrictions. You should also wonder how a real-world application could get very far if it did rely on tables that did not have any triggers. You should wonder about referential integrity and the like. You need to realize that the performance and tuning theory is fine and will get you to think about the process, but it will not provide some magic answer that will speed up the server a great deal overnight.

With that said, you should understand some very practical points about the SQL Server. With these points covered, you can proceed to the many full texts that assume you are building the application from scratch and that you as a DBA have complete control over the way the users and the developers will create and maintain the applications that your business depends on. You probably see a problem right away. Many of the applications you deal with these days are from third-party vendors. The applications may well be the best in their fields, but they are also likely to be ports from some other database system to SQL Server. This means that even less of the theory of performance and tuning will apply, because the application was not designed, either logically or physically, for the particular needs of the SQL Server. Therefore, the options remaining for you as a DBA to dramatically improve server performance are few.

9.2   What You Can Do in the Real World

You need to separate temporary performance degradations due to your business cycle or the day of the week or month from an ongoing downward trend. Then, you need to determine if a temporary slowdown is worth the effort to investigate, let alone cure. This is a business decision: Does the business invest enough resources to provide a certain performance level no matter where in the business cycle you are, or does the business prefer to have less spare capacity being maintained all the time?

In the real world you need to realize you can't make the server run faster for everyone. In fact, you need to first decide which users you are going to please and which users you are going to disappoint. You will probably get rid of the latter users by moving them to another server where their queries can run without slowing down everyone else.

First, you need to get as many of the transactions that the server is trying to satisfy to be as short as possible. This will reduce the blocking as various server processes don't stay connected as long and don't need to hold locks for as long. This again goes back to the design of the application. You can't simply make the transactions shorter; the design of the application has to be changed. This also means that you need to identify who is doing what in the server and limit access to the server to those who really need to have the highest throughput. Other users must be moved off the server, especially those users that need to run reports or other uncontrolled queries. The remaining short queries should be executed as stored procedures by the application. You should not have multiple applications running against the same server, because you can't tune the server layout for multiple conflicting priorities. What you are doing here is limiting the number of kinds of queries the server has to respond to. This will require that the users do not have open access to the server and can only execute queries that are part of a fixed set of queries available through the one application running against the server via stored procedures. This implies no users are allowed to run isql or use any other application to access the server directly. Depending on the corporate culture you are dealing with, this can be a real shock.

Assuming you can get past the previous step, prioritize the queries for which you are trying to tune the server. This implies that some queries are more important than others. While your users will not agree with this, it is more important that transactions that make money directly for the business (like entering an order) get through the server more quickly than transactions that don't (like looking up the last five years of orders for some executive committee). If you are going to improve the performance of the server at all, you must get some control over what the server is being asked to do. Only then can you begin to apply the methods that come from the theory. You need to minimize the number of different types of queries because even if you tune the server for the most important queries, it takes only one user running a long and low priority query (like requesting the last five years of sales data) to slow down and outright block all the short and important queries.

The lower priority queries must be moved off the OLTP server to a decision support server. Depending on the needs of the user base, you may want to create more and different indexes on the tables of the report server to support more complex queries. You will need to establish a host of procedures and processes to maintain a decision support server that will supply the best performance for most of that server's users.

Once you have settled on a set of queries you are worried about, you can work on creating the best set of indexes that will cover most if not all of the important queries. This is a case where some of the theory is really useful (see below). Be careful in your selection of indexes; it is easy to create too many and spend all the server's time simply updating and maintaining all the various indexes.

With a good set of indexes, you can improve the server's performance simply by getting all these indexes into cache. With enough server machine memory, you can keep the nonclustered indexes in memory, thus eliminating all the physical I/O for the queries that are covered by these indexes. Note that you also want to get most, if not all, of the stored procedures into cache as well, and the server assigns a percentage of the server machine memory that is available to the server to the procedure cache. Hence, more cache is good which means more memory is good for server performance. All of this goes back to capacity planning (see Chapter 10).

A very basic, powerful, and often ignored process that will help server performance more than all the theories put together is archiving. This simply means that you have a process that systematically identifies data in the server that is no longer needed in the OLTP server and moves that data to an archive database on another server. This keeps the databases on the OLTP server as small as possible, facilitating everything from performance to recovery (see Chapter 8). The process of archiving is discussed in the section titled "Archiving" below.

These techniques are not glamorous and will not win you any awards for theoretical database design, but they do work. They are also unpopular if the server environment has been allowed to evolve with users doing whatever they want whenever they want. As with so many problems in the real world, the biggest hurdles to solving them are political (and all too often they become personal), not technical. You can do little more than understand what can be done and work to make it happen within your environment.

;-)

> The high-priced consultants arrive amid great fanfare. As the ticker-tape parade fades into the distance, you, the DBA who couldn't attend the long lunch for management and the consultants because you had to attend to the production systems, are left with the wisdom of the ages, delivered for about 4x what you make. You are told to drop the mirrors on all the production server devices and remirror with the **noserial** option, that is, with parallel mirroring. You are assured that this will improve performance by 100 percent by replacing the **serial** mirroring that you had set up because it provides maximum data integrity (see Chapter 4). Fine, you drop the mirrors and you can't see any improvement in the application performance, but not all the users are on the system, so you proceed to mirror everything again, using the **noserial** option. After a week of waiting, even management agrees that the application is as slow as ever, and in fact, there was no speedup when there was no mirroring at all.

You can't fool ignorant people, no matter how much they charge in the process. The logic was flawless but irrelevant. If your application is slow, it may not be as simple as turning off mirroring to get a 100 percent speedup. You need to keep this in mind when you are given "advice." Only you and your users know your system, and only you and your users live and die by its performance. Try anything you like, but the odds are that you will have to look long and hard to find the real sources of the slow performance you are trying to find and fix.

And, just as a footnote, the expensive out-of-town help couldn't come back to explain your situation because they charge so much you can't afford them any more.

9.3 Indexes and Queries

This discussion does not replace the very detailed and lengthy discussions available in other sources regarding the SQL Server query optimizer and how it selects the index(s) it will use to satisfy a given query (see Chapter 16).

As mentioned previously, all the important queries for the database should be covered by an appropriate index on each table. This refers to a nonclustered index whose key is built on the field or fields of the table that the queries need to access.

A nonclustered index builds index pages that make it easy to find the individual rows of the table that contain the data in the key for the index. Eventually, the nonclustered index will point to the individual rows of the table spread throughout the table. But, for the fields (columns) of the table that form the key of the index, the nonclustered index will actually contain an ordered set of the key fields. The nonclustered index, as far as the table data in the columns that make up the key is concerned, forms a clustered index for the fields that make up the key, since the index stores this subset of table data in order of the key. Thus, for queries that need data only from the columns that make up the key of the index, so-called covered queries, the server need not go to the data page to retrieve rows of the table. Instead, the data that will satisfy the covered query is available within the index pages. For a covered query, the index pages contain many more 'rows' of the table data relevant to the query on a given data page since only the data that forms the index key is stored on the index page. This means there is more data relevant to the covered query per page in the index, thus reducing the I/O needed to satisfy the query. For a covered query, the server can satisfy the query by just accessing the values of the key that the index maintains in order.The index also has a pointer to the full row of the table for each value of the key, but for a covered query the server need not access the full row.

You need to keep many things in mind whenever you start thinking about server performance. Even with the best indexes in the world, if your query is going to return more than about 20 percent of the rows of the table, the optimizer will just table scan (retrieve all the rows of the table) anyway. If you are looking at the query plans (see "set showplan" in SQL Server Performance Tools, below) and an unexpected table scan appears, you need to determine how many rows were returned relative to the size of the tables. If you are retrieving a lot of rows, you need to review why this query is even running against the OLTP machine. You should move all such transactions to the decision support server. Note that there really isn't a good index for a query that needs lots of rows returned.

All the indexes in the world won't help much if more than one user wants to update the same data page. This usually comes up when all the data in a table is ordered by some unique number like an order number. Assuming that the table has a clustered index on the order number and that the order numbers increase linearly with time, you are guaranteed that every user who is trying to enter a new order (a very important query for your business) will be fighting over the last few data pages of the table. In order to prevent this, you can assign an artificial (i.e., doesn't have anything to do with the order or the time it was created) key to each row of the table in a random manner. Then, recreate the clustered index so that it is based on this artificial key column that is randomly distributed throughout the rows of the table. This means that even for new orders the rows will be spread randomly throughout the database. Users that need access to these new rows will be trying to access pages throughout the table, not just at the very end of it. This greatly reduces the blocking users see while they wait for the data page they need. Blocking is very costly in terms of server performance because it represents time during which nothing useful is being done for the process that is being blocked. (You can see which server users, if any, are being blocked in the output of **sp_who**.) Note that you need lots of disk space to recreate a clustered index. The other way to do this is to bcp out the table data, truncate the table, drop and recreate the clustered index and bcp the table data back in, but this approach is very slow.

Another real-world problem that you must be aware of: The query plans for stored procedures are done once when the stored procedure is first compiled. A stored procedure is always compiled the first time it is called after the server has started up. The query plan is then retained and will be used for all subsequent executions of the stored procedure. This is what makes the use of stored procedures useful for speeding up queries, but it implies that you are always running the queries in the stored procedure against the same set of data every time. The problem is that the query plan may not be appropriate the next time the stored procedure is executed.

Consider a stored procedure that takes in a parameter called "order number" and runs against a table with a million rows, each row representing an order. Assuming that the primary key is order number, a query that retrieves all the order rows—where order number is greater than the order number supplied to the stored procedure at execution—will return vastly different numbers of rows, based on the order number that is passed to the stored procedure. If your application passed order number = 999,990 to the stored procedure the first time it was executed (and therefore was recompiled) since the server was last started, the query plan will probably make use of any available indexes, just as you expect. But, you need to remember that if the next execution of the stored procedure is passed order number = 100, the query plan using the index(s) will result in much worse server performance than if the query simply did a table scan, because virtually the whole table must be returned. For queries that return lots of data, the use of an index may be worse than just table scanning because of the overhead of traversing the index levels for each value of the index key.

You must also note that if you manually execute the query or queries in the stored procedure to examine the query plan, you may think everything is fine, but you are not executing the stored procedure's query plan and therefore are not seeing what the stored procedure is planning on doing. This can be very confusing and can lead to lots of lost time.

Finally, again, you must reduce the number of queries that your application submits to the server, and you should eliminate any queries that require lots of data returned. Such queries should be moved off the OLTP server to the decision support server.

You can use the **with recompile** option in the stored procedure so that it is recompiled each and every time it is executed. However, you will have a hard time telling if this improved things, because you will then have the added overhead of always recompiling, which may slow the query down as much as the use of an improper query plan did. This all leads to an observation that even if you identify a set of queries that the application makes and even if all of those queries are made through stored procedures, you can still get some killer queries if the application allows users to pass anything they want to the stored procedures. This gets back to fixing the application rather than the server.

You will be tempted to create every table with the clustered index the same as the primary key. This is not always a good idea and, in some cases, can ruin server performance. Consider a table where the primary key is order number. All the new orders will have the highest order numbers, and if the clustered index is created on the primary key, then all the data records are ordered by order number. This means all your users that are entering new orders will be contending for the last pages in the table, which will lead to lock contention and poor server performance. You must spread the user access out across all the data pages of the table to improve performance. On the other hand, if your users wanted to look at old order data and create reports based on ranges of order numbers, then this clustered index may be ideal, especially for a decision support server where the users are not updating, but only selecting.

Finally, you must not ignore the basics while you delve into the theory of performance and tuning. All of your indexes are examined by the query optimizer in the SQL Server to determine the best one (if any) to use. The way the query optimizer does this is to decide how many pages would have to be read by using the index or simply by scanning the whole table. The query optimizer makes this decision based on the distribution page that exists for each index. Without getting into how the query optimizer uses the distribution page to select an index, the point here is that the statistics information on the distribution page must be current or the optimizer will be making uninformed decisions. You must run **update statistics** and **sp_recompile** on all the tables in each database. Note that **sp_recompile** is executed on a table and, when executed, causes any and all stored procedures that reference the table to be recompiled. Even if a table is static, it still must have the distribution page updated at some point after the table is created and loaded. As part of your regular server maintenance, you should update all the user tables in the server, as well as updating the active tables more often. You can't check to see how recent the distribution page is for a given index; that is why it is better to just update them all regularly rather than trying to remember which tables were updated and when. You can detect indexes that have not had any distribution page created at all; that is, **update statistics** has never been run since the table or index was created or last truncated and loaded. The query to do this is—

```
select object_name(id) from sysindexes where
distribution = 0 and indid > 0 and id > 100
```

—which selects the rows of *sysindexes* that have *distribution* = 0, indicating no distribution page. Note that you eliminate system tables by specifying *id* > 100. Tables that don't have a clustered index will have *indid* = 0, but they don't have a distribution page so you eliminate them with *indid* > 0.

9.4 Spreading Segments Over Server Devices

One of many aspects of server performance that is argued about revolves around how to place the database segments on or over the available server devices. Consider the example below before you dive into a complex segmentation scheme.

Imagine that you have a database *db1* that consists of three segments. The first segment is the combined *system* and *default* segments, the second is the *logsegment* for the transaction log, and the third is called *ncindexes* where all the non-clustered indexes are stored. You can also assume that you are told that spreading each of these segments so that a part of each segment is on a different server device will help improve performance by speeding up the I/O for each of multiple users. The logic can be taken further by requiring that the multiple server devices of each segment be attached to separate controllers to provide multiple parallel I/O paths to portions of each segment. We take each of the segments in turn and explain why this advice is dubious at best.

You can start with the *logsegment* segment. Each transaction makes changes to the database. And all these changes are recorded in the transaction log, whether the transaction commits or is rolled back. Hence, the transaction log will always be a performance bottleneck because all users who are changing the database (i.e., causing changes to the database, all of which must be recorded in the transaction log) wait in line while the server records each user's changes on the last data page of the current extent of the transaction log segment. All the user changes that need to be recorded in the transaction log will be contending for access to the end of the transaction log while waiting for their log records to be written. There is nothing you can do to change this behavior, so there is no performance gain by spreading the transaction log across multiple server devices on different controllers. All you can do is determine how large the transaction log should be and allocate that much space on server devices on the same physical disk. You shouldn't normally need a transaction log larger than a whole physical disk, so the *logsegment* should always be on one physical disk, occupying multiple partitions if necessary.

Consider the *ncindexes* segment next. This segment contains the nonclustered indexes for the largest or most heavily accessed tables in the database. As such, these indexes should be used by most, if not all, queries that are run against this database. Further, the most important queries should be covered by the indexes you create on the table. This means that the server doesn't have to go to the data page to retrieve rows of the table; the data needed to satisfy the query is available within the index pages. Since the index pages contain only the table data from the columns that make up the index key (versus all the columns of the table) there will be more data relevant to the query on each index page compared to the pages that store the table data. This reduces the I/O needed to satisfy the query. Further, if you have sufficient memory on the server machine and you don't have too many indexes, you should have most, if not all, of the data pages for the *ncindexes* segment in the server's cache, so that no physical I/O is needed at all. Whereas the tables themselves may well be far too large to fit in any practical amount of memory, carefully chosen indexes will often fit within the server's data cache. Such indexes cover the most important queries— those that must run the fastest and are needed by most of your users to support the business—and are based on keys that are made up of as few of the table's columns as possible. Getting most of the most frequently used index pages into cache makes spreading the *ncindexes* segment irrelevant.

Now for the remaining segment that supports the *system* and *default* segments. To gain any benefit from spreading this segment around, you are assuming that the tables in this segment are heavily accessed, which means they should be properly indexed (a few indexes that cover the important queries) and these indexes should all be created on the *ncindexes* segment discussed above. This means that for the important queries these tables should not be accessed much at all, because the indexes will satisfy the queries and the indexes are all in cache.

Given this discussion, you should conclude that rather than pursue some arcane segment and server device allocation scheme, you should go back to the real cause of all the problems—the set of queries that the application is asking the server to satisfy—and buy as much memory as possible.

You should also consider the difficulties you and your fellow DBAs will have maintaining any complex segmentation scheme. If it isn't clear where to add space to a given segment, you can count on it being done wrong. Any performance gains due to a complex segmentation scheme can be wiped out by one careless addition of space for a segment on the inappropriate server device.

9.5 Spreading Individual Tables

If, for whatever reason, you can't cover all the queries with non-clustered indexes, then you can take individual tables that are heavily accessed, create a segment for each, and spread that segment over several physical disks, preferably on separate controllers. But, this requires that the data in such a table will be accessed in a random pattern, that is, the user access will occur throughout the table space, not just at the end where new data pages are added. You will probably require some form of artificial key or random number that is one column of this table (not related to any attribute of the entity, i.e., not a real piece of information about the data stored in the table) and build the clustered index of this table on that randomly distributed number. This ensures that the query access will be spread out across the table space, minimizing hot spots where user contention for the same data pages causes slow overall server performance.

9.6 Archiving

Of all the server performance enhancing techniques available, perhaps the most powerful is quite simple and requires more of a cultural shift for the users than anything technical to do with the server. This technique is archiving. You identify the database(s) that hold the data that represents your business. These database(s) are the ones that grow all the time as your business moves along. You set up a process that will scan these database(s) and identify all the data that is older than some time span. The data that is too old is moved to another database. The benefits of this process are many and varied. First, the size of the database(s) that are in use every day does not keep growing, which means you can establish processes to handle dumps, **dbcc** checks, and so on, that will work for a long time. Also, all of these processes run much faster on a smaller database. You need to maintain only the indexes over the current data, and that means smaller indexes (due to smaller tables); more indexes will fit in the same amount of cache, which means you get more use out of the server machine memory you have available to the server. Even a table scan, when necessary, will run faster on smaller tables.

In order to make archiving work, you must set up a process that can be run regularly to archive the production database(s). This process must be complete, so you don't have to worry about it each time you run it. The process could involve a script that runs once a day to determine which rows in the database are old enough to be archived, then indicates that fact in a column added to the tables for that purpose. Another approach is to simply add the date and time when the row was added to the database and let the script compare that information with the current date. You could also archive data based, not on how old the data is, but how big the database is. Either way, you will have to examine the current logical and physical design of your database(s) to see how best to archive the data.

Once the data to archive has been identified, you then need to move that data out of the database and into a separate archive database that is created for each archiving period. If you are archiving quarterly, you would set up a database for the present quarter where you would archive data until the next quarter starts. You need to decide whether you need all the data online at all. If so, you will need one large database that will grow over time as more and more business history is added to it. If not, you can decide how many previous archive periods you need online and keep only that many archive databases in the server. This arrangement means that at each archiving period one old database would be dropped from the OLTP server, see Figure 8.12 in Chapter 8, "SQL Server Recovery."

At the end of each archive period, you will either have created a new archive database for the next archiving period or you will have increased the size of the one ongoing archive database. In either case, you should run a full **dbcc** check against the archive database and fix any problems that you find, then dump the database to tape. This assures you that you have all of this data on a known, clean dump, so you only have to worry about corruption and other problems in the current data, which is a smaller database. Depending on the nature of your business, the current data set may be very much smaller, saving you a great deal of time. In this way archiving also helps you by speeding and simplifying recovery, see Chapter 8.

Archiving is well worth the effort but will require some changes to existing applications. Your application will need to know that only data for the current archiving period is stored in the database(s) that the application is used to accessing. The application needs to be able to detect requests for older data and know how to access the appropriate archive database. Depending on how many archive periods you keep online the application may need to know about the location of very old archive databases that should be on the decision support server. You will want to minimize the number of archive databases that are kept on the OLTP server. Ideally only the archive database that is being filled for the current archive period would be there, because any access to any database takes resources that the server should be applying to current transactions. Note that the need for application changes is a theme throughout this discussion. For archiving, the time invested in making such changes is very well worth it.

9.7   Decision Support Server

Along with archiving, setting up a decision support server will help you improve the performance of the OLTP server more than almost anything else. As has been mentioned repeatedly, to make any progress in server tuning you must first identify the short, important transactions that the applications on the OLTP server need to run as fast as possible, then move anything else off to a decision support server. This will allow you to reduce the number and type of queries you are trying to tune for. Further, with a copy of the production data on the decision support server, you can also improve the response for the longer-running, more complex queries by setting up more and different indexes on the tables than you should have on the OLTP server.

The decision support server needs to have a copy of the production database data that is on the OLTP server and that is refreshed at some regular interval. Your determination of the proper refresh interval will be a taxing political question. You must identify who needs what data and how current it must be. Some of your users will say that their queries must be run against data that is absolutely up-to-date, but you need to filter this a great deal. There is a trade-off between how many users can get a certain level of performance running against the OLTP server. In order to improve performance for some users, you may have to force the others to use data that is somewhat out of date on the decision support server.

Note that using a decision support server to off-load the OLTP server is a very good approach, but as with other proposed solutions discussed here, it may well involve changing your applications. Consider an application that allows users to query all the sales orders ever entered into the system: You decide to archive all but the last three months of the sales order data to an archive database on the decision support server; you also dump the OLTP sales order data and load it into the decision support server on a nightly basis; the application now needs to examine the user's request and send queries to three places, depending on the data needed. Or, you modify the application to simply only access either the OLTP server or the decision support server. This will prevent users from trying to access both up-to-date data and archive data at the same time. Either you must modify the applications or your users must run the applications twice, once on the OLTP server and again for any data older than the archiving period.

This raises the question of how to keep the decision support server up-to-date with the OLTP server. You can do this by loading the database dumps you normally make on the OLTP server into the decision support server right after the dumps are complete. If you are dumping your OLTP server once a day, then your decision support server will always be one day behind, at worst. The use of database dumps is relatively simple, because you already go to the trouble of making the OLTP server database dumps; by loading the dumps into the decision support server, you are also verifying that the dumps are good. Note that you must maintain the decision support server databases as the same size as (or larger than) the OLTP server databases that are being dumped and loaded. This means that any time you add space to the OLTP server databases, you will need to add the same amount of space to the decision support server. Also, the process of loading the decision support server will take longer and longer as the database dumps become larger or you add more databases. You have to decide at what point the downtime of the decision support server due to database loading cuts too much into the benefit of having the decision support server at all. You can speed the process of dumping and loading: If you have enough server machine disk space on the OLTP and decision support servers, you can dump the database to a disk file, copy that file to disk on the decision support server machine, and then load the dump. This technique is limited because you can only dump to a single disk file, which limits the maximum dump size to around 2 GB. (For System 10 you can use disk striping (dump to multiple disk files at once) with the Backup Server to speed the dumping process and to dump databases where the dump would be larger than a single UNIX file system.) Your users will become increasingly frustrated that the decision support server is available less and less often. You are also setting up another server that should be on a separate server machine which means more of all the software, hardware, facilities, and personnel resources that are always in short supply.

As the time to load all the necessary OLTP dumps becomes too long, there is another approach you can implement. This involves loading the OLTP dumps into the decision support server once and from then on moving the transaction logs (which you should be dumping regularly on the OLTP server anyway) to the decision support server and applying them to the databases there. This process still involves some downtime, but it is less time than for a complete load of the entire database. This approach does require more monitoring, and when it fails, you have to load the entire database from dumps, which will lock out your users for an extended period of time. Remember, for both a **load database** or a **load transaction** command, the database in question can't have any users in the database. Although you would think the method of loading transaction logs would allow you to keep the decision support databases in sync with the OLTP databases to within the transaction log dump interval on the OLTP server, this isn't practical. Since you have to get rid of any users in the database to load the transaction logs, you won't be able to load any transaction logs until off-hours; then you will need to load all the transaction logs that have accumulated from the OLTP databases since the last time you updated the decision support databases, as illustrated in Figure 9.1.

Both of these approaches to keeping the decision support server in sync suffer from another problem that may actually limit the decision support server performance even though it off-loads and helps the OLTP server performance. You must move any user queries that are not short, important transactions to the decision support server. This allows you to create only the indexes needed to support the reduced set of queries that will run on the OLTP server. This should help you speed up the performance of the OLTP server. But, these indexes are just the opposite of what you want for indexes on the decision support server. The decision support server is for longer-running, complex queries that may need to retrieve large amounts of data from various databases for reporting or data analysis. The server performance for this sort of data access can be improved significantly by creating more and different indexes on the tables in the databases. These indexes may be built on more, and sometimes all, of the columns in a table. On the OLTP server, you should reduce the number of indexes on each table to minimize the time the server spends maintaining indexes and to fit as many of the indexes into cache as possible. Since you are dumping and loading from the databases on the OLTP server, you are forcing the decision support server to have the same minimal set of indexes as the OLTP server. The only way around this is to keep the users off the decision support server even longer, while you build the different indexes after each database load. This will further reduce the time the decision support server is available to your users.

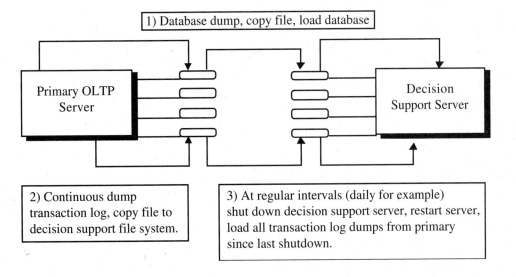

Figure 9.1   Keeping decision support server in sync using transaction logs- - - - - - - - - - -

For the transaction log approach to work you must maintain all the databases on the decision support server as read-only, because any activity in the database causes the next transaction log load to fail. This means you can't create new indexes and it also means the users can't run any queries that would update or write any data in the databases.

The load database approach doesn't have to have the databases in read-only mode, but each load will overwrite any changes made, such as new indexes.

Both approaches will maintain all parts of the databases affected, but this doesn't include the *master* database. Since you can't just load the *master* database from the OLTP server to the decision support server, that means many of the system tables will not be in sync. The server logins, for example, will not be maintained between the two servers. Even if you were willing to load the *master* database every time, you shouldn't unless all the server devices have the same physical names, and so on. You can't really keep the *master* database of the decision support server in sync with the OLTP server.

The dump and load database approach is the simplest and works well for small databases. It prevents you from maintaining any indexes different from the OLTP server, but again, for small databases that will load quickly, you will have time to build indexes each time you load, because the tables in the databases will also be smaller. As the databases involved get bigger, you will spend more and more time loading and creating indexes than you will letting users use the server. At some point, you will need to decide if it is time to go without the indexes or move to the transaction log loading process. Replication Server may provide a better way to maintain the decision support server. Replication Server can replicate the tables you need from the OLTP server into the decision support server without any downtime on the decision support server at all, while you maintain a unique set of indexes as well. As described in Chapter 2, it can be a major project to replicate all the tables in all the databases of your OLTP server, but the benefits can be many. You could also replicate data from multiple servers so that the decision support server can support reporting queries that are more complex than any that could ever be run on the OLTP server.

9.8 Standard Set of Application Transactions

Although you can measure server performance in several ways, it is still difficult for you, the DBA, to really measure server performance from the users' perspective. From their point of view, the server is "slow," based on how long it takes for them to run their various queries. Whether or not the number of writes to disk is higher than normal doesn't really interest them, only the overall throughput shows up in their world. You can save yourself a lot of troubleshooting time if you can agree with the users what exactly the server performance is before it gets worse. The best way to do this is to establish some set of transactions that you can run through the application to see what the overall server performance is at any given time. For example, although SQL Monitor will tell you a great deal about the server, it slows the server down by some amount while it is running. A set of transactions allows you to measure the server performance without any other processes to affect the results. Further, it is good to have timing data for such a set of transactions before the users complain. Without a baseline of how the application's transactions were behaving in the past, you don't have much to go on when the users tell you the application is slow.

Establishing a standard set of transactions is also part of the whole tuning process. The standard set of transactions should be the same set of transactions that you identified as the most important queries for which you are trying to improve server performance.

It isn't always practical to establish such a set of transactions, but if you can do so, you should run them when server performance is good or at least acceptable. Then you should run them at some regular interval to measure server performance over time and throughout your business cycle. When you upgrade the server or alter any part of the logical or physical database design, you can run these same transactions in your development environment to detect any performance problems early in the development process. Then, when you do roll out the new application changes to production, you should again run these transactions to get a measure of performance that you can compare with the data from the past.

9.9   SQL Monitor

SQL Monitor™ is a Sybase product that works with the SQL Server to provide you with a graphical display of the server's performance. The data displayed is very useful for tracking down server performance problems.

The SQL Monitor consists of two portions: the server portion, which runs on the same server machine as the SQL Server and reads the shared memory of the server; and the client portion, which can run anywhere and reads the data that is in the server portion and displays it to you. Note that you now have another process running that can take resources away from the SQL Server.

When you start SQL Monitor, disable the checking of memory that uses the **dbcc memusage** command, which can slow down the SQL Server substantially. You do this by using the -nomem option when you execute sqlmon, which is the client portion of the product.

The default configuration of SQL Monitor can support up to five connections between the server portion and all client portions. This means that five different SQL Monitor Clients can be connected to one SQL Monitor Server, but each client can only have one window open. Or, one client can be connected that can open five windows. You can have only a total of five windows open among all clients. You can increase the maximum number of connections to 20 by using the -n20 option of the SQL Monitor Server startup script, but you must also change the shared memory start address, which involves running buildmaster. You must not do this procedure when the SQL Server is running. Consult the SQL Monitor Server Supplement for the details of this process.

The SQL Monitor product does have some limitations. First, it can show performance data only for a limited number of server devices in the bar chart used for showing disk I/O rates, and so on. This is a problem for a large server with numerous server devices. You also have no control over which server devices are shown, and you can't switch between sets of server devices. The text display that comes along with the bar graphs does tell you about all the server devices, but it gives you only the total I/O data for each server device. This is especially frustrating on a larger server where you purposely create lots of server devices to support multiple user-defined database segments to improve performance, but you can't see them all with your performance monitoring tool.

SQL Monitor doesn't provide a time history for the performance data for nearly long enough. It will display data for 60 intervals; depending on the interval you have selected for the performance parameter in question, that may be sufficient, but it doesn't help you correlate performance from a month or a year ago with what is happening right now. You can print the windows, but then you are forced to keep a file of hardcopy output for comparison. You really need to be able to call up data that spans your business cycle and be able to compare data from several previous business cycles to put the current server performance into any useful perspective.

Since the use of SQL Monitor can slow the SQL Server performance somewhat, you need to determine the performance impact for your SQL Server on your specific hardware and operating system platform. A good way to determine this is to run your standard set of transactions (described above) with and without the SQL Monitor server running on the server machine. Note that even if you have stopped all the SQL Monitor Clients, the SQL Monitor Server is still running on the server machine and should be stopped as well.

There are several windows that can be displayed by SQL Monitor. Each one provides you with data about a different aspect of server performance. The windows are described in Table 9.1.

Table 9.1   SQL Monitor Windows

SQL Monitor (Main Window)	Lists the windows that are available. If you did not specify the -nomem option when you started the SQL Server Client (sqlmon), the pie chart of server machine memory usage will also be displayed.
Cache	Displays graphs of the data cache and procedure cache performance. From observing the physical and logical reads for the data cache, you can determine whether most of the requests for data pages are being satisfied with data pages already in the data cache. From this and the similar graph for the procedure cache, you can tune the amount of server cache and the balance between data and procedure cache.
Device I/O	Displays graphs and summary data for the number of disk accesses, as well as the rate of disk access. This data can help you optimize the load balancing across the server devices. This is another reason to name server devices after their physical disk partition names. As you watch the display of disk access rates for each server device, you need to be able to tell which server devices are attached to which controller.
Performance Summary	Shows you the overall performance of the entire SQL Server. Metrics include CPU use, transactions per second, network load, locking, and device I/O.
Performance Trends	Displays a continuous graph of the same performance measurements as the Performance Summary window.
Process Activity	Isolates one or a series of server processes for monitoring; you can watch the CPU usage and disk access rates for the chosen processes.
Process Detail	Provides more detail about a single server process.
Process List	Shows the current server processes and status, very similar to the output of the **sp_who** server command.
Transaction Activity	Provides a bar chart showing a summary of all transaction rates by transaction type. For example, you can use this to see what percentage of your transactions are being done as updates in place.

9.10 SQL Server Performance Tools

Several tools enable you to monitor and refine server performance that are built into the SQL Server.

sp_monitor

sp_monitor is a stored procedure that will output the current status of various server performance parameters. Typical output for two successive executions is shown below. Note that for each parameter there are two numbers. The first number is the measure of the parameter since the server was last started. The second number, in parentheses, is the measure of the parameter since the last time **sp_monitor** was executed. By making runs of **sp_monitor** at regular intervals, you can look at the change in a parameter over the interval and see the rate of change for the parameter. For example, you can take the data for total_write, which measures the number of disk writes made by the server. Since the server was last started, there have been 3,472,865 disk writes, but we are more interested in the performance of the server recently. Looking at the second set of output we see for total_write 3472895(30); note the value for seconds for the second set of output of 28 seconds. This tells you that in the last 28 seconds there have been 30 writes to disk by the server. This is very close to a server disk write rate of 1 per second.

You can run this stored procedure as a cron job at some regular interval during the operating hours of the server. This data can be output to a disk file on the server machine, and these files can be kept on disk for some period of time. When you run into a server performance problem, you can look through these files and see what the server has been doing in the recent past. This data is also useful for simply monitoring server performance before there is any problem.

```
1> sp_monitor
2> go
last_run                current_run                seconds
------------            ------------               -----------
Apr 1 1995  1:20PM      Apr 1 1995  1:21PM         35


cpu_busy                io_busy                    idle
-----------             -------------              --------
```

```
18489(0)-0%            74797(1)-2%            1707049(34)-97%

packets_received       packets_sent           packet_errors
----------------       -------------          -------------
 740556(10)            1056871(10)            0(0)

total_read       total_write    total_errors     connections
----------       -----------    -------------    ---------------
-
2141401(2)       3472865(83)    0(0)             19377(1)

(return status = 0)
...
...
...
1> sp_monitor
2> go
last_run               current_run            seconds
--------------         --------------         -----------
Apr 1 1995  1:21PM     Apr 1 1995  1:22PM     28

cpu_busy               io_busy                idle
----------             ----------             ---------
18491(2)-7%            74801(4)-14%           1707072(23)-82%

packets_received       packets_sent           packet_errors
 --------------        -------------          ---------------
-
 740562(6)              1057195(324)           0(0)

 total_read      total_write    total_errors     connections
 -----------     -----------    -------------    ---------------
-
2142628(1227)   3472895(30)     0(0)             19378(1)

(return status = 0)
```

set showplan

You can execute **set showplan** before executing a store procedure, SQL script, or individual statement, and the server will display the query plan that it will use to satisfy the query or queries. Note that **set showplan** doesn't display any activity that would go on due to triggers on the table(s) that would be activated by the queries you are executing. Further, as noted above for indexes, examining the query plan for a stored procedure manually may not help you track down the performance problems you are after. Recall that the query plan for a stored procedure is created once when the stored procedure is first created, and after that, only when the stored procedure is recompiled.

Remember, also, that server locking can lead to blocking, which will severely degrade server performance. The server locks each page as it is accessed until the user accessing that page is done with it. If a query wants over 200 pages for update, the server will simply escalate to a table lock. The table lock can block lots of users on a big table. This is yet another reason you must avoid queries that return lots of data if you are going to be able to improve performance. Note that for big tables, 200 pages is not much; thus, if you are doing queries that do updates, you may be locking the whole table each time they run. Queries that cause locking problems are another performance problem you need to watch out for. Keep in mind that escalating to a table lock will not be displayed by **set showplan,** so you won't detect this behavior when you examine the query plan manually.

set noexec

When you are trying to find a performance problem, it can be useful to examine the query plan without actually executing the query. You can get this behavior by executing **set noexec** along with **set showplan** before you execute the query.

set statistics

You can get the server to display the reads and writes for the query, both those to cache and those to disk. You get this behavior by executing **set statistics io on** or **set statistics time on**. You can use both of these at the same time.

9.11 Application-Transparent Server Tuning

While much of the preceding discussion involved ways to identify changes that need to be made to the application and the resulting queries, there are things that you can do to the SQL Server directly that can improve performance and require no changes to the application(s) at all. These changes are not going to cure problems with the application(s), but you should be aware of them. You probably can't tell what the overall effect of any of these would be without trying them out. Only then can you tell if one of these changes would have a real impact versus the performance problems inherent in the application(s). We discuss the following topics:

More Memory is Good
Solid State Device
File System Server Devices
Mirroring
More Server Devices are Better
vdevno and Performance

More Memory is Good

Most server performance and tuning work attempts to reduce the amount of physical disk access that must go on to satisfy a query. The more parts of the database you can squeeze into cache in server machine memory, the better. For the database pages that represent these objects, whether they are data, indexes, triggers, or stored procedures, the more that are in memory, the more that simply won't require any physical disk I/O to access. Try getting more server machine memory before trying much else.

Given the memory on the server machine, you will need to decide how to allocate it between data cache and procedure cache. Data cache is where the data pages are held while being read or changed. Procedure cache is where stored procedures are held. In both cases, the more times the server can find what it needs in memory (cache) the faster everything will go. The only way to really figure out the correct allocation for both kinds of cache is to use SQL Monitor and see how often the server finds what it needs in each cache (hit rate). You then alter the allocation by changing the percentage of SQL Server memory that will be allocated to procedure cache, using

sp_configure with the procedure cache option (20% is the default). The server will allocate all the memory needed for its own operation and then allocate 20 percent of the remaining memory to the procedure cache. This means you don't directly allocate the data cache; it gets whatever isn't allocated to the procedure cache.

All of this simply means that you should get as much memory as possible and then, after the server is up and running, adjust the allocations for data and procedure cache.

Solid State Device

This change simply takes the advice of "More memory is good" to its logical conclusion. A solid state device (SSD) is simply a server device that is supported physically in RAM rather than on a physical disk partition. This makes all access to the database objects in the SSD very fast. Using what you learn from SQL Monitor, you can determine which server devices are most heavily accessed and move them to an SSD. Frequently, you will find that *tempdb* is very heavily accessed, as are the transaction logs of the most popular databases on the server. If it is pretty obvious that one or a few databases or database segments are being hit much harder than the rest, you may realize a very significant increase in server performance by moving them to SSD.

File System Server Devices

As discussed in detail in Chapter 4, you don't want to assign server devices to file system files because the I/O is buffered and therefore you can't guarantee that the data is recoverable. For *tempdb,* you don't ever try to recover the database, so you can move it off to a file system server device and the buffered I/O will speed up access to *tempdb*. Often, it is the transaction log of *tempdb* that benefits most from such a move. Try this; if it doesn't improve things, just revert to the way it was. Since *tempdb* is cleared out each time the server is restarted, you can move it around from one server device to another much more easily than a user database.

Mirroring

Mirroring of server devices (and thereby, databases) has been discussed in detail in Chapter 4, and is done primarily to prevent server downtime and enhance recoverability. From a performance and tuning point of view, if you have a situation where you are reading from a database a great deal, you may benefit from the fact that the server can read in parallel from both physical devices that make up the server device and the mirror.

More Server Devices are Better

Many times the question comes up of why it is better or worse to have more or fewer server devices supported by any one physical disk. This translates into a question of how best to partition the physical disk. There are three reasons you want to use more partitions not fewer. Two of the reasons will benefit you in your performance and tuning efforts.

- More partitions of a physical disk, with a server device assigned to each partition, make it more meaningful and therefore more useful to identify which server device is being used the most. You can determine which server device is most heavily used by using SQL Monitor (see above), but if you only have one huge server device assigned to all the space on the physical disk, that could mean any of the databases on the huge server device has a problem. Your ability to monitor, identify, and fix server performance problems is much better with more granular observations. You get more granular performance data because you have more server devices. Certainly, this can be taken too far, but for SunOS you only have eight partitions maximum, with two of those unavailable for server devices (see Chapter 1). Using six partitions for six server devices is better than just one huge partition and server device.

- Internally, the SQL Server maintains a queue of access requests for each server device. The fewer the number of server devices to handle all the server device access requests, the more that pile up waiting for each server device. More server devices help to minimize any waiting that would go on due to these internal queues.

- This reason relates more to preventing server downtime and enhancing server recovery, but that, too, is a form of improved server performance. When a physical disk goes bad, usually only a piece of it does. The rest of the disk may be fine. The fewer partitions and server devices you have on a single physical disk, the more of your database is lost for any single disk problem. If you have six server devices on six physical disk partitions and the disk develops a bad block in one partition, only the one server device is lost. With only one server device for the whole physical disk, all of the database(s) on that server device are lost, even if only one block of the disk goes bad.

vdevno and Performance

This section is related to the second bullet, above. While the SQL Server maintains a queue for each server device, it also checks the list of server devices to see if an I/O request has been satisfied. The server checks this list in order of *vdevno*. If the server makes an I/O request of server device 10 (i.e., *vdevno* = 10) and then wants to check to see if that I/O request has been completed, the server has to first check server devices 0 through 9. If the server device in question were 1, this process would be faster. You can identify the server devices that support the most I/O activity and see which database segments are supported by those server devices. You could try shuffling the *vdevno* values so that the most heavily accessed server devices have the lowest possible values. But, in order to change the *vdevno* value of a server device, you have to drop the server device and then do a new **disk init**. This also means dropping the server device that currently has the lower *vdevno* value, as well as whatever database segments were supported on both the server devices.

This sort of tuning is best done when first installing or rebuilding the server. The performance gains from this sort of change are not great, and the work involved in shifting existing *vdevno* values around is considerable, as is the risk that you won't get everything back quickly.

9.12 Preventing Downtime

Preventing server downtime may not seem like a server performance issue to you, but it is. Your users will always want better server performance, but they say that assuming that the server is always available. You have the unpopular job of getting in the way by running **dbcc** checks, making database and transaction log dumps, mirroring server devices, and so on, to prevent downtime. Remember that any downtime lowers the overall average server performance, and all the things that you do to prevent server downtime are just as important, if not more so, than efforts that might improve performance, especially if those efforts involve any risk of server downtime.

9.13 Servermap and Performance and Tuning

While you are going through the process of analyzing what is wrong with the performance of your server and how to improve it, don't forget the servermap (see Chapter 5). You should examine the servermap for the server and make sure it is up-to-date before you go any farther. Make sure the segmentation for all the databases has been maintained properly. Look for databases that you don't remember or segments of known databases that you don't remember. Look at the database creation dates to be sure nobody has somehow gotten 'sa' access and recreated any of the databases, which could indicate the database was not recreated with the proper segmentation for performance, not to mention who is doing this to your server.

Reviewing the servermap should also remind you to check that the hardware configuration of the server machine is the same as you thought it was when you first prepared the servermap. You should ask the server machine SA to verify the memory, disks, controllers, OS patches, and anything else regarding the configuration of the server machine. You should also verify that there haven't been any network changes recently, such as new server machines being put on the network that could slow your server down as it interacts with the rest of the database system.

Finally, you need to think about the overall load balancing of the server. Using the outputs from SQL Monitor, look for the most heavily used server devices and relate that to the disk partitions of the servermap to determine what is using those disks so much. Reviewing the servermap should also help you identify your options for curing the problem. The servermap is ideal for determining what is running on the less heavily accessed disk partitions and where you might move segments of a database to improve performance, where you might add database space to create a new clustered index, and so on.

Chapter 10

Capacity Planning

The need for capacity planning is almost always overlooked. You guess how big a few of the databases on the server will be, get some vague comments from the application developers, and order the machine. You will need more disk space before the machine hits your receiving dock. Often, if not every time, you will inherit the machine(s) and have had no input as to their initial configuration. At the same time, no matter how you get stuck with the poor decisions of others, you invariably get a chance to change at least part of it.

;-)

> It is the end of the business cycle. The server crashes. You need to replace the old worn out disks and controllers. You need more disk space. You keep getting errors from the old disks. You know it's bad this time because the CIO has decided to watch you recover the server. He/she sits in your cubicle and pretends to take an interest in you as a human being. You get tense. The CIO, after exhausting the small talk, turns to you and asks, "What do you need to prevent this in future?" That is the time to have a good answer. Be prepared to lay out the server the way it should be done (that is, your way). You will get a chance; you just never know when that chance will come. Be prepared to tell the CIO what you need. At least be prepared to figure out what you need.

All too often the little capacity planning that is discussed is endless, detailed equations of how to figure out, to the nearest kilobyte, how big a table will be. You then order disks at 2 Gb each. The table will probably grow exponentially anyway. You need to think about the capacity of your database system to support the business. This does not mean the size of individual tables or indexes. It means the capacity to support the applications, their backups, their development, and test environments, as well as the ability to support maintenance of the whole system.

We discuss capacity planning from the following perspectives:

10.1	The Overall Database System
10.2	The Individual Server
10.3	Real World Example
10.4	Capacity Planning for The Database System

10.1 The Overall Database System

You are used to thinking of the capacity of your server. As your server grows and other servers are added to your database system, you need to think of the capacity of the whole system. You can't support your business on one server on one machine any more. You will need to consider the ability of your database system to provide the services as listed below to support your business. Note that you will need to move data between multiple servers all the time. You must ensure that you can move files between the server machines that make up your database system. This may or may not require that all the server machines are made by the same vendor.

Primary OLTP Server
Standby Server
Decision Support Server (DSS) or Report Server
Development Server
Test Server
DBCC Server
Previous Release Server
Replication Server
Support for the Database System

Primary OLTP Server

You will need a server to support the OLTP applications that support your business. This server should have the capacity to support all the functions described in the following sections. This server should be configured to support a high rate of small transactions with a limited number of indexes on each table. Access to this server should be very limited to prevent ad hoc user queries that can cause server performance to slow to a crawl.

Standby Server

Depending on the nature of your business, you may need a standby server that you can fail over to in a short period of time. How fast you need to fail over depends on the cost to your business of downtime. You also must determine if such a standby system needs to support all the databases of the primary or just a subset of critical databases that would allow the most important business functions to continue until the primary was repaired. You may or may not need the same capacity on the standby server as on the primary OLTP server. A big factor in this is whether the standby server is required to replace the primary OLTP server for an indefinite period of time. If so, the standby server should be virtually identical to the primary OLTP server in terms of processor power, memory, and disk space. Keeping the standby server in sync with the OLTP server is a labor-intensive process.

Decision Support Server (DSS) or Report Server

One of the fundamental things you must do to improve and maintain the performance of the primary OLTP server is force all (absolutely ALL!) ad hoc or decision support queries to a separate server. This decision support server (DSS) or reporting server must be kept in sync with the primary OLTP server. This can be done by periodically loading database dumps from the primary server. This method is fine as long as the lag time between the primary and DSS server is acceptable to the users of the DSS server. If you dump the databases on the primary every day, the DSS server will be behind the primary by a full day, because it has no further updates between the daily database loads. Another method is to dump the transaction log of each of the databases on the primary and apply these transaction log dumps to the databases on the DSS server. This process will keep the DSS server up-to-date to within the interval between primary server database transaction log dumps. Note that either of these methods will require considerable disk space capacity on both the primary and DSS server machines. Further, these same techniques would be used to keep the standby server in sync with the primary OLTP server. The standby server will also require the same disk space capacity as the primary and DSS servers to support synchronization of the servers. Keeping the DSS server in sync with the OLTP server is a labor-intensive process.

Development Server

You must not allow the primary OLTP server in your database system to be used to support any form of application development or testing. You must provide a separate server dedicated to supporting the needs of application development. This server should have sufficient capacity to support copies of the databases that exist on the primary server. Certainly, such a development server does not need the capacity of the primary for such things as mirroring or for storing database or transaction log dumps to ensure recoverability. Still, the development server must have sufficient disk capacity to support copies of however many of the primary server's databases are involved in the applications being developed. In general, you should assume that all the databases on the primary server may need to be loaded on the development server. Also, the development server will need disk space to support moving large datasets into and out of the server, as well as any logical dumps that are very useful in the development environment since database objects change frequently as application development moves along.

Test Server

Depending on the nature of your database system and the complexity of the applications that are being developed, you should consider another separate server to support application testing. This server should be sized similarly to the development server. You would perform final acceptance testing of applications by using copies of the primary databases on this server. Having the test server separate from the development server supports realistic performance testing of a given application without interference from development work going on for other applications. Further, application testing on a separate server will not delay development work.

DBCC Server

As the databases on the primary server grow and as your business expands across the country and around the world, you will not have time to perform much, if any, maintenance on the primary server. Your databases do not have to become very large before a complete **dbcc** run will take many hours to complete—and you still should fix the errors uncovered by the **dbcc** run before making a database dump. Your business can't afford to be down long enough to allow all this activity to go on. You will need to set up yet another separate server to support **dbcc** runs. This server, the DBCC server, supports **dbcc** runs, loading old dumps, experiments like logical dump times, striping across multiple drives, and so on.

Previous Release Server

As you upgrade the servers in your database system to the latest release, you reach the point where all the servers are at the new release. You should still have a server at the previous release to retrieve data from dumps made prior to the upgrade. Depending on the nature of your business and the time between database dumps, you may need a server at the previous release level for a year or more. Such a server does not have to be a large powerful machine, and it could even be installed on the DBCC server machine. Still, this server will need sufficient disk space to hold the largest database from which you might need to retrieve data.

Replication Server

Replication Server will require a dedicated server machine of its own. You certainly can install the product on one of your other server machines, but the performance of the SQL Server on that machine may suffer. You will also have an easier time maintaining your replication system if most or all of the components run on a dedicated server machine. Note that Replication Server requires a SQL Server database to hold information about other Replication Servers, subscriptions, and so on. Hence, the machine dedicated to Replication Server will also be supporting a SQL Server to hold this database. You will need to consider the performance of this dedicated machine because Replication Server requires considerable CPU cycles to carry out its functions. Further, you will need to size the disk space for Replication Server to support storing transactions (stable queues) for whatever period of time your system requires. The longer you need to be able to operate while one of the nodes in your replication system is down, the more disk space you will need (see Chapter 2).

Support for the Database System

You will need to consider the support you will require for the database system. Although this is often overlooked, it is vital. You can downsize to client-server all you want, but you will need support from various persons and/or organizations. Your database system will require support from tape operators for database and file system dumps, restores, and archiving of tapes off site. You will need sufficient SA support to install, repair, and modify all the server machines in your system. You will need sufficient facilities to house, air-condition, power, and keep secure all of your server machines and their data. All of these support considerations need to be compared against your business needs. All of these support functions must have the capacity to support all the servers of your system for all the hours your business requires. To expect the system to be available at almost all hours is a major capacity planning problem as your database system grows and your business grows.

10.2 The Individual Server

For each of the SQL servers in your database system, you need to consider many factors, listed below, that will require various amounts of capacity. Here, we are primarily concerned with disk space because that is always in short supply. You are encouraged to waste your time arguing about the merits of various processor architectures (this is a joke!). You need to be more practical. There aren't that many high-end platforms that you are really going to consider for your mission-critical business applications. Further, benchmarks are well known to be virtually useless in determining the ability of any platform to support your applications in your environment. If all the other issues surrounding capacity planning for your system are so completely figured out that which processor you are running is all that is left, you are way ahead of most of the world. We discuss various issues regarding disk space on a given individual SQL Server. This issue will drive most, if not all, of the practical capacity problems. If you find you are truly CPU bound, then you can consider changing platforms, but you will still need all the disk space you needed before.

Databases
Number of Segments
Mirrors
Memory
File System Space
Database Dumps to Disk
Transaction Log Dumps to Disk
Tuning
Moving Data Around
Logical Dumps to Disk
Inter-server Needs
Server Machine Limitations
Replication Server
Server Machine Tape Drives

Databases

At a minimum, you should have planned database capacity for your server. You should have a good idea how big all the databases on your server need to be. If this is an existing server and you need to look at capacity planning for the future, you have the existing databases and some history of how fast they grow. If this is a new server installation, you need to know what the most important applications are that the new server will support. The application developers should have some idea how much space their product(s) require, although their idea of a big business environment and yours may be shockingly different.

Number of Segments

The number of segments needed by each database is where you probably tuned out when you did your capacity planning. You ordered enough disks to support the total size of all the databases and a little more and that was it. You need to think more about what you will be doing with the disk space. See Chapter 4 for more discussion of segments.

If the applications need to have any user-defined segments, those segments ought to be kept on server devices separate from the rest of the database for performance reasons. This means you need more server devices, which in turn means more disk partitions, and that can mean more physical disks.

You also need to factor in how these database segments are going to be spread over the controllers. For example, the server devices supporting the transaction log segment (*logsegment*) and the partitions supporting their mirrors should not be on physical disks that are connected to the same controller. You must have some idea how large the segments of the database will be and how they need to be separated from each other over controllers. Also, you don't want to place more than one heavily accessed segment of any database on a given disk or, ideally, one controller. If you need to separate a segment for performance reasons, adding another heavily accessed segment to the same physical disk will just reduce the I/O throughput. You need to know which segments are most heavily accessed and when. At the same time you can't predict most of this very well.

You need to be aware of segments as well as overall database space when laying out or expanding a server. Once you have some performance history, you can further expand your server's disk space to support segmentation refinements to further improve performance. Note that it may take considerably more disk space to support the existing and near-term growth of separated database segments than to support just the overall database size.

Mirrors

Mirroring will take a little or a lot of disk space, depending on how much of the database you mirror. See Chapter 4 for details of the mechanics of mirroring. You should consider not only the recovery issues but also your ability to maintain the mirroring of your server devices. You should consider mirroring all of the database segments in your server if only to simplify the maintenance of the mirrors. If you mirror only a select set of server devices, you will constantly have to check that any space added to the databases is still mirrored. Even if a database is static and could be recovered completely from previous database dumps, you should consider mirroring the database to ensure that your server could continue operating through a disk failure.

Memory

The amount of memory you have installed in the server machine will directly impact the server performance. In general, you can't have too much memory. The amount of memory needed is equal to all the database objects you would like to have in cache (memory) at all times. You should have memory equal to the size of all the non-clustered indexes in the server. If the majority of the queries are covered (see Chapter 9) by these indexes, then all the data pages needed for the queries will be in cache which will greatly reduce the amount of physical disk I/O that must be performed. You also need memory for the procedure cache which will contain stored procedures. If at all possible, buy as much memory as the server machine will allow. Memory is one of the cheapest and fastest ways to improve server preformance with no impact on existing applications or database structure.

File System Space

File system disk space is often overlooked. You left that to the server machine SA person, who assumes you need only enough file system space to support the server machine operating system and some swap space. You need to reconsider. You will need file system space to support all of the SQL Server files and any other products you need on the server. The server files include all the files necessary to install the server as well as various optional files for character sets. When you upgrade from one server release to another you will need sufficient file system space to hold another set of installation files for the new release (see Chapter 13). You will need to keep all the files for the previous release until the upgrade is complete and you are convinced you don't need to regress. You will need duplicate sets of files anytime you upgrade any of the related server products. Note that you must determine the actual space available on disk before you can perform any capacity planning. Depending on the specifics of your platform, you may have 10 percent less disk space after formatting.

Database Dumps to Disk

As part of your recovery plan, you will be dumping the databases in your server. You can dump them to tape, but you should consider dumping them to disk. Dumping them to disk is faster than tape, which frees up the server and allows other server users to get their work done sooner. Dumping to disk allows you to capture all the database dumps to tape at once with a file system dump done at the server machine operating system level (see Chapter 8). You may need to move database dumps from one server machine to another for various reasons. This means you may also need file system space for database dumps from other servers. Dumping databases to disk takes a great deal of disk space because you now need enough file system space to hold copies of all the databases you need to dump.

Transaction Log Dumps to Disk

Your server will need to dump the transaction log of various databases periodically (see Chapter 8 for details). Dumping the transaction log(s) to disk is a good idea; they will be done more quickly than if dumped to tape, which means you can dump the transaction log more often and disturb the server users for briefer periods. You need to decide on your backup and recovery plan. This plan will describe how often you dump the transaction log and how often you dump the databases to disk and to tape. You also need to know how long to keep the transaction log dumps on disk. You certainly need to keep all the transaction log dumps made since the last database dump, but you may also need the previous set, in case the most recent database dump is not usable for some reason. You need to examine the size of the transaction log dumps for each of your databases throughout your business cycle (day, week, month, quarter, year) to decide how much file system space is required to hold all the transaction log dumps you need according to your recovery plan.

The tape drives on your server machine are not perfect and will fail from time to time. You should plan additional file system space to hold the additional transaction log dumps that would pile up while you had a failed tape drive replaced. Also, if your dumping of the transaction log is delayed for any reason, you will have a very large transaction log dump when you resume dumping, and your file system will need to have the free space to absorb the large dump file. Note that in the event of such a failure you could move the transaction log dumps to any other machine in your system, but you still need to have such space available even if only on a remote machine. Depending on your recovery plan and how you handle the process of making tape dumps, you may not have a tape operator on duty through weekends or holidays to change tapes. This is another case when you would need extra file system space for transaction log dumps.

;-)

Your server has been running normally for months with transaction log dumps being made to disk every hour during the business day. Suddenly the transaction log dumps grow quickly to twice and then three times their normal size. You will eventually find out that a new application was applied to the databases on your server. This new application had the interesting habit of dropping and creating any required stored procedures every time a user ran the application. This resulted in a very large increase in the logged activity in the databases. The application developers didn't realize this, because the part of their application that did this was an "off-the-shelf" module supplied by another division of your own company. You had been able to store a week's worth of transaction log dumps on the existing file system space, but now can't keep even two days' worth before the file system is full. You have to change your recovery plan immediately. The point here is that a lack of disk space can cripple your operation very quickly, and it isn't just a lack of database space that you need to worry about.

Tuning

After the server is up and running you may, sooner or later, find that you need to either add or change some of your indexes. This will need to be done as you try various experiments to tune the performance of your server. Consider that if you need to create a new clustered index on a table, you will need to add disk space to the database equal to about 120 percent of the size of the table.

;-)

Your server runs a little slower all the time. An analysis reveals that for reasons best known to themselves, the original database designers decided not to create a clustered index on one of the largest tables on the server. Over time, the table and the other databases on the server have grown to fill almost all the space available. Now, to improve performance you need to create the clustered index, but you don't have that kind of disk space available. You are now in the position of needing to add disks just to create the index. Moreover, these disks will be empty after the new index is created, because the process of creating a clustered index essentially builds a copy of all the data in the table in the new sort order and when that is complete, drops the original set of data. As a side issue, your server machine does not have any more room to accept more disk controllers or more disks. You start to think that capacity planning is important after all.

As part of your efforts to improve the performance of your server, you may need to build more indexes or drop and recreate others. Either way, you will need to be able to add enough disk space to the database segment(s) that support these indexes before you can create new indexes. You should allow for this in your overall capacity planning because the space to perform these index creations is so large. Without this kind of capacity, you may not be able to do some fundamental performance tuning.

Moving Data Around

Your server may need to import and/or export data to/from other servers or systems. Frequently, you will need to dump/load portions of the database to/from disk files. Whether these files originate on your server or not, you need to have sufficient file system space to support whatever quantity of data you expect. If you need to import a 10-Mb file and store copies of this file for a week, you need to have 70 Mb of file system space for this data. You also need to understand the impact to your business of any failure during the process of moving this data through your database system. If the network is down for a day, do you need to store the same files for a longer period of time? If so, you would need to plan for more file system space.

Logical Dumps to Disk

You must plan on being able to retrieve objects or data from your database dumps. For various reasons, you will need to do this without reloading a dump into an existing database on the server. If you need to retrieve ten rows of a user table from a database dump made a month ago, you can't just load the dump into the existing database because that would wipe out all the database changes made in the last month. The database dumps that you make to tape or disk, using SQL Server, are physical dumps. They are a simple copy of everything in the database and the transaction log. When (note that we don't say "if") you need to retrieve an object from the database dump, there is no way to do this directly. You must load the entire database somewhere on your server, or on another server in your system, and then retrieve the object from this database. Clearly, this will require a lot of database disk space in order to be able to load a complete copy of your largest database. This process is also very slow and requires creating the database on the same or another server.

The alternative is to make logical dumps of your databases. A logical dump means that the definition of each object is retrieved from the server and dumped to a file system file. This file can be used to rebuild the object(s) on the same or other servers. In fact, the logical dump of a database object is independent of the server version and hardware platforms because it is the Transact-SQL definition of the object. You need to plan enough file system space to support whatever logical dump plan you deem appropriate. Such a plan may call for a logical dump once a week or only when significant changes are made to the data or objects in a given database. The ability to make logical dumps is not supported by Sybase SQL Server. You would have to install a third-party software product such as DataTools SQL BackTrack™ (see Chapter 8 for details).

Inter-server Needs

The servers in your database system may need to transfer large files among themselves. For example, you may keep a copy of a database on another server as a standby in case the primary database or server fails. One way to do this is to move the transaction log dumps of the primary database to the secondary server machine and apply the transaction log dumps to the database on the secondary server. This requires sufficient file system space on both server machines to store enough transaction log dumps to span the longest interval you expect to go between transfers between server machines. Note that for smaller databases you may perform this process by periodically transferring a full database dump rather than a set of transaction log dumps.

Server Machine Limitations

You need to think about the limitations of the server machine itself. Although you need to be aware of things like the CPU and memory of the server machine, here we continue to focus on the disk space capacity of the server machine. This takes several forms.

First, you need to know how many disk controllers the machine can accept. This number and the maximum number of physical disks that can be attached to each controller without causing an I/O bottleneck will tell you the maximum disk space you can ever have.

Second, you need to consider the physical space where the server machine is installed. You will need more rack space to install more disks. If the existing rack(s) are full, you will need to add a new rack or racks to have room to install any new disks. Remember that just because the server machine will accept more disk doesn't mean you can put them in. You should consider this as part of your capacity planning.

Replication Server

If you plan on installing Replication Server on your server, you need to take that into account in your capacity planning. We discuss what Replication Server is and what it does in Chapter 2. Briefly, Replication Server requires what is called a stable queue to store transactions while they are being moved from the primary database to the replicate database(s). This stable queue is assigned to one or more raw disk partitions similarly to the way server disk devices are supported by physical disk raw partitions. You need to have an estimate of how large a stable queue you will need for your server. The size of the stable queue you need is based on how long you estimate Replication Server will have to function while part of the replication system is unavailable (the network, for example). It is not unreasonable to need 1 Gb or more for a stable queue for production systems. Further, while the current release of Replication Server does not support mirroring of the stable queue, that feature may be available in soon-to-be-released versions of the product. You should plan on having disk space equal to twice the size of the stable queue you require.

Server Machine Tape Drives

You need to think about the tape drives on your server machine. You may think this is a minor problem. You may be wrong. If you are dumping multiple databases to tape, you need to think about how many of your databases will fit on one tape. If the total size of all the databases on the server that you need to dump to tape exceeds the capacity of your tape drive, you will have to wait for the first tape to fill up, then eject it and insert a second tape. This means considerably more time and more possible errors than a single tape dump would entail. Even if you plan on dumping your databases to disk and capture them all with a file system dump to tape at the operating system level, you should consider how much will fit on one tape. You pay a lot for somebody to be available to insert that second tape. Further, in a disaster situation it is much easier to be able to make a dump on the fly if you need only one tape to do it.

Another factor to consider is the overall time it takes your server to make dumps to tape or disk. If your business runs around the clock, you will have a narrow window for daily database and file system dumps. If you can't make the complete dump within that window of time, you will have to change your dump plan. The speed of your tape drives as well as their capacity is a factor in your capacity planning.

10.3 Real-World Example

The preceding discussion may seem unreasonably complex. We consider a real-world example. The server described below is typical of a large production system. We discuss real-world needs as they follow each of the sections described in the previous section. We first discuss the capacity planning required for the basic database system that supports one primary OLTP server. For each server in the database system we discuss the general operational needs of the server, the disk capacity needed and the server machine performance requirements. We then discuss the capacity planning issues surrounding the primary OLTP server in detail in the next section.

Capacity Planning Case Study—the Overall Database System

We consider these capacity issues:

Primary OLTP server
Standby server
Decision support server (DSS) or report server
Development server
Test server
DBCC server
Previous release server
Replication server

Primary OLTP server

The primary OLTP server supports the mission critical applications that support your business. The OLTP server is where the majority of your day-to-day on-line processing occurs. It is the primary site of the data that represents your business. Your users are attached to this server to perform their business tasks. You must not allow users to perform anything but the OLTP that your business runs on. You must optimize the indexes on this server to support OLTP, that is, short, fast transactions that are quickly committed to minimize blocking and maximize throughput.

Your primary OLTP server is supporting 17 databases. The details of the disk space for this machine are discussed below. The total size of all the server devices set up for the server is 12 Gb, with 8 Gb actually assigned to databases at the moment. This leaves 4 Gb for growth of the existing databases. You may think that 4 Gb is a lot of free space. When you consider the number of segments of the largest databases and that each needs to grow on a server device connected to a separate controller, the space free for each of those segments is only a portion of the total free space. Also, when the largest production database is 5 Gb and you are adding space to that database, as needed, in 100 Mb chunks, 4 Gb doesn't seem like very much at all. Further, all of the database segments are mirrored, and one-quarter of the available physical disks are assigned to the operating system and to supporting file systems. The primary OLTP server has 16 2.4 Gb physical disks, with four of these disks attached to one controller. Of the four disks attached to each controller, one disk is assigned to supporting file systems. This provides more controllers to spread the server devices over than a configuration where all the disks for file systems were assigned to one controller. Overall, after formatting and so on, the server machine has 32 Gb of disk space. Of that 32 Gb, 8 Gb (one-quarter) supports file systems, the largest being the directories that store transaction log dumps and database dumps. This leaves 24 Gb for the server itself with 12 Gb assigned to server devices and the other 12 Gb used for mirrors of all the server devices. Recall that you want to use a whole physical disk for server devices and a whole physical disk for the mirrors of those same physical devices.

The OLTP server machine needs the CPU, memory, network interfaces, and so on necessary to support the response time and number of concurrent users that your business applications require. We focus on capacity planning of disk space in the following discussion. You need to assess the capacity of the server machine in other ways as well. You must estimate how many users will need to use the server at one time and use that to plan for sufficient memory, not only to support that many user connections but also the data and procedure cache needed to support the databases. Overall, you need to know what kind of transaction rate is needed and whether your server machine can supply the processing power needed to keep up.

Standby server

The standby server (PSS) and its server machine should be identical to the primary machine as far as CPUs and memory. The term "hot standby" is often abused. To really be a hot standby, the server would have to be capable of detecting a failure on the primary and immediately switching over to the hot standby with virtually no interruption in service. This is hard to achieve. A standby machine will have to be capable of supporting the full business load for some period of time. If you require that the standby server support all your production applications for an indefinite period of time, you need to make this server machine as powerful as the primary. In any case, the standby machine, however warm you think it is, will need the same amount of disk space as the primary because it will have a complete copy of all the production databases and should be mirrored just as the primary. The standby machine will be expected to support all production functions that the primary does and therefore should have the same file system space as the primary. You can reduce this to some extent, but the savings in hardware will be small compared to the complexity of switching over to the standby if it isn't set up similarly to the primary. Further, when you need to fail over to the standby, you really can't control how long you will need to stay on the standby. You must consider the trade-off between hardware for the standby now versus the later cost to your business of depending on a slower standby machine for some period of time.

To support the business in the same way as the primary does, the standby machine needs the same amount of disk space, that is, 32 Gb, and it should be assigned to controllers in the same way as for the primary. The layout of the disks and controllers should be identical to that of the primary. You can then use the same scripts for creating server devices (**disk init**) and databases (**p_dbcreate**) on both machines, which is a significant time-saver.

The processing capacity requirements of the standby server machine will depend on how you intend to recover from a failure of the primary. If you plan on running on the standby only long enough to complete repairs on the primary, then the standby may not need to have the processing capacity of the primary. If you choose to have a less powerful standby machine, then you need to make sure your users understand this. You will also need to be ready to repair the primary OLTP server quickly, because your business will suffer as long as you are running on the standby. You should plan on having the same server machine performance capacity on the standby as you have on the primary. This means you can fail over to the standby, and your business can function normally for the indefinite future while the primary is repaired.

Decision Support Server (DSS) or Report Server

The decision support server (DSS or report server) should be able to support a full copy of all the production databases that are on the primary OLTP server. The DSS server should be used for all user queries that are not strictly OLTP. If you allow users to do anything but OLTP on your primary server, you will suffer intolerable performance degradation. Worse, you won't have any way of curing the performance problems because you won't have any idea what is running on the server at any given time. Any one user could log in and start scanning all the tables on the server. The DSS server should have a very different set of indexes optimized for decision support queries. These indexes will be very different, and there should be more of them than for the primary OLTP machine.

Since the DSS machine is not used to directly support the business transactions, you don't need to mirror every database segment. Further, if you have a failure on this server, you can recreate the database and reload from dumps from the primary OLTP server. Therefore, you only need half the server disk space of the OLTP server, but you should still have the same file system capacity. You will need this capacity to support the database and transaction log dumps to disk that you will need to apply to the DSS server to keep its databases in sync with the primary OLTP server. For this example, that means you need 20 Gb of disk space, with 8 Gb supporting file systems and 12 Gb assigned to server devices. Note that you always need to mirror the master device. The DSS server may not need the same layout of disks per controller as the OLTP/PSS servers do. You will save a great deal of time creating databases on the DSS server if you have the same number of physical disks supporting databases on both the DSS and OLTP servers. If you partition these disks on the DSS server the same way as on the OLTP server, you can simply dump the definition of a database on the OLTP server (using **p_dbcreate**), edit in the different server device names, and create the database on the DSS server. See Chapter 11 for a full discussion of this process.

The DSS server machine performance capacity you need is debatable. If your users require fast turnaround on their decision support queries, you may need the same level of CPU capacity as you need for the primary server. Usually, this is not the case because decision support users can wait longer for a response. Generally, a longer response time is expected for these sorts of queries, because you can't optimize server performance for queries you can't see ahead of time. You will probably be fine using a server machine with significantly less processing power than the primary OLTP server.

Development server

The development server is for application development work. It needs to have sufficient disk capacity to support whatever development work your organization is supporting. Assuming that this development server is supporting development of applications that will eventually run on the OLTP server, you need the disk capacity to hold a complete copy of the databases currently on the OLTP server, allow for the growth of the existing databases on the OLTP, disk space for any and all versions of the software under development, and space for large datasets that are frequently needed from other sources to populate tables during development. If you have a separate test server (as described in the next section), you should make sure that all final testing of applications is done on the test server. This will allow development work to move ahead while final testing is done in a separate controlled environment independent of the sometimes wild and uncontrollable environment that is necessary for application development to proceed.

Given all this, the development server should have 20 Gb of disk space: 8 Gb for file system space and 12 Gb for the databases. Note that you need to determine if you can support applications development for servers other than the OLTP server on this single development server machine. You are better off to have a single machine dedicated to the development server for each large OLTP server in your system. You don't want developers working on too many applications on the same server because they may block each other and can slow the server down substantially. Also, developers have a habit of crashing the server and oftentimes the server machine itself. You must keep all development work off the OLTP server and the OLTP server machine.

The development server machine does not require the same number of disk controllers as the OLTP server. Again, you will save a great deal of time creating databases on the development server if you have the same number of physical disks supporting databases on both the development and OLTP servers. If you partition these disks on the development server the same way as on the OLTP server, you can simply dump the definition of a database on the OLTP server (using **p_dbcreate**), edit in the different server device names, and create the database on the development server.

The required performance of the development server machine is again debatable. You need to run the applications at a reasonable rate to assess performance of the queries that make up the application, but supplying too much server machine performance can actually fool the developers into thinking the application doesn't need tuning. Generally, the development server machine will be a machine that is not the latest technology; rather, it will be a machine that was new a few years ago and became a development server machine after being replaced by the latest OLTP server machine.

Test server

The test server is similar to the development server but even less controlled. Your database system may not require a separate test server. You need to assess the development process that you are supporting. Frequently, there is a need to quickly prototype an application or a modification to an existing application, such efforts need to go on as quickly as possible. This work should be done on the development server. Once the application is ready to roll out to the production system, it should move to the test server, where it can be run against a current copy of the data on the OLTP server. This provides a final test environment that is isolated from other development activities. With a separate test server you can test one application while development continues on other applications on the development server.

The disk space requirements of the test server are the same as for the development server: You will need to support a copy of all the databases on the OLTP server and have room for database and transaction log dumps from the OLTP server to keep the data on the test server up-to-date. For our example database system, the test server would need 20 Gb of disk space, 8 Gb for file system space and 12 Gb for database space. As with the development server, you will save a great deal of time creating databases on the test server if you have the same number of physical disks supporting databases on both the test and OLTP servers. If you partition these disks on the test server the same way as on the OLTP server, you can simply dump the definition of a database on the OLTP server (using **p_dbcreate**), edit in the different server device names, and create the database on the test server.

As with the development server machine, the performance required for the test server machine does not have to be incredible.

DBCC server

For a database system that supports even one large database, you will need a dedicated DBCC server. In an ideal world, you would have sufficient downtime whenever you needed it to run a full set of database consistency checks (**dbcc**) on each database before you make each database dump. As database size grows, the time it takes to make a **dbcc** run and the database dump grows as well. Soon your business can't afford to have the system off line for the hours that it would take to run **dbcc**s before each dump, let alone to run **dbcc**s again to fix any corruptions found in the database. See Chapter 8 for more discussion of these factors. At that point, you need a server where you can load the database dumps of your production databases and run the full **dbcc** set without interfering with your business. A DBCC server is also a good place to load older database dumps when you need to retrieve data or database object information that has been lost from the production system. Note that Sybase SQL Server does not support dumping or recovering anything smaller than the entire database. For a large database, this can be a real problem, and a DBCC server is a good place to retrieve such information. Further, the very act of loading a database into the DBCC server can serve another function within your recovery plan. If you can load the database from a database dump made to tape, you are verifying that the dump tape is good.

The DBCC server will need enough disk space to support all the databases on the OLTP server and any other databases that are large enough to require **dbcc** runs on a separate machine. For our example, the DBCC server needs 20 Gb of disk space, with 8 Gb for file system space and 12 Gb for database space. As always, you will save a great deal of time creating databases on the DBCC server if you have the same number of physical disks supporting databases on both the maintenance and OLTP servers. If you partition these disks on the DBCC server the same way as on the OLTP server, you can simply dump the definition of a database on the OLTP server (using **p_dbcreate**), edit in the different server device names, and create the database on the DBCC server.

The performance of the DBCC server machine can be significantly less than that of the other server machines discussed so far. Simply doing **dbcc** runs over and over does not require large amounts of processing power. You need to have a dedicated server machine for this server so the **dbcc** runs don't interfere with other server work. You don't need a very fast server machine for this work.

Previous release server

As your database system moves along, you will upgrade the servers from one release to the next. While most releases are backward compatible, not all of them are. Clearly, the relevant example is that of upgrading from Sybase SQL Server 4.9.x to System 10. All the database dumps made when 4.9.x was running are no longer useable with System 10. You can't recover any data from the 4.9.x dumps without maintaining a server at the 4.9.x level. You should be ready to maintain a server at the previous release level whenever you consider upgrading the servers in your database system. Always verify that the upgrade will work with the pre-upgrade dumps that you have (see Chapter 13).

A previous release server would need only enough disk capacity to support the largest database dump you think you might need for recovery before the System 10 upgrade. For our example, the largest database is 5 Gb, so the previous release server should have 10 Gb of disk space to support this database and the file systems needed to support a 4.9.x SQL Server. Note that you may be able to run this server on one of the other server machines in your system, specifically, the DBCC server.

The performance of the server machine to support a previous release version of the server is not an issue. This server is only for loading database dumps and retrieving data.

Replication server

If your database system is going to include the use of Replication Server, you need to consider the capacity planning issues regarding the product. You aren't going to find any accurate performance information about Replication Server because it depends too much on your individual servers, the transaction load on those servers, how much of that load is being replicated, network load, and the performance of each server machine involved in the Replication Server System. You should consider a dedicated server machine to support Replication Server and the associated SQL Server that it requires (see Chapter 2 for more details).

The disk space needed for the Replication Server machine depends entirely on the number and size of the stable devices required to store all the transactions that Replication Server must store during the replication process. There are many factors that go into determining the size of the stable devices required, but for our example, you can assume that the Replication Server machine needs 10 Gb of disk space: 4 Gb for file system space and 6 Gb for the stable devices. Note also that if you are using Replication Server in your database system, you should plan on supporting at least one and perhaps two development Replication Servers. You need a development Replication Server environment to test the process of creating subscriptions, the time it takes for subscriptions to materialize for large tables, and how to recover from the crash of any of the components of Replication Server. You would have to add more disk space to support the Replication Server development environment on the development server machines involved.

The performance required for the Replication Server machine will depend on the amount of data that is being replicated and how fast your users need to see each transaction replicated. There are many variables in predicting the performance of Replication Server; the only true measure is to install it on a machine and let it run your applications.

Capacity Planning Case Study—the Individual Server

We now discuss the various factors that you must consider when estimating the disk space capacity required by the primary OLTP server in your database system. Because the disk capacity required for each of the other server machines depends on the capacity required of the OLTP server, this detailed estimation for the OLTP server is required. We cover the disk capacity required for the following:

Databases
Number of segments
Mirrors
Memory
File system space
Database dumps to disk
Transaction log dumps to disk
Tuning
Moving data around
Logical dumps to disk
Interserver needs
Server machine limitations
Replication server
Server machine tape drives
Summary

Databases

You must determine the size of each database that your OLTP server will support, or for an existing server, is supporting. For either case, you need to estimate how much each database will grow in the future. You may think that some historical data will be helpful, but often your databases are growing exponentially, so looking at past growth may hurt more than it helps. You need to decide how long you want your current configuration to be adequate, say, a year. You must determine what disk capacity will be required to support each database for the next year.

In our example, we presently have a total of 8 Gb database space used and we have 12 Gb of overall database space. This allows for 50 percent growth, although, as we have discussed, placing segments on separate devices, and so on, will reduce the effective capacity. Note that if we look at the history of the largest database over the last year we observe that it was around 2.5 Gb a year ago, whereas the current size is 5 Gb. It has doubled in size and the business has been growing at an even faster rate this year compared to last. You will have a hard time predicting what the size of this database will be in a year.

Number of segments

You need to consider how many segments your most important database requires. For our example, the most important databases are the three largest ones.

Consider the largest first. It needs *default* and *system* segments as well as a *logsegment*, nonclustered index (*ncindexes*), and a *data* segment for several of the largest tables. These separate segments were created to improve performance. Therefore, place each of them on a different controller. So, you need four controllers. For the OLTP server machine in our example, we have 16 physical disks and, as discussed in Chapter 1, we allow only 4 physical disks per controller, a value which may vary, depending on the hardware platform your server is running on. The OLTP server machine has four controllers.

You also need to consider the needs of the other two critical databases. Each of them has *default/system* segments, *logsegment,* and a nonclustered index segment (*ncindexes*). For each database, these segments should be placed on disks attached to different controllers. Unless you are going to install a disk controller for each segment of every database on the server, you need to balance the load over the controllers you have. You need to place the segments of different databases on the controllers you have to minimize contention for the disk controller. By placing each segment of the most important database on a separate controller, you have optimized the disk I/O for that database, but be aware that you will be placing segments of other databases on those same controllers.

You must be aware of two different and competing capacity requirements. First, one database needs some number of segments, each of which should be on a different controller. Second, each database requires some number of segments, but your server machine only has so many controllers. At some point, segments from different databases will compete for disk I/O with segments of other databases. You need to balance the two requirements and monitor the disk I/O over time to see if the load balancing is being maintained.

Mirrors

Determine your mirroring plan. As we have discussed previously, the simplest plan to set up and maintain is to mirror all segments of every database and to assign whole physical disks to either server devices or their mirrors. You need to assess the needs of your business and the time it will take you to maintain the mirrors. If you decide to mirror only selected devices of selected databases, be prepared to check frequently to prevent database space being added to a segment in such a way that the segment is no longer fully mirrored. Note that we said "mirror only selected devices": You can only mirror a server device; you can't mirror a segment without mirroring all the devices that support that segment. For our example, we need to mirror all the segments of all the databases, so we need the same amount of disk space for mirroring that we need for the database space itself, namely 12 Gb (see Chapter 4).

Memory

As described earlier, the more memory the better. At a minimum, you should determine the maximum amount the server machine can accomodate, and trade that cost against the cost to the business of slower server performance. Install no less than 128 Mb, and preferably 500 Mb. Memory only looks expensive until compared with the cost of server performance and the personnel resources to perform server tuning.

Within the memory you have on the server machine, you will need to decide how to allocate it between data cache and procedure cache. Data cache is where the data pages are held while being read or changed. Procedure cache is where stored procedures are held. In both cases, the more times the server can find what it needs in memory (cache), the faster everything will go. The only way to really figure out the correct allocation for both kinds of cache is to use SQL Monitor and see how often the server finds what it needs in each cache (hit rate). You then alter the allocation by changing the percentage of SQL Server memory that will be allocated to procedure cache using **sp_configure** with the procedure cache option (20 percent is the default). The server will allocate all the memory needed for its own operation and then allocate 20 percent of the remaining memory to the procedure cache. This means you don't directly allocate the data cache; it gets whatever isn't allocated to the procedure cache.

File system space

The amount of file system disk space you will need is larger than you like to think. Here we consider the file system space that is not called out in the items below. This file system space includes disk space for the operating system software, swap space (discuss this with your server machine SA to determine required space), all the files needed to install and maintain the SQL Server, all other products that you may need to run on the server machine, and all the files needed to upgrade the server, server machine, or any of the other products running on the machine. A good rule of thumb is to assign one-quarter of all the physical disks on the server machine to file system space. You will need this much file system space for various uses. You need to increase the amount of file system space to allow for the following specific items that require large amounts of space.

Database dumps to disk

You need to plan ahead if you are going to dump the large databases on your server to disk. You can dump the smaller ones to the file system space you examined above, but for the largest databases you need to specifically plan for enough file system capacity. For our example, the largest three databases on the server are 5 Gb, 2 Gb and 1 Gb in size for a total of 8 Gb. In order to dump each of these to disk, you will need 8 Gb of file system space and these 8 Gb must be dedicated to database dumps and should not be used for anything else. If you allow other files to occupy any of this space the database dumps may not succeed.

For System 10, database dumps are made through the Backup Server. This allows you to dump to multiple disk files or tape drives. This can dramatically reduce the time it takes to dump a database. For tape drives or disk files that are in file systems on physical disks that are attached to separate controllers, you can reduce the dump time by the number of disk files or tape drives you are using. Hence, you can dump a database to four tape drives or disk files in one-fourth the time of the same dump made to a single tape drive or disk file. Note that this means you need to plan the number of disk file systems or tape drives and their location over the available controllers.

Transaction log dumps to disk

You need to allow for dumping the transaction log of your most important databases throughout your database dump cycle. If you dump the databases once per day, you should be dumping the transaction log throughout each day. You need to determine how long you need to retain the transaction logs on disk and make an educated guess as to the average size of the transaction log dump files. Using all this, you can come up with the file system capacity needed. Take into account the business cycle your business goes through. Make sure you are allowing for the periods of peak activity. For our example server, an entire physical disk is dedicated to storing the transaction log dumps for just the largest database. During periods of low business activity, this is plenty of room. However, at the end of the business cycle, there is only room for three days of transaction log dumps. For our example server, we would prefer to be able to store a full week's worth of transaction log dumps.

Tuning

Although the database space allowed for previously may be sufficient for the current size of the databases, you may need additional space for tuning the server. When you need to improve server performance, one of the factors to consider is the indexes on tables in each database. In order to create new indexes or any index, if none was created initially, you need more database space. Creating a clustered index is very costly in terms of space. You will need about 120 percent of the table size for creating a clustered index. For our example server, the largest table is roughly 800 Mb, so you would need to plan sufficient disk space capacity for the data segments of the database to allow for 1.2 Gb of additional database space. This disk space, for building non-clustered indexes, needs to be available to the index segment of the database, which means it has to be located on the devices supporting the index segment of the database. The additional space for building the new index needs to be on the index segment of the database, or else the completed index won't be on the index segment. The index segment was created to isolate the indexes to one controller for improved performance. Note that while the database space used to create a clustered index is free after the index is built, you can't shrink the database back down without the considerable effort of rebuilding the database. Further, you may well need to build a different clustered index at some later time, so the space may be needed again in the future.

;-)

> A third-party application is installed in a great hurry. No one bothers you with it because that would take time. Turns out the application was written a long time ago for another platform and was ported again in a great hurry. Things run for a while and then performance drops through the floor. Suddenly they have time to hunt you down. You look at the tables and discover there isn't a single index on the tables the application is using. Clearly, it is time to create some indexes but that will take a lot of space, space the server doesn't have. You now need to add disks just to have room to create new indexes, with the clustered indexes taking the most space.

Moving data around

You will need additional file system space for storing data that is going to or being received from the outside world. Frequently, the databases on your server will need to import or export data to other systems. For example, you may be receiving customer data from an outside vendor each night. You must know about this activity on your server and supply sufficient capacity to store any such data for the required duration. Depending on the nature of your business, data files like this can be very large or may need to be retained for a long period of time. Both factors can lead to a need for large amounts of file system space.

Logical dumps to disk

Along with your normal database dumps, you must consider the need to make logical dumps. A logical dump of a database allows you to retrieve individual data or objects. See Chapter 8 for more discussion of logical dumps. If you are planning to make logical dumps of your database, you should plan on sufficient file system space to store the latest logical dump of each database. You will need to determine which databases justify a logical dump being stored on disk and for how long. Typically, a logical dump will occupy significantly less disk space than the actual database, because a logical dump does not capture any of the index structure of the database, only the index definitions. For our example server, we need to store only the latest logical dump, and we need to have logical dumps of all the databases on the server. Using a factor of 50 percent to estimate the space required for a logical dump of the databases on our example server, we should plan on having 6 Gb of file system space for the logical database dumps of all our databases (12 Gb total database space x 50%).

Interserver needs

You need to consider additional file system space to allow for interserver file transfers. You may need to dump a database on one server and move it to another server in your system or outside. Any server in your system that needs to move dumps or other files to another server will need space to store the files. Note that this is different from the need for storing data that is being imported or exported. Here, we refer to dump or data files that are being moved between servers. You need to examine the way your database system functions to determine if you need file system space to support such transfers. For example, the DBCC server will need file system space to allow database dumps from other servers (principally, the primary OLTP server) to be copied to the DBCC server, where they are stored until needed for **dbcc** runs. In the discussion of the DBCC server, we allowed 20 Gb of disk space—12 Gb for databases and 8 Gb for file system space. This is sufficient if we are going to load the database dumps into the DBCC server from tapes. If you plan to automate the process you must be able to copy the database dumps you want from their home server to the DBCC server. For our example server, the largest database is 5 Gb so the DBCC server would need 5 Gb of file system space to store a copy of the dump. You need to determine if the existing file system capacity of 8 Gb is sufficient to support a 5-Gb database dump file and all the other needs of the DBCC server.

Server machine limitations

We have been discussing server machine disk space as if we can add disks without limit. You must determine how many controllers can be physically installed in each server machine in your database system. With the maximum number of disks per controller, you have the upper limit on how much disk space you can install on each machine. As you reach the upper limit on disk space, you will have to decide whether to replace the server machine or off-load some of its disk space to another server. Further, this applies not only to the physical limitations of any one server machine but the area where the machines are installed as well. You must have sufficient rack space to install more disks, as well as the power and air conditioning to support all these devices.

Replication server

For our example server, Replication Server would be running on a dedicated machine and would not impact the disk space capacity planning of the primary OLTP server machine.

Server machine tape drives

You need to examine your database system to ensure you can move data tapes between server machines. You may have to move database dump tapes to load a database on the reporting server or on the DBCC server. In either case, you must be sure the tape dump made on one server machine is readable by the tape drive on the other server machine. Note that this doesn't just mean the tape drives are from the same vendor or have the same capacity. The device file used to dump to a tape drive will affect the amount of compression used during the dump. If the other tape drive does not support that level of compression using the same compression techniques, the tape may not be readable. Experiment to be sure you can move tapes between server machines.

Also, look at the capacity of the tape drives on each server machine relative to the databases you will need to dump to tape. As the databases grow, you will approach the capacity of the tape drive. You can put each database dump on a separate tape, but doing so takes lots of operator time and lots of tapes. If you are dumping multiple database dumps to a single tape (this is not supported for 4.9.x SQL Server, but can be done, see Chapter 15) or if you are dumping databases to file system disk files and then dumping the file system to tape, you will eventually fill the entire tape. Now the operators need to load a second tape, and so on. You need to be planning for tape operator capacity as well if you are going to be able to support multitape dumps.

Summary

In summary you have a primary OLTP server that supports databases that occupy a total of 8 Gb of disk space. However, to support the OLTP users, the DSS users, the need for a standby server, a DBCC server, and a development and test environment you now need to have six servers running on six separate server machines (assuming the previous release server runs on one of these six machines as well) and you will need a seventh server machine to support Replication Server. Overall, you are now in need of 164 Gb of disk space. You need to plan for this kind of growth and get used to the idea that you need hundreds of gigabytes of disk space. Keep in mind that you now have many things growing in parallel. If one of the databases grows by 1 Gb, then the file system space for the database dump on this server machine has to grow by the same amount, as does the room on the dump tape. The size of the transaction log dumps may grow as well. Any server machines where the database disk dump file will be copied have to grow also. And so on.

You should also think about the number of people that will be required to install, support, and upgrade all this equipment. You alone can't handle all these tasks. Even if you do support all these functions for your current database system, consider what is coming as your business grows.

;-)

Note that the example OLTP server discussed would need to have 48 Gb of disk space to accommodate all the possible needs. However, the server machine only has a maximum of 32 Gb of disk space physically available. This example is taken from real-world systems and points out how you have to change your outlook to be ready for the demands of your overall database system. The OLTP server machine was considered huge when it was installed only a few years ago, and it was purchased with all the disks it could handle. Now the machine can't physically accept any more disk drives. The machine will have to be replaced just to add the disk capacity that the server already needs. Note that until the server machine is replaced, it simply can't support all the activities that are desired. Dumping databases to disk, for example, simply can't be done. This means you as DBA must continue physically moving database dump tapes between machines until the server machine is replaced.

10.4 Capacity Planning for the Database System

We have been discussing the capacity planning process for each of the servers in the system. You also need to plan for adding servers. As the needs of your business grow, so will the databases on your servers. At some point, you will need to move some of the data off one server and set up another server. Frequently, you will set up a server for each major application group as each one becomes large enough to require a separate server and machine. Often, you will want to move the databases to be located nearer the users of that data, and politics will play a big role in deciding which database lives on which server and where the server is located geographically. You need to be aware of this process and be planning how you will handle the movement of these databases to other locations. Note that each location will then need all the capacity that we have discussed here—server, machines, disk space, physical environment, and support personnel.

Chapter 11

Operational Details of SQL Server

There are many aspects of the operation and use of SQL Server that you need to understand. We discuss several of them because they come up often while you are performing your DBA duties.

Specifically, we discuss these topics:

11.1	Interfaces File
11.2	Communication Among Servers
11.3	Creating Stored Procedure from SQL Script or defncopy Output
11.4	What *sysusages* Means
11.5	Reading the Errorlog
11.6	Impacts of Creating a New Database
11.7	Modifying System Tables Manually
11.8	bcp Command
11.9	Full Transaction Log or Other Segment (1105 Error)

11.1 Interfaces File

The interfaces file is very important to the operation of the SQL Server and related products. Basically, the interfaces file is a list of all the SQL Servers, Open Servers, and related products like the components of Replication Server (and Backup Server for System 10). This list documents the names of all these servers, the server machine name, and port number where they run. For each server in the interfaces file, you will find one or more lines that begin with "master" or "query" or "console" (there are a few other possibilities but they are rare). The interfaces file is used in three different ways, each of which is discussed below.

First, the interfaces file is read by the SQL Server when the server is started. As the server starts, it reads the interfaces file to find the servername specified in the startup script. The servername is either specified by the value of the DSLISTEN environment variable or is specified as a command-line option (-s) to the execution of the dataserver binary itself (see Chapter 15). When the server finds the servername, it uses the server machine name and port number information specified for the "master" entry to determine where it is supposed to start up. The SQL Server will also use the information in the "console" entry to determine where the console process is to be started. Note that the server should be using the server version of the interfaces file, which contains all of the information for the master, query, and console entries for SQL Servers. as shown in Figure 11.1.

Other servers, like the SQL Monitor Server (*<servername>*_MSV in the interfaces file) only need master and query entries. (For System 10, the console program goes away, so this entry in the interfaces file is no longer needed; see Chapter 14.) Note that the SQL Server doesn't have to be started with the same servername as is stored in *sysservers* for the local server. The SQL Server really doesn't have a name and will start up as whatever name is in the startup script. This can cause confusion. When you start the server, you tell it a servername that the server uses to locate a machine name and port number in the interfaces file. This does not affect the "name" of the server, which is simply an entry in *sysservers* and is returned by **select @@servername**.

Second, the interfaces file is read by an operating SQL Server whenever it needs to communicate with any of the other servers on the network. Note that which servers appear to be on the network is limited by those servers that appear in the interfaces file that the SQL Server looks at. The SQL Server can communicate only with the servers listed in the interfaces file that you specify in the startup script or that is specified by the environment variable SYBASE. Note that the environment variable SYBASE specifies only the *directory* where the file called *interfaces* is located, not the actual interfaces file itself. If you don't specify the location of the interfaces file, the server assumes it is located in the directory that is specified in the environment variable SYBASE. When the SQL Server needs to communicate with a remote server it looks for the remote server in the interfaces file; when it finds the remote servername, it uses the associated server machine name and port number for the query entry to know where to communicate with the remote server.

Third, any client that needs to communicate (login) to a SQL Server must look through the interfaces file to find the desired servername and use the information it finds in the query entry to determine where to look for the SQL Server. Note that all clients should be using the client version of the interfaces file, as shown in Figure 11.1. You need to understand that the environment variable DSQUERY simply specifies the servername. If you run isql or some other application and you don't specify which server you wish to access, then the servername is taken to be the value of DSQUERY. At that point, the interfaces file that the client has access to will be scanned for the information about the servername = DSQUERY. If you have problems with an application that can't login to a server, check the way that the DSQUERY or the servername is being set up and check the interfaces file that is being used.

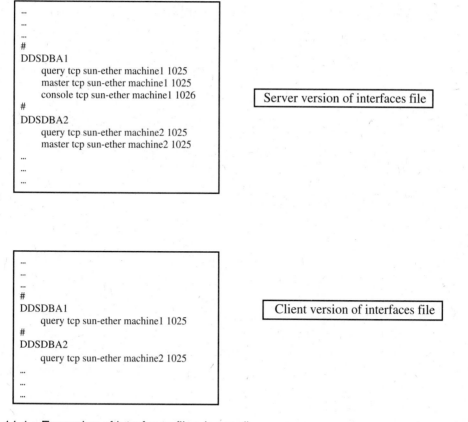

Figure 11.1   Examples of interfaces files (normal) -

Because the interfaces file is so intrinsic to the startup and operation of the SQL Server and because it must contain the information (server machine name and port number) for all the servers and related products that need to talk to each other, you should maintain a master copy of both the server and client versions of the interfaces file in one location on your database system. The master copy of the server version should then be copied to all the server machines in your database system, and the master copy of the client version should be copied to all the clients or the file servers that support clients. In this way, each server machine has a local copy of the server version of the interfaces file that has information for all the other servers in the database system. The clients all have a copy of the client version of the interfaces file, which contains only the query entry for those servers that you as DBA want the clients to know about.

You may think that having two versions of the interfaces file is unnecessary, but an example of their use will show the value of this approach. When you need to isolate a server from the users, it is much better to isolate it via changes to the server version of the interfaces file. You can isolate the server by restarting the server in single-user mode, but that doesn't guarantee that you as DBA will be the single user and you can find yourself locked out of your own server. You can further put all the databases into 'dbo' use only, but that prevents you from doing any real-world testing where you need to log in to the server as individual server users to test permissions and the like. It is easier for you to simply edit the server version of the interfaces file and change the servername and the port number for the server you wish to isolate. An example of such changes is shown in Figure 11.2.

Now you edit your server startup script to start the server as DDSDBA1_TESTING, and the server finds that this server should be started on machine1 port 1925. The server will start up and be available to those persons that you have informed about the new servername and port number. Users that will assist you in the testing will need to be granted access to the server machine where they can use the local modified copy of the server version of the interfaces file, or they will need to create their own temporary interfaces file on their client machine. Users trying to log in through the client version of the interfaces file will try in vain, as there is no server called DDSDBA1 operating on machine 1 port 1025. This scheme allows you to test the server in its normal operating state while you control who gains access to the server.

```
...
...
...
#
DDSDBA1_TESTING
      query tcp sun-ether machine1 1925
      master tcp sun-ether machine1 1925
      console tcp sun-ether machine1 1926
#
DDSDBA2
      query tcp sun-ether machine2 1025
      master tcp sun-ether machine2 1025
...
...
...
```

```
Server version of interfaces file
            (modified)
```

```
...
...
...
#
DDSDBA1
      query tcp sun-ether machine1 1025
#
DDSDBA2
      query tcp sun-ether machine2 1025
...
...
...
```

```
Client version of interfaces file
```

Figure 11.2   Examples of interfaces files (DDSDBA1 isolated from users) - - - - - - - - - - -

It is safer for you to change both the servername and the port number in the server version of the interfaces file. If you change only the port number and then some other person or process were to redistribute the master copy of the server version of the interfaces file, that action would overwrite your change to the port number while the servername remained the same. Suddenly the server would be available to all the users without your knowledge. To prevent this, you should change both the server-name and the port number in the local copy of the server version of the interfaces file on the server machine that supports the server you are isolating. If the master copy of the interfaces file gets distributed now, it will change both the servername and the port number to their original values. The users still can't get in because the server will still be (in our example) DDSDBA1_TESTING while they are trying to access

DDSDBA1. Of course, you won't be able to access the isolated server, either. You will try to access DDSDBA1_TESTING and get a "server not found in interfaces file" error. At that point, being a DBA, you should pretty quickly figure out that the entry in the interfaces file has been overwritten. You can change the local copy of the server version of the interfaces file again and again access the isolated server, which will be just as you left it, without any changes made by users.

Be sure that you do not use spaces before the text of the lines for the master, query, or console entries in the interfaces file. These lines must be preceded by a single tab character. If you use spaces, the server will not read the entry and it will appear that the server is not in the interfaces file. This error is especially frustrating because there is no way to see it as you examine the interfaces file on the screen. Further, note that this can crop up in some unintended ways. For example, if you use ftp to move the interfaces file from one server machine to another, you must use the binary mode. Otherwise, the interfaces file will be moved but the tabs will be replaced by spaces. If you are having problems with a server and it appears to be related to the interfaces file, check for spaces before the entries for the server that is having problems.

11.2 Communication Among Servers

In order for two SQL Servers to communicate with each other by using remote procedure calls (one server executes an RPC to the other), several things must be set up. You need to understand what these steps are and how to check the status of this communication process.

First, the remote server must be configured to allow remote connections (that is, **sp_configure "remote access", 1**), as shown in Figure 11.3.

Second, both servers must have entries in their interfaces file for the other server. This is another reason to maintain one master copy of the server version of the interfaces file and distribute a copy to each server machine. The client version of the interfaces file doesn't need all the information about all the servers. A client only needs to have an interfaces file that contains information about the servers the users need to access. If a user is accessing a server and needs to execute an RPC to another server, that request is handled by the server itself, which will use the server version of the interfaces file to find out about the other server.

```
1> sp_configure
2> go
name           minimum    maximum    config_value run_value
--------------- ----------- -------------- ----------------- -----------

...

...

...
devices          4           256        30          30
remote access    0             1         1           1
remote logins    0      2147483647      64          64
remote sites     0      2147483647      10          10
remote connections 0    2147483647     128         128
pre-read packets 0      2147483647       0           0
upgrade version  0      2147483647     491         491
...

...

...
```

Configuration of ServerB

```
1> select * from sysservers
2> go
srvid srvstatus srvname  srvnetname
------ ---------- ----------- --------------
  0      0      serverB   SERVERB
  1      1      serverA   SERVERA
  2      1      serverC   SERVERC
```

sysservers on ServerB

```
1> select * from sysremotelogins
2> go
remoteserverid remoteusername  suid status
----------------- ----------------------- ------ --------
    1           NULL         -1    0
    2           NULL         -1    0
```

sysremotelogins on ServerB

Figure 11.3   Remote server logins from server A to server B

Third, each server must have an entry for the other server in the system table *sysservers,* as shown in Figure 11.3. The system table *sysservers* contains the information the server uses to determine what the remote server is called. The server then uses this information to find the remote server in the interfaces file. This allows each server to have two names: one that the server uses internally to call a remote server, and the other the name that appears in the interfaces file for the remote server. Thus, you could have an application running on several servers that is hard-coded to call servername1, and in *sysservers* for each server, you have an alias that assigns a unique servername to servername1. So, for each server, the same application that calls servername1 would then be calling the individual server on that server machine.

A good example of this rather confusing process is the System 10 Backup Server. With the System 10 SQL Server, the only way to make dumps (or loads) is through the Backup Server. The Backup Server is an Open Server application and therefore is a remote server to the SQL Server. However, the SQL Server is hard-coded to call SYB_BACKUP whenever the SQL Server needs to dump or load. As soon as you have more than one System 10 SQL Server in your database system, you have a problem. All the System 10 SQL Servers will be calling SYB_BACKUP when they need to dump and load. By default, when you install the SQL Server and Backup Server (using sybinit, see Chapter 3) the entry in *sysservers* for the Backup Server is SYB_BACKUP for both *srvname* and *srvnetname*. If you don't change this, all the servers will be calling SYB_BACKUP (*srvname*). The servers will then all look at the associated SYB_BACKUP (*srvnetname*), then go out to their interfaces file (server version) and all call for the Backup Server that is running at the machine and port number specified in the interfaces file for the server (Backup Server) named SYB_BACKUP. If all the servers have a Backup Server running on the server machine, and if the interfaces file on each server machine points to the Backup Server running on that server machine for the entry SYB_BACKUP, then all is well.

However, as soon as you have a common interfaces file, things get confused. Multiple servers will be calling SYB_BACKUP, which in the common interface file points to one server machine and port number. To cure this problem, you must change the *srvnetname* in *sysservers* for each server to reflect a unique name for each Backup Server. The easiest way to do this is to change *srvnetname* to <servername>_BCK. Now, each SQL Server will call SYB_BACKUP (the *srvname* in *sysservers* for the Backup Server), which will be associated with <servername>_BCK (*srvnetname* in *sysservers*) and will appear in the interfaces file as a unique server machine and port number, since all the different <servername>_BCKs will be in the common interfaces file. Note that you must not change the *srvname* (SYB_BACKUP) for the Backup Server. If you do, the SQL Server will not be able to communicate with any Backup Server at all.

Fourth, each server must have an entry in the system table *sysremotelogins* that tells the server how to treat remote logins from the other (remote) server, as shown in Figure 11.3. In the example, the value of *suid* = -1 and *status* = 0. This means that for any of the server logins on serverA that execute an RPC to serverB, the server login from serverA will be compared with the same server login on serverB and the passwords must match. If they don't or if the server login from serverA doesn't exist on serverB, then the execution of the RPC fails. This is the most secure way to handle remote logins, but it does require that you maintain the server logins and their passwords on both servers. Further, you can set up other configurations where some server logins on serverA are mapped into different server logins on serverB. Also, you can set up the trusted mode by using **sp_remotelogin,** which will drop the requirement that the server login passwords agree between the two servers. Be aware of these options and how each of your servers is configured. You must know what level of security you have on your servers.

Note that each remote server in *sysservers* has a *srvid* that is joined with *remoteserverid* in *sysremotelogins* to get the permissions for remote logins from each remote server. For our example, as far as serverB is concerned, serverA has *srvid* = 1 in *sysservers;* this corresponds with *sysremotelogins* column *remoteserverid* = 1 which has *suid* = -1 and *status* = 0 as discussed above.

Fifth, the server executing the RPC (that is, the local SQL Server) must be named, which means there is an entry in *sysservers* for the local server (*sysservers srvid* = 0) and **select @@servername** will return the name of the local server (non-NULL).

With this configuration, it is required that the server login on serverA that executes the RPC to serverB must also exist as a server login on serverB, and the server login must have the same password on both serverA and serverB. If the options were set differently, there might not be such a requirement.

To test such a link, access serverA using isql, and **execute serverB...sp_who**, and see what happens. If you get reasonable results back (that is, you believe the returned results to be from serverB), then the link is working from serverA to serverB. If you need to have the link working both ways, you should also isql into serverB and **execute serverA...sp_who** to see if you get reasonable results. Note that the *servername* you use with **...sp_who** will depend on the entries in *sysservers* for each server. For serverA, the entry in *sysservers* for the remote server should be serverB for the syntax **serverB...sp_who** to function correctly. Note that in *sysservers,* serverB would be the value of *srvname*, whereas the associated value of *srvnetname* could be anything. It is the value of *srvnetname* that the server uses to scan the interfaces file to find the remote server.

11.3 Creating Stored Procedure from SQL Script or defncopy Output

You will often need to write a script and then move it into a database, where it will be a stored procedure. Once you have the SQL script working the way you want, you need to add to the top of the script the statement—

```
create procedure <stored_procedure_name> as
```

—and you need to add the statement **go** at the end of the script. Additionally, if you are making changes to an existing stored procedure, you should add the statement—

```
drop procedure <stored_procedure_name>
```

—and **go** before the create procedure statement.

Note that when you use the utility defncopy to copy out the SQL that defines a database object and then need to use the resulting output file to create a stored procedure or trigger, you also need to edit the file and make sure the **drop procedure, create procedure** (or **create trigger**, **drop trigger**), and the necessary **go** statements are in the correct places before you try to create the database object.

11.4 What *sysusages* Means

The system table *sysusages* (in the *master* database) is very important and very misunderstood. This table stores the information about where all the pieces of each database are stored on disk. More specifically, each row of *sysusages* represents the assignment of some chunk of disk space to a database in the server. When you execute the **create database** or **alter database** commands, you are adding rows to *sysusages*. Further, each row of *sysusages* tells you exactly where the chunk of database space is located out on the server devices (that is, physical disks), and each row of *sysusages* has a *segmap* value that tells you which segments have been assigned to the chunk of database space.

The way all this information is stored in *sysusages* is very confusing, and we discuss various aspects of each row of *sysusages*.

Which Database Is Affected
Amount of Database Space
Location of Database Space
Segments Assigned to Database Space
Can't Remove Database Space (Except for *tempdb*)
Updating *sysusages* Manually
load database and *sysusages*

See Figure 11.4 for an example of the data in *sysusages* and related system tables.

Which Database Is Affected

The *dbid* column in *sysusages* joins with the *dbid* column in *sysdatabases* to relate the *dbid* of each chunk of disk space (space fragment) to a database *name*. You can see which rows of *sysusages* support which database based on the *dbid* value. Using *db1* as an example in the data from system tables, as shown in Figure 11.4, the last three lines of the *sysusages* table belong to *db1*, which has a *dbid* of 4. Keep in mind that the order of the rows in *sysusages* for a given *dbid* reflects the exact order in which the database space was created. So, for *db1* the three rows of *sysusages* represent a complete record of the size and order of each chunk of database space assigned to *db1*.

Amount of Database Space

Each row of *sysusages* identifies a chunk of disk space. The size of each chunk is stored in each row of *sysusages* in the *size* column. For *db1*, the three rows of *sysusages* that represent the disk space of the database have sizes of 5120, 2560, and 5120 respectively; these are all in 2K pages. The total disk space for *db1* is then 12,800 2K pages or is 25 Mb.

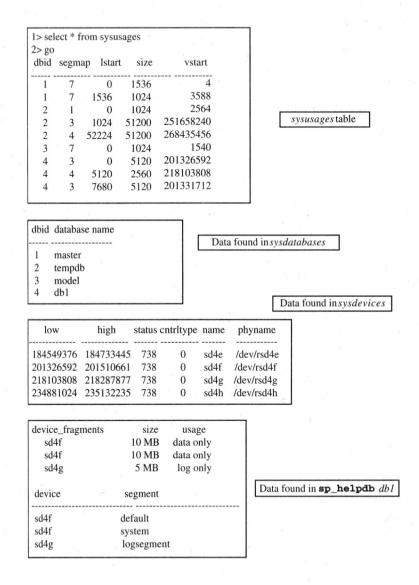

```
1> select * from sysusages
2> go
dbid  segmap  lstart  size    vstart

------ -------- ------- ------- ----------
  1      7        0     1536           4
  1      7      1536    1024        3588
  2      1        0     1024        2564
  2      3      1024    51200   251658240
  2      4     52224    51200   268435456
  3      7        0     1024        1540
  4      3        0     5120   201326592
  4      4      5120     2560   218103808
  4      3      7680     5120   201331712
```

sysusages table

```
dbid  database name
------ -----------------
  1     master
  2     tempdb
  3     model
  4     db1
```

Data found in *sysdatabases*

Data found in *sysdevices*

```
 low          high        status cntrltype name    phyname
-------------- -------------- ------- ----------- ------- -----------
184549376  184733445   738      0       sd4e   /dev/rsd4e
201326592  201510661   738      0       sd4f   /dev/rsd4f
218103808  218287877   738      0       sd4g   /dev/rsd4g
234881024  235132235   738      0       sd4h   /dev/rsd4h
```

```
device_fragments      size      usage
   sd4f              10 MB    data only
   sd4f              10 MB    data only
   sd4g               5 MB    log only

device                segment
-----------------     ------------------------
sd4f                  default
sd4f                  system
sd4g                  logsegment
```

Data found in **sp_helpdb** *db1*

Figure 11.4   Example of *sysusages* and related tables- -

Location of Database Space

You can tell where each piece of the database is located from the value of the *vstart* column of *sysusages*. This is where the virtual device number (*vdevno*) comes into play. Recall that *vdevno* came up during the **disk init** command. Now you can see why. Each data page (2K page) in the entire server needs to have a unique page number. Each data page also has a unique page number within the database. So, for each row in *sysusages* we have within the database the unique page number that is the value of *lstart* (logical starting page). Note that for each database, *lstart* simply jumps from row to row by the size of each row's chunk of database space. For the example of *db1*, you can see that *lstart* starts out at 0 for the first chunk of disk space, which is 5120 data pages, and the next row of *sysusages* for *db1* has *lstart* of 5120. The first data page for *db1* is *lstart* = 0, so 5120 pages starting from page 0 is 5119. The next chunk of disk space for *db1* starts at page 5120 and has size 2560, which bring us to 7679, and so on. You will see that whereas the *lstart* values for *db1* are marching along sequentially, the *vstart* values are not. For each row of *sysusages* that represents disk space for *db1*, the unique page number within the whole server is the value of *vstart*. The *vstart* value is a combination of the *vdevno* and the *lstart* value for each chunk of disk space. This explains why *vdevno* can't be reused among **disk init** commands. The value of *vdevno* must be unique among all server devices because the *vstart* values are based on *vdevno*, and the *vstart* values must be unique within the server.

You are finally ready to determine where each chunk of disk space is located. To do this, you must look at the data in *sysdevices*. For each server device, which is a physical disk partition (or a disk file), *sysdevices* has a *low* and a *high* value. These values tell you the starting (*low*) data page number and the ending (*high*) data page number for the server device. By comparing these ranges of data pages to the *vstart* page number in *sysusages,* you can determine which server device is associated with each chunk of database space. Note that a row in *sysusages* will never overlap a server device. Each row in *sysusages* represents a piece of disk space from a **create database** or an **alter database** command; these commands require that you add space to one or more server devices, but you are required to define how much space goes on each device. The server will make an entry in *sysusages* for the space assigned to each server device. If one of the server devices fills up, then the server fills all of the server device but does not try to assign space on another server device. All this means is that you don't need to worry about the size of the disk space in a row of *sysusages*; you only need to locate the *vstart* value between the *low* and *high* values in *sysdevices,* and you have located the server device that has the chunk of database space.

For the example of *db1*, we see that the first row of *sysusages* for *db1* has a *vstart* of 201326592 and looking at the data from *sysdevices* in Figure 11.4, we see that this value for *vstart* is between the *low* (201326592) and the *high* (201510661) data page values for the server device sd4f. In fact, this chunk of database space is the first chunk of database space on the server device sd4f.

Segments Assigned to Database Space

Segments have been discussed fully in Chapter 4. Each chunk of database space, or each row of *sysusages*, supports a set of segments for the database. The value of *segmap* for each row of *sysusages* tells you what segments are assigned to each chunk of database space. The way in which multiple segment assignments are encoded into the *segmap* value is not very intuitive. The encoding involves the logical OR of the bitmaps of the numbers of all the segments that are assigned to the chunk of disk space. The numbers for segment assignments are listed in Table 11.1.

Table 11.1   Segment Assignment Numbers

Segment Type	Segment Number	Segment Number Bitmap
system	1	000001
default	2	000010
logsegment	4	000100
first user-defined	8	001000
second user-defined	16	010000
third user-defined etc.	32 etc.	100000

The segment numbers jump from 2 to 4 and from 4 to 8 because they are the decimal version of the binary bit map of the segment number. When you combine segment assignments, you add the segment numbers together. For a piece of database disk space that has the segment assignments of *system*, *default,* and *logsegment*, which are the assignments you get when you simply create a database, the *segmap* value is 7. For pieces of the database that are supporting the *logsegment* only, the *segmap* value is 4. Note that the segment number for user-defined segments increases rapidly from 8 to 16 to 32 and then 64 and 128. If you have a lot of user-defined segments you will have very large segment numbers and *segmap* values. You must realize that just because you might have a *segmap* value of 128 does not mean there are 128 segments; the *segmap* value cannot range continuously from 1 to 128 but steps between 1 and 128, jumping from the various combinations of 1 and 2 and 4 and 8 and so on.

Can't Remove Database Space (Except for tempdb)

Now that you have some idea what each row in *sysusages* tells you, you need to remember that you can't just delete rows from *sysusages* to reduce the size of a database. The one exception to this is *tempdb*. If you need to reduce the size of *tempdb,* you can delete some or all of the rows of *sysusages* that represent the chunks of disk space assigned to *tempdb*, except for the first 2 Mb on the master device, which should never be removed. You then restart the server, and *tempdb* will have been reduced. Consult the Sybase SQL Server Troubleshooting Guide for the details of this process.

Updating sysusages Manually

Note that anytime you are manually updating system tables, you must observe various warnings about such a procedure, see "Modifying system tables manually" below.

WARNING:

- Updating system tables in not supported by Sybase—there is no guarantee that the system table schema will be maintained between releases, which means manual updates that work for one version may not work on another version.

- Do not perform such updates without first consulting with Sybase Technical Support.

- Make sure you have dumps of everything you might need to rebuild the server, in case the manual updates destroy something.

- After updating system tables, you should restart the server to copy the changes into memory.

When you execute **sp_addsegment**, **sp_extendsegment**, or **sp_dropsegment**, you are running stored procedures that look at *sysusages* and determine all the rows that belong to the server device specified in the execution of the stored procedure and the database in which the stored procedure was executed. Then, the *segmap* value is altered for all the appropriate rows. This is how a server device is assigned to the *logsegment* and only the logsegment, that is, the *segmap* value is set to 4. This also explains why you must set up such a device before any data for any other segment is written to the server device. When the database space on the server device was originally assigned through the **create database** or **alter database** commands, the *segmap* value was set up to be 7 or 3, respectively (that is, *default*, *system*, and *logsegment* segments, or *system* and *default*). If any objects are created on this device on the *default* or *system* segments, the data pages of those objects will be marked as belonging to the *default* or *system* segments. If you then tried to assign all future allocations of space on the server device to the *logsegment* alone by manually changing *segmap* to 4 for the relevant rows of *sysusages*, the server will now allow only data pages that belong to the *logsegment* to be written to the server device; there will still be those data pages that already existed for the objects that belong to the *default* and *system* segments. The server will still refuse to perform a **dump transaction** command because the server device must contain only *logsegment* data pages for the command to work. Until all the pages can be assigned to the *logsegment,* you can't simply change the *segmap* value to 4 and get the effect of having only *logsegment* data pages on the server device.

Now we reach a contradiction. If you use the stored procedures, you can't assign the *segmap* value to 4 until all the data pages are free to be assigned to *logsegment*. You can, however, go into *sysusages* manually and update anything you like. You must not do this without a good reason and a good plan and a good backup. You must realize that although you can manually update the *segmap* values in *sysusages*, that won't necessarily get you the effect you want. The stored procedures are there for a reason and you should use them.

There are situations when you will want to manually alter the *segmap* values in *sysusages*. This process is not supported by Sybase, but you should understand that it exists and when you might use it.

If you need to recreate a database quickly, use the **for load** option of the **create database** command. However, after that command completes, you are left with all the correct chunks of space in the correct order in *sysusages* for loading the database dump, but the *segmap* value for all the rows for the database is set to 3, except for one, assuming that one line of the **create database** statement contained the **log on** clause, which means the *segmap* value would be 4 for that row. Now you are supposed to wait for the **create database** (with the **for load** option) to complete, load the database dump and then manually use the **sp_addsegment**, **sp_extendsegment**, and **sp_dropsegment** to correctly recreate the same *segmap* values for the rows of *sysusages* as existed previously for the database. Manually performing all these stored procedure executions, in the correct order with no mistakes, can be very tedious for large databases that have data spread out over many server devices. You can update the *sysusages* tables manually by using the *lstart* values of the rows for the database. Note that the *vstart* values are based on the *vdevnos* of the server devices; as such they could change if you were rebuilding the server and didn't do all the **disk inits** in the same order. However, the *lstart* values will be the same as long as all the chunks of space for the database are created in the same order and size as existed in the original database. So, you can update the *segmap* values based on the *lstart* values by specifying that for *lstart* greater than x and less than or equal to y, the *segmap* value should be z.

Take *db1* again as an example. Assume you are recreating *db1* on the server. You can run **create database** using the **for load** option to create the exact same three rows in *sysusages* as in the original. Update the rows of *sysusages*, where *dbid* = 4, as follows:

- For *lstart* greater than or equal to 0 and less than 5120, *segmap* = 3.

- For *lstart* greater than or equal to 5120 and less than 7680, *segmap* = 4. (The value of *lstart* of the next row of *sysusages* for *db1*. Note that the data page numbers for the current row of *sysusages* run from *lstart* = 5120 to 7679.)

- For *lstart* greater than or equal to 7680, *segmap* = 3.

You must use > or = and < because you can't control how the server will create the chunk of database space. For example, if you request 10 Mb of space on a server device, the server may create it in one shot and only one row will appear in *sysus-*

ages, or the server will create two rows in *sysusages* for, say, 7 Mb and 3 Mb. By using the approach shown above, you avoid any problems caused by this server behavior.

Of course, you need to have the data from *sysusages* before you can use this approach, but manually rebuilding the database by using the **sp_createsegment** and relevant commands would require the same data to know what size chunks of the database to create in which order. Note that this process is done for you by the script **p_dbcreate** described in Chapter 15. This script will generate the commands for a database to create the database with the **for load** option and to update the *sysusages* rows for the database to recreate the exact same segmentation. This is very useful and fast when you need to rebuild a database on the same server. It is also useful when you need to recreate the database on another server, because you still need to recreate the same size chunks of space in the same order only on the new server. If the new server has the same server devices with the same names (and sufficient free space), you can execute the output of **p_dbcreate** directly. The more likely event is that you have different server devices. In that case, you need to determine a conversion map between the original server devices and the new server devices and edit the new server device names into the output of **p_dbcreate** before executing. This is a very good approach for creating the databases on a reporting or standby server.

load database and sysusages

There is another reason you need to understand what the rows in *sysusages* mean. As mentioned previously, the order of the rows in *sysusages* for a given database tells you the exact order in which the chunks of space were allocated for that database. This is also the order in which the database will be dumped. When you load the database from dump, this is also the order in which the pages of the database will be brought into the database. All this means that when you recreate the database, either on the same server or on another server, you must recreate the database such that the same chunks of space are created in the same order and in the same size. For the example of *db1,* this means that you must recreate the database such that there are rows in *sysusages* that show a 10-Mb chunk assigned to *system* and *default* segments (*segmap* = 3), followed by a 5-Mb chunk assigned to *logsegment* (*segmap* = 4), and finally a row of *sysusages* that shows a 10 Mb chunk of database space with a *segmap* = 3. Note that it doesn't matter how many rows of *sysusages* there are for the newly created database as long as the overall size and order of the chunks are the same. Note the dump of *db1* will bring in 10 Mb of *segmap* = 3 data followed by 5 Mb of *segmap* = 4 data, and so on. This means that *sysusages* can show two rows of *segmap* = 3 database space as long as the following conditions are met: the size of these two chunks adds up to 10 Mb; the next bunch of rows in *sysusages* for *db1* adds up to 5 Mb, all of which have *segmap* = 4; followed by any number of rows in *sysusages* that are all *segmap* = 3 and that add up to 10 Mb of space overall.

If you don't recreate the database so that the overall size and order of the chunks of database space recreate the size and order of the original, the load from dump will place data pages from the transaction log on server devices that the server thinks are for *system* and *default* segment objects (and vice versa). This is fine until you try to write something to one of these segments; the server will be confused because it will try to write a change to an object of the *default* segment that is on a server device that is marked as *logsegment* only (*segmap* = 4) in *sysusages*. This form of corruption may not be recoverable. You must be careful when recreating database that will be loaded from a dump.

11.5 Reading the Errorlog

The SQL Server errorlog contains a wealth of information that you will need during times of crisis. Since the server may not be available because of a crash you may need to extract information from the errorlog. We discuss the following items that can be found in the errorlog, and we flag each of these same items in the example errorlogs that are shown in the following sections for a 4.9.x and System 10 server, respectively.

Table 11.2   Items Found in the Errorlog

Item	Description/Recommendations
1. SQL Server version	Displays the SQL Server version and EBF level that is being executed. This is the first line of the errorlog.
2. Location of errorlog	If you are looking at an old errorlog, then you already know where it is kept, but this information is useful when you start a server; you should check that the errorlog is being sent where you think it is.
3. Maximum user connections	Displays the maximum possible number of file descriptors, which tells you the maximum number of user connections that the server can support. Note that this doesn't mean the server is configured for this many user connections. Further, if you see a small number of file descriptors, you know that you need to allow more file descriptors. See the *Sybase SQL Server Installation Guide* and *System Administration Guide Supplement* for your server machine platform.
4. Master device	Shows the physical disk partition that supports the master device. This information is vital if you need to run **buildmaster** or other procedures to fix the master device and the server itself is down. This is also the only way to determine what the disk partition is for the master device if you have never mirrored the master device. As discussed in Chapter 7, until the master device is mirrored, *sysdevices* doesn't reflect the actual physical device. Note that the errorlog shows you the physical disk partition that is supporting the master device as "virtual device 0", which means *vdevno* = 0 and that is the master device.
5. Master device is mirrored	If the master device is mirrored (you should mirror the master device always) that will be reported in the errorlog. You must check this each time the server starts to make sure the mirror of the master device is functioning properly.
6. Interfaces file information	Reports the server machine name and port number where the server is running.
7. Servername	Reports the name of the server, which means the entry in *sysservers* for the local server. Recall that this is the only way a server can be named, that is, by making an entry in *sysservers* by means of **sp_addserver** with the **local** option. If the server (the local server) has not been named by using **sp_addserver** with the **local** option, the errorlog will simply say "server is unnamed". Even though you specified the name of the server during installation (sybconfig or sybinit for System 10), that name was only used for the creation of the RUN_<*servername*> script to start the server.

Table 11.2   Items Found in the Errorlog (Continued)

Item	Description/Recommendations
8. Server devices and mirrors	Displays each of the server devices along with its *vdevno*. Note that the errorlog will refer to each server device as a virtual device. If the server device is mirrored, there will be an additional line "mirror: *<physical_name_of_mirror>*".
9. Asynchronous I/O in use for server devices	As each server device is displayed, so is the fact that asynchronous I/O is being used for the device. You should check that all the server devices are using asynchronous I/O. If you create a server device on a file system, the errorlog will display that fact for the server device. Make sure you see the correct I/O method being used for each server device.
10. Recovery of databases	As the server recovers each database, the errorlog will contain messages about how many transactions were rolled forward or back. This is also where you should look for any error messages regarding recovering a database.
11. Default sort order and character set	Shows the ID number for the default sort order and the default character set after the server has recovered. These numbers are important; you should compare all the servers in your database system that need to share database dumps and verify that they all use the same default sort order and character set.

Example of 4.9.x SQL Server Errorlog

Each of the items in Table 11.2 is shown in the errorlog below. Each item is marked with a comment line /* <item> */ above the relevant portion of the errorlog.

```
/dba/DDSDBA1/errorlog 57 % more errorlog
/* 1) SQL Server Version */
00: 95/04/01 14:53:42.20 kernel: SQL Server/4.9.2/EBF 2825
   Rollup/Sun4/OS 4.1.2/1/OPT/Sat Apr  9 10:25:53 PDT 1994
/* 2) Location of Errorlog */
00: 95/04/01 14:53:42.27 kernel: Logging SQL Server messages
   in file '/dba/DDSDBA1/bin/errorlog'.
00: 95/04/01 14:53:42.27 kernel: Using config area of disk
   for boot information
00: 95/04/01 14:53:42.39 kernel: kdconfig: opening secondary
   master device
00: 95/04/01 14:53:42.43 kernel: Using config area from
   primary master device.
/* 3) Maximum User Connections */
```

```
00: 95/04/01 14:53:42.69 kernel: Using 2048 file
   descriptors.
00: 95/04/01 14:53:42.69 kernel: Network and device
   connection limit is 2043.
00: 95/04/01 14:53:42.71 kernel: Dump/Load buffers
   configured with 8 pages.
/* 4) Master Device */
00: 95/04/01 14:53:42.99 kernel: Initializing virtual
   device 0, "/dev/rsd4b"
/* 5) Master Device is Mirrored */
00: 95/04/01 14:53:43.00 kernel: mirror: /dev/rsd5b
00: 95/04/01 14:53:43.00 kernel: Virtual device 0 started
   using asynchronous i/o.
00: 95/04/01 14:53:43.10 kernel: network name ddsdba1,
   type sun-ether, port 1025
00: 95/04/01 14:53:43.23 server: Number of buffers in buffer
   cache: 5393.
00: 95/04/01 14:53:43.23 server: Number of proc buffers
   allocated: 1797.
00: 95/04/01 14:53:43.23 server: Number of blocks left for
   proc headers: 1943.
00: 95/04/01 14:53:43.81 server: Opening Master Database ...
00: 95/04/01 14:53:44.17 server: Loading SQL Server's
   default sort order and character set
/* 6) Interfaces File Information */
00: 95/04/01 14:53:44.19 kernel: network name machine1, type
   sun-ether, port 1025
00: 95/04/01 14:53:44.26 server: Recovering database
   'master'
00: 95/04/01 14:53:44.33 server: Recovery dbid 1 ckpt
   (2391,23)
00: 95/04/01 14:53:44.33 server: Recovery no active
   transactions before ckpt.
/* 7) Servername */
00: 95/04/01 14:53:44.59 server: server name is 'ddsdba1'
00: 95/04/01 14:53:44.65 server: Activating disk 'sd1d'.
/* 8) Server Devices and Mirrors */
00: 95/04/01 14:53:44.65 kernel: Initializing virtual device
   18, "/dev/rsd1d"
```

```
00: 95/04/01 14:53:44.65 kernel: mirror: /dev/rsd10e
/* 9) Asynchronous I/O in use for Server Devices */
00: 95/04/01 14:53:44.66 kernel: Virtual device 18 started
  using asynchronous i/o.
00: 95/04/01 14:53:44.66 server: Activating disk 'sd1e'.
00: 95/04/01 14:53:44.66 kernel: Initializing virtual device
  19, "/dev/rsd1e"
00: 95/04/01 14:53:44.67 kernel: Virtual device 19 started
  using asynchronous i/o.
...
...
...
/* 10) Recovery of Databases */
00: 95/04/01 14:53:44.84 server: Recovering database
  'model'.
00: 95/04/01 14:53:44.86 server: Recovery dbid 3 ckpt
  (266,25)
00: 95/04/01 14:53:44.86 server: Recovery no active
  transactions before ckpt.
00: 95/04/01 14:53:45.01 server: Clearing temp db
00: 95/04/01 14:53:57.38 server: Recovering database 'db1'.
00: 95/04/01 14:53:57.43 server: Recovery dbid 4 ckpt
  (6401,1) oldest tran=(6401 ,0)
00: 95/04/01 14:53:57.50 server: 1 transactions rolled
  forward.
00: 95/04/01 14:53:57.84 server: Recovering database 'db2'.
00: 95/04/01 14:53:57.90 server: Recovery dbid 5 ckpt
  (51206,23) oldest tran=(51206 ,22)
00: 95/04/01 14:53:57.91 server: 1 transactions rolled
  forward.
...
...
...
00: 95/04/01 14:53:57.84 server: Recovering database 'dbn'.
00: 95/04/01 14:53:57.90 server: Recovery dbid 5 ckpt
  (51206,23) oldest tran=(51206 ,22)
00: 95/04/01 14:53:57.91 server: 1 transactions rolled
  forward.
00: 95/04/01 14:59:42.38 server: Recovery complete.
```

```
/* 11) Default Sort Order and Character Set */
00: 95/04/01 14:59:42.38 server: SQL Server's default sort
   order is:
00: 95/04/01 14:59:42.38 server:          'bin_iso_1' (ID = 50)
00: 95/04/01 14:59:42.38 server: on top of default
   character set:
00: 95/04/01 14:59:42.39 server:          'iso_1' (ID = 1).
```

Example of System 10 SQL Server Errorlog

Each of the items discussed in Table 11.2 is shown in the errorlog below. Each item is marked with a comment line /* <item> */ above the relevant portion of the errorlog.

```
/dba/DDSDBA1/errorlog 53 % more errorlog
00:95/04/01 14:26:02.69 kernel  Using config area of disk
   for boot information
00:95/04/01 14:26:02.89 kernel  Using config area from
   primary master device.
/* 1) SQL Server Version */
00:95/04/01 14:26:03.05 kernel  SQL Server/10.0.2/P/Sun4/OS
   4.1.x/1/OPT/Fri Oct 28 10:22:26 PDT 1994
/* 2) Location of Errorlog */
00:95/04/01 14:26:03.07 kernel  Logging SQL Server messages
   in file '/dba/DDSDBA1/errorlog/errorlog'.
/* 3) Maximum User Connections */
00:95/04/01 14:26:03.07 kernel  Using 2048 file descriptors.
00:95/04/01 14:26:03.08 kernel  Network and device
   connection limit is 2045.
/* 4) Master Device */
00:95/04/01 14:26:03.45 kernel  Initializing virtual device
   0, '/dev/rsd4h'
/* 5) Master Device is Mirrored --> note that the master
   device is NOT mirrored in this example */
00:95/04/01 14:26:03.46 kernel  Virtual device 0 started
   using asynchronous i/o.
00:95/04/01 14:26:03.46 server  Disk I/O affinitied to
   engine: 0
00:95/04/01 14:26:03.60 server  Number of buffers in buffer
   cache: 4978.
```

```
00:95/04/01 14:26:03.60 server  Number of proc buffers
  allocated: 1659.
00:95/04/01 14:26:03.61 server  Number of blocks left for
  proc headers: 1518.
00:95/04/01 14:26:04.83 server  Opening Master Database ...
00:95/04/01 14:26:05.08 server  Loading SQL Server's default
  sort order and character set
/* 6) Interfaces File Information */
00:95/04/01 14:26:05.15 kernel  network name machine1, type
  sun-ether, port 1025
00:95/04/01 14:26:05.18 server  Recovering database 'master'
00:95/04/01 14:26:05.21 server  Recovery dbid 1 ckpt
  (1385,19)
00:95/04/01 14:26:05.24 server  Recovery no active
  transactions before ckpt.
/* 7) Servername */
00:95/04/01 14:26:05.67 server  server name is 'ddsdba1'
00:95/04/01 14:26:05.73 server  Activating disk 'sd4b'.
/* 8) Server Devices and Mirrors -- devices are NOT
  mirrored */
00:95/04/01 14:26:05.73 kernel  Initializing virtual device
  36, '/dev/rsd4b'
/* 9) Asynchronous I/O in use for Server Devices */
00:95/04/01 14:26:05.74 kernel  Virtual device 36 started
  using asynchronous i/o.
00:95/04/01 14:26:05.74 server  Activating disk 'sd4d'.
00:95/04/01 14:26:05.74 kernel  Initializing virtual device
  10, '/dev/rsd4d'
00:95/04/01 14:26:05.75 kernel  Virtual device 10 started
  using asynchronous i/o.
...
...
...
00:95/04/01 14:26:06.04 server  Activating disk
  'sybsecurity'.
00:95/04/01 14:26:06.04 kernel  Initializing virtual device
  2, '/dev/rsd6h'
00:95/04/01 14:26:06.05 kernel  Virtual device 2 started
  using asynchronous i/o.
```

```
00:95/04/01 14:26:06.05 server  Activating disk
   'sysprocsdev'.
00:95/04/01 14:26:06.05 kernel  Initializing virtual device
   1, '/dev/rsd5h'
00:95/04/01 14:26:06.06 kernel  Virtual device 1 started
   using asynchronous i/o.
/* 10) Recovery of Databases */
00:95/04/01 14:26:06.18 server  Recovering database
   'sybsecurity'.
00:95/04/01 14:26:06.21 server  Recovery dbid 5 ckpt (365,2)
   oldest tran=(365,1)
00:95/04/01 14:26:06.23 server  1 transactions rolled
   forward.
00:95/04/01 14:26:06.64 server  audproc: Loading global
   audit options from sysauditoptions.
00:95/04/01 14:26:06.66 server  audproc: Global audit
   options successfully loaded.
00:95/04/01 14:26:06.69 server  Recovering database 'model'.
00:95/04/01 14:26:06.70 server  Recovery dbid 3 ckpt (323,7)
00:95/04/01 14:26:06.70 server  Recovery no active
   transactions before ckpt.
00:95/04/01 14:26:06.82 server  Clearing temp db
00:95/04/01 14:26:09.94 server  Recovering database
   'sybsystemprocs'.
00:95/04/01 14:26:09.95 server  Recovery dbid 4 ckpt
   (4122,27)
00:95/04/01 14:26:09.95 server  Recovery no active
   transactions before ckpt.
00:95/04/01 14:26:10.40 server  Recovering database 'db1'.
00:95/04/01 14:26:10.41 server  Recovery dbid 6 ckpt
   (5299,6)
00:95/04/01 14:26:10.41 server  Recovery no active
   transactions before ckpt.
00:95/04/01 14:26:12.46 server  Recovering database 'db2'.
00:95/04/01 14:26:12.48 server  Recovery dbid 7 ckpt
   (2381666,9)
```

```
00:95/04/01 14:26:12.48 server  Recovery no active
  transactions before ckpt.

...
...
...
00:95/04/01 14:26:36.72 server  Recovering database 'dbn'.
00:95/04/01 14:26:36.75 server  Recovery dbid 8 ckpt
  (42729,5)
00:95/04/01 14:26:36.75 server  Recovery no active
  transactions before ckpt.
00:95/04/01 14:26:57.56 server  Recovery complete.
/* 11) Default Sort Order and Character Set */
00:95/04/01 14:26:57.56 server  SQL Server's default sort
  order is:
00:95/04/01 14:26:57.58 server           'bin_iso_1' (ID = 50)
00:95/04/01 14:26:57.58 server  on top of default character
  set:
00:95/04/01 14:26:57.58 server           'iso_1' (ID = 1).
```

11.6 Impacts of Creating a New Database

You certainly know how to create a new database, and Chapters 4 and 6 discussed details of the process and planning where to put a database. You need to complete the task by remembering all the impacts of a new database and how to deal with them.

If appropriate, you must add the new database to the cron script that dumps data-bases, updates statistics, performs **dbcc** checks, and so on. Further, you must check that the server machine has sufficient disk space or tape capacity to handle the additional database dump.

11.7 Modifying System Tables Manually

From time to time you will need to manually update data in the system tables. You should review your plan for doing this with Sybase Technical Support before you begin. Also, make sure you have a good dump of the *master* database before you make changes.

WARNING:

- Updating system tables in not supported by Sybase—there is no guarantee that the system table schema will be maintained between releases, which means manual updates that work for one version may not work on another version.

- Do not perform such updates without first consulting with Sybase Technical Support.

- Make sure you have dumps of everything you might need to rebuild the server in case the manual updates destroy something.

- After updating system tables, you should restart the server to copy the changes into memory.

You must use **reconfigure** to enable the **allow updates** option for the server. Without this done, you can't make updates to a system table.

You should select all the data from the system table before making any changes. This provides a record of what was there before you changed anything. You then begin a transaction and perform your updates. Before you commit the transaction, select all the data from the system table again to be sure you made the change you intended and only that change. Then, commit the transaction; you should now select all the data again to document the changes.

You must remember to reset the **allow updates** option, that is, turn it off so that nobody else can update any of the system tables.

This process is demonstrated in "Moving Master Device to Larger Partition" in Chapter 7.

11.8 bcp Command

The bcp command is very important for various operations. The command has many options, and the format files in particular require a great deal of explanation. We do not cover the many aspects of the bcp command syntax here because the Sybase SQL Server Utility Programs for UNIX manual covers the subject very well.

11.9 Full Transaction Log or Other Segment (1105 Error)

The effects of a full transaction log have been discussed in Chapter 8 "Capacity Planning" and Chapter 10 "SQL Server Recovery." When you encounter an 1105 error, you need a step-by-step process that you can follow to verify exactly what the problem is before you can fix it. We discuss such a procedure below.

The procedure boils down to verifying that you indeed have a repeatable 1105 error, verifying which segment of which database is full, and resolving the problem. Note that it is entirely possible that the transaction that encountered the 1105 error may have been rolled back as a result of the 1105 error itself. When you try to verify the segment being full, you may find that there is some space available. At that point you must decide whether to try to free up more space in the segment or whether to wait for the user to encounter the 1105 error again, at which time you would repeat the process here. Also, while the 1105 error itself will report which segment in which database is full, you must verify this for yourself. Following are the steps for error verification and resolution.

1.	Verify Which Database Is Involved
2.	Determine Which Database Segment Is Full
3.	Deal with a Full Transaction Log
4.	Deal with a Full Database Segment
5.	Deal with Multiple Segments on a Server Device

1. Verify Which Database Is Involved

You must first verify which database encountered the 1105 error. You should be able to determine this from the user reports and from the server errorlog. If you are unable to determine which database had the 1105 error, then proceed to step 2.

2. Determine Which Database Segment Is Full

If you know which database had the 1105 error, proceed as described below for that database.

If you are not sure which database had the 1105 error, then repeat the process described here for each and every database on the server.

Checkpoint to verify transaction log is full
Create table to verify that *system* and *default* segments are full
Create table to verify that user-defined segment is full

Checkpoint to verify transaction log is full

First, enter the database and execute **checkpoint**. If the **checkpoint** command returns normally, the transaction log is not completely full. This means you must not use the **dump transaction** command with the **no_log** option. Using **dump transaction** with **no_log** when the transaction log is not completely full can cause corruption and other problems. The fact that the transaction log is not full tells you one of three things:

- **Wrong Database**
  If indeed it is a transaction log (*logsegment*) that filled and caused the 1105, you are not looking at that transaction log. You need to determine the database that encountered the 1105 error.

- **Transient 1105 error**
  It is entirely possible that the transaction that encountered the 1105 error may have been rolled back as a result of the 1105 error itself. Now you need to decide whether to free up more transaction log space or simply wait for the 1105 problem to reoccur.

- **1105 on some other segment**
  You may be in the database that encountered the 1105 error, but it wasn't the transaction log that filled.

  If the **checkpoint** command does not return normally and produces an 1105 error, then the transaction log is completely full; there isn't even enough room to write the checkpoint record. You need to deal with the full transaction log (see step 3, "Deal with a full transaction log").

Create table to verify that *system* and *default* segments are full

Try to create a table in the database. You should create a small table with a table name that is very unusual, something like

```
create table psychol(a int)
```

This practice makes it easy to remove the table later on, because the table name will stand out among the names in *sysobjects* (in case you forget to remove it immediately after this experiment). If the **create table** completes normally, then you have verified that there is space to create objects in the database. Note that for a simple database, one that does not have any user-defined segments, this verifies that the *default* and *system* segments are not full.

If the **create table** command fails and you get the 1105 error again, then the segment in which you were trying to create the table is full. You must add space to the segment (see step 4, "Deal with a full database segment").

Once you are done with this segment, drop the table you just created. Be very careful to ensure that you are dropping the correct table, that is, the table you just created while verifying which segment was full.

Create table to verify that user-defined segment is full

Try to create a table in the user-defined segment that you suspect is full. If the database does have user-defined segments and you suspect that a user-defined segment is full, attempt to create a table in each user-defined segment to verify exactly which segment is full. The syntax is

```
create table psychol (a int) on <segment_name>
```

If the **create table** command fails and you get the 1105 error again, then the segment in which you were trying to create the table is full. You must add space to the segment (see step 4, "Deal with a full database segment").

Once you are done with this segment, drop the table you just created. Be very careful to ensure that you are dropping the correct table,that is, the table you just created while verifying which segment was full.

3. *Deal with a Full Transaction Log*

At this point, you should attempt a **dump transaction** without any options, that is, a normal transaction log dump. Doing so will make a copy of the transaction log and truncate any transaction log pages that contain completed (committed or rolled back) transactions. After the **dump transaction** command completes, try **checkpoint** again. If it works normally, then the transaction log is not completely full. You should check how full the transaction log is by using

```
sp_spaceused syslogs
```

Compare the results with the size of the transaction log for the database. If the comparison shows that the transaction log is close to full, you need to decide whether to wait for further 1105 errors or to try to free up more transaction log space. Since you have already dumped the transaction log, any completed transactions should have been truncated. This means you have an on-going transaction that needs to be completed (committed or rolled back) so that more of the transaction log can be truncated.

If the second attempt at **checkpoint** still fails with the same 1105 error, you have no choice: you must free up space in the transaction log before the database can accept any more changes. You can **dump transaction** with the **no_log** option, which will truncate the log without trying to write the checkpoint record in the transaction log. After this command completes, try **checkpoint** yet again.

If this **checkpoint** completes normally, use **sp_spaceused** to check how much space in the transaction log was freed up. If the transaction log is now close to empty, you are done. Note that you have broken the sequence of transaction logs, and that affects your ability to recover the database (see Chapter 8).

If this **checkpoint** command does not succeed and you still get an 1105 error, then the transaction log is still completely full and can't be truncated at all because there is an on-going transaction (one that has not committed or been rolled back) at the very beginning of the transaction log. Recall that even one on-going transaction in the transaction log prevents the truncation of any of the following pages of the transaction log, whether or not they contain completed or on-going transactions.

At this point, you need to kill the server process that generated the on-going transaction or have the associated user log out of the server, which would kill and roll back the on-going transaction. The problem here is how to identify which user is responsible for the on-going transaction. Unless you have some way of telling which user(s) might be responsible, perhaps through the way your application(s) interact with the user, you have little choice other than to kill user processes and hope that clears things up. Or, you can simply shut down and restart the server, which will effectively kill all the server users and roll back any on-going transactions.

Note that you can always add space to the transaction log (*logsegment*) to clear up the 1105 error, but this usually doesn't help, and you don't want to have the size of the transaction log constantly increasing (see Chapter 6). Unless you have a good reason to increase the size of the transaction log, you should clear up the 1105 error by freeing space within the current transaction log.

4. Deal with a full database segment

Once you have verified that a specific database segment is full, you must add space to the segment before any further changes can be made to objects in that segment. Note that we are assuming the full segment is not the transaction log (*logsegment*). You must be careful whenever you add space to the database. If you are adding space to a segment, on a server device that is already supporting that database segment, you can proceed without too much concern.

If this is not the case, or if you need to add space to a user-defined segment, you must be very cautious. User-defined segments are generally created to isolate specific database objects (tables or indexes) to specific server devices for performance reasons. If you start adding space to such a segment on the wrong server device(s), you may be setting up a situation where a given server device is supporting multiple segments and any performance benefits of isolating the objects on the user-defined segment (that is, the whole reason for bothering with the user-defined segment in the first place) may be lost. See Chapter 4 for discussion of the problems with adding space to database segments; and see Chapter 10 for discussion of the need to plan ahead to provide server devices to support adding space to database segments.

5. Deal with Multiple Segments on a Server Device

As a final note, you should be aware that if a server device supports multiple database segments (this is very normal), it is possible that the segment reported to be full in the 1105 is only one of the segments that is full. For example, it is very normal for a database to be created with the transaction log (*logsegment*) on a separate device. This means the other two segments that are always created for any database, the *default* and *system* segments, are both supported by the other server devices assigned to the database. Hence, you may get an 1105 error that tells you the *system* segment is full, but if you try to create a table in the database, which would try to create the table in the *default* segment, you would get an 1105 error also. This simply means you may get 1105 errors reporting multiple segments being full. If those segments are supported by the same server devices, then, indeed, all those segments are full, and adding space on any of the server devices that support these multiple segments will add space to all the segments of that server device at the same time.

Chapter 12

Database Administration Versus Database System Size

The way you will administer your database system changes dramatically as the size of the system grows. In fact, the size of your system will soon dictate the way you work.

We cover the following topics.

12.1	Small Database Systems
12.2	Large Database Systems
12.3	Very Large Database Systems
12.4	Summary

We discuss the same set of basic database administration issues, listed below, for small, large, and very large database systems. Generally, there are a few large databases in any given system and they will dictate the way you work. Hence, in order to handle the needs of one large database you will be working with a large database system.

Objects
Recovery
Maintenanc
Security
Business Importance

12.1 Small Database Systems

A small database system is one that can be administered by one DBA without losing control, and one that can follow all the recommendations of the Sybase SQL Server Administration guide. As you read through the sections below you'll realize that very few truly small database systems exist. For the few that do, they either don't justify the expense of their existence or they will very quickly grow to the point of being large.

Objects

For a small database system there are few enough database objects (databases, tables, stored procedures, triggers, rules, and so on) so that you can maintain all of them by using a set of scripts that you (DBA) maintain. Anytime an object is added, deleted, or changed, the change is handled by the DBA and the scripts are kept up to date. These scripts allow for recovery of any object at any time. Further, these scripts allow for a logical rebuild or migration of the database system from one machine to another. Even if the DBA is not the one who maintains the scripts, the number of objects is small enough that one person can be responsible for keeping the scripts up to date.

Recovery

In a small database system the process of making and applying database and transaction log dumps can be handled by a single DBA. You have the time to dump the databases and the transaction logs. You have time to perform the full **dbcc** runs before you make each database or transaction log dump. Further, you have time to correct any problems that are uncovered by the **dbcc** runs before you make any database or transaction log dumps. You can wait for all user activity to stop before you start the **dbcc** and dump process.

Maintenance

A small database system is not impacted by maintenance procedures. The time it takes to run the full **dbcc** suite does not affect the business that the database system supports. The time it takes to fix all problems found by the **dbcc** runs each and every time they are run does not affect the business. You as the DBA have time to do all of this and make the dump(s) within your normal working hours.

Other maintenance procedures such as **update statistics** and **sp_recompile** on all tables in your database system can be performed as often as recommended, based on the amount of activity in the tables of each database.

Maintenance required for the server machine, such as periodic rebooting or tape drive maintenance, can always be performed as soon as it is required without affecting your business.

Security

The number of users is small enough that you as DBA can determine what their permissions should be throughout the database system. You have time to add and drop all users needed to support your business. You can review and verify that all user permissions on all database objects are correct to support the business. As users change jobs within the business and as the scope of individual jobs change, you can effect these changes quickly and accurately.

Business Importance

The business you support can function efficiently (profitably?) with the database system that you alone can support. The business will not be impacted by the database system being down for the length of time needed to replace a disk, recover from dumps, or to rebuild the system completely from the complete and up-to-date set of scripts that you maintain.

;-)

> I maintain such a system all the time—then I wake up! If you truly believe you have a small database system, then the business you support isn't growing and your career won't either, or you're about to be fired for being incompetent!

12.2 Large Database Systems

A large database system is one that can't be administered by one DBA without losing control, and one that can't follow all the recommendations of the Sybase SQL Server Administration guide. As you read through the sections below, you'll realize that most database systems fit this category. Most database systems have databases that are large enough, or have enough users, or support a business that must operate around the clock; hence, most database systems are large in that they require you to administer them in a very different manner than that described in the Sybase manuals. From the section below you will realize that a single DBA can't possible keep up with a large database system. Your function will change. You will need to plan much more than in the past. You will need to automate and delegate many tasks you are used to performing and controlling personally.

Objects

As your database system grows, the amount of data you are responsible for grows. Along with this, the number of objects within the databases will grow also. Frequently, businesses will not want to develop their own version of standard applications. These applications will be purchased through a vendor that specializes in software for the business function in question, accounting, for example. This application software will often be modified to suit the specific needs of your business. When your business purchases such an application, you have no idea how the logical or physical data models were developed, or if there was any formal development at all. As your system grows, you will lose the ability to track each object, the script that creates it, the users that can access it, and so forth. Further, the people within your organization that maintain the applications will not be willing to wait for DBA to have time to install a new version of a trigger. You will be forced to allow other users to create objects. You lose all control over object creation and maintenance.

Further, you don't have any idea what the impact of changes to objects will be. You will be tasked with restoring a table definition from a month ago and the data that was present at that time because some object change has corrupted (logically, not a corruption within the server) the data. You will not have a current script to create the old, let alone the new, table. The best you can do is load a complete dump of the database from a month ago and let the applications persons look through it for what they need.

Note that you can't fight this progression. It is in the best interests of your business to minimize the in-house application development effort. As the business moves from existing systems to in-house client-server systems, many applications will move to your database system very quickly. The users that depend on these applications will not be interested in providing DBA with a complete script for each and every object, nor will they accurately document the changes they will make. You must recognize this change—the old ways that worked for a small database system may serve as a basis for administering a large database system, but by themselves, are largely useless for that task.

Recovery

Database dumps for a large database system take longer. The time needed will gradually overwhelm the daily downtime available. If your business only needs to be supported for eight hours a day five days a week, database dumps that take two hours each will have to be run late at night. You can't be there to cover the full day and then make the database dumps yourself.

Transaction log dumps must be done much more frequently. Once your business is depending on the database system for revenue, you can't afford to lose a day's data. You will need to plan transaction log dumps to run often enough to minimize the data lost if the system crashes during the business day.

If a database dump fails, there may not be enough time to make another dump until the next business day is complete. In this case, you must be prepared to store transaction logs for the entire period between database dumps.

If the transaction log fills, you can't stop the business to make a database dump. It becomes very important that you plan ahead for database space (disk space) and the like. You won't have very much downtime anymore, and what you have will be steadily reduced by business needs that move around the world.

All of this becomes critical as your business needs support 24 hours a day. Even though your business may only need on-line access to the database system for normal business hours, you will be expected to support a growing amount of decision support activity that will demand the database system be available at all hours.

Maintenance

While every aspect of your system is growing, so does the time it takes to perform routine maintenance. You will have less and less time to run **update statistics** and **sp_recompile** on tables that have had changes. You won't have much of an idea what tables need this done, and you won't have time to do them all.

While you would like to run **dbcc** for all databases before you make a database dump, the time required for **dbcc** runs will quickly overwhelm your daily maintenance window, assuming you have any downtime at all each day. As this process unfolds, you are forced to move maintenance activity to the weekends. As your business grows and you must support offices in other states and countries, even the weekend shrinks.

The business impact of any downtime grows. Simple things like rebooting the server machine become highly political, and you will need to have a notification procedure in place.

;-)

A specific example will make this clear. Suppose your database system must support OLTP business operations in North America and Europe (with offices in Asia scheduled to open next year). This means the system must be available from midnight to 6:00 p.m. your time each day. Such a system can easily have several databases that contain several gigabytes of data each. A full **dbcc** suite on such a database can run 30 hours on a 4.9.x SQL Server. A database dump for such a database can take 2 hours. You will barely have time to make a database dump for each production database between the time North America shuts down and Europe starts up again. Any other maintenance procedures must be done in the time between Friday at 6:00 p.m. and Sunday midnight, assuming your business doesn't need the system all weekend. Once the offices in Asia open, your system will be required 24 hours a day. How will you handle this? What will you do when you have a failure? How long will recovery take and how much will the recovery time cost your business in lost revenue?

Troubleshooting will take longer as the number of interacting users and objects grows. You won't have a set of scripts to tell you what each object does and what other objects it depends on. You will have to figure all this out in real time.

Security

Along with an increase in database size and the number of objects comes an increase in the number of users. A growing business will need to support a growing user base, whether they are internal users or external. You will no longer be able to track each of them. Nor will you be able to track the proper permissions for the many new objects that these new users and their new applications will require.

You must plan for some systematic approach to adding and dropping users, user permissions, object permissions, and so on. You also will need to keep user passwords in sync across multiple servers and plan for migrating and restoring all these permissions as part of recovery or upgrading.

As you lose the ability to know all your users, you also need to be more aware of threats to the security of your database system (and thereby to your business). You will need a plan for systematically changing passwords when a user leaves the company. You will need to enforce many security procedures that your users will not like.

Business Importance

Now that your small database system has moved from a development or pilot project to a system that supports the business in real time, you must change your entire focus. You are no longer in control of many aspects of your system. You must depend on many other persons to get the job done. Your business is not looking at your system as an interesting development for future use, they are looking at it to support their paychecks, bonuses, stock price, and ultimately their future.

Your users will no longer be impressed with how clever you are, since most of them will never know you exist, unless you make a big mistake. The DBA role in a large database system is more about responsibility than control. You have the responsibility to make sure the system is under control, but you can no longer do it alone.

12.3 Very Large Database Systems

A very large database system (a system that supports very large databases or VLDBs), just like a large database system, has no clear-cut definition. This book does not attempt to cover the unique problems of administering very large databases in detail. What follows are the issues that come up as your system grows beyond the structure and procedures that are covered in this book. In general, very large databases have the same problems as large databases, just a whole lot worse. We cover the areas where very large databases diverge from large databases. As the size of the average business database system grows, new products will become available to help DBA with these problems. We don't cover solutions to these unique problems in this book; rather, we point out the problems of very large databases in the context of systems of SQL Servers to give some perspective to the current and future problems that you will face.

;-)   We assume you are going to survive the transition from small to large database systems. We'll let very large databases wait for now.

Objects

A database system that supports very large databases may not have any more objects than any other system. But, it will have a much larger amount of data. The logical model for a 40-Gb (or 400-Gb) database may not have any additional objects compared with a 4 Gb database. However, as a practical matter, you may be forced to split up objects across multiple servers to reduce the recovery and maintenance time to a reasonable duration. Hence, you may be dealing with multiple sets of objects.

Recovery

Along with maintenance, recovery is the big issue for very large databases and the systems that support them. If your database takes a week to dump, what exactly is your database dump strategy? How do you plan to recover your 40-Gb (or 400-Gb) database?

Maintenance

Routine tasks that you could perform at will on a small database system are truly incomprehensible for a very large database system. How will you run **dbcc** on this database? And if you do run **dbcc**, how will you fix any errors you find? Can you picture running **update statistics** on a table that contains 800 million rows?

Security

As with objects, the security issues may not change much at all as your databases grow from large to very large. The security needs of such a system will be very similar to those you must have in place for a large database system.

Business Importance

As the databases that your business relies on grow beyond the ability of a single SQL Server to handle, the business impacts of failures grow as well. The revenue lost from needing to restore a 40-Gb (or 400-Gb) database is huge.

12.4 Summary

We covered the way a DBA must look at the job of database administration for three different cases. The first is the ideal, Sybase manual case of a small database system that consists of databases small enough that they can be taken care of during normal business off-hours. The second case is the most common, as it represents the transition of your system from a development effort to a system that the company relies on for revenue. The third case shows you where you are headed as the endless demand for more and better access to more and more data continues. This book covers the large database system case, a system where databases are not split across SQL Servers but wherein you have many SQL Servers to support your various business activities.

Chapter 13

Upgrading SQL Server

Upgrading the SQL Server is a routine part of your job as the DBA. Upgrading comes in many forms. The simplest is applying an EBF (Emergency Bug Fix—note that 'emergency' is overstated since EBFs come out on a regular basis), followed by a rollup that is an update of the server containing many bug fixes that have been developed over some period of time and finally a version upgrade that generally involves modifying portions of the databases in a manner that prevents going back to the previous version of the server.

We discuss the following topics.

13.1 Installation Guide, Release Notes, and EBF Cover Letter

Whenever you install an EBF for the SQL Server, you must have available the various documents related to installing and configuring the server. The *Sybase SQL Server Installation Guide* and the Release Notes for the version of the server to which you are applying the EBF are very useful. The EBF cover letter tells you what bugs are fixed in the EBF and other information relevant to the upgrade process. These documents will also alert you to operating system patches required to support the upgrade.

If you are going to perform a version upgrade (examples include 4.9.2 to System 10.0 and System 10.0 to 10.0.1), there will be a whole separate installation guide (or a Release Bulletin) for the upgrade. Obtain, read, and retain this material. Version upgrades can be deadly, and the information contained in these documents can save you and your users from untold disaster.

13.2 Sybase Technical Support

Before you actually install any EBF or other upgrade, you must establish what version of the server you are currently running. The best way to do this is to access the server using isql and execute

```
select @@servername
```

Note that you must establish not only the server version (such as 4.9.2) but also the EBF level.

Once you know the server version and EBF level, you need to contact Sybase Technical Support and ask them to review what bug fixes (features?) are in the EBF you are running and tell them which EBF you are planning to apply to your server. You must verify that the new EBF and the current EBF are indeed compatible.

This becomes very important if you have a "one-off" EBF. A one-off EBF means an EBF that was created for your site to fix a special set of bugs that you are encountering. This also implies that the bug fixes you have in your current EBF may not be compatible with the new EBF, especially if the new EBF is a rollup EBF, that is, it contains many bug fixes that may or may not include the special bug fixes you needed at your site. Reviewing the current and new EBF in this much detail is the only way to prevent problems.

You need to ask if the current EBF you have is part of the codeline (that is, the set of SQL Server source code that most of the customer base is running). If you have any special bug fixes that are not part of the codeline, you may be affected in two ways. First, you can still upgrade (apply the new EBF), but you may lose the special bug fixes you needed (called regression). Second, you can still upgrade, but some of the new bug fixes may not have been tested against the one-off bug fixes in your current EBF; you may find the new EBF will actually make things worse, that is, you may end up with new bugs.

13.3 Risks of the Upgrade Process

Before you attempt any form of server upgrade, you should understand why you are applying the upgrade and what you will do if it fails. For most EBF upgrades, you can regress (go back to a previous EBF) simply by reinstalling the previous EBF. For version upgrades, this is often not possible. You must be prepared to deal with the possibility that the upgrade may fail, and you must have a plan to get back to a functioning and stable server. Even if the upgrade succeeds, it is possible that due to conflicts between bug fixes in EBF levels, and so on, the data currently in your server becomes corrupted. Even though you can go back to the previous EBF level, you will still have to fix the data corruption.

These concerns are all the more acute when you are dealing with a version-level upgrade, such as 4.9.2 to System 10. In the event that the upgrade fails, you can find yourself in a state where the data in the databases has been irreversibly modified to be compatible with System 10, but the upgrade didn't complete so you don't have a functioning server. You can't just reinstall the 4.9.2 server because the data itself was modified. You need to discuss these possibilities with Sybase Technical Support before you upgrade, and you must have a plan for recovery in the event of a failed upgrade before you begin.

13.4 EBF Upgrades

The process of upgrading the SQL Server from one EBF level to another is not complicated. However, since it comes up often, you should standardize the process so that any of the DBAs can do it as needed. Further, by standardizing the process, you can easily, quickly, and safely move back to a previous EBF if needed. You should set up the same process on all of your servers, both production and development, so that any of the DBAs can be trained once and will be able to install a new EBF or regress to an old EBF on any machine in your database system. Following are the steps of an EBF checklist.

1.	Obtain Documents
2.	Load the New EBF
3.	Verify Current Server Version and EBF Level
4.	Archive the Current Server Binary
5.	Shut Down the Server
6.	Copy New EBF into Server Binary File
7.	Restart Server
8.	Verify that Server is Executing New EBF
9.	Document the EBF Installation

1. Obtain Documents

Obtain and read the Release Notes or Bulletin or Cover Letter that explains the new EBF fixes and any details of the installation process. It is always a good idea to review the Installation Guide for the server version you are currently running to ensure that all the server machine operating system patches are in place and any other parameters of the hardware have been set up before applying the new EBF.

2. Load the New EBF

Load the new EBF from tape or copy it from another server machine in your database system into the standard directory for storing server binaries. Note that for the standard environment discussed previously (see Chapter 1), you need to get the new EBF executable file into /dba/<*servername*>/bin. Note also that the server executable filename should be standardized to make locating any EBF easy and error-free. Such a standard would be s_*<servername-lowercase>*.*<version>*datasvr.*<EBFlevel>* and an example would be s_ddsdba1.492datasvr.3121.

3. Verify Current Server Version and EBF Level

You must verify the current server version and EBF level that you are running. You need to access the server using isql and execute

```
select @@ servername
```

An example of the output of this command is shown below.

```
/dba/DDSDBA1 % isql -Usa -SDDSDBA1
Password:
1> select @@version
2> go


    ---------------------------------------------
SQL Server/10.0.1/EBF 3434/Sun4/OS 4.1.x/1/OPT/Tue Apr  1
   17:30:20 PDT 1995

(1 row affected)
```

This output tells you that you are running the System 10.0.1 version of the server at the 3434 EBF level. Note that if this isn't the EBF level (or the server version) you thought you were running, you need to stop and reassess what has been going on. You should not proceed with the upgrade until you are sure the new EBF will not cause problems when applied to the current server. Or, you need to get the server running at the EBF (and version) level it should be before you can plan the EBF upgrade.

4. Archive the Current Server Binary

Now that you know the current server version and EBF level, archive the currently executing server binary by copying the file that is actually executed when you start the server into a file that reflects the EBF level. Recall that in the standard environment, you start the server by executing /dba/ *<servername>*/RUN_*<servername>*, which actually executes the server binary file which has a filename like s_<*servername-lowercase*>.<*version*>datasvr; an example would be s_ddsdba1.1001p2datasvr. Thus, each time RUN_<*servername*> is executed, the file s_ddsdba1.1001p2datasvr is executed to actually start the SQL Server. In addition, the file s_ddsdba1.1001p2datasvr contains the binary for the currently executing server version and EBF level. This file should be copied to a filename of s_<*servername-lowercase*>.<*version*>datasvr.<*EBFlevel*>; an example would be s_ddsdba1.1001p2datasvr.3434. Copying the file preserves the currently executing server in case you need it later. If you have followed the standard procedure, the currently executing server should already exist in such a file; if so, you don't need to copy it again.

5. Shut Down the Server

Shut down the currently executing server. As with any normal (nonemergency) shutdown of the server, you should follow the steps described in Chapter 8 to ensure that the server and its databases are stable before shutting down the server.

6. Copy New EBF into Server Binary File

With the server shut down, you now move the new EBF server executable into the file that is executed each time RUN_<*servername*> is executed, that is, the file s_<*servername-lowercase*>.<*version*>datasvr. An example would be s_ddsdba1.1001p2datasvr. Applying the new EBF really boils down to copying the new EBF server executable (binary) file to this file (that is, s_ddsdba1.1001p2datasvr). The next time RUN_<*servername*> is executed, the new EBF will be executed as the server.

This approach makes it very easy to install a new EBF or to regress to an older EBF level. Note that no editing of files is involved. This means the whole EBF upgrade process can be accomplished by simple UNIX commands. This approach is very valuable when you need to perform EBF upgrades during off-hours from a remote terminal.

7. Restart Server

Restart the server watching the errorlog to verify that the new server EBF is really executing. See Chapter 11 for more discussion of watching the errorlog during server startup.

8. *Verify that Server is Executing New EBF*

Once the server has fully recovered you should run isql against the new server and run **select @@servername** to verify that the new EBF level is being executed as you expect.

9. *Document the EBF Installation*

Finally, document what you did, so the other DBAs will know that this server was upgraded to this new EBF level.

13.5 Version Upgrades

A version upgrade is an upgrade that involves more than simply restarting the server with a new binary. It may also mean an upgrade for which you can't regress to the previous version in any easy way. Examples of a version upgrade would be 4.2 to 4.8 and 4.9 to System 10. In these cases, the actual data in the databases is reworked; this means that dumps of the previous version can't be loaded into the upgraded server. A version upgrade is more involved than an EBF upgrade for these reasons. A version upgrade may also require changes to your applications. Changes such as SQL syntax or feature changes to be compliant with one of the ANSI standards can wreak havoc with an existing application. Only through application testing against the new version of the server will you determine the impact of the new version on your application(s).

You must be aware of the risks to your database system if the upgrade goes poorly. You must think of how to recover the previous version if needed. Further, you need to think of the impacts on other servers. You may need to upgrade other servers in the system immediately to support a reporting server, for example, that takes its data from the primary OLTP server. Once you upgrade the primary server, you must upgrade the report server as well or you can't keep the report server up to date. Further, you may need to have a separate dedicated server at the older version level somewhere in your system to support loading of dumps made at the previous version. You must be prepared to recover data from objects in the database at the previous version.

Version upgrades involve much more planning and testing prior to the actual upgrade. We discuss the process of upgrading from SQL Server 4.9.x to System 10 below.

13.6 Preparing to Upgrade 4.9.x to System 10

The following steps are taken with the server at the 4.9.x level. Some of these steps are simply to prevent trouble during the upgrade. These steps should be done well before the actual upgrade begins. For that reason, the set of steps includes restoring the databases to their original options so that normal processing can resume while the results of the pre-upgrade checks are reviewed. Note, however, that the steps for dropping mirrors and so forth should not be performed until you are ready to proceed with the complete upgrade.

You will notice the discussion of mirrors throughout the upgrade process. The use of mirrors allows you to regress to the 4.9.x server quickly in case the upgrade to System 10 fails. This regression method requires that any database you wish to regress quickly be mirrored. Databases that are not mirrored would have to be dropped, recreated and loaded from dumps if they are not mirrored before the upgrade begins. You should mirror all the databases on your server for many reasons, but here the reason is to provide a quick regression path for all the databases of the server. Following is a check list for upgrade preparations.

1.	Reset All Database Options
2.	Use sybinit for Preupgrade Database Check
3.	Review the Log of sybinit During Preupgrade Database Check
4.	Use sybinit for Pr-upgrade Reserved Word Check
5.	Examine the Output of sybinit Reserved Word Check
6.	Reset All Database Options
7.	Drop Mirrors and Devices for New System 10 Devices
8.	Check Remaining Server Device Mirrors
9.	Check Partitions for New System 10 Devices
10.	Perform **dbcc** Checks on All Databases
11.	Check Free Space in All Databases
12.	Check for Objects Related to Indexes
13.	Dump Transaction Logs and Checkpoint All Databases

1. Reset All Database Options

Set all the databases on the server to have no options set. Note that you do not want to remove the **select into/bulkcopy** option on *tempdb*. Other than that, all databases should show no options set in the output of **sp_helpdb**.

2. Use sybinit for Pre-upgrade Database Check

In order to run the pre-upgrade checks of the 4.9.x server, you must run sybinit. Note that you are not running sybconfig. When you start sybinit, you must be UNIX user 'sybase.' See Chapter 3 for details of becoming UNIX user 'sybase' and changing file permissions as required so that the 'sybase' user can execute sybinit. When you start sybinit, select the 'upgrade an existing SQL Server' option and then select the pre-upgrade check "Test SQL Server upgrade eligibility now." See the sections below for the actual output from the sybinit session.

3. Review the Log of sybinit During Pre-upgrade Database Check

The following output is from the sybinit session during which the upgrade eligibility test is run. Note that the directory /dba/1001p2 is the location of the new System 10 files, whereas the current 4.9.x server files are located in the normal installation (or home) directory of /dba/sybase. After the upgrade is complete, move the files in /dba/1001p2 into /dba/sybase.

```
machine1 % $SYBASE/install/sybinit
The log file for this session is
   '/dba/1001p2/init/logs/log0401.002'.

SYBINIT

1.   Release directory: /dba/1001p2

2.   Edit / View Interfaces File

3.   Configure a Server product
4.   Configure an Open Client/Server product


Ctrl-a Accept and Continue, Ctrl-x Exit Screen, ? Help.
```

Enter the number of your choice and press return: 3

CONFIGURE SERVER PRODUCTS

Products:

Product	Date Installed	Date Configured
1. SQL Server	Apr 01 95 12:51	Apr 01 95 12:51
2. Backup Server	Apr 01 95 12:51	Apr 01 95 12:51

Ctrl-a Accept and Continue, Ctrl-x Exit Screen, ? Help.

Enter the number of your choice and press return: 1

NEW OR EXISTING SQL SERVER

1. Configure a new SQL Server
2. Configure an existing SQL Server
3. Upgrade an existing SQL Server

Ctrl-a Accept and Continue, Ctrl-x Exit Screen, ? Help.

Enter the number of your choice and press return: 3

UPGRADE EXISTING SQL SERVER

1. Release directory for previous release /dba/1001p2

Ctrl-a Accept and Continue, Ctrl-x Exit Screen, ? Help.

Enter the number of your choice and press return: 1
Enter the pathname of the release directory to use (default
is '/dba/1001p2'):
/dba/sybase

UPGRADE EXISTING SQL SERVER

1. Release directory for previous release /dba/sybase

Ctrl-a Accept and Continue, Ctrl-x Exit Screen, ? Help.

Enter the number of your choice and press return:

CONFIGURE EXISTING SQL SERVER

Select one of the following servers:

1.   DDSDBA1

/* note that sybinit displays all the servers that have
entries in the interfaces file and if the number of
servers fill more than one screen you will see
<More>
Ctrl-f Scroll Forward, Ctrl-b Scroll Backward.
be careful and use control-f (^f) to keep scrolling through
all the servers */

Ctrl-a Accept and Continue, Ctrl-x Exit Screen, ? Help.

Enter the number of your choice and press return: 1

ENTER SA ACCOUNT NAME AND PASSWORD

1. SA Account: sa

2. SA Password:

Ctrl-a Accept and Continue, Ctrl-x Exit Screen, ? Help.

Enter the number of your choice and press return: 2
Enter the password to this account:

ENTER SA ACCOUNT NAME AND PASSWORD

1. SA Account: sa

2. SA Password: #######

Ctrl-a Accept and Continue, Ctrl-x Exit Screen, ? Help.

Enter the number of your choice and press return:

SQL SERVER UPGRADE

1. Test SQL Server upgrade eligibility now
2. Check for reserved word conflicts
3. sybsystemprocs database configuration

4. Upgrade SQL Server now

Ctrl-a Accept and Continue, Ctrl-x Exit Screen, ? Help.

Enter the number of your choice and press return: 1
Testing SQL Server 'DDSDBA1' for eligibility to upgrade to
release '10.0.1'.
....
....
....D
one

Server 'DDSDBA1' passed Preupgrade eligibility test.
Press <return> to continue.

/* you would exit sybinit at this point */
/* the log file output for sybinit during the Pre-upgrade
eligibility test is shown below */

The log file for this session is
'/dba/1001p2/init/logs/log0401.002'.
04/01/95 03:25:43 PM Sybinit/10.0.1/P2/Sun4/OS
  4.1.x/1/OPT/Wed Mar 30 13:09:47
                    PST 1994
04/01/95 03:25:43 PM BEGIN ENVIRONMENT INFORMATION

USER ENVIRONMENT
----
user name: dba

```
current directory:            /dba/1001p2/init/logs
character set:                iso_1
language:                     us_english
sybinit release directory:    /dba/1001p2
working release directory:    /dba/1001p2


04/01/95 03:25:43 PM END ENVIRONMENT INFORMATION
04/01/95 03:28:14 PM Copying entry 'DDSDBA1' from interfaces
   file
              '/dba/sybase/interfaces' to interfaces file
              '/dba/1001p2/interfaces'.
04/01/95 03:28:15 PM Calling the shell with
   '/dba/1001p2/upgrade/preupgrade
              -SDDSDBA1 -P
              -N > /dba/1001p2/init/logs/tmp 2>&1 '.
04/01/95 03:28:15 PM Testing SQL Server 'DDSDBA1' for
   eligibility to upgrade to release '10.0.1'.
04/01/95 03:36:49 PM Done
04/01/95 03:36:49 PM Begin output from 'preupgrade':
         Starting preupgrade of SQL Server
         Checking status in all existing databases.
         Checking space in all existing databases.
                   Database db1 has sufficient space.
                   Database db2 has sufficient space.
                   Database db3 has sufficient space.
....
....
....
                   Database dbn has sufficient space.
Clearing reused columns in all existing databases.
            Preupgrade of SQL Server to 10.0 is complete.
04/01/95 03:36:49 PM End output from 'preupgrade'.
04/01/95 03:38:09 PM Server 'DDSDBA1' passed preupgrade
   eligibility test.
04/01/95 03:38:17 PM Exiting.
04/01/95 03:38:17 PM The log file for this session is
                   '/dba/1001p2/init/logs/log0401.002'.
04/01/95 03:38:17 PM Log close.
```

4. *Use sybinit for Pre-upgrade Reserved Word Check*

In order to run the pre-upgrade checks of the 4.9.x server, you must run sybinit. Note that you are not running sybconfig. When you start sybinit, you must be UNIX user 'sybase.' See Chapter 3 for details of becoming UNIX user 'sybase' and changing file permissions as required so that the 'sybase' user can execute sybinit. When you start sybinit you select the "upgrade an existing SQL Server" option and then select the pre-upgrade "Check for reserved word conflicts." See the sections below for the actual output from the sybinit session.

5. *Examine the Output of sybinit Reserved Word Check*

The following output is from the sybinit session during which the reserved word conflict check is run. The output shown below starts from the SQL SERVER UPGRADE menu.

```
SQL SERVER UPGRADE

1.  Test SQL Server upgrade eligibility now
2.  Check for reserved word conflicts
3.  sybsystemprocs database configuration

4.  Upgrade SQL Server now


Ctrl-a Accept and Continue, Ctrl-x Exit Screen, ? Help.

Enter the number of your choice and press return: 2
The log file for sp_checkreswords output is
'/dba/1001p2/init/logs/checkres.dmp'.

Warning: 53 conflicts with 10.0 reserved words were found.
Sybase suggests that you resolve these conflicts before
upgrading the SQL Server.  Run 'sp_checkreswords' on each
database for more information.
Press <return> to continue.

/* you would exit sybinit at this point */
```

```
/* the output file containing the reserved word conflicts is
shown below */

/dba/1001p2/init/logs 5 % more checkres.dmp
Reserved Words Used as Database Objects for Database 'db1'
------------------------------------------------------------
-
------------------------------------------------------------
-
Owner
-------------
dbo
Object Type                       Object Name
------------------------          --------------------
Table                             Column
------------------------          --------------------
sysobjects                        schema
------------------------------------------------------------
============================================================
=
Database-wide Objects
--------------------

User names
------------------------------
public
Reserved Words Used as Database Objects for Database 'db2'
------------------------------------------------------------
-
------------------------------------------------------------
-
Owner
------------------------------
dbo
Object Type                       Object Name
------------------------          ----------------------
Table                             Column
------------------------          ----------------------
sysobjects                        schema
------------------------------------------------------------
```

```
===============================================================
=
Database-wide Objects
---------------------

User names
------------------------------
public
Reserved Words Used as Database Objects for Database 'db3'
-------------------------------------------------------------
-
-------------------------------------------------------------
-
Owner
------------------------------
dbo
Object Type                     Object Name
------------------------------  ----------------------
Table                           Column
------------------------------  ----------------------
sysobjects                      schema
-------------------------------------------------------------
===============================================================
==
Database-wide Objects
---------------------
User names
------------------------------
public
....
....
....
Reserved Words Used as Database Objects for Database 'dbn'
-------------------------------------------------------------
-
-------------------------------------------------------------
-
Owner
------------------------------
dbo
```

```
Object Type                     Object Name
------------------------------  ---------------------
Table                           Column
------------------------------  ---------------------
sysobjects                        schema
bugs                              user
syb_breaks                        level
------------------------------------------------------------
-
============================================================
=
Database-wide Objects
--------------------


User names
-------------------------------
public
```

You need to be aware of several things in the output of the reserved word conflict check. The file of reserved words simply tells you of objects in databases in the server that are reserved words in System 10 SQL Server. These words can't be used in Transact-SQL statements, and so on, once the server is upgraded to System 10. However, you must understand that each and every database in your 4.9.x server will have a column of the system table *sysobjects* called *schema*. The column named *schema* is fine in the 4.9.x SQL Server, but *schema* becomes a reserved word in the System 10 server. You don't need to do anything about this conflict because the upgrade process itself will automatically change the column name to *schema2*. If you look at the server documents for the system table *sysobjects* for both the 4.9.x and System 10 servers, you will see that the column *schema* in 4.9.x becomes *schema2* in System 10.

Now for the other reserved word conflicts. Note that the reserved word conflicts will not prevent you from upgrading to System 10. You can complete the upgrade without changing the object names (table, column, and so on) that are causing the conflict. However, once you try to access the object (table, column, and so on) the server will complain and generate an error. Note that you can also turn on an option within the server (see **set quoted identifier on**) to allow reserved words that are enclosed in double quotes. The point you must retain is that the reserved word conflicts don't prevent you from upgrading, but they may prevent you from executing all the queries of your business after the upgrade.

For the other reserved word conflicts, you need to determine how many other objects depend on the objects that use reserved words. If possible, you should change the objects as soon as possible. If the objects that have reserved word conflicts are vital to your business, you may need to delay the upgrade until these conflicts can be worked out or until you are confident you can operate by using the reserved words in double quotes. This is another reason you must perform these pre-upgrade checks well in advance of the actual upgrade.

In the output shown above for the reserved word conflict check, we see that the table *bugs* has a column named *user* and the table *syb_breaks* has a column named *level*. Both *user* and *level* are reserved words in System 10. You need to determine the impact to your applications if queries can't access these columns of these tables, and determine the work needed to change the object and all objects that depend on it.

;-)

> You will also find that the reserved word conflict check may flush out objects that are not owned by server user 'sa'. If this is the case you should simply notify the user that does own the object and simply inform them that their object(s) will not be usable after the upgrade. That will motivate them. If they never reply just delete the objects. Paybacks are hell!

6.   *Reset All Database Options*

Since you are performing these pre-upgrade checks well ahead of the actual upgrade, you will need to reset all the database options to what they were before you performed the pre-upgrade checks. Note that, as always, this is another time when you will appreciate the fact that you are dumping the system tables of your server regularly. You may need the output of this process to check what the database options were.

7. Drop Mirrors and Devices for New System 10 Devices

The System 10 SQL Server requires a separate server disk device, called sysprocs-dev, to support the *sybsystemprocs* database, which houses all the system stored procedures for the System 10 SQL Server. If you are installing the auditing capabilities available under System 10, you will also need a separate server disk device, called sybsecurity, to support the *sybsecurity* database. Although you can place both the *sybsystemprocs* and *sybsecurity* databases on any available server device, it is best if you place each of them on a separate server device created just for this purpose. Specifically, it is best not to place these databases on the master device. The master device should be supporting as little as possible to simplify recovery. Both of these devices must be 30 MB, must be separate from other server devices, and should be mirrored. See Chapter 1 for details of disk partitioning to support the System 10 server. Set up the disk partitions to support these devices before you begin the upgrade process. Since these devices (and their databases) get created by the sybinit process, you must drop the devices (and their mirrors, if they are mirrored) that currently occupy the disk partitions that will support these new devices and databases. If you don't have any 30-MB partitions available, you need to decide where to locate the new server devices needed, then drop the devices and mirrors, if there are any on those partitions.

;-)

> If you don't have the 30-MB partitions that you need, then you haven't been doing the capacity planning for disk space that you should have. Note that capacity planning is not just about total disk space. In this case, it is about having the appropriate disk partitions for the needed System 10 devices and their mirrors on physical disks that are separate from the disk housing the master device and so on. Note that the standard disk partitioning scheme discussed in Chapter 1 would make it very easy to accommodate the devices needed by the System 10 SQL Server.

8. Check Remaining Server Device Mirrors

Now that you have dropped the mirrors and devices on the partitions needed to support the new System 10 devices, check that all the other devices in your server are currently mirrored. As discussed in Chapter 1, it is simply easier for you to administer a server where each and every server disk device is mirrored. As we shall see later, these mirrors provide a good regression path in case you need to move back from System 10 to the 4.9.x server.

9. Check Partitions for New System 10 Devices

Ensure that the partitions you have selected for the new System 10 devices to be created during the sybinit process (sysprocsdev and sybsecurity) are the size you think they are (to be passed along to sybinit) and that they are owned by UNIX user 'sybase' during sybinit.

10. Perform dbcc Checks on All Databases

Ensure that all the databases are free from corruption before upgrading.

11. Check Free Space in All Databases

The upgrade will remap database objects, such as stored procedures and triggers, that are compiled. The remapped objects will take up more space in each database, so you need to check the free space in each database. If the free space in a given database is less than 10 percent of the total size of the database, you should add space to increase the free space to 10 percent of the total database space. Run **sp_spaceused** in each database to determine how much free space is available. Note that you should perform this step even though the pre-upgrade check of the database (performed by using sybinit) told you there was sufficient space in each database.

12. Check for Objects Related to Indexes

Here you need to perform two queries in each and every database in the server. If either query returns more than zero rows, you have an object that doesn't have a corresponding entry in *sysindexes* or an index that doesn't have a corresponding entry in *sysobjects*. Note that **dbcc** may not catch such problems, and the upgrade can fail when it hits such an object or index. If you find any problems like this, contact Sybase Technical Support for the procedure to properly delete the offending object or *sysindexes* entry.

The queries are shown below:

```
select id from sysobjects
where (type = 'U' or type = 'S')
and id not in (select id from sysindexes)
```

```
select id from sysindexes
where id not in (select id from sysobjects)
```

13. *Dump Transaction Logs and Checkpoint All Databases*

You must dump the transaction log for each and every database and run **checkpoint** in each database. This will provide a copy of the transaction log in case you must recover, and it frees up space in the transaction log to support the upgrade. If there is a standby server of the server being upgraded, apply these transaction log dumps to the standby server. This will keep the standby server as up-to-date as possible in the event of a problem with the upgrade.

13.7 Upgrading 4.9.x to System 10

Now you are ready to perform the actual upgrade of your server from 4.9.x to System 10. There are many steps that you need to perform, many of which will seem unnecessary to you. These steps are to protect you, your users, and the data from becoming partially upgraded with no way to return to the 4.9.x version of the server. You should review all the steps listed below before you start upgrading.

The detailed steps below assume you are upgrading a SQL Server from the 4.9.2 level to System 10. As with all specific procedures, you should contact Sybase Technical Support for a review of your server's specific hardware, software, EBF level, and configuration before starting the upgrade. You may need to modify the series of steps shown below to deal with the specifics of your server and server machine. Following is a checklist for the task.

1.	Isolate Server from Users
2.	Dump Transaction Log Again
3.	Verify Transaction Log Is Empty
4.	Dump All Databases to Tape
5.	Dump Server Configuration to Disk Files
6.	Dump Contents of *syslogins* System Table
7.	Dump *master* with Devices Mirrored
8.	Check Mirrors

9.	Drop Secondary Side of Mirrored Devices
10.	Check that All Mirrors Dropped
11.	Turn Off All Database Options
12.	Set 'sa' Password NULL
13.	Test 'sa' Password
14.	Verify *master* as Default Database for 'sa'
15.	Dump *master* without Mirrors
16.	Increase TIMEOUTCOUNT in Upgrade Script
17.	Reconfigure Server for Upgrade
18.	Add Entry to Interfaces File for *<servername>_SYS10*
19.	Restart Server
20.	Dump *master* for New Configuration
21.	Use sybinit to Start Server Upgrade
22.	Perform sybinit Pre-upgrade Database Check
23.	Perform sybinit Reserved Word Check
24.	Perform *sybsystemprocs* Database Configuration
25.	Upgrade Server
26.	Install Backup Server and Auditing

1. Isolate Server from Users

Before you start the actual upgrade, you need to isolate the server from the users. The best way to do this is to shutdown the server (after notifying the users) and then restart the server but on a different port number. (See Chapter 11 for details of how the interfaces file works and how to change port numbers.) This will prevent any user from logging into the server while the upgrade is underway. The basic idea here is to bring the server up on a server machine port that is different from the port number the users have in their copy of the interfaces file. This assumes that the server machine has its own version of the interfaces file separate from the interfaces file(s) used by the users (see Chapter 1). You should note the time it takes for the server to recover on the new port number.

2. Dump Transaction Log Again

You must dump the transaction log for each and every database and run **checkpoint** in each database again. This will flush out any transactions that were completed by users after the previous transaction log dump and before the server was shut down. If there is a standby server of the server being upgraded, apply these transaction log dumps to the standby server. This will keep the standby server as up-to-date as possible in the event of a problem with the upgrade.

3. Verify Transaction Log Is Empty

For each database, execute **sp_spaceused syslogs** to determine the used and free space in the transaction log. Since the server has been restarted and the users isolated, there shouldn't be any open transactions that could hold the transaction log full.

4. Dump All Databases to Tape

Once you have the server isolated from the users, you should not be making any changes to the user data. Now you must dump all the databases, including *master* and *model,* to tape. If you prefer to dump to disk, make sure a dump to tape of the disk dump files is made before you proceed with the upgrade. To be really safe, you should try to load these dumps on another server. You will think this is paranoid and you will be correct. You need to decide what the cost to the business would be if the last dump of the databases at the 4.9.x level were bad and the upgrade failed. If that occurs, you can only recover the server to the point of the previous database dump(s).

5. Dump Server Configuration to Disk Files

You must dump the system tables that are dumped by the script dump_systables to disk files (see Chapter 15). The easiest way to do this is to simply execute the cron job script manually. Check that the output file is created and that the output file is from the latest execution of the script. In addition, you must dump the output of executing **sp_helpdb** within each and every database on the server. This means you must execute isql into the server, **use db1**, **sp_helpdb db1**, then repeat this for every database in the server and dump the output to a disk file.

6. Dump Contents of syslogins System Table

Use the bcp utility to dump the contents of the *syslogins* table to a disk file. This dump will be needed if there are any problems later with user accounts. This disk file will tell you what the user's *suid*, login *name*, *password*, and default database were on the 4.9.x server. This information should be available in case you need to rebuild the server. Note that you must use bcp with the -c option so that you can edit the output. You will need to edit out the information for the 'sa' and 'probe' server logins before you can bcp the file into the *syslogins*.

7. Dump master With Devices Mirrored

You must now dump the *master* database to disk. Since you are running a 4.9.2 server at this point, you must dump *master* to a disk dump device and then rename the file so that the dump is not overwritten by subsequent dumps. You should name this dump of the *master* database dump_<*servername*>_master_4.9.2_withmirrors_ date_time.out to make it easy to rebuild the server if needed. Note that this dump of the *master* database contains data from the system table *sysdevices,* reflecting the primary and secondary (mirror) server disk devices that contain 4.9.2 data. See Figure 13.1(A).

8. Check Mirrors

Check the mirrors of all the server devices to make sure none of them had failed before you made the dump of the *master* database in the previous step. You should document the mirrors (save the output of **p_mirror**—see Chapter 15) of the server devices for later use.

9. Drop Secondary Side of Mirrored Devices

For each of the server devices that has a mirror (see Chapter 1 for reasons why you should mirror all the server disk devices), perform the following command:

```
disk unmirror name = '<devicename>',
side = secondary,
mode = remove
```

This command will permanently drop the secondary side (the mirror) of the device pair. Note that both the primary server device and the secondary server device of the pair contain server data at the 4.9.2 version level. You can put the commands to drop the mirror of each server device into a script to make dropping all the mirrors more efficient.

10. Check That All Mirrors Dropped

Run **p_mirror** again to verify that all the server disk devices do not have mirrors.

11. Turn Off All Database Options

Make sure that all database options are turned off, except for the **select into/bulk copy** option for *tempdb,* which must always be turned on.

12. Set 'sa' Password NULL

Reset the server user 'sa' password to NULL.

13. Test 'sa' Password

Verify that the server user 'sa' password is indeed NULL by using isql and logging into the server as 'sa.'

14. Verify master as Default Database for 'sa'

Verify that the default database for the server user 'sa' is *master.*

15. Dump master without Mirrors

You must now dump the *master* database to disk again. Since you are running a 4.9.2 server at this point, you must dump *master* to a disk dump device and then rename the file so that the dump is not overwritten by subsequent dumps. Name this dump of the *master* database dump_<*servername*>_master_4.9.2_nomirrors_ date_time.out to make it easy to rebuild the server if needed. Note that this dump of the *master* database contains data from the system table *sysdevices,* reflecting the primary server devices only, which still contain 4.9.2 data. see Figure 13.1(B).

16. Increase TIMEOUTCOUNT in Upgrade Script

If your server takes a long time to recover even with no user access, you may need to increase the parameter TIMEOUTCOUNT in the upgrade script. Consult Sybase Technical Support for the details of making this change. A long time is defined to be more than ten minutes to recover.

17. Reconfigure Server for Upgrade

The upgrade process takes a significant portion of the server machine memory available to the server. To make room for this you should reconfigure the server to reduce the user connections to 10 and the stack size to 286720. You will have to restart the server to make these configuration changes take effect.

18. Add Entry to Interfaces File for *<servername>_SYS10*

Now that you are about to begin the actual upgrade process, you should rename the server to make it clear that you are no longer accessing a 4.9.2 server. Make a new entry in the interfaces file on the server machine for this new server; modify your RUN_*<servername>* script as well.

19. Restart Server

Restart the server as *<servername>_SYS10*.

20. Dump master for New Configuration

You must now dump the *master* database to disk again. Since you are running a 4.9.2 server at this point, you must dump *master* to a disk dump device and then rename the file so that the dump is not overwritten by subsequent dumps. You should name this dump of the *master* database dump_*<servername>*_master_4.9.2_nomirrors_ newconfig_date_time.out to make it easy to rebuild the server if needed. Note that this dump of the *master* database contains data from the system table *sysdevices* reflecting the primary server devices only which still contain 4.9.2 data.

21. Use sybinit to Start Server Upgrade

Start sybinit just as you did for the pre-upgrade checks done previously.

22. Perform sybinit Pre-upgrade Database Check

Repeat the pre-upgrade database check to verify that nothing has changed since the previous check.

23. Perform sybinit Reserved Word Check

Repeat this check just in case there have been changes in any of the objects since the last reserved word check. Compare the output from this run of the reserved word check with the previous output. If there are new reserved word conflicts, you must determine whether or not the upgrade can proceed.

24. Perform sybsystemprocs Database Configuration

Now that you are really upgrading the server, you need to provide sybinit with parameters defining which disk partition will support the *sysprocsdev* and how big it will be, as well as size of the *sybsystemprocs* database.

25. Upgrade Server

Select "Upgrade SQL Server now" from the SQL SERVER UPGRADE menu in sybinit. You are now performing the actual upgrade of your server.

26. Install Backup Server and Auditing

With the upgrade complete, you must install the Backup Server and should install the auditing capabilities of the System 10 SQL Server as well. You can restart sybinit or simply stay within the same sybinit session and go back to the NEW OR EXISTING SQL SERVER menu.

13.8 Post Upgrade 4.9.x to System 10

Once you have successfully completed the upgrade of your server to System 10, you have several tasks remaining before you can go home. These tasks are listed and described below.

1.	Dump *master* Database after Upgrade
2.	Set 'sa' Password
3.	Reset All Database Options

4.	Reset Server Configuration
5.	Reset Server Name
6.	Restart Server as 'dba'
7.	Install Thresholds
8.	Install Roles for All DBA and Operator Users
9.	Dump *master* Database Again
10.	Dump All Databases
11.	Check All Production Scripts
12.	Mirror Primary Devices
13.	Update Table Statistics
14.	Allow User Access

1. Dump master Database after Upgrade

You must now dump the *master* database to disk again. Since you are running a System 10 server at this point, you must use the Backup Server for dumping *master* to disk. Note that with System 10 and the Backup Server you can now dump a database or transaction log directly to a file on disk—you don't have to (although you still can) use a server dump device. You should name this dump of the *master* database dump_<servername>_master_10x_date_time.out to make it easy to rebuild the server if needed. Note that this dump of the *master* database contains data from the system table *sysdevices* reflecting the primary server devices only, which now contain System 10 data, see Figure 13.1(C).

2. Set 'sa' Password

You must reset the server user 'sa' password immediately. Recall that you set the 'sa' password to be NULL before the upgrade began. Note that System 10 encrypts passwords, so the entries for password in the system table syslogins will no longer be human readable. Hence, you can't even check to see if the 'sa' password is NULL. You will have to remember what the 'sa' password was before the upgrade to reset it or look it up on one of the other servers in your database system that is still at the 4.9.x version level.

3. Reset All Database Options

Check each database on the server to reestablish any and all database options that were in effect before the upgrade took place. This is another time when you need to have dumped the server system tables to disk (see Chapter 15).

4. Reset Server Configuration

Now, reset the stack size and the number of user connections to their pre-upgrade values. Recall that before the upgrade process began, you changed the configuration of the server to have only 10 user connections and a stack size of 286720. You may not be able to reconfigure both of these parameters at once. Using the configuration of the server that was upgraded above as an example, you would be increasing the number of user connections from 10 to 800 while reducing the stack size from 286720 to 40960. If you try to change both parameters at once, the server may not start if there is not enough memory to support 800 user connections and the stack size of 286720 while the server reduces the stack size. You may need to reduce the stack size, restart the server, verify the server configuration, then repeat the process for the user connections.

5. Reset Server Name

During the upgrade you changed the server name to <servername>_SYS10 to make sure you couldn't run scripts that called for <servername> and to make sure you were aware that you were no longer running a 4.9.x server. Now that you are preparing the server for online use, you need to reset the server name in the startup scripts and in the interfaces file to the pre-upgrade server name, or to a new server name, if appropriate for your applications. Note that this does not involve changing the name of the server as it has been in the system table *sysservers*. See Chapter 11 for more details of how a server is named permanently.

6. Restart Server as 'dba'

You should copy the existing 4.9.x server files from /cis1/sybase to some other directory for archiving. Copy the new System 10 files from, in the example, sybinit output /dba/1001p2, to /cis1/sybase. You also need to be executing the System 10 server binary file that was in /dba/1001p2/bin; it is a file called dataserver and must be renamed to the file that is executed by the RUN_<servername> script. Then start the server as UNIX user 'dba' by using RUN_<servername>. You need to verify that the server is running as the pre-upgrade server did, with the old name and so forth. Check the errorlog as the server recovers to verify that the new System 10 server is being executed (you can isql into the server and execute **select @@servername** also).

;-)

> You're the only DBA who isn't a senior DBA in the group. You make a big deal about how you must be allowed to do one of the upgrades from 4.9.x to System 10. You get management to agree to this, and they force one of the senior DBAs to come in on one of their (very rare) days off. You then try to upgrade and find it isn't working. You panic and page the senior DBA at lunch. The senior DBA takes one look at the errorlog of the new server and points out that you have started the 4.9.x server executable on the System 10 master device. You look like an idiot. You are shuffled off to a do-nothing job on a server that no one cares about in another building. You should not be surprised. Read the errorlog when things go wrong.

7. Install Thresholds

With System 10 you can have thresholds on all databases. More specifically, you can set up the last-chance threshold for each database. You must note that the last-chance threshold is not automatically set up when you upgrade a database to System 10. You must use the **select lct_admin ("lastchance", db_id())** command to establish the last-chance threshold for each database that is upgraded. This threshold will prevent the transaction log from filling up completely. You do need to review the material in the Sybase manuals to learn about thresholds and determine if you need any additional thresholds for your user databases. Note that the default behavior under System 10 is to suspend all user transactions in a database once the transaction log fills to the point of the last-chance threshold. If you prefer to have user transactions aborted while generating the familiar 1105 error (segment full), you can use **sp_dboption** to set the **abort tran on log full** option for the database.

8. Install Roles for All DBA and Operator Users

You will need to learn about "roles" as part of System 10. You can now assign the role of operator (**oper_role**) to a set of server logins. Those logins will be able to dump and load databases without you having to grant permission to execute those commands in the individual databases, as you had to under 4.9.x. You also need to determine how you want to handle the whole question of the 'sa' account. You can assign **sso_role** and **sa_role** to any of the logins that previously had the 'sa' password. This allows you to audit the individual login that is performing 'sa' work in the server. On the other hand, you need to watch for problems stemming from not using 'sa' to perform 'sa' tasks. An example would be any scripts that are hardwired to run as server user 'sa.' Such scripts will need to be changed manually, and then you have to determine what server user should be used when the script logs in to the server as part of the script.

9. Dump master Database Again

You must now dump the *master* database to disk again. Since you are running a System 10 server at this point, use the Backup Server for dumping *master* to disk. Note that with System 10 and the Backup Server, you can now dump a database or transaction log directly to a file on disk—you don't have to (although you still can) use a server dump device. You should name this dump of the *master* database dump_<*servername*>_master_10x_oldconfig_date_time.out to make it easy to rebuild the server if needed.

10. Dump All Databases

Now, dump all the databases in the server to tape (or to disk files and then make a file system dump to tape). These will be your first dumps made at the System 10 version level, and you can't use any of the dumps made at the 4.9.x version level any more.

11. Check All Production Scripts

Now that you have upgraded to System 10 and are about to allow user access, you must ensure that any and all scripts (or cron jobs) that were operating before the upgrade are again operating. You may have to modify these scripts to work with the System 10 features like server user roles, encrypted passwords, and so forth.

12. Mirror Primary Devices

Ever since the server was isolated from the users before the upgrade, the business data in the server has been unchanged. This is necessary in case you have to regress to mirrored 4.9.x level data or if you have to rebuild the server, using dumps made at the 4.9.x version level. Ever since then, you have not allowed any changes to the business data because those changes could not be recovered if you regressed to the 4.9.x version level. Now that you are ready to allow user access and hence allow changes to the business data that you must be able to recover, you need to determine if you are committed to the System 10 server. This means you should have tested your applications against the upgraded server to ensure that they function properly and that all the data appears to be present. Once you allow user access to the System 10 server, you must stay at System 10 or you will lose data when you regress.

As part of this, mirror the primary server devices that have System 10 data to the partitions that were mirrors of these server devices before the upgrade. Note that this will wipe out the 4.9.x data that is stored on the partitions that once again become mirrors of the primary server devices.

13. Update Table Statistics

Execute **update statistics** and **sp_recompile** on all tables in the server. You can use the script described in Chapter 15.

14. Allow User Access

You need to restart the server (the System 10 server) on the pre-upgrade port number that is in the client's interfaces file. See Chapter 1 for details of the two versions of interfaces files and Chapter 11 for details of how the interfaces file works and changing port numbers. This should allow user access just as before the upgrade, that is, same server name and port number as was in the client version of the interfaces file before the upgrade began.

13.9 Actual Upgrade Output 4.9.x to System 10

This section presents actual outputs from upgrades, as listed in the following table. The starting page of each output is also listed for convenience.

Output from sybinit during SQL Server Upgrade	page 467
sybinit Log File during SQL Server Upgrade	page 474
Output From sybinit during Backup Server and Auditing Installation	page 478
sybinit Log File during Backup Server and Auditing Installation	page 487
Upgrade Status Log	page 488

Output from sybinit during SQL Server Upgrade

Here is the actual output from the sybinit upgrade process. Note that $SYBASE is pointing to the upgrade directory /dba/1001p2, not /dba/sybase. This is correct because the upgrade needs the files that are in /dba/1001p2.

```
machine1 %echo $SYBASE
/dba/1001p2
machine1 %$SYBASE/install/sybinit
The log file for this session is
'/dba/1001p2/init/logs/log0401.002'.

SYBINIT

1. Release directory: /dba/1001p2

2. Edit / View Interfaces File

3. Configure a Server product
4. Configure an Open Client/Server product


Ctrl-a Accept and Continue, Ctrl-x Exit Screen, ? Help.

Enter the number of your choice and press return: 3

CONFIGURE SERVER PRODUCTS

Products:

    Product         Date Installed   Date Configured
1.  SQL Server       Apr 01 95 12:51  Apr 01 95 12:51
2.  Backup Server    Apr 01 95 12:51  Apr 01 95 12:51


Ctrl-a Accept and Continue, Ctrl-x Exit Screen, ? Help.

Enter the number of your choice and press return: 1

NEW OR EXISTING SQL SERVER
```

```
1.  Configure a new SQL Server
2.  Configure an existing SQL Server
3.  Upgrade an existing SQL Server


Ctrl-a Accept and Continue, Ctrl-x Exit Screen, ? Help.

Enter the number of your choice and press return: 3

UPGRADE EXISTING SQL SERVER

1. Release directory for previous release /dba/1001p2


Ctrl-a Accept and Continue, Ctrl-x Exit Screen, ? Help.

Enter the number of your choice and press return: 1
Enter the pathname of the release directory to use
  (default is '/dba/1001p2'):
/dba/sybase

UPGRADE EXISTING SQL SERVER

1. Release directory for previous release /dba/sybase


Ctrl-a Accept and Continue, Ctrl-x Exit Screen, ? Help.

Enter the number of your choice and press return:

CONFIGURE EXISTING SQL SERVER

Select one of the following servers:


1.  DDSDBA1_SYS10
```

/* note that **sybinit** displays all the servers that have entries
in the interfaces file and if the number of servers   fill
more   than   one   screen   you   will   see
<More>
Ctrl-f Scroll Forward,   Ctrl-b Scroll Backward.
be careful and use control-f (^f) to keep scrolling through
all the servers */

Ctrl-a Accept and Continue, Ctrl-x Exit Screen, ? Help.

Enter the number of your choice and press return: 1

ENTER SA ACCOUNT NAME AND PASSWORD

1. SA Account: sa

2. SA Password:

Ctrl-a Accept and Continue, Ctrl-x Exit Screen, ? Help.

Enter the number of your choice and press return:

SQL SERVER UPGRADE

1. Test SQL Server upgrade eligibility now
2. Check for reserved word conflicts
3. sybsystemprocs database configuration

4. Upgrade SQL Server now

Ctrl-a Accept and Continue, Ctrl-x Exit Screen, ? Help.

Enter the number of your choice and press return: 1
Testing SQL Server 'DDSDBA1_SYS10' for eligibility to
upgrade to release
'10.0.1'.

```
.........................................................
.........................................................
....................Done
```

Server 'DDSDBA1_SYS10' passed preupgrade eligibility test.
Press <return> to continue.

SQL SERVER UPGRADE

1. Test SQL Server upgrade eligibility now
2. Check for reserved word conflicts
3. sybsystemprocs database configuration

4. Upgrade SQL Server now

Ctrl-a Accept and Continue, Ctrl-x Exit Screen, ? Help.

Enter the number of your choice and press return: 2
The log file for sp_checkreswords output is
'/dba/1001p2/init/logs/checkres.dmp'.

Warning: 53 conflicts with 10.0 reserved words were found.
Sybase suggests that you resolve these conflicts before
upgrading the SQL Server. Run 'sp_checkreswords' on each
database for more information.
Press <return> to continue.

SQL SERVER UPGRADE

1. Test SQL Server upgrade eligibility now
2. Check for reserved word conflicts
3. sybsystemprocs database configuration

4. Upgrade SQL Server now

Ctrl-a Accept and Continue, Ctrl-x Exit Screen, ? Help.

Enter the number of your choice and press return: 3

SYBSYSTEMPROCS DATABASE CONFIGURATION

1. sybsystemprocs database size (Meg): 10

2. sybsystemprocs logical device name: sysprocsdev

3. create new device for the sybsystemprocs database: yes

4. physical name of new device:

5. size of the new device (Meg): 10

Ctrl-a Accept and Continue, Ctrl-x Exit Screen, ? Help.

Enter the number of your choice and press return: 4
Enter the physical device name for the sybsystemprocs database :
/dev/rsd9h

SYBSYSTEMPROCS DATABASE CONFIGURATION

1. sybsystemprocs database size (Meg): 10

2. sybsystemprocs logical device name: sysprocsdev

3. create new device for the sybsystemprocs database: yes

4. physical name of new device: /dev/rsd9h

5. size of the new device (Meg): 31.951172

Ctrl-a Accept and Continue, Ctrl-x Exit Screen, ? Help.

Enter the number of your choice and press return: 5
Enter the size of the new device:
31

SYBSYSTEMPROCS DATABASE CONFIGURATION

```
1. sybsystemprocs database size (Meg): 10

2. sybsystemprocs logical device name: sysprocsdev

3. create new device for the sybsystemprocs database: yes

4. physical name of new device: /dev/rsd9h

5. size of the new device (Meg): 31


Ctrl-a Accept and Continue, Ctrl-x Exit Screen, ? Help.

Enter the number of your choice and press return:

SQL SERVER UPGRADE
 1. Test SQL Server upgrade eligibility now
 2. Check for reserved word conflicts
 3. sybsystemprocs database configuration

 4. Upgrade SQL Server now


Ctrl-a Accept and Continue, Ctrl-x Exit Screen, ? Help.

Enter the number of your choice and press return: 4

Enter the NEW pathname of the SQL Server's errorlog (default is
'/dba/1001p2/install/errorlog'):
/dba/DDSDBA1/errorlog
Running task to upgrade the SQL Server.

Checkpointing all databases.
Upgrading SQL Server DDSDBA1_SYS10 to release 10.0.1
.................................................................
.................................................................
.................................................................
.................................................................
.................................................................
```

```
.............................................................
.............................................................
.............................................................
.............................................................
.............................................................
.............................................................
.............................................................
.............................................................
.............................................................
.............................................................
.............................................................
.............................................................
.............................................................
.............................................................
.............................................................
.............................................................
.............................................................
.............................................................
.............................................................
.............................................................
.............................................................
.............................................................
.............................................................
.............................................................
.............................................................
.............................................................
.............................................................
.............................................................
.....................Done
Upgrade of server 'DDSDBA1_SYS10' to release '10.0.1'
               succeeded.
Task to upgrade the SQL Server succeeded.
Running task to update the SQL Server runserver file.
Task to update the SQL Server runserver file succeeded.
Running task to boot the SQL Server.
waiting for server 'DDSDBA1_SYS10' to boot...
Task to boot the SQL Server succeeded.
Running task to create the sybsystemprocs database.
sybsystemprocs database created.
Task to create the sybsystemprocs database succeeded.
Running task to install system stored procedures.
.......................................................Done
Task to install system stored procedures succeeded.
```

```
Running task to set permissions for the 'model' database.
Done
Task to set permissions for the 'model' database succeeded.

Configuration completed successfully.
Press <return> to continue.
```

sybinit Log File during SQL Server Upgrade

```
/dba/1001p2/init/logs % more log0401.002
04/01/95 09:12:41 PM Sybinit/10.0.1/P2/Sun4/OS
4.1.x/1/OPT/Wed Mar 30 13:09:47
                    PST 1994
04/01/95 09:12:41 PM BEGIN ENVIRONMENT INFORMATION

USER ENVIRONMENT
--------------------------
user name:                      dba
current directory:              /auto/usr/u/dba
character set:                  iso_1
language:                       us_english
sybinit release directory:      /dba/1001p2
working release directory:      /dba/1001p2


04/01/95 09:12:42 PM END ENVIRONMENT INFORMATION
04/01/95 09:14:02 PM Copying entry 'DDSDBA1_SYS10' from
                interfaces file
                '/dba/sybase/interfaces' to interfaces file
                '/dba/1001p2/interfaces'.
04/01/95 09:14:03 PM Calling the shell with
'/dba/1001p2/upgrade/preupgrade
                -DDSDBA1_SYS10 -P -N >
/dba/1001p2/init/logs/tmp 2>&1 '.
04/01/95 09:14:03 PM Testing SQL Server 'DDSDBA1_SYS10' for
                eligibility to upgrade to release '10.0.1'.
04/01/95 09:20:37 PM Done
04/01/95 09:20:37 PM Begin output from 'preupgrade':
```

```
Starting preupgrade of SQL Server
Checking status in all existing databases.
Checking space in all existing databases.
        Database db1 has sufficient space.
        Database db2 has sufficient space.
        Database db3 has sufficient space.
....
....
....
        Database dbn has sufficient space.
Clearing reused columns in all existing databases.
Preupgrade of SQL Server to 10.0 is complete.
04/01/95 09:20:37 PM End output from 'preupgrade'.
04/01/95 09:20:42 PM Server 'DDSDBA1_SYS10' passed preup-
grade eligibility test.
04/01/95 09:28:50 PM The log file for sp_checkreswords
                output is
                '/dba/1001p2/init/logs/checkres.dmp'.
04/01/95 09:35:39 PM Running task to upgrade the SQL Server.
04/01/95 09:35:47 PM Copying entry 'DDSDBA1_SYS10' from
                interfaces file
                '/dba/sybase/interfaces' to interfaces file
                '/dba/1001p2/interfaces'.
04/01/95 09:35:47 PM Checkpointing all databases.
04/01/95 09:35:48 PM Calling the shell with
'/dba/1001p2/upgrade/upgrade100
                DDSDBA1_SYS10 /dev/rsd1h /dba/sybase
                /cis1/1001p2  >
                /dba/1001p2/init/logs/tmp 2>&1 '.
04/01/95 09:35:48 PM Upgrading SQL Server DDSDBA1_SYS10 to
release 10.0.1
04/01/95 11:17:00 PM Done
04/01/95 11:17:00 PM Begin output from 'upgrade100':

>>> Running upgrade100 with the following configuration:
SERVERNAME=DDSDBA1_SYS10
MASTERDEVICE=/dev/rsd1h
OLDSYBASEDIR=/dba/sybase
NEWSYBASEDIR=/dba/1001p2
```

```
>>> PHASE 1 begins.......

>>> Saving current configuration in
/dba/1001p2/upgrade/DDSDBA1_SYS10.ocon file.
>>> Saving the database segment information in
/dba/1001p2/upgrade/DDSDBA1_SYS10.log file.

>>> Upgrading from 4.9.1.

>>> Saving previous stack size.

>>> Stack size is set to 286720. This is more than
>>> or equal to the default stack size of 28672.
>>> Leaving the stack size of 286720 unchanged.

>>> Saving previous memory size.

>>> Memory size is set to 61440. This is more than
>>> or equal to the default memory size of 5120.
>>> Leaving the memory size of 61440 unchanged.


>>> PHASE 1 completes.......

>>> Shutting down the existing SQL Server.

>>> Booting the new 10.0.1 SQL Server.


>>> PHASE 2 begins.......

>>> Final phase to upgrade to 10.0.1 SQL Server.


>>> PHASE 2 completes......

>>> Upgrade to 10.0.1 SQL Server is now complete.

04/01/95 11:17:00 PM End output from 'upgrade100'.
04/01/95 11:17:00 PM Upgrade of server 'DDSDBA1_SYS10' to
```

```
                       release '10.0.1' succeeded.
04/01/95 11:17:00 PM Task to upgrade the SQL Server
                     succeeded.
04/01/95 11:17:00 PM Running task to update the SQL Server
runserver file.
04/01/95 11:17:18 PM Task to update the SQL Server runserver
file succeeded.
04/01/95 11:17:19 PM Running task to boot the SQL Server.
04/01/95 11:17:19 PM Calling the shell with
                     '/dba/1001p2/install/RUN_DDSDBA1_SYS10 >
                     /dba/1001p2/init/logs/tmp 2>&1 '.
04/01/95 11:17:20 PM waiting for server 'DDSDBA1_SYS10' to
                     boot...
04/01/95 11:17:31 PM Task to boot the SQL Server succeeded.
04/01/95 11:17:31 PM Running task to create the
                     sybsystemprocs database.
04/01/95 11:17:32 PM Created device 'sysprocsdev'.
04/01/95 11:17:55 PM Created database 'sybsystemprocs'.
04/01/95 11:17:55 PM sybsystemprocs database created.
04/01/95 11:17:55 PM Task to create the sybsystemprocs
                     database succeeded.
04/01/95 11:17:55 PM Running task to install system stored
                     procedures.
04/01/95 11:17:55 PM Installing Sybase system stored
                     procedures
04/01/95 11:24:54 PM Done
04/01/95 11:24:54 PM Task to install system stored
                     procedures succeeded.
04/01/95 11:24:54 PM Running task to set permissions for the
                     'model' database.
04/01/95 11:24:54 PM Setting the permissions for the 'model'
                     database
04/01/95 11:24:55 PM Done
04/01/95 11:24:55 PM Task to set permissions for the 'model'
                     database succeeded.
04/01/95 11:33:28 PM Configuration completed successfully.
04/01/95 11:36:55 PM Exiting.
04/01/95 11:36:55 PM The log file for this session is
                     '/dba/1001p2/init/logs/log0401.002'.
04/01/95 11:36:55 PM Log close.
```

Output from sybinit during Backup Server and Auditing Installation

```
machine1 % $SYBASE/install/sybinit
The log file for this session is
'/dba/1001p2/init/logs/log0401.003'.

SYBINIT

1. Release directory:  /dba/1001p2

2. Edit / View Interfaces File

3. Configure a Server product
4. Configure an Open Client/Server product


Ctrl-a Accept and Continue, Ctrl-x Exit Screen, ? Help.

Enter the number of your choice and press return: 3

CONFIGURE SERVER PRODUCTS

Products:

     Product          Date Installed   Date Configured
  1. SQL Server       Apr 01 95 12:51  Apr 01 95 23:33
  2. Backup Server    Apr 01 95 12:51  Apr 01 95 12:51


Ctrl-a Accept and Continue, Ctrl-x Exit Screen, ? Help.

Enter the number of your choice and press return: 2

NEW OR EXISTING BACKUP SERVER

1. Configure a new Backup Server
2. Configure an existing Backup Server
```

Ctrl-a Accept and Continue, Ctrl-x Exit Screen, ? Help.

Enter the number of your choice and press return: 1

ADD NEW BACKUP SERVER

1. Backup Server name: SYB_BACKUP

Ctrl-a Accept and Continue, Ctrl-x Exit Screen, ? Help.

Enter the number of your choice and press return: 1
Enter the name of the new Backup Server (default is
'SYB_BACKUP'):
DDSDBA1_BCK

ADD NEW BACKUP SERVER
1. Backup Server name: DDSDBA1_BCK

Ctrl-a Accept and Continue, Ctrl-x Exit Screen, ? Help.

Enter the number of your choice and press return:

BACKUP SERVER CONFIGURATION

1. Backup Server errorlog: /dba/1001p2/install/backup.log
2. Enter / Modify Backup Server interfaces file information
3. Backup Server language: us_english
4. Backup Server character set: iso_1

Ctrl-a Accept and Continue, Ctrl-x Exit Screen, ? Help.

Enter the number of your choice and press return: 2

SERVER INTERFACES FILE ENTRY SCREEN

    Server name: DDSDBA1_BCK

```
1.  Retry Count:  0
2.  Retry Delay:  0

3.  Add a new listener service


Ctrl-a Accept and Continue, Ctrl-x Exit Screen, ? Help.

Enter the number of your choice and press return: 3

EDIT TCP SERVICE

1.  Hostname/Address: machine1
2.  Port:
3.  Name Alias:

4.  Delete this service from the interfaces entry


Ctrl-a Accept and Continue, Ctrl-x Exit Screen, ? Help.

Enter the number of your choice and press return: 2
Enter the port number to use for this entry (default is ''):
1030

EDIT TCP SERVICE

1.  Hostname/Address: machine1
2.  Port: 1030
3.  Name Alias:

4.  Delete this service from the interfaces entry


Ctrl-a Accept and Continue, Ctrl-x Exit Screen, ? Help.


Enter the number of your choice and press return:
Is this information correct? y
```

SERVER INTERFACES FILE ENTRY SCREEN

   Server name: DDSDBA1_BCK

1. Retry Count: 0
2. Retry Delay: 0

3. Add a new listener service

Modify or delete a service

Listener services available:

   Protocol Address   Port   Name Alias
4. tcp   machine1   1030
Ctrl-a Accept and Continue, Ctrl-x Exit Screen, ? Help.

Enter the number of your choice and press return:
Write the changes to the interfaces file now? y

BACKUP SERVER CONFIGURATION

1. Backup Server errorlog: /dba/1001p2/install/backup.log
2. Enter / Modify Backup Server interfaces file information
3. Backup Server language: us_english
4. Backup Server character set: iso_1

Ctrl-a Accept and Continue, Ctrl-x Exit Screen, ? Help.

Enter the number of your choice and press return:
Execute the Backup Server configuration now? y
Running task to update the Backup Server runserver file.
Task to update the Backup Server runserver file succeeded.
Running task to boot the Backup Server.
waiting for server 'DDSDBA1_BCK' to boot...
Task to boot the Backup Server succeeded.

```
Configuration completed successfully.
Press <return> to continue.

NEW OR EXISTING BACKUP SERVER

1.  Configure a new Backup Server
2.  Configure an existing Backup Server


Ctrl-a Accept and Continue, Ctrl-x Exit Screen, ? Help.

Enter the number of your choice and press return:

CONFIGURE SERVER PRODUCTS


Products:

    Product          Date Installed   Date Configured
1.  SQL Server         Apr 01 95 12:51  Apr 01 95 23:33
2.  Backup Server      Apr 01 95 12:51  Apr 01 95 23:44


Ctrl-a Accept and Continue, Ctrl-x Exit Screen, ? Help.

Enter the number of your choice and press return: 1

NEW OR EXISTING SQL SERVER

1.  Configure a new SQL Server
2.  Configure an existing SQL Server
3.  Upgrade an existing SQL Server


Ctrl-a Accept and Continue, Ctrl-x Exit Screen, ? Help.

Enter the number of your choice and press return: 2

CONFIGURE EXISTING SQL SERVER
```

Select one of the following servers:

1. DDSDBA1_SYS10

Ctrl-a Accept and Continue, Ctrl-x Exit Screen, ? Help.

Enter the number of your choice and press return: 1

ENTER SA ACCOUNT NAME AND PASSWORD

1. SA Account: sa

2. SA Password:
Ctrl-a Accept and Continue, Ctrl-x Exit Screen, ? Help.

Enter the number of your choice and press return:

SQL SERVER CONFIGURATION

1.	CONFIGURE SERVER'S INTERFACES FILE ENTRY	Unchanged
2.	MASTER DEVICE CONFIGURATION	Unchanged
3.	SYBSYSTEMPROCS DATABASE CONFIGURATION	Changed
4.	SET ERRORLOG LOCATION	Unchanged
5.	CONFIGURE DEFAULT BACKUP SERVER	Unchanged
6.	CONFIGURE LANGUAGES	Unchanged
7.	CONFIGURE CHARACTER SETS	Unchanged
8.	CONFIGURE SORT ORDER	Unchanged
9.	ACTIVATE AUDITING	
10.	Remap the query trees in all databases	

Ctrl-a Accept and Continue, Ctrl-x Exit Screen, ? Help.

Enter the number of your choice and press return: 9

ACTIVATE AUDITING

1. Install auditing: no

2. sybsecurity database size (Meg): 5

3. sybsecurity logical device name: sybsecurity

4. create new device for the sybsecurity database: no

Ctrl-a Accept and Continue, Ctrl-x Exit Screen, ? Help.

Enter the number of your choice and press return: 1

ACTIVATE AUDITING

1. Install auditing: yes

2. sybsecurity database size (Meg): 10

3. sybsecurity logical device name: sybsecurity

4. create new device for the sybsecurity database: no

Ctrl-a Accept and Continue, Ctrl-x Exit Screen, ? Help.

Enter the number of your choice and press return: 4

ACTIVATE AUDITING

1. Install auditing: yes

2. sybsecurity database size (Meg): 10

3. sybsecurity logical device name: sybsecurity

4. create new device for the sybsecurity database: yes

5. sybsecurity physical device name:

6. size of the new device (Meg):

Ctrl-a Accept and Continue, Ctrl-x Exit Screen, ? Help.

Enter the number of your choice and press return: 5
Enter the physical name of the device to use for the
sybsecurity database (default is ''):
/dev/rsd13h

ACTIVATE AUDITING

1. Install auditing: yes

2. sybsecurity database size (Meg): 10

3. sybsecurity logical device name: sybsecurity

4. create new device for the sybsecurity database: yes

5. sybsecurity physical device name: /dev/rsd13h

6. size of the new device (Meg): 31.951172

Ctrl-a Accept and Continue, Ctrl-x Exit Screen, ? Help.

Enter the number of your choice and press return: 6
Enter the size of the new device:
31

ACTIVATE AUDITING

1. Install auditing: yes

2. sybsecurity database size (Meg): 10

3. sybsecurity logical device name: sybsecurity

4. create new device for the sybsecurity database: yes

5. sybsecurity physical device name: /dev/rsd13h

6. size of the new device (Meg): 31

Ctrl-a Accept and Continue, Ctrl-x Exit Screen, ? Help.

Enter the number of your choice and press return:

SQL SERVER CONFIGURATION

```
1.  CONFIGURE SERVER'S INTERFACES FILE ENTRY     Unchanged
2.  MASTER DEVICE CONFIGURATION                  Unchanged
3.  SYBSYSTEMPROCS DATABASE CONFIGURATION        Changed
4.  SET ERRORLOG LOCATION                        Unchanged
5.  CONFIGURE DEFAULT BACKUP SERVER              Unchanged
6.  CONFIGURE LANGUAGES                          Unchanged
7.  CONFIGURE CHARACTER SETS                     Unchanged
8.  CONFIGURE SORT ORDER                         Unchanged
9.  ACTIVATE AUDITING                            Changed
10. Remap the query trees in all databases
```


Ctrl-a Accept and Continue, Ctrl-x Exit Screen, ? Help.

Enter the number of your choice and press return:
Execute the SQL Server Configuration now? y
Running task to install auditing capabilities.
.......Done
waiting for server 'DDSDBA1_SYS10' to boot...
Auditing capability installed.
Task to install auditing capabilities succeeded.

Configuration completed successfully.

```
Press <return> to continue.

The log file for this session is
'/dba/1001p2/init/logs/log0401.003
```

sybinit Log File during Backup Server and Auditing Installation

```
/dba/1001p2/init/logs 83 % more log0401.003
04/01/95 11:37:00 PM Sybinit/10.0.1/P2/Sun4/OS
4.1.x/1/OPT/Wed Mar 30 13:09:47
                PST 1994
04/01/95 11:37:00 PM BEGIN ENVIRONMENT INFORMATION


USER ENVIRONMENT
-------------------------
user name:                    dba
current directory:            /auto/usr/u/dba
character set:                iso_1
language:                     us_english
sybinit release directory:    /dba/1001p2
working release directory:    /dba/1001p2



04/01/95 11:37:00 PM END ENVIRONMENT INFORMATION
04/01/95 11:41:08 PM Running task to update the Backup
                Server runserver file.
04/01/95 11:41:09 PM Task to update the Backup Server
                runserver file succeeded.
04/01/95 11:41:10 PM Running task to boot the Backup Server.
04/01/95 11:41:10 PM Calling the shell with
                '/dba/1001p2/install/RUN_DDSDBA1_BCK >
                /dba/1001p2/init/logs/tmp 2>&1 '.
04/01/95 11:41:12 PM waiting for server 'DDSDBA1_BCK' to
                boot...
04/01/95 11:41:17 PM Task to boot the Backup Server
                succeeded.
04/01/95 11:44:29 PM Configuration completed successfully.
04/01/95 11:47:52 PM Running task to install auditing
```

```
                        capabilities.
04/01/95 11:47:53 PM Created device 'sybsecurity'.
04/01/95 11:48:16 PM Created database 'sybsecurity'.
04/01/95 11:48:18 PM 'sp_auditinstall' succeeded.
04/01/95 11:48:49 PM Done
04/01/95 11:48:50 PM Rebooting SQL Server 'DDSDBA1_SYS10' to
                        activate audit process.
04/01/95 11:48:56 PM Calling the shell with
                        '/dba/1001p2/install/RUN_DDSDBA1_SYS10 >
                        /dba/1001p2/init/logs/tmp 2>&1 '.
04/01/95 11:48:57 PM waiting for server 'DDSDBA1_SYS10' to
                        boot...
04/01/95 11:49:09 PM Auditing capability installed.
04/01/95 11:49:09 PM Task to install auditing capabilities
                        succeeded.
04/01/95 11:49:31 PM Configuration completed successfully.
04/01/95 11:50:43 PM Exiting.
04/01/95 11:50:43 PM The log file for this session is
                        '/dba/1001p2/init/logs/log0401.003'.
04/01/95 11:50:43 PM Log close.
```

Upgrade Status Log

This output file shows you what the upgrade process is actually doing while all those
dots are moving across the screen (see "Output From sybinit During SQL Server
Upgrade" above to see the dots). You can lose your mind if you just watch the dots
so it is good to check this output file while the upgrade is moving along.

```
/dba/1001p2/upgrade 90 % more DDSDBA1_SYS10.u92
/dba/1001p2/upgrade/upgrade -SDDSDBA1_SYS10
    Starting upgrade to SQL Server 10.0.1.
    Dropping system stored procedures from master.
    Adding new messages to sysmessages.
    Adding new configuration variables to sysconfigures.
    Adding new columns to system tables in all existing
    databases.
    Adding new sqlstates to sysmessages.
    Adding new datatypes to all existing databases.
```

Changing name of system catalog columns in all existing databases.
Renaming previously spare system columns to new names.
Removing obsolete columns from system tables.
Recalculating sysindexes.maxlen.
Executing following commands in all existing databases.

> Adding new column colid2 in syscomments for larger texts.
> Deleting old index syscomments on syscomments.
> Creating new index syscomments on syscomments.
> Creating system catalog: sysreferences and indexes.
> Creating system catalog: sysconstraints and indexes.
> Creating system catalog: sysusermessages and indexes.
> Updating type, length and usertype of the status2 field of the sysobjects table.
> Resetting status2, objspare fields of the sysobjects table.
> Creating system catalog: systhresholds and index.
> Creating system catalog: sysroles and indexes.
> Inserting rows to Sysroles and Sysusers.
> Adding new columns to sysreferences.
> Dropping existing indexes on sysreferences.
> Creating new indexes on sysreferences.
> Inserting values in new dbname columns in sysreferences.

Upgrading the Sysprotects tables and protection information.
Configuring system for connection to Backup Server.
Setting hierarchy value for datatypes in Systypes table.
Setting Password Expiration Interval to 0 (no check).
Setting Audit Queue Size to 100.
Creating system catalog: syssrvroles and indexes.
Creating system catalog: sysloginroles and indexes.
Inserting rows to syssrvroles.
Inserting rows to sysloginroles.
Initializing sysusages unreservedpgs column

```
Initializing sysdatabases status2 column
Creating system catalog: syslisteners.
Deleting 'diskdump' Sysdevices entry.
Initializing systypes ident column
Updating master device name
Updating sysconfigures
Modifying 'open databases' configuation
Updating dynamic configured variables in sysconfigures
Drop any existing password conversion procedure
Creating password conversion procedure.
Converting all plaintext passwords to encrypted passwords.
Dropping password conversion procedure.
Setting upgrade version to 10.0.1.
Upgrading the following objects in sysprocedures:
        procedures, triggers, rules, defaults, and views.
Remapping objects in database, master.
        Remapping object, sp_dircontext.
...
...
...

Completed upgrade of master: 22 succeeded and 0 failed.
Remapping objects in database, tempdb.
Completed upgrade of tempdb: no objects in sysprocedures
to remap.
Remapping objects in database, model.
Completed upgrade of model: no objects in sysprocedures
to remap.
Remapping objects in database, db1.
...
...
...

Completed upgrade of db1: 102 succeeded and 0 failed.

Completed upgrade of aedb: 14 succeeded and 0 failed.
Upgrade to SQL Server 10.0.1 is complete.
```

13.10 Regressing from Failed System 10 Upgrade

If you fail to upgrade your server to System 10 successfully, you can fall back or regress to your 4.9.x server by using one of the master database dumps you made during the upgrade process and using the mirrors you had of the 4.9.x server databases before you began the upgrade. The process of this regression is discussed below. Note that this approach will recover only those databases that were fully mirrored at the 4.9.x version level. All other databases could be recreated and reloaded from dumps, assuming you can recover the master database to its 4.9.x condition. The steps of the recovery are listed below.

If you have attempted to upgrade your server to System 10 and have failed to do so, contact Sybase Technical Support for a review of the situation. You must make sure that the regression plan shown below is the best alternative for your system before you start regressing. It may turn out that you can easily fix the cause of the upgrade failure and complete the upgrade. You must not try to regress in haste. On the other hand, you must know about this regression process before you begin upgrading so you can take the steps necessary to make this regression process viable. We discuss these steps:

1.	Shutdown Server
2.	Install 4.9.x Server on Same Master Device
3.	Load Dump of *master* (4.9.x version)
4.	Change Permissions on Primary Server Devices
5.	Restart Server
6.	Recover Server at 4.9.x

1. Shutdown Server

If the server is still running after the failed upgrade attempt, you must shut it down. The server must be shut down so that you can reinstall the 4.9.x master device on the existing System 10 master device.

2. Install 4.9.x Server on Same Master Device

You need to load the dump of the *master* database you made before the upgrade when the server was at the 4.9.x version level. In order to do this, you must have a 4.9.x server running; this requires that you reinstall the 4.9.x master device by running buildmaster. Note that the master device at this point is at the System 10 version level and you will be overwriting the existing master device with the 4.9.x version. You do this by executing buildmaster -d /dev/*<partition_of_master_device>* -s *<size_of_master_device_in_2K_pages>*. Note that you must run the 4.9.x version of buildmaster, not the System 10 version.

3. Load Dump of master (4.9.x version)

You must add the -m option to your RUN_*<servername>* script to start the server in single-user mode. And you must ensure that you are starting the 4.9.x server, not the System 10 server. At this point, you should still have the server isolated from the user community so that no one but you can login to the server as the "single user." You restart the server in single-user mode and load the dump of the *master* database that you made during the upgrade attempt (see step 7 in Section 13.7). The name of this *master* database dump should be —

dump_*<servername>*_master_4.9.2_withmirrors_date_time.out

—and you must be sure you are loading the correct *master* database dump. The SQL Server Troubleshooting Guide has details on the process of loading a dump of the *master* database. Loading a dump of *master* will shutdown the server.

Note that the idea here is to load the *master* database dump that was made while the server was at 4.9.x and had the server devices mirrored. After the load of the *master* database dump is complete, the *master* database will again contain the information about the server devices and their mirrors, just as it did early in the upgrade process when all the server devices had data at the 4.9.x version level. At this point, the mirrors of the server devices are no longer dropped because the master database (specifically, the system table *sysdevices*) has now been restored to reflect the server configuration before the mirrors were dropped.

Note further that at this point the primary side of each mirrored pair has data that is at the System 10 version level, whereas the mirrors of these mirrored pairs were dropped just before the upgrade started. This means you have primary devices with data at the System 10 version level and mirrors of those server devices with data at the 4.9.x version level. See Figure 13.1(D).

4. Change Permissions on Primary Server Devices

You must change the ownership and/or file permissions on the files that control the access to the disk partitions that support the primary server devices of each server device mirrored pair. The point is that you make it so that the UNIX user that is starting the server (should be UNIX user 'dba') can't gain access to the primary server devices.

5. Restart Server

When the server is started the next time, it will open the restored *master* database, look in the system table *sysdevices,* and find the names of all the server devices and their mirrors, which will appear to have never been dropped. But, when the server tries to access the primary server devices (which contain data at the System 10 version level), the file ownership and/or permissions will prevent that access from happening. The server will detect this and will then fail over to the mirrors of the primary server devices. At this point, you have your server running on a primary master device and on secondary server devices that all contain data at the 4.9.x version level. See Figure 13.1(E).

6. Recover Server at 4.9.x

At this point, you would decide what your plan is regarding the upgrade. If you plan to operate at the 4.9.x version level for any length of time, you should drop the primary side of each of the mirror pairs to get rid of the server devices that have System 10 data on them. You could then remirror from the former secondary (now the primary and unmirrored server devices) server devices to restore the mirrored pairs at the 4.9.x version level.

Note that you can only use this regression process if you had mirrors of the server devices and you made the dump of the *master* database at the right time and you dropped the mirrors of the server devices at the right time (before upgrade process started). See Figure 13.1 for illustration of the flow of the regression process.

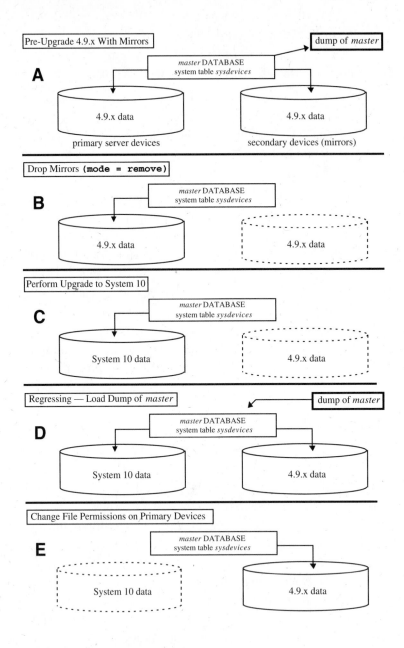

Figure 13.1   Regression to 4.9.x -

13.11   Dependencies

We have been discussing the upgrade process for a single server. Your database system consists of many servers. You must determine what the plan will be for upgrading the other servers in your database system. Further, you must determine the impact all this will have on the applications that your servers support. This means you must know all the applications that you are supporting and which servers they run against now, as well as which servers they will run against in the case of a failure of one of the primary servers.

For more details of these and other issues involved with upgrading your database system to System 10, see Chapter 14.

Chapter 14

Transitioning to System 10

There are many changes to the SQL Server in System 10. Read the manual *What's New in Sybase SQL Server Release 10.0?* that is part of the System 10 SQL Server documentation set. This manual gives details of the many changes that may affect your applications and the way you perform your DBA duties.

We discuss the changes listed below, but you must read the manual to see all the changes, some of which are subtle, that may force you to change portions of your existing database system.

14.1	System 10 Changes to SQL Server
14.2	Transition to System 10 Won't Happen All at Once
14.3	SQL Server Upgrade Dependencies
14.4	Changes that Affect Existing Applications
14.5	Changes that Affect DBA
14.6	Compatibility with Other Sybase Products
14.7	Server Login Passwords
14.8	Server Login 'sa' versus Server Logins with **sa_role**
14.9	Backup Server

14.1 System 10 Changes to SQL Server

The biggest change you will encounter with System 10 as a DBA is the Backup Server. The Backup Server is a separate process that runs on the server machine and makes all dumps and loads for the SQL Server. Note that the Backup Server does not have to run on the same server machine as the SQL Server, but for fastest performance the SQL Server and the Backup Server should be on the same server machine.

497

If you use one Backup Server on one server machine to dump and load for several SQL Servers on other server machines, you run the risk that any problem with the Backup Server machine or the network will prevent you from making any database or transaction log dumps or loads. Since dumping the transaction log is the only way to free up space in the transaction log, being able to dump the transaction log periodically is critical to your production databases.

Due to the increase in the number of system stored procedures, the *master* database would not be able to handle them all without growing, and, as discussed in Chapter 7, you can't expand the *master* database beyond the master device, so these stored procedures have been moved to a new system database *sybsystemprocs* on the sysprocsdev server device. Similarly, for the new auditing functions, another system database, *sybsecurity*, has been created on the sybsecurity server device. Note that the *sybsystemprocs* database is required for installing the System 10 SQL Server, whereas the *sybsecurity* database is optional but highly recommended. Further, these two new databases need to be on their own server devices and should be separated from the master device and each other; they both should be mirrored.

System 10 has thresholds that will execute a user-supplied stored procedure when the free space available in any segment for a given database falls below a specified value. You can set up multiple thresholds for each database, and several new stored procedures help you create and maintain them. Note that the stored procedures that are executed when thresholds are crossed are not supplied, and you must create and assign a stored procedure to each threshold manually.

Roles allow various permissions to be granted to individual server logins. The server user 'sa' account still exists, but you can assign **sa_role**, **sso_role**, or **oper_role** to individual server logins. Several stored procedures come along with this new feature. Note that **sa_role** is not like 'sa' in 4.9.x. The **sa_role** can't add or drop server logins, only database users. Hence, if you need to have the functions of 'sa' as you are accustomed to under 4.9.x, you will need to assign **sa_role**, **sso_role**, and **oper_role** to the individual server login in question. The **oper_role** allows the user to dump databases, and this is much easier than having to add the user to each database and grant permission to dump the database to that user.

In addition to roles that can increase security by associating 'sa' events with individual server logins, you also have new auditing features. When you enable the auditing functions, the server will record the login that is performing selected actions within the server. The auditing features rely on the presence of the *sybsecurity* database on the sybsecurity server device, and you must manually activate the auditing functions. If the transaction log of the *sybsecurity* database fills up, that can stop all activity on the entire server. Security is also enhanced by encrypting the server user passwords that are stored in the server.

System 10 also provides cursors that allow retrieval of individual rows of data from the server to a client. There are many new statements and stored procedures that support the creation and manipulation of cursors.

14.2 Transition to System 10 Won't Happen All at Once

The transition of any of your servers from 4.9.x to System 10 will not happen overnight. First you must be sure that the applications that your databases support are ready to run against a server at the System 10 version level. The only way to really determine this is to move the data (or at least a subset of the data) to a development server, upgrade the development server to System 10 and run the application there for some period of time. If at all possible, you should simulate the load that is present on the production application, that is, you should have multiple users running the application concurrently. You must test the application against the System 10 development server for obvious problems, like reserved word conflicts, and the like, and you must also test the application with multiple users to look for performance problems caused by blocking, and so on.

14.3 SQL Server Upgrade Dependencies

The process of upgrading one SQL Server to System 10 has been discussed in detail in Chapter 13. You need to consider the dependencies that exist between the servers in your database system. Consider the typical database system shown in Figure 14.1.

If you are considering upgrading the primary OLTP server to System 10, you must understand that you can no longer dump and load data from the primary OLTP server to the standby server or any other server in the system until the other server(s) are also at the System 10 version level. You must consider the business impact of not having the standby or decision support server (reporting server) available during the time it takes to upgrade the other server(s). You also need to determine whether you will proceed with upgrading the other servers immediately after upgrading the primary OLTP server, or if you will wait for some period of time to make sure you don't need to regress to 4.9.x. During this period of time, the business would be relying on the one server.

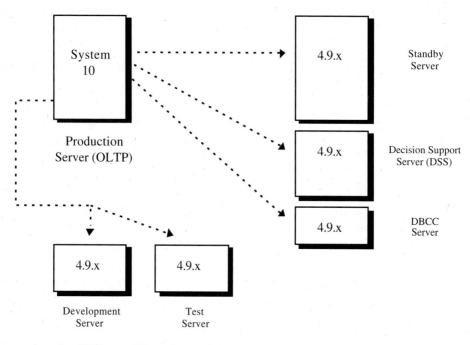

Assuming OLTP server is first to be upgraded to System 10, data cannot be distributed to other servers until they are also upgraded.

Figure 14.1   The multi-server database system transitioning to System 10 - - - - - - - - - - - -

You should have tested your business applications on a development server before upgrading the primary OLTP server. This means you need a development server that has been loaded with some or all of the production data and is then upgraded to System 10. Unless you obtain a new server machine, you need to realize that the server you use to support this upgrade and testing will have to be taken out of service as far as the rest of the existing database system is concerned. After the existing development server is upgraded, you will not be able to move data to and from other 4.9.x servers in the database system.

Also note that you can save a great deal of effort if you simply upgrade one server to System 10 and once you have decided to upgrade the other servers, simply destroy the other server(s) (after making complete dumps of everything, of course). You can easily do this by simply installing the System 10 SQL Server from scratch on whatever disk(s) you choose. The former server(s) will be wiped out; after the databases have been created, you can simply dump and load the databases from the one server that was upgraded to System 10. It is much faster to install a System 10 SQL Server than it is to upgrade to System 10.

If the databases on your primary server are large enough that **dbcc** runs take too long (that is, your business can't be down long enough to run the **dbcc** checks on the production system) and you are dumping and loading these databases to a separate, dedicated DBCC server, you need to realize that once the primary server is upgraded you can no longer run **dbcc** checks on the existing DBCC server. And, once you upgrade the DBCC server, you can only run **dbcc** checks on System 10 databases, which excludes any large databases in your database system that have not been upgraded yet. To keep all the functionality of your database system, you would need two DBCC servers and two development servers (and perhaps even two test servers), all of which should be running on separate server machines. You need to have an upgrade plan for all the servers in your database system. You must plan ahead for supporting all the existing functions on servers that are upgraded and those that won't be upgraded, or at least won't be upgraded in the near term.

One other minor point is that the upgrade to System 10, as described in Chapter 13, assumes that the server machine has sufficient disks and partitions to support the new server devices, sysprocsdev and sybsecurity, and their mirrors. Since these new server devices and their mirrors should be placed on physical disks that are separate from the master device and each other, this implies that you need to have at least six physical disks each having a small partition (the 'h' partition) of 30 Mb. You need to plan ahead to support these new server devices and their mirrors.

14.4 Changes that Affect Existing Applications

There are many changes in the System 10 version of SQL Server that can impact your existing applications. We discuss the major areas that have changed, but you must review the entire *What's New in Sybase SQL Server Release 10.0* document to determine all the changes that could affect your applications. There is no simple script or process to examine all of your applications and all the databases that they run against to see what all the conflicts will be. The best practical approach is to simply test your applications against System 10 data and see what happens. Tracking down all the possible problems takes time and can be the longest single step in the whole upgrade process.

The System 10 SQL Server has new reserved keywords that can cause problems if your existing applications try to access objects whose names are among these reserved words. The upgrade of the SQL Server to System 10 can complete successfully with reserved word conflicts unresolved; it isn't until your applications try to access database objects that are named with words that are now reserved that you will see the problems. You must test your applications against a System 10 server. There is no correlation between a successful upgrade of the SQL Server and your applications running successfully against the System 10 SQL Server. See Chapter 13 "Upgrading SQL Server" for discussion of checking for and dealing with reserved word conflicts.

Some of the existing datatypes have different precision that may affect the results of computations performed on these datatypes.

Similarly, there have been some changes in the way conversions between some datatypes are handled.

The use of table correlation names (table aliases) has become more restrictive. Under 4.9.x, after declaring a table correlation name, you could use either the correlation name or the table name in the following portions of the query. Under System 10, you lose this flexibility because only the table correlation name is permitted. Note that this kind of problem can be buried deep within the Transact-SQL code of your application; again, there is no script to find all these potential problems for you.

With the move of user-created stored procedures from the *master* database to the *sybsystemprocs* database, any such procedures that reference system tables located in the *master* database must now explicitly specify that the system table in question is in the *master* database. Further, if you have changed any of the default permissions on system stored procedures, the default permissions will be reset by the upgrade process. Finally, you need to decide where you will locate any of your own procedures. If they were in the *master* database, the upgrade process will leave them there, but you may want to have them in the *sybsystemprocs* database along with all the system stored procedures.

A major change in System 10 involves subqueries. The changes are many and some are subtle. You must review all the details of these changes. The two biggest changes are to correlated subqueries that use the **in** or **any** clauses and subqueries using the **not in** clause when NULL values are returned. You need to look over the many changes to subqueries. Also, the System 10 server may not generate an error for conflicts in the way you use subqueries and the way System 10 analyzes them, but you will see severely degraded performance. Again, testing your application against a System 10 server is the only practical approach that will allow you to identify which queries are taking the most time; those are the queries you must fix first.

14.5 Changes that Affect DBA

The very basic **alter database** command has changed in a way that can be very confusing. Under 4.9.x you simply altered a database by adding space on a device; the new space was assigned the same segments as any existing space for that database on that device. If the device was not previously supporting the database, then the space was given the segment assignments of *system* and *default*. If you altered a database to add space on a device that was supporting the *logsegment* alone (the transaction log on a device or devices separated from all other segments of the database), then the new space was also supporting the *logsegment* only. Under System 10 the **alter database** command now has the **log on** clause, just as the create database command has had all along. The impact is that when you use **alter database** to increase the size of the transaction log, you must use the **log on** clause even though you are adding space to a device that already supports only the *logsegment* for the database. This change isn't difficult, only confusing when you are under pressure and the old (and very similar) syntax doesn't work anymore.

With the addition of the *sybsystemprocs* and *sybsecurity* databases, the process of recovering the *master* database has changed, although not by much. The process of restoring the *master* database is the same as before, but you may now need to restore the *sybsystemprocs* database as well, depending on the problem that required restoring the *master* database. Recreating the *sybsystemprocs* involves running installmaster, which is not very intuitive since you aren't doing anything to *master* at all.

These new system databases should be included in whatever process you use to run **dbcc** checks on all the databases in the server. You will also need to decide where to locate any DBA stored procedures that were in *master* under 4.9.x. The upgrade won't move them, but you may want to have all of them in *sybsystemprocs*. As discussed in Chapter 1, it is better to put your DBA stored procedures into a separate database dedicated to supporting the DBA function (*dbadb*).

Several of the supplied system stored procedures have changed. Specifically, **sp_addsegment**, **sp_dropsegment**, and **sp_extendsegment** now require the database name of the database being affected. This can be confusing because the 4.9.x versions did not allow you to specify the database; you had to be in the database before you could execute any of these commands.

The stored procedures **sp_helpdb** and **sp_helpsegment** now return the free space in each segment of the database. This change is very useful to the DBA because it makes it very easy to determine which segments of a database are full or are getting there. This feature allows you to become much more proactive about database space.

The output of **sp_who** now shows more status values for a given process, and you can kill processes in more of these states than in 4.9.x. You will soon find that you still can't kill process nearly as much of the time as you need to.

Identity columns can now be used in tables for generating sequence numbers. Under 4.9.x you had to come up with the code to generate these numbers on your own.

The query optimizer has been improved so that it is more accurate when choosing the best index for a given query. Under 4.9.x the query optimizer only computed statistics for a table based on the whole key, but now keeps statistics on each subset of columns that make up the key. On the other hand, this improvement depends on you running **update statistics** regularly. Also, you must run **update statistics** before the new optimizer functionality will take effect.

The **create table** command now has additional syntax to allow definition of integrity constraints. This can save a great deal of time that would be needed for coding triggers to handle the same constraints. You need to understand the limitations of these built-in integrity constraints since they do not completely replace the need for triggers in every situation. Specifically, you should make sure you understand what **sp_primarykey** really does and does not do. Further, be aware that integrity constraints or the so-called declarative referential integrity will not support things like cascading deletes. You must still create triggers to take care of things like cascading deletes. Carefully review what these new features can do for you, but be sure that you really understand what is going on before you rely on them.

Thresholds have been mentioned previously. They monitor the free space in each segment of each database. When the free space falls below the specified number of pages, the threshold will execute the associated threshold procedure. You must create and assign the stored procedure that will be fired when each threshold is crossed. Note that there is no default or supplied threshold procedure. Although you will immediately think of using this new feature on the transaction logs (*logsegment*), you should consider using thresholds for the other segments of your databases as well. When a threshold is crossed, the associated stored procedure is executed and any **print** or **raiserror** statement(s) will send messages to the SQL Server errorlog.

There are two types of thresholds. The first is the type that you create by specifying what database and segment the threshold applies to, the threshold itself as the number of remaining free pages, and the name of the stored procedure to be executed when the threshold is crossed. The second type is called the "last-chance" threshold and refers to the transaction log (*logsegment*) only of each database. This threshold will ensure that there is always enough free space left in the transaction log to allow a **dump transaction** command to be executed. This last-chance threshold is automatically set up when you create a database under System 10 and the *logsegment* is on a separate server device from the rest of the database. Further, the point at which this threshold is activated (that is, the number of free pages remaining in the transaction log) is automatically adjusted each time you add space to the transaction log. When the free space in the transaction log falls below the level of the last-chance threshold, it executes the stored procedure **sp_thresholdaction**. By default every last-chance threshold fires the stored procedure called **sp_thresholdaction**, unless you modify this behavior for a database by using **sp_modifythreshold** to specify a different stored procedure. This stored procedure is not supplied and if you don't create **sp_thresholdaction** in the database, nothing will happen when the last-chance threshold is crossed. Typically, you create a stored procedure (call it **sp_thresholdaction**, create it in the *sybsystemprocs* database, and then all the last-chance thresholds in the server will use it) that contains a **dump transaction** or other commands and a **print** or **raiserror** statement, which will cause the associated message(s) to be printed to the server errorlog.

There is a vital part of the threshold story that can easily go unnoticed. While the last-chance threshold is automatically created for any database that is created under System 10, this does not apply to any databases that were upgraded to System 10. This means that after the upgrade from 4.9.x to System 10 (see Chapter 13) the databases in the server will not have a last-chance threshold. You have to execute the following command in each such database to create the last-chance threshold:

```
select lct_admin ("lastchance", db_id())
```

There are new stored procedures to help you administer thresholds, including **sp_addthreshold**, **sp_modifythreshold**, **sp_dropthreshold**, and **sp_helpthreshold**.

Along with roles in System 10 come the stored procedures **sp_displaylogin**, **sp_locklogin**, and **sp_modifylogin**, which allow you to display information about a server login and to lock that login. Locking a server login saves you the effort of dropping any objects owned by that user as well as dropping the user from the database before dropping the login. You can lock a user server login rather than dropping it; the *suid* of the user server login is preserved. Hence, the *suid* will not be reused by another server login. Depending on how you maintain server user logins, this may help by keeping the *suid* in sync between servers because once a login is assigned to a *suid*, it doesn't ever have to change—even when you want to deny access to a login.

The **sp_dboption** now includes a parameter **default network packet size** so that you can set the packet size larger for things like bcp and then set it smaller for normal operations consisting of small transactions.

14.6 Compatibility with Other Sybase Products

You also need to consider all the other products that are running on your database system that may need to communicate with the server you have just upgraded. A good example is Open Server™. If you upgrade a SQL Server that makes calls to an Open Server, you may need to upgrade the Open Server as well. Note that System 10 SQL Server version 10.0.1 requires that the Open Server be upgraded to the 10.0.1 version of the Open Server. You need to realize that even within the System 10 version level, there are different releases. Make sure the upgrade you are performing will not break the functional links you currently need between servers and other products.

;-)

You upgrade one of your System 10 (10.0.0) SQL Servers to 10.0.1. The SQL Server upgrade goes well. The next day various applications are failing. You find out (for the first time) that there is a production application whose functioning depends on using the Open Server. It seems that the SQL Server version 10.0.1 is not compatible with the Open Server 10.0 version that you had been running successfully against SQL Server 10.0.0 (enough different version numbers for you?). You noticed that the upgrade instructions for the SQL Server version 10.0.1 state that you must upgrade Open Server, but you didn't care because you didn't know there was an Open Server that your SQL Server needed to support a production application. You now need to order the new version of Open Server, which will take some time to arrive. Meanwhile, you can't support the application and you can't regress to SQL Server 10.0.0 because the upgrade to 10.0.1 modifies the data. In order to regress you would have to have all databases mirrored and so forth, as described in Chapter 13. Note that similar dependencies exist between the SQL Server and the Backup Server versions. You must determine all the products that are running on or depend on the SQL Server you are upgrading and you must determine how to make all of them work with the upgraded System 10 SQL Server.

You also need to realize that other products may have an upgrade procedure of their own that needs to be followed before you upgrade the SQL Server to System 10. An example of this is the Sybase product Report Workbench. It turns out that this product, as part of its normal operation, creates tables with column names, some of which are reserved keywords in System 10. The Report Workbench product has an upgrade procedure that is available from Sybase Technical Support, but it should be run before the SQL Server is upgraded to System 10. If you don't track down all the reserved word conflicts before you upgrade the SQL Server, you won't realize that some of the conflicts are due to other products that need their own upgrade process before the SQL Server is upgraded. In this particular example, it was difficult to make the changes to Report Workbench after the server was upgraded, and while the problems were being worked out Report Workbench could not be run against the upgraded SQL Server.

Also, you must uncover and understand any interserver dependencies. Make sure you don't need to dump or load data to or from a 4.9.x SQL Server before you upgrade a server to System 10. After the server is upgraded is not the time to discover that some part of your business depends on a dump from that server being loaded into a 4.9.x server elsewhere in the company.

14.7 Server Login Passwords

You will need to understand the way the System 10 SQL Server handles server login passwords. Then, assess the impact this will have on the way you currently manage such passwords, both on the individual server and among all the servers in your database system. Under System 10 the server login passwords are stored in the *syslogins* tables in encrypted form. Therefore, you can't look up a password anymore, as you could under 4.9.x. If you are used to looking up a server login password on one server and then comparing it to the passwords for the same login on other servers, you can't do that any more. Since this is a good way to keep server login passwords in sync between servers and since the same server login on two servers must have the same password to support communication between the two servers, you need to determine how you are going to perform this sort of checking in the future.

Even if you don't regularly check server login passwords between servers, you will run into this problem when you need to add a server login. If the server login already exists on any other server in your database system, you can't determine if this particular login will or will not need, now or in the future, to communicate with other servers. Hence, you should assume that the login will need to communicate between servers, and you need to make the password the same on all servers. But if the login already exists on another server and that server is at System 10, you have no way to determine the existing password. One way to handle this is to add all server logins to one server in your database system and use that set of server logins whenever you install a new server. Again, that works until that central server is upgraded to System 10 and any 4.9.x (or earlier) servers remain in your database system. At that point, you can't use this one server as a source of all login data for a new server unless the new server is also a System 10 server. Loading the contents of *syslogins* from a System 10 server to a 4.9.x server won't work because the 4.9.x server doesn't know how to interpret the encrypted passwords.

Finally, you can improve the login password security on System 10 servers by setting up a password expiration interval so that each login must change its password every so often.

14.8 Server Login 'sa' versus Server Logins with sa_role

Although it appears better to lock the server user 'sa' login and have individual server logins with **sa_role** perform all 'sa' tasks, there can be problems with this approach. Under 4.9.x you want all objects in your databases to be created by server user 'sa' to avoid permissions problems and to simplify the DBA job. If under System 10 you now have individual logins with **sa_role**, then you have a group of server logins that create database objects. When a server login is aliased to 'dbo,' that server login inherits the *suid* of the dbo. If this is not the server login 'sa' and you need to communicate with another server where the database is owned by some other server login, you may not be able to perform remote procedure calls (RPCs) due to a mismatch between the server login passwords of the two different dbos of the databases involved. This is the sort of problem that is only found through testing your applications and procedures for creating database objects. Note that this makes it more difficult for you to test applications or procedures, because you not only need a development server at System 10, but you also need other servers to simulate communication between a System 10 server and any other server version(s) you have in your database system.

You will face similar questions when you set up cron jobs on the server machine that supports the System 10 SQL Server. You must determine which server login these cron job scripts will use. You may want to create a server login just for this purpose and give that server login **sa_role**. Or you may want to simply run all cron job scripts as server login 'sa'—but then you can't lock the 'sa' login.

14.9 Backup Server

Backup Server is a separate process that runs on the server machine. Note that this means you have another process to check on to make sure it is running and another errorlog to check as well. It also means you need to have a separate startup script for the Backup Server. The Backup Server is an Open Server application and as such requires that the SQL Server be configured to allow remote access during any dump or load. The Backup Server is installed by using sybinit, just as for the SQL Server; sybinit will configure the SQL Server to allow remote access as part of the installation.

You must have the Backup Server running before you can make any dump or load from or to the SQL Server. However, you don't need to restart the Backup Server when you restart the SQL Server. Anytime you do restart the SQL Server or the Backup Server you should verify that the two servers are communicating by executing—

```
SYB_BACKUP...sp_who
```

—from within the SQL Server. If this command returns, then you don't need to restart the Backup Server. If the command does not return, then you should kill the Backup Server if it is running and restart it. You must then check again for communication between the SQL Server and the Backup Server. You should make starting the Backup Server part of the RUN_<*servername*> script that starts the SQL Server (see Chapter 15). This will ensure that any restart of the SQL Server will look for a running Backup Server; if it doesn't see one, it will restart the Backup Server automatically.

Backup Server must be running or any scripts or cron jobs that perform dumps or loads in the server will fail.

Backup Server is always called SYB_BACKUP from within the SQL Server. If you go into the system table *sysservers* and change the value of *srvname* for the Backup Server from SYB_BACKUP to anything else, you can't make any dump or load from or to the SQL Server. When you install the Backup Server by using sybinit, you are asked for the name of the Backup Server. If you accept the default, then the value of the *srvnetname* in *sysservers* will also be SYB_BACKUP. You should not do this because the *srvnetname* is what a client calls when it wants to communicate with another server. If more than one SQL Server in your database system were set up with a Backup Server that had a *srvnetname* of SYB_BACKUP, then anytime any SQL Server tried to make a dump, it would call SYB_BACKUP and it would not be clear which Backup Server actually gets the call. (See Chapter 11 for details of how *sysservers* works.) You must have a unique name for each Backup Server.

Backup Server allows you to dump to a server logical device just like 4.9.x does, but it also allows you to dump to a specific tape or disk device without having the device already defined as a dump device to SQL Server. This is a very big improvement for the DBA, because you can specify any tape drive on the server machine you want without maintaining server dump devices for each one. More importantly, for dumps made to disk files, you can specify the specific disk filename directly so you don't have to dump to a server disk dump device and then copy the disk file to another file name. This was required under 4.9.x when dump devices were used to prevent the next dump from overwriting the dump file.

You can install Backup Server on a remote server machine and dump from a SQL Server on another server machine, but the process is very slow. If you want to do this, you must test it out in your particular environment. This capability is still useful for installation or disaster recovery when you may need to dump or load between server machines.

Backup Server allows you to dump to multiple devices at once (striping). This means you can dump a database to four disk devices at once and the dump completes in roughly one-fourth the time. This applies to striping to tape devices as well. One example: A 5-Gb database that takes 2.5 hours to dump to a single tape takes only 20 minutes to dump to five disk devices.

Backup Server supports multiple dumps to a single tape. Since the Backup Server allows multiple dumps to a single tape, it assigns a filename to each dump, or you can specify a filename as part of the **dump database** syntax. If you don't specify a dump filename, the Backup Server generates one for you that is very difficult to comprehend. The **load database** command now has the **with listonly** option that will list all the filenames of all the dumps on a tape for you. You then must use the filename when loading from the dump tape, unless there is only one dump on the tape. Note that if you make repeated runs of existing scripts that dump to tape and you don't change tapes between runs, you may wind up with multiple dumps on one tape.

You must change any scripts that you run that make dumps (or loads) to reflect the new syntax of the **dump database** and **dump transaction** server commands. For dumps to tape, you must specify the **capacity** of the tape device; for the first dump to a tape, you must include **with init** to start writing to the tape.

Backup Server does away with the need for the console process. You don't need an entry in the interfaces file for the console port number, either.

Under 4.9.x you could see a **dump database** or **dump transaction** command executing simply by looking at the output of **sp_who**, and by looking at the I/O count for the process, you could determine how far along it was. With Backup Server, this feature doesn't work anymore. Once the Backup Server is working on the request to dump or load, the only way to see if a dump or load is in progress is to look for a process, called sybmultbuf, running on the server machine supporting the Backup Server. This process is running while the dump or load is in progress.

Chapter 15

Scripts

Here we discuss the details of some standard scripts. These scripts will be useful to you in several ways. First they provide a set of scripts that you should have on each of your servers. Second each script provides the basic syntax you need to build other scripts.

Note that these scripts are from a Sun OS environment and were written for the C shell. However, they are commented profusely to enable you to convert them to your particular environment. We discuss scripts that accomplish the following tasks:

15.1	Dump Database Transaction Log (dumplog)
15.2	Dump Databases for SQL Server 4.9.x (dumpdb)
15.3	Load Databases for SQL Server 4.9.x (loaddb)
15.4	**update statistics** on All Tables (update_statistics_all_tables)
15.5	Dump Commands to Recreate Databases (dump_db_create)
15.6	Run **dbcc** Checks (checkdb)
15.7	Dump Data from System Tables (dump_systables)
15.8	Create Stored Procedure to Generate Database Creation Script (**p_dbcreate**)
15.9	Create Stored Procedure to Check Mirrors (**p_mirror**)
15.10	Create Stored Procedure to Output Device Space (**p_devspace**)
15.11	Create Stored Procedure to Output All Segments on Devices (**p_servermap**)
15.12	Dump Databases for SQL Server System 10 (dumpdb_sys10_tape_disk)
15.13	Load Databases for SQL Server System 10 (loaddb_sys10)
15.14	Server Startup Script RUN_*<servername>*

For each script the text of the script is shown with explanations for each part. The comments in the script are lines that start with a #. Also, once a command or syntax has been commented on in one script, the comment is not repeated in the following scripts.

15.1 Dump Database Transaction Log (dumplog)

The dumplog script will dump the transaction log for each of the database names given. This script would normally be executed as a cron job. When executed as a cron job, the server user 'sa' password should be placed in a file that only UNIX user 'dba' has permission to see. Then, the contents of this password file should be used in the crontab entry for the script. Assuming the password file is /usr/dba/<*server-name*>, the crontab entry to execute the dumplog script every hour from 10 a.m. to 10 p.m. would look like this

0 10-22 * * * /dba/<*servername*>/scripts/dumplog `cat/usr/dba/.<*servername*>` db1

This entry in the crontab would execute the dumplog script on the hour (0 minutes after the hour) every hour from 10 a.m. to 10 p.m.; each time the script is executed, it would dump the transaction log for the database called *db1*.

To execute the dumplog script, enter—

```
dumplog <sa_password> <db1, db2, db3, ... , dbn>
```

—which will dump the transaction log to a disk file for each database listed.

```
#!/bin/csh -f

# this first line is very important -- it identifies this script as
# being a C shell script and yes, the first line appears to be a
# comment line
# now test to see if enough arguments were supplied, the 0th
# argument is the name of the script that is being executed, the
1st
# argument is the password and the 2nd argument is the list of
# database names
```

```
if ($#argv < 2 ) then

# echo sends the text to the screen and echo ${0} sends the 0th
# argument to the screen which is the name of the script followed
by
# the rest of the text specified
# if the script isn't supplied the correct number of arguments, it
# simply outputs the required parameters and exits

        echo ${0}: invalid  format: $#argv parameters provided, at
            least 2 required
        echo ${0}: required format: ${0} '<sa password> <data-
            base(s)...>'
        exit(1)

# exit(1) means the script exits and returns a status of 1
#indicating an error -- this is useful when executing this script
# as part of a larger script

endif

# here we test to see if the server user is 'dba' -- if not, exit
# with error status

if (`whoami` != "dba") then
        echo you must be UNIX user dba to dump the transaction log
        exit(1)
endif

# umask specifies the permissions to be set up for any files cre-
ated
# in the script
# note that the umask value (in this case 006) will be XORed with
# 666 to arrive at the file permissions
# unalias removes any alias for the rm command -- often the UNIX user
# accounts have rm aliased so that you have to confirm each rm
# execution

umask 006
unalias rm

# here we set up various parameters needed later
# the SYBASE variable points to the SYBASE directory where all
```

```
# product files are installed

setenv SYBASE /dba/sybase
# the SERVER variable is set to the name of the SQL server we need
# to access

setenv SERVER PDSOPS21

# the BIN variable points to the subdirectory of the SYBASE
# directory where the executables are stored

set BIN=${SYBASE}/bin

# the variable logdir is the directory where the transaction log
# dumps will be created
# the variable outfile is the location of the errorlog for the
# execution of the script
# the variable password is set to the first argument supplied when
# the script was executed
# shift simply shifts the arguments supplied -- remaining arguments
# are all database names


set logdir=/diskdump
set outfile=${logdir}/dumplog.out
set password=$1
shift

# the variable dmptime contains the date and time

set dmptime=`date +%y%m%d%H%M%S`

# test to see if another dumplog is already executing -- if so,
exit
# with error status and send mail
# this is useful -- it prevents multiple dumplog executions -- if
# one dumplog is running and gets hung up for any reason, the
# following cron executions will abort themselves. If one dumplog is
# running, there is no point in having another execution start up,
# as it will simply be blocked by the previous execution.
# ps -xauw lists all the processes running on the machine
# grep will extract only the processes that are running that contain
# 'dumplog' and
```

```
# wc -l returns the word count, but the -l flag returns the line count
# of the grep output

ps -xauw > /tmp/ps.dumplog
set cnt = `grep dumplog /tmp/ps.dumplog | wc -l`

# subtract 2, 1 for the current execution and 1 for the cron
# expr causes the expression inside the ` ` to be evaluated

set cnt1 = `expr $cnt - 2`
if ($cnt1 > 0) then

# the mail command uses -s to specify subject of mail and dba is the
# user the mail is sent to

        mail -s "${SERVER} dumplog aborted" dba < /tmp/ps.dumplog
exit 1
endif

# remove the temporary file used to hold the listing of the cron jobs
# running

rm /tmp/ps.dumplog

# set up the list of databases that will have a transaction log
dump

set dbs_to_trandump=($argv)

# write to the output file the date when the looping over the
# databases starts

echo "dumplog:${SERVER}: started at `date`." > $outfile

# set up the set of databases, and for each one dump the
# transaction log to disk

foreach dbname ($dbs_to_trandump)

# create the disk file name that will contain the transaction log
# dump

set logfile=${dbname}.log_${dmptime}
```

```
# execute the utility program isql -- note that you need to include
# the path to the isql executable since the cron execution may not
# have the same path you have when you run isql. The -e option
# echos the input to the output file. Note that there is an output
# file created for each database that is dumped. Once isql is
# executed, continue to send commands to isql until we reach the
# finish_sql label.

${BIN}/isql -Usa -S${SERVER} -I$SYBASE/interfaces -e >
   ${dbname}_logdump.out << finish_sql
$password
dump tran $dbname to '${logdir}/${logfile}'
go
exit
finish_sql

# if the execution of isql returns with status=1 then something went
# wrong, send mail to dba

        if ($status) then
                echo dumplog:${SERVER}: log dump of $dbname failed
                    at `date`. >> $outfile
                mail -s "${SERVER}: log dump of $dbname failed"
                    dba < $outfile
        endif

# if the transaction log dump completed write out the time of the
# completion

        echo dumplog:${SERVER}: completed xact log dump of $dbname
            at `date` >> $outfile
end

# whatever happened during the execution, output the date when the
# cron job finished and send the entire output file to dba.

echo "dumplog:${SERVER}: exiting at `date`." >> $outfile
mail -s "${SERVER}: log dump cronjob complete" dba < $outfile
exit
```

15.2 Dump Databases for SQL Server 4.9.x (dumpdb)

WARNING:
Dumping multiple databases to a single tape is not supported as part of the Sybase SQL Server product.

The dumpdb script dumps one or more databases to a tape device. As noted above, Sybase SQL Server version 4.9.x does not support dumping multiple databases to one tape. However, as shown in the script, you can dump multiple databases to a nonrewinding tape device. As one database dump finishes, the next dump starts up; as long as the tape device doesn't try to rewind, things will work out fine. Note again that dumping multiple databases to one tape is not supported by Sybase—use at your own risk.

Since this script is designed to dump to tape, it is assumed that a tape operator will be executing the script manually, because the tape must be loaded in the drive before the script can begin. For this reason the script prompts for the server login and password of the user who is executing the script. Thus, any user who needs to execute this script must have permission to dump the databases. This requires that all such users be granted **dump database** permission in each database. As discussed in Chapter 1, you should set up all such users in the *model* database before creating all the user databases so that these users will have **dump database** permission in all the user databases.

This script can be executed as a cron job if desired. You would have to change the script to assign the command-line arguments for user name and password to the appropriate variables, because the script currently will prompt and wait for the input of both parameters.

To execute the script, after loading the tape in the correct tape drive, enter the following:

```
dumpdb <username> <password>
```

```
#!/bin/csh -f
umask 006
setenv SYBASE /dba/sybase
```

```
# here the script prompts for the username and password
# echo-n simply writes to the screen without a new line character
# at end of text and the user input is assigned to the variable by
# set username = $<
# stty echo simply echoes the text to the screen
# clear simply clears the screen
echo -n Please enter your SQL Server login:
set username = $<
stty -echo
echo -n Please enter your SQL Server password:
set password = $<
stty echo
clear


# set up the output file for this script

set outfile=/diskdump/PDSOPS21_dumpdb.out

# write to both screen and output file the date when the dump
script
# started

echo "dumpdb:PDSOPS21: started at `date`."
echo "dumpdb:PDSOPS21: started at `date`." > $outfile

# mt is the UNIX command to control the tape drive. Here we use the
# -f option to specify the tape device nrst8 which is a nonrewinding
# tape device. This means it doesn't rewind until we explicitly ask
# it to. We then specify that we want to rewind the tape. This
# positions the tape for the first database dump.

mt -f /dev/nrst8 rewind

# write a file to the tape as a tape header -- since SQL Server
# 4.9.x doesn't provide this feature we do it manually. This tape
# header will tell you the name of the server machine and the date
# the dump script was started. This can be very useful when you
need
# to determine the date and source of an old dump tape.
# we echo the server machine name and the date to a temporary file
# called dumptape_header
# uname -a outputs the hostname and operating system version
```

```
# dd is the UNIX command for copying and converting data files -- if
# is input file, of is output file, bs is the block size of both
# input/output files, count=n specifies copy only n input records

echo `/usr/bin/uname -a`" "`/usr/bin/date` >/tmp/dumptape_header
dd if=/tmp/dumptape_header of=/dev/nrst8 bs=80 count=1

# now we start dumping each of the databases. Note that the list of
# databases to dump is hardcoded in the script. This script is
# designed to be executed by a tape operator who should not need to
# determine which databases to dump. Further, for a production
# system you shouldn't be changing which databases are being dumped
# very often.

foreach dbname (master db1 db2 db3 db4 model)
        echo "dumpdb:PDSOPS21: dump of $dbname started   at `date`."
        echo "dumpdb:PDSOPS21: dump of $dbname started   at `date`."
        >> $outfile

# note that the databases are being dumped to logical device
# ntapedump8 which refers to the server machine device nrst8 -- you
# need to change this to the  appropriate logical dump device for
# your server machine
# note that here we don't use $SYBASE/bin/isql because this script
# won't be executed by UNIX user 'dba' -- the tape operator should
# not have access to the filesystems set up for 'dba' -- the tape
# operator will need to execute the isql code that is available to
# the workstation -- you will have to change this based on your
# specific environment.

/usr/local/sybase/bin/isql -U$username -SPDSOPS2 -e >> ${outfile}
  <<finish_sql
$password
dump database $dbname to ntapedump8
go
exit
finish_sql

# if the isql execution returns with status=1 then something failed
# write to the tape operator's screen and the output file

if ($status) then
    echo "dumpdb:PDSOPS21: database dump of $dbname has FAILED at
```

```
        `date`."
    cat   ${dbname}_dbdump.out
    echo "dumpdb:PDSOPS21: database dump of $dbname has FAILED at
        `date`." >> $outfile
    cat   ${dbname}_dbdump.out >> $outfile
else
    echo "dumpdb:PDSOPS21: database dump of $dbname completed at
        `date`."
    echo "dumpdb:PDSOPS21: database dump of $dbname completed at
        `date`." >> $outfile
endif
end


# when all of the databases have been dumped to tape write the date
# to both the operators screen and the output file

echo "dumpdb:PDSOPS21: exiting at `date`."
echo "dumpdb:PDSOPS21: exiting at `date`." >> $outfile


# send the output file to dba

mail -s "dumpdb:PDSOPS21: output" dba < $outfile


# here we use the UNIX mt command to rewind and eject the tape
# the mt command takes several options; here offline will rewind and
# eject the tape

mt -f /dev/nrst8 offline                    # rewind tape
exit
```

15.3 Load Databases for SQL Server 4.9.x (loaddb)

The loaddb script loads one or more of the database dumps you made using the
dumpdb script. Recall that the dumpdb script allows you to dump more than one
database to a tape, which is not a supported feature of the 4.9x Sybase SQL Server.
Now that you have a tape with multiple database dumps on it, we discuss how to
load a database from the tape. The SQL server has no idea that the tape has multiple
database dumps on it. In fact, when you issue the server command load database *db1*
and specify the tape drive, the server will just start reading the tape, assuming that
the database dump for *db1* is there. The script must take care of positioning the tape

such that the database dump for *db1* is the very next file on the tape. Recall that the dumpdb script put a header on the tape to identify the date and server machine where the tape was created, then the script dumped the requested databases to tape. This means we need to know where the dump of database *db1* is on the tape and position the tape to that file before we tell the server to begin loading *db1*.

Each database dump on the tape is a file. Therefore, if we know how many databases were dumped before *db1* was dumped, we know the number of the file we need to load *db1* from the tape. For example, let's assume you used the dumpdb script to dump databases *db0*, *db1*, *db2*, and *db3* to tape. Recall that the dumpdb script puts a header file on the tape. The header file is the first file on the tape, but this is the 0th file or count = 0 for the UNIX mt command. Hence, the database dump of *db0* is the count = 1 file, and the database dump of *db1* is the count = 2 file. Using this count, you can use the UNIX command mt with the fsf or fast-forward option to position the tape to the beginning of the third file (count = 2), which is the beginning of the *db1* database dump.

Since this script is for loading a database dump, it would not normally be used as a cron job. Usually, the need to load a database from tape comes up only if there has been a major problem. Therefore, the script should be executed manually.

To execute the loaddb script manually

```
loaddb <servername> <sa_password> <databases_to_load>
```

The script takes the names of the databases to load and equates the name of each with a count value. The script can then position the tape for loading. This approach has some dependencies you need to be aware of. The number of databases being dumped and the order in which they are dumped must remain fixed between the dumpdb and loaddb scripts. Also, if one or more of the dumps should fail to start for any reason during the execution of the dumpdb script, the total number of files on the dump tape will be off by one, and you would need to edit the loaddb script to change the count value(s) for the database(s) you are trying to load. This is where the mail that is sent to UNIX user 'dba' after the dumpdb script comes in. Before loading a database dump from tape, examine the mail message that was generated when the dump tape was made. If there are any failures before the database dump that you need to load, you need to make changes to the loaddb script.

```
#!/bin/csh -f

umask 006              # make our files -rw-rw----

# here we test to see if we have all the required parameters;
# if not, we read the header file off the tape and write
# to the screen what all the required parameters are and exit
# with status=1, which indicates an error condition.

if !($#argv) then
        dd if=/dev/rst8 bs=80 count=1
        echo loaddb: format: loaddb.PDSOPS21 '<Server Name>
<Server Password> <Database(s)>'
        exit (1)
endif
setenv SYBASE /dba/sybase
setenv SERVER PDSOPS21
set BIN=${SYBASE}/bin

# here we assign the servername and password parameters. The
# use of shift just moves us along the string of arguments
# supplied when the script was executed.

set srvname = $1
shift
set password = $1
shift
set databases_to_load = ($argv)
echo "loaddb: started at `date`."

# rewind the tape to position it at the very first file on
# the tape. Note that we are specifying the rewinding tape
# device here and that you need to change rst8 to whatever
# the nonrewinding tape device is on your server machine.

mt -f /dev/rst8 rewind                    # rewind tape

# here we set up the databases that we need to load. For each
# one we use the database name to determine the count value,
```

```
# i.e., how many files into the tape is the dump of database
# dbx? If the database name requested isn't in the script's
# list of possible databases to load the script will exit
# with status=1 (error condition).

foreach dbname ($databases_to_load)
        echo loaddb: beginning load of $dbname
        switch ($dbname)
                case db0:
                        set counter = 1
                        breaksw
                case db1:
                        set counter = 2
                        breaksw
                case db2:
                        set counter = 3
                        breaksw
                case db3:
                        set counter = 4
                        breaksw
                default:
                        echo invalid database name $dbname
                        exit (1)
        endsw

# here we fast-forward the tape to the beginning of the nth
# file where n=counter+1 -- recall the first file on the tape
# is the 0th file, so the 5th file on the tape is counter=4

        mt -f /dev/nrst8 fsf $counter

# if positioning the tape returns an error condition, the
# script exits, advising the user to get help from the dba.

        if ($status) then
            echo database load script failed during
                positioning of tape -- contact DBA for help
                exit (1)
        endif
```

```
# write the date the load started to the output file

echo "loaddb: started at `date`." > /dba/${SERVER}
  /diagnostics/${dbname}_loaddb.out
# execute isql for the first database to be loaded. You will
# need to change the logical tape device from ntapedump8 to
# the appropriate tape device for your server.

${BIN}/bin/isql -Usa -S${srvname} -e >> /dba/${SERVER}
  /diagnostics/${dbname}_loaddb.out <<finish_sql
$password
load database $dbname from ntapedump8
go
exit
finish_sql

# if the isql execution fails, write that out to the output
# file and exit with status=1

        if ($status) then
                echo load of $dbname failed at `date`.
output to output file
                exit (1)
        endif

        echo load of $dbname completed at `date`
output to output file

# rewind and eject the tape

        mt -f /dev/rst8 off                     # rewind tape
end

# write out date of end of loaddb script and send output file
# to dba

echo "loaddb: ended at `date`." >> /dba/${SERVER}
  /diagnostics/${dbname}_loaddb.out
```

```
mail -s 'load of database complete' dba <
    /dba/${SERVER}/diagnostics/${dbname}_loaddb.out
exit
```

15.4 update statistics on All Tables (update_statistics_all_tables)

The update_statistics_all_tables script will execute the server command **update statistics** and the server stored procedure **sp_recompile** for each and every user table on the entire server. This script is very useful because it is difficult to keep track of which tables on the server have been updated or should be updated. Even though you may have a list of several critical tables that must be updated frequently, you should regularly use this script to make sure that all the tables in the server are updated. You need to prevent the situation where you run across tables that have never had update statistics performed. This can happen if it was never done, but also when a table is truncated. Until you run **update statistics** for such a table, it will appear to the server that it was never done.

The crontab entry would look like this:

0 21 6 * *   /dba/*<servername>*/scripts/update_statistics_all_tables
                    <servername> `cat/usr/dba/*<servername>*`

This entry in the crontab would execute the update_statistics_all_tables script at 21:00 (09:00 p.m.) on the sixth day for every month and every year. Note that crontab days start with 0 for Sunday and run through 6 for Saturday.

You can manually execute this script, as follows:

```
update_statistics_all_tables <servername> <sa_password>
```


```
#!/bin/csh -f

# set up various parameters and the output file

unalias rm
```

```
setenv SYBASE /dba/sybase
setenv BIN ${SYBASE}/bin
set SERVER = $1
set PASSWORD = $2


set outfile=/dba/${server}/diagnostics/update_statistics.out
cp /dev/null $outfile
# first we need to generate a list of all the databases in the
# server

set TEMPFILE=/tmp/${SERVER}_databases.list
cp /dev/null $TEMPFILE
${BIN}/isql -Usa -P$PASSWORD -S$SERVER -I$SYBASE/interfaces <<
    finish_sql >> $TEMPFILE
use master
go
select name from sysdatabases where name != "tempdb" order by name
go
finish_sql

# append the output of all the databases to the output file
# select the servername and date/time to the output file

echo " " >> $outfile
echo "all databases in server...." >> $outfile
echo " " >> $outfile
cat $TEMPFILE >> $outfile
echo " "
${BIN}/isql -Usa -P$PASSWORD -S$SERVER -I$SYBASE/interfaces <<
    finish_sql >> tfile
select @@servername
go
select getdate()
go
finish_sql

# see the dump_db_create script discussion for details of the
# following part of the script

set num_lines=`wc -l $TEMPFILE | cut -c1-9`
set last_line=`expr $num_lines - 2`
set first_line=`expr $last_line - 2`
```

```
set databases_list=`tail -$last_line $TEMPFILE | head -$first_line`
rm -f $TEMPFILE

# Finally we can set up the list of databases

foreach dbname ($databases_list)
# now repeat the process but this time generate a list of all the
# user tables in each database

set TEMPFILE2=/tmp/${dbname}_tables.list
cp /dev/null $TEMPFILE2
${BIN}/isql -Usa -P$PASSWORD -S$SERVER -I$SYBASE/interfaces -e <<
    finish_sql >> $TEMPFILE2
use $dbname
go
select name from sysobjects where type="U" order by name
go
finish_sql

echo " " >> $outfile
echo "@@@@@@@@@@@@@@@@@@@@@@@" >> $outfile
echo "all tables in database $dbname...." >> $outfile
echo "@@@@@@@@@@@@@@@@@@@@@@@" >> $outfile
echo " " >> $outfile
cat $TEMPFILE2 >> $outfile
echo " " >> $outfile

# cut out the first 4 and last 2 lines of the listing of all the
# user tables in this database

set num_lines=`wc -l $TEMPFILE2 | cut -c1-9`
set last_line=`expr $num_lines - 4`
set first_line=`expr $last_line - 2`
set tables_list=`tail -$last_line $TEMPFILE2 | head -$first_line`
rm -f $TEMPFILE2

# now we start updating statistics and executing sp_recompile for
# each user table in each database

echo "@@@@@@@@@@@@@@@@@@@@@@@@@@@@@@@@@@@@@@@@@@@@@" >> $outfile
echo "updating statistics for tables in database $dbname" >>
    $outfile
echo "@@@@@@@@@@@@@@@@@@@@@@@@@@@@@@@@@@@@@@@@@@@@@" >> $outfile
```

```
echo " " >> $outfile
foreach table_name ($tables_list)
${BIN}/isql -Usa -P$PASSWORD -S$SERVER -I$SYBASE/interfaces -e <<
finish_sql >> $outfile
use $dbname
go
select getdate()
go
update statistics $table_name
go
sp_recompile $table_name
go
select getdate()
go
finish_sql

# the first end is for the loop for each user table
# the second end is for the loop for each database in the server

end
end

mail -s "$SERVER update statistics" dba < $outfile
exit(0)
```

15.5 Dump Commands to Recreate Databases (dump_db_create)

This script dumps to a disk file the Transact SQL commands needed to recreate each database on the server. The commands that are generated can be used to recreate each database on the same server or to recreate the database on another server. To recreate the server on another server, you must first edit the output to change the server device names from those of the source server where the **p_dbcreate** SQL script was run to the server device names of the target server. The crontab entry to execute this script would look like this;

```
0 23 * * *    /dba/<servername>/scripts/dump_db_create <servername>
              `cat/usr/dba/<servername>`
```

This entry in the crontab would execute the dump_db_create script at 23:00 hours (11:00 p.m.) every day.

To execute the dump_db_create script manually, enter

```
dump_db_create <servername> <sa_password>

#!/bin/csh -f

# setup various parameters and the output file

unalias rm
setenv SYBASE /dba/sybase
setenv BIN ${SYBASE}/bin
set SERVER = $1
set PASSWORD = $2
set outfile=/dba/${SERVER}/diagnostics/dump_db_create.out
cp /dev/null $outfile

# first we need to generate a list of all the databases in the
# server -- we want to generate the commands necessary to
# (re)create all of the databases on the server

set TEMPFILE=/tmp/${SERVER}_databases.list
cp /dev/null $TEMPFILE
${BIN}/isql -Usa -P$PASSWORD -S$SERVER -I$SYBASE/interfaces <<
    finish_sql >> $TEMPFILE
use master
go
select name from sysdatabases where name != "tempdb" order by name
go
finish_sql

# append the output of all the databases to the output file
# select the servername and date/time to the output file

echo " " >> $outfile
echo "all databases in server...." >> $outfile
echo " " >> $outfile
cat $TEMPFILE >> $outfile
echo " "
${BIN}/isql -Usa -P$PASSWORD -S$SERVER -I$SYBASE/interfaces <<
```

```
    finish_sql >> $outfile
select @@servername
go
select getdate()
go
finish_sql

# after we generate the list of databases on the server, we need to
# edit out the first two lines and the last two lines of the output
# -- they contain the column names and the number of rows
# selected, respectively. The output of the select for the
# databases goes to a temporary file. We remove the lines we don't
# want by determining the number of rows in the temporary file.
# Note that the output of the wc -l command gives us the number of
# lines (wc is the word count command, and the -l option counts
# lines, not words) and the name of the file. We use the cut command
# with the -c option to cut out only columns 1 through 9 that
# contain the number of rows in the temporary file. With that done
# we can set a parameter for 2 lines less than the total number of
# lines and another parameter for the first parameter -2. Now we
# feed the temporary file through the tail command specifying that tail
# output the last x lines of the file, where x = num_lines - 2
# -- this will give us a the temporary file without the first two
# lines, then we feed that into the head command telling it
# to only output the first x - 2 lines, which gives us all the
# previous lines but not the last two lines. This gets rid of the
# first 2 and last 2 lines of the temporary file.

set num_lines=`wc -l $TEMPFILE | cut -c1-9`
set last_line=`expr $num_lines - 2`
set first_line=`expr $last_line - 2`
set databases_list=`tail -$last_line $TEMPFILE | head -$first_line`
rm -f $TEMPFILE

# Finally we can setup the list of databases
# then execute the stored procedure p_dbcreate for each database

foreach dbname ($databases_list)
${BIN}/isql -Usa -P$PASSWORD -S$SERVER -I$SYBASE/interfaces <<
    finish_sql >> $outfile
use dbadb
go
p_dbcreate $dbname
```

```
go
finish_sql
end
exit(0)
```

15.6 Run dbcc Checks (checkdb)

This script is used to run the full **dbcc** set. This script would be used after loading a database from a dump tape onto the DBCC server and assumes that the database to be loaded, database *db1* in the script below, has already been created on the DBCC server. This would be a good place for you to use the **p_dbcreate** SQL script described previously, inasmuch as that script will dump the database definition from the source server. After you edit the **p_dbcreate** output to reflect the actual server device names on the DBCC server, you can create the database with the **for load** option on the DBCC server and execute the checkdb script shown below.

You can execute the script manually as well, as follows:

```
checkdb <sa_password>
```

Note that this script is hardcoded for running the **dbcc** checks for a single database. You could modify the script to accept the database name as a parameter input at execution time. You need to determine how you want to run the **dbcc** checks for each database on your server. For the largest databases, you may not want to run **dbcc** checks on all of the database, only on selected tables, etc. In that case, you would need a separate script set up for each database.

```
#!/bin/csh -f

# select @@servername returns the name of the server you are
# connected to
# select db_name() returns the current database
# select getdate() returns the current date/time
# dbcc traceon (3604) causes the output of the dbcc runs to be
# sent to your screen or in this case to the output file of
# the script
# the script outputs the date/time as each dbcc run completes
```

```
# -- this timing information is very important when planning
# dbcc runs on your production servers to fix corruptions
# found after running dbcc checks on the DBCC server


isql -Usa -P$1 -SDDSMAIN1 > dbcc_db1.out << finish_sql
select @@servername
go
use db1
go
select db_name()
go
select getdate()
go
dbcc traceon (3604)
go
dbcc checkalloc (db1)
go
select getdate()
go
dbcc checkdb (db1)
go
select getdate()
go
dbcc checkcatalog (db1)
go
select getdate()
go
finish_sql
mail -s "dbcc runs for db1 completed" dba < dbcc_db1.out
exit(0)
```

15.7 Dump Data from System Tables (dump_systables)

This script is executed as a cron job to dump various server system tables to a disk file. This script should be executed daily; it will record the configuration of the server. Then, the file system dump to tape that should be done each day on the server machine will capture this file, giving you a daily record of the configuration of the server. This script should be run on each of the server machines in your database system that supports an SQL Server. It is crucial that you dump this information to disk regularly. When (not if) you have a crisis, you will need this information to recover, and once the crisis has arrived, you generally won't have any way to retrieve the information.

0 20 * * * /dba/<servername>/scripts/dump_systables `cat/usr/dba/<em>&lt;servername&gt;</em>`

This entry in the crontab would execute the dump_systables script on the hour (0 minutes after the hour) at 8 p.m. each day. Each time the script is executed, it will dump the selected system tables to the specified disk file. The disk file is overwritten each time the script is executed.

To execute the dump_systables script manually, enter—

```
dump_systables <servername> <sa_password>
```

—which will dump the system tables specified in the script to the file specified in the script.

```
#!/bin/csh -f
if ($#argv < 2) then
        echo ${0}: invalid format, $#argv parameters given, 2
          required.
        echo ${0}: required format: ${0} '<svrname> <password> .'
        exit (1)
endif
umask 006                                   # make our files -rw-rw----
setenv SYBASE /dba/sybase
setenv BIN   ${SYBASE}/bin
set SERVER=$1
shift
set PASSWORD=$1
shift

# set the directory where the output of the script will be placed

set dir=/dba/${SERVER}/diagnostics
```

```
cd $dir

# execute isql as server user 'sa', send output to the file specified
# use the master database to select all data from the system tables
# shown then execute the stored procedure sp_configure to document
# the server configuration
# next use the database called dbadb which should be part of the
# standard configuration of your server -- dbadb is where stored
# procedures, etc., that are dedicated for DBA use are stored
# execute the stored procedures p_mirror and p_devspace to record the
# status of all server device mirrors and the server device space
# respectively
# finally select all the data in the syslogins system table -- this
# allows you to  record all the users of the server -- very
# important when rebuilding a server

${BIN}/isql -Usa -S${SERVER} > ${dir}/${SERVER}_dump_systables.out
    << finish_sql
$PASSWORD
use master
go
select * from sysusages
go
select * from sysdevices
go
select * from sysdatabases
go
select * from sysservers
go
select * from sysremotelogins
go
exec sp_configure
go
exec sp_helpdevice
go
exec sp_helpdb
go
select * from syslogins
go
use dbadb
go
exec p_mirror
go
exec p_devspace
```

```
go
exec p_servermap
go
exit
finish_sql

# append the date to the output file

date >> ${dir}/${SERVER}_dump_systables.out

# the following command is commented out. Use it to dump and append
# to results of buildmaster -yall -- this command will dump out a much
# more detailed version of the server configuration
# than sp_configure. However, you must specify the master server
# device (/dev/rsd1h in this example) which will vary from server to
# server. You must be familiar with buildmaster and understand how
# to specify the master server device. If you execute buildmaster with
# the wrong options, you can wipe out the master device for the
# server. Dumping this information is very good when you need
# to rebuild or reconfigure your server. Be careful with buildmaster!

# ${BIN}/buildmaster -d/dev/rsd1h -yall >>
#     ${dir}/${SERVER}_dump_systables.out

# the chmod 600 sets the permissions on the output file so that
only
# UNIX user 'dba' has the ability to use it. This is done because
# the output of the syslogins system table will contain the
# passwords of all the server users in plain text for SQL Server
# 4.9.x

chmod 600 ${SERVER}_dump_systables.out
exit
```

15.8 Create Stored Procedure to Generate Database Creation Script (p_dbcreate)

This script will create the stored procedure **p_dbcreate**, which will dump the commands needed to recreate a database on the server. This stored procedure is called by the dump_db_create script described above. The stored procedure should be created in the server database *dbadb*.

The commands that are generated use the **for load** option of the **create database** command. This is much faster than the **create database** command alone because the server assumes (in fact, requires) that you immediately load the database from a database dump after you create the database with the **for load** option. Using the **for load** option prevents the server from initializing all the data pages, as it would with the normal **create database** command. This can save you a great deal of time for large databases.

This script also outputs the Transact SQL commands necessary to update the system table *sysusages* in the *master* database to set up all the segments on the proper devices once each database has been (re)created. For a full discussion of *sysusages* and what it does, see Chapter 11. You can achieve the same effects by using only the **create database** portion of the **p_dbcreate** output and then manually adding, dropping, and extending segments as necessary to make *sysusages* for the new database match the segmentation of *sysusages* on the source server.

This script should be loaded into *dbadb*. If you want to be able to execute this stored procedure from any database, then install the stored procedure in the *master* database (for System 10, you would install it in *sybsystemprocs*) and name it **sp_dbcreate**. If you want server users other than 'sa' (or users who have been granted **sa_role** in System 10) to be able to execute the stored procedure, then execute the following server command:

```
grant execute on p_dbcreate to public
```

The script can be executed manually, as follows:

```
isql -Usa -S<servername> -P<sa_password>
use dbadb
go
p_dbcreate <database_name>
go
```

```
create proc p_dbcreate @dbname varchar(40) as

# start by selecting or outputting the text of the create database
```

```
#   command
# next, select all the rows from sysusages for the database and
# convert the number of logical pages in each row of sysusages to
# MB -- one page is 2 KB for SunOS servers and 1024 squared is 1 MB
# the way we get the name of the server device for each row in
# sysusages is by noting that each server device has a low and high
# virtual page number and each row in sysusages has a virtual page
# number indicating the starting virtual page number of the
# fragment of disk space described by the row

select 'create database ' + @dbname + ' on'
select
name + '=' + convert(char(4),(size*2048)/(1024*1024)) +
',' from master..sysusages u, master..sysdevices d
where u.vstart >= d.low
and u.vstart <= d.high
and d.cntrltype = 0
and u.dbid=(select dbid from master..sysdatabases where
    name=@dbname)
order by u.lstart
select 'for load'

# here we generate the commands necessary to update the system
# table sysusages to reflect the segments assigned to each server
# device in the original database. We do this by generating
# commands that will update the segmap value of the rows in
# sysusages on the target server to have the same values as the
# original server. We again use the virtual page start, low and
# high values to determine which rows in sysusages should get which
# segmap value.

select 'update sysusages set segmap=' +
convert(char(4),u.segmap) + ' where
dbid=(select dbid from master..sysdatabases where name="'
+ @dbname +
'") and lstart >= ' + convert(char(9),lstart) +
'and lstart < ' +
convert(char(9),lstart+size) from
master..sysusages u, master..sysdevices d
where u.vstart >= d.low
and u.vstart <= d.high
and d.cntrltype = 0
```

```
# throughout this script we must only effect changes to those rows
# of sysusages that belong to the database in question -- here we
# limit the rows of sysusages that will be affected to those that
# have the dbid of the database we are (re)creating -- we select
# dbid = (select dbid ... name = database in question) because the dbid
# may not be the same on the target server as on the primary even
# though the databases will have the same name

and u.dbid=(select dbid from master..sysdatabases where
    name=@dbname)
go
```

15.9 Create Stored Procedure to Check Mirrors (p_mirror)

This script will create the stored procedure **p_mirror** that is used to check the *status* of the mirror for all server devices. It is called as part of the dump_systables script.

This stored procedure simply lists all of the server devices currently set up and the mirror for each server device, if any, along with the *status* of each server device. You should examine this output to see that all the server devices that should be mirrored are indeed mirrored. The *status* column is also important. Once you have all your server devices and mirrors set up, the *status* for all server devices with mirrors should be the same, and all server device without mirrors should have the same *status* as well. Scanning the *status* column will show you any devices that have changed status. Note that a server device that has a mirror may have failed over to the mirror, and, while the server device and the mirror will show up in the **p_mirror** output as if everything were normal, it is the *status* output that will tell you that the server device has failed over to the mirror device.

This script should be loaded into *dbadb*. If you want to be able to execute the stored procedure from any database, you need to install the stored procedure in the *master* database (for System10, you would install it in *sybsystemprocs*) and name it **sp_mirror**. If you want server users other than 'sa' to be able to execute the stored procedure, you need to execute the following server command:

```
grant execute on p_mirror to public
```

This stored procedure can also be run manually, as follows:

```
isql -Usa -S<servername> -P<sa_password>
use dbadb
go
p_mirror
go
```

The sql to create the stored procedure **p_mirror** is shown below. Note that the stored procedure simply selects each server *device name, phyname, mirrorname,* and *status* from the system table *sysdevices* in the *master* database. This information is not selected for devices where *status* = 16 because that *status* indicates a dump device, that is, a disk (file system) or tape device, and dump devices are not server devices and don't have mirrors.

```
create procedure p_mirror as
select getdate()
select @@servername
select db_name()
select "logical"=substring(name,1,10), "physical"
  =substring(phyname,1,20), "mirror"=substring
  (mirrorname,1,20), status from master..sysdevices
  where status!=16
go
```

15.10 Create Stored Procedure to Output Device Space (p_devspace)

This script creates the stored procedure **p_devspace** which outputs the total, used, and free space for all server devices. This stored procedure is called from the script dump_systables. This output is useful when you are generating a servermap, adding database space, or checking how much free space you have on the server.

This script should be loaded into *dbadb*. If you want to be able to execute this stored procedure from any database, you need to install the stored procedure in the *master* database (for System10 you would install it in *sybsystemprocs*) and name it **sp_devspace**. If you want server users other than 'sa' to be able to execute the stored procedure, you need to execute the following server command:

```
grant execute on p_devspace to public
```

You can execute the stored procedure manually

```
isql -Usa -S<servername> -P<sa_password>
use dbadb
go
p_devspace
go

create procedure p_devspace as
select device_name = sysdev.name,
total_Mb = (sysdev.high - sysdev.low + 1) / 512,
used_Mb = sum(sysuse.size)/512,
free_Mb =
(sysdev.high - sysdev.low + 1)/512 -
sum(sysuse.size)/512
into #space_on_devices
from sysdevices sysdev,
sysusages sysuse
where
sysdev.cntrltype = 0
and
sysuse.vstart
between
sysdev.low
and
sysdev.high
group by
sysdev.name
/* now for any devices that have been
initialized but not yet in use by any
databases... */
insert #space_on_devices
select sysdev.name,
total_Mb = (sysdev.high - sysdev.low + 1) / 512,
used_Mb = 0,
free_Mb = (sysdev.high - sysdev.low + 1) / 512
from sysdevices sysdev, sysusages sysuse
where
sysdev.cntrltype = 0
```

```
and not exists
(select * from sysusages sysuse2
where sysuse2.vstart between sysdev.low and sysdev.high)
/* now output the total results */
select distinct * from #space_on_devices
order by device_name
compute sum(total_Mb),
sum(used_Mb), sum(free_Mb)
return
go
```

15.11 Create Stored Procedure to Output All Segments on Devices (p_servermap)

This script will create the stored procedure **p_servermap** which will output the various database segments that are on all of the server devices. This stored procedure is called by the script dump_systables. This output will list all the server devices that have database segments on them. The output also shows the size of each database segment and the total space on each device that is taken by database segments. This output and the output of **p_mirror** and **p_devspace** will allow you to generate the entire servermap. The output of **p_servermap** shows you each server device, the database segments on each device, the segment number of each segment, and the size of the segment. Note that the segment number is unique within each database. This means that you would need to execute the following server commands to find out the segment names for each segment number in each database. Note that this script outputs information only for those server devices that have database segments —server devices that have been created but not yet assigned to any database will not appear. You need to use the output of **p_devspace** to determine the complete set of all server devices.

```
isql -Usa -S<servername> -P<sa_password>
use <dbname>
go
select * from syssegments
go
```

This script should be loaded into *dbadb*. If you want to be able to execute this stored procedure from any database, you need to install the stored procedure in the *master*

database (for System10, you would install it in *sybsystemprocs*) and name it
sp_servermap. If you want server users other than 'sa' to be able to execute the
stored procedure, you need to execute the following server command:

```
grant execute on p_servermap to public
```

This script can be executed manually, as follows:

```
isql -Usa -S<servername> -P<sa_password>
use dbadb
go
p_servermap
go


# we first select the devices and for each device the relevant
# entries from sysusages
# we select this data into temporary table #smap

create procedure p_servermap as
select device_name =substring( sysdev.name,1,11),
database_name=substring(sysdb.name,1,20),
seg#=substring(convert(char(4),sysuse.segmap),1,4),
size_Mb = substring(convert(char(7),sysuse.size/512),1,7)
into #smap
from sysdevices sysdev,
sysdatabases sysdb,
sysusages sysuse
where
sysdev.cntrltype = 0
and
sysuse.vstart
between
sysdev.low
and
sysdev.high
and
sysuse.dbid = sysdb.dbid
```

```
# next we select from #smap to #smap2 summing up all the entries
# for each database, segment and segment number on each device.
# This means that multiple entries in sysusages for one segment of
# one database will be summed into one entry for the segment

select device_name,database_name,
seg#,space_per_seg=sum(convert(int,size_Mb))
into #smap2
from #smap
group by device_name,database_name,seg#

# we output the meaning of the segmap numbers. The segmap numbers 1
# through 7 are the same for all databases. For segmap values
# greater than 7, you need to look at the data in syssegments for
# each database to see the segment name for each user-defined
# segment. Note that for System10 the auditing database
#(sybsecurity) has a segment called auditsegment and the segmap
# value is 8 -- since this segment is on the same server device as
# the system, default and logsegment, the segmap value will be 15.

set nocount on
select "segmap values 1 through 7
seg# and segment name
 1 -- system
 2 -- default
 3 -- default/system
 4 -- log only
 5 -- log/system
 6 -- log/default
 7 -- log/system/default
 8 -- user defined
15 -- audit/log/sys/def
16 -- user defined"
set nocount off

# select the final output from #smap2 and this time compute the
# total space used by all database segments on each server device

select device_name,database_name,
seg#,space_per_seg
```

```
from #smap2
order by device_name,database_name,seg#
compute sum(space_per_seg)
by device_name

return
go
```

15.12   Dump Databases for SQL Server System 10 (dumpdb_sys10_tape_disk)

The dumpdb_sys10_tape_disk script uses the features of Sybase SQL Server System 10 Backup Server to dump databases to tape and to disk. The reason for this is the same reason you will probably need to dump databases both to tape and to disk. You want to dump all your databases to disk, but you don't have sufficient disk space because you (more likely, your predecessor(s)) didn't bother with capacity planning. So, for the databases that are small enough, you dump to disk; for the large databases, you still have to dump to tape. This script points out the differences in dumping a database using System 10 Backup Server versus 4.9.x. For this script we assume that database *db1* is so large it requires its own tape, then database *db2* is still too large to dump to disk so it is dumped to a second tape along with the *master* database. The remaining databases are dumped to disk files. Note also that anytime you are dumping databases to disk files, you must ensure that a file system dump is made immediately following the completion of the database dumps to disk to ensure that the disk dumps are captured to tape.

You should also note the database dump of the *master* database is followed by the truncation of the *master* transaction log. The *master* database does not allow the transaction log to be on a separate server device, which means you can't dump the transaction log separately from the *master* database. Dumping the transaction log is the normal way to truncate or remove the inactive portion of the transaction log. Since you can't dump the transaction log for the *master* database, the log will continue to grow until it eventually fills up and stops the server. The only way to truncate the transaction log of the *master* database is to execute the **dump transaction** with the **truncate_only** command, as shown in the script. Note that this command needs to be executed after the **dump database** *master* command (see Chapter 7 for more details). Make sure you are truncating the *master* database transaction log periodically. You don't have to do it as part of the dump database script, but you must make sure it happens regularly.

As with the previous dumpdb script (for SQL Server 4.9.x), this script is designed to be run by the tape operator and therefore is not normally executed as a cron job. The script assumes the tape operator is available to load the two tapes needed for the large database dumps. For this reason, the script prompts for the server login and password of the user who is executing the script. Note that this means any user who needs to execute this script must have permission to dump the databases. This requires that all such users be granted **oper_role**.

To execute the script manually, enter

```
dumpdb_sys10_tape_disk <username> <password>
```

```
#!/bin/csh -f
umask 006
setenv SERVER PDSOPS21
setenv SYBASE /dba/sybase

# here we set up a tape device number -- this makes it easier to
# change the tape device number as you move this script to other
# server machines
# you only need to change the tape device number here

setenv TAPEDEVNO  8
setenv REWINDINGTAPE    /dev/rst${DEVNO}
setenv NONREWINDINGTAPE  /dev/nrst${DEVNO}
echo -n Enter Your Server Username:
set username = $<
stty -echo
echo -n Enter Your Server Password:
set password = $<
stty echo
clear
echo dumpdb:${SERVER}: beginning dump of ${SERVER} system 10 server
set dir=/diskdump
```

```
set outfile=${dir}/${srvname}_dumpdb.out

# the C shell command tee copies standard input to standard output
# and copies the input to a file specified. This means all the
# commands in the script are echoed to the user's screen and to the
# output file specified

setenv COPYINPUT '/bin/tee -a '${outfile}
mt -f ${NONREWINDINGTAPE} rewind

# set the first database to dump to the first tape -- this is the
# only dump going to the first tape because the database dump will
# almost fill the tape

set dbname=db1
echo "dumpdb:${SERVER}: [${dbname}] started at `date`." >
   ${outfile}

# dump database db1 to the first tape
# note the System 10 dump database command requires the new options
# capacity=5000000 which tells the Backup Server that the tape
# drive has a capacity of 5 GB
# with init tells the Backup Server to initialize or overwrite this
# tape -- this is only specified for the first dump to a given tape

$SYBASE/bin/isql -U${username} -S${SERVER} -e <<finish_sql_tape1 |
    $COPYINPUT
${password}
dump database ${dbname} to '${NONREWINDINGTAPE}'
capacity=5000000
with init
go
exit
finish_sql_tape1

# if the database dump of the first database fails do not go on to
# the second tape -- exit with status=1 (error condition)

if ($status) then
        echo "dumpdb:${SERVER}: database dump of ${dbname} has
            FAILED at `date`." | $COPYINPUT
        cat  ${dbname}_dbdump.out | $COPYINPUT
        exit(1)
```

```
else
        echo "dumpdb:${SERVER}: dump of ${dbname} completed at
            `date`." | $COPYINPUT
endif
# rewind and unload the first tape

mt -f ${NONREWINDINGTAPE} off

# request load of second tape before continuing

echo -n "Load 2nd PDSOPS21 server tape.  Press return when ready to
    continue. "
set waiting = $<
echo -n "Are you sure the 2nd tape is loaded?  Press return if ready
    to continue. "
set waiting = $<
mt -f ${NONREWINDINGTAPE} rewind                        # rewind tape

# set the second database and the master database to dump to the
# second tape
# note that after db2 is dumped to tape you don't use the with init
# option when dumping the master database

set dbname=db2
set dbname2=master
echo "dumpdb:${SERVER}: [${dbname}] started    at `date`." |
  $COPYINPUT
$SYBASE/bin/isql -U${username} -S${SERVER} -e <<finish_sql_tape2 |
    $COPYINPUT
${password}
dump database ${dbname} to '${NONREWINDINGTAPE}'
capacity=5000000
with init
go
dump database ${dbname2} to '${NONREWINDINGTAPE}'
capacity=5000000
go
dump tran master with truncate_only
go
exit
finish_sql_tape2
if ($status) then
        echo "dumpdb:${SERVER}: database dump of $dbname has FAILED
```

```
            at `date`." | $COPYINPUT
        cat  ${dbname}_dbdump.out | $COPYINPUT
else

        echo "dumpdb:${SERVER}: dump of $dbname completed at
            `date`." | $COPYINPUT
endif


# rewind and unload the second tape

mt -f ${NONREWINDINGTAPE} off                    # rewind tape

# set up the remaining databases to dump to individual disk files
# note that for a database dump to a disk file you simply specify
# the disk filename -- you don't have to worry about server dump
# devices unless you prefer to

foreach dbname (db3 db4 db5 db6 db7)
echo "dumpdb:${srvname}: [${dbname}] started  at `date`." | $TEE
$SYBASE/bin/isql -U${username} -S${SERVER} -e
    <<finish_sql_diskdumpdb | $COPYINPUT
${password}
dump database ${dbname} to "/diskdump/${dbname}_databasedump.out"
go
exit
finish_sql_diskdumpdb
if ($status) then
        echo "dumpdb:${SERVER}: database dump of $dbname has FAILED
            at `date`." | $COPYINPUT
        cat  ${dbname}_dbdump.out | $COPYINPUT
else
        echo "dumpdb:${SERVER}: dump of $dbname completed at
            `date`." | $COPYINPUT
endif


# here is the end of the loop for the databases dumped to disk

end

echo "dumpdb:${SERVER}: exiting at `date`." | $COPYINPUT

# mail the output file from the dump to dba
```

```
mail -s "dumpdb:${srvname}: output" dba < $outfile
clear
exit
```

15.13 Load Databases for SQL Server System 10 (loaddb_sys10)

There is no script needed to load databases from a dump tape as there is for SQL Server 4.9.x. SQL Server 4.9.x didn't think there could be more than one dump per tape, so it just loaded whatever file was on the tape at the time the load database command was executed. SQL Server System 10 allows for multiple database dumps on a single tape; therefore, the server requests the filename before it will load a dump. If you have only one dump file on a tape, you don't have to specify the file-name of the file; just load the database or transaction log dump. Also, System 10 doesn't require that you use a server dump device to dump or load. You can use the physical device name or the actual filename for a database dump or load to or from a disk file. To load from a dump tape, execute—

```
load database db1 with listonly
```

—which will give you a listing of all the dumps on the tape and the filename for each dump. Unless you specify a filename when you create the dump, the server will generate the filename itself. The filenames the server creates are not good. They involve the day of the year and the number of seconds since midnight. You will end up simply listing out the filenames as described above. You can't figure out what the filename should be. You can look at the output of whatever process you used to create the dump and the filename will be there.

To automate this process, change the script dumpdb_sys10_tape_disk to use specific filenames, that is, the **file='filename'** option for the dump database command. Then, for the load script, you could have a switch statement and, depending on the database to load, specify the filename used for that database dump. This would require that you set up the file names and don't change them unless you change both the dump and load scripts.

15.14   Server Startup Script RUN_*<servername>*

This script provides one location to set up the startup of all the Sybase products that need to be running on the server. If you are running only one SQL Server on the server machine, you can use the RUN_*<servername>* script that is generated by syb-config (sybinit for System 10). However, as explained in the next section, there are good reasons not to use RUN_*<servername>* as it is generated by sybconfig but to leave it alone as part of your server documentation. Further, you should modify a copy of the RUN_*<servername>* script so that it will execute the startup scripts for the other products that run with the SQL Server, such as SQL Monitor, Backup Server for System 10, and the various components of Replication Server. As your database system becomes more complex, you will need to have one script on each server machine that can be executed by any of the DBAs and that will bring up all the processes needed on the server machine. The RUN_*<servername>* script per-forms this. By having a script called RUN_*<servername>* on each server machine in your database system, you make it very easy for any DBA to log in to the server machine, find the standard directory /dba/SERVERNAME, and execute RUN_*<servername>*.

The RUN_*<servername>* script could also be executed automatically as part of the process of the server machine starting up.

To illustrate this process of copying and modifying the RUN_*<servername>* script, we follow the example below for the server DDSDBA1. You should begin by mov-ing the RUN_DDSDBA1 script that was created by sybconfig (sybinit for System 10) to RUN_DDSDBA1_orig. Leave this file as it is in the $SYBASE/install directory where it was created, which for our example is /dba/sybase/install. Renaming the file prevents accidentally running the original, unmodified version of the startup script. This file, along with the errorlog file, both of which were created by the installation process, will become part of the documentation of the server as it was installed. These files document the location and size of the master device, the initial server ver-sion and configuration, and so on. Next, copy RUN_DDSDBA1_orig to RUN_DDSDBA1 but in the directory /dba/DDSDBA1 as part of the standard file sys-tem configuration of the server machine. You should make all modifications to this copy of the startup script.

We follow the process, starting with the original RUN_DDSDBA1 script in the /dba/sybase/install directory. The script is shown below before any modifications have taken place.

```
/dba/sybase/install% more RUN_DDSDBA1
#! /bin/sh
# Server name:     DDSDBA1
# dslisten port:
# master name:     /dev/rsd1h
# master size:     15360

DSLISTEN=DDSDBA1; export DSLISTEN

/dba/sybase/bin/dataserver -d/dev/rsd1h
   -e/dba/sybase/install/errorlog_DDSDBA1
```

Next, copy this script to RUN_DDSDBA1 but in the /dba/DDSDBA1 directory. Now you can modify the startup script.

You then add the command—

```
mv /dba/DDSDBA1/errorlog  /dba/DDSDBA1/errorlog.`date
   +%y%m%d%H%M%S`
```

—to copy the server errorlog to a separate file each time the server starts. This makes it easy to review the latest errorlog without wading through lots of older errorlogs. It also prevents the file system from filling up. As the file system becomes full, you can easily delete the oldest individual errorlog files without shutting down the server. Normally, as the errorlog grows, you just have one massive errorlog file. When the file system gets too full, you must shut down the server and remove the whole error-log. This makes it more likely that you will remove errorlogs that document important events. You should use the modified startup script below to make each server start up a separate errrolog file.

Include in RUN_DDSDBA1 any trace flags that you need in your environment. This way, the server will start up with the same trace flags every time it starts up. Who-ever actually starts the server does not need to know which trace flags to use, since that information is in the startup script. Also, you should change the part of the script that actually executes the binary so that it uses the -s, -i, and -M options of the dataserver command. Note that the dataserver command is simply the execution of the server binary. As explained for the server upgrade process (see Chapter 13), the server binary should be renamed to reflect the server version and EBF level. In the startup script, you don't need to execute dataserver; instead, you can execute whatever the dataserver file is called.

For the example shown below, we execute the file s_ddsdba1.491datasvr, which is the dataserver file for the 4.9.1 version of SQL Server (note that the only difference between a 4.9.1 and a 4.9.2 SQL Server is the EBF level). The -s option allows you to name the server; as the server starts, it will use the name from the -s option to look in the interfaces file and determine which server machine and port number to start up on. This means you don't have to set up the environment variable DSLISTEN, and it simplifies the process of determining which UNIX process ID belongs to the SQL Server. Normally, if you simply execute the RUN_<*servername*> script as is you will see a UNIX process ID for the RUN_<*servername*> script and then the SQL Server process itself will appear separately. However, the servername is not in the name of the process. This isn't a problem when you have only one server running on any server machine. But, as you add SQL Monitor, Backup Server (for System 10), and the various components of Replication Server, you will find it more and more difficult to quickly and accurately determine which process is which Sybase product. When you need to kill a server for any reason, you must be able to identify the correct UNIX process ID. By use of the -s option, the name of the server appears in the name of the process in the output of ps. This makes it much easier to identify the process ID of any server or related product.

Similarly, the -i option allows you to specify the location of the interfaces file, and the -M option allows you to specify where the server shared-memory files will be located. With the -e option, you can place the errorlog and the shared memory files in the appropriate directories, rather than having them located in the default location of $SYBASE/install. The actual binary is stored (along with all the other EBFs and other binary server files) in /dba/DDSDBA1/bin. The interfaces file must remain in the $SYBASE directory for use by isql, etc.

This is very important. You want to have everything needed to start up the server outside the $SYBASE directory. The $SYBASE directory gets overwritten any time you load a major upgrade of the server; moreover, any additional Sybase products are also loaded to this directory. This means you should protect the server by moving all the files it needs out of the $SYBASE directory.

Note that the -s, -i, and -M options are not documented under the dataserver command in the Sybase manuals but are in the Sybase Answerbase CD-ROM product. Refer to SYBASE TechNote "SQL Server Command Line Flags."

```
/dba/DDSDBA1% more RUN_DDSDBA1
#! /bin/sh
# Server name:DDSDBA1
# dslisten port:
# master name:/dev/rsd1h
# master size:15360
#
# from here on we have altered the script to add features.
# set up the trace flags for the server
#

TRACE_FLAGS = "-T4013 -T4016"

# document what the trace flags mean....
# from trace.h:
# **      DATASERV, 13    4013    log loginrec in errorlog.
# **      DATASERV, 16    4016    log an informational message to
# errorlog
#
# move current errorlog to a new file
#

mv /dba/DDSDBA1/errorlog  /dba/DDSDBA1/errorlog.`date
   +%y%m%d%H%M%S`

#
# now actually execute the server binary with the -s option
# see the dataserver command under the UNIX utilities in the Sybase
# manuals
#
```

```
exec /dba/DDSDBA1/bin/s_ddsdba1.491datasvr -d/dev/rsd1h -sDDSDBA1\
 -e/dba/DDSDBA1/bin/errorlog -i/dba/sybase -M/dba/DDSDBA1/bin
    $TRACE_FLAGS &

# wait for 5 minutes
# this is to allow the SQL Server to fully recover before the SQL
# Monitor starts up
sleep 300

/dba/DDSDBA1_MSV/RUN_DDSDBA1_MON

# if System 10 server, add command to start up Backup Server if it
# is not already running

if (`ps -ef | grep DDSDBA1_BCK | wc -l` <2) then
    /dba/DDSDBA1_BCK/RUN_DDSDBA1_BCK
# end of System 10 specific portion of server startup script

# end of startup script
```

In summary, there are several advantages to using the various options of the **dataser-ver** command. Using them means that the server is not dependent on the values of any environment variables. This will prevent confusion later if the value of $SYBASE were changed before a server was started. Using these options also makes it easy to determine the actual location of the errorlog and interfaces file that the server is using, because the entire **dataserver** command line, including all the options, will be displayed by the **ps** command. If there are problems, you can look at the **ps** output to see exactly where the server got the interfaces file it used to start up and where the errorlog is currently being generated.

Chapter 16

Recommended Reading

As you execute your many duties as a DBA, you will run across bits and pieces of many other jobs and functional areas. These will include data modeling, logical and physical database design, system administration, UNIX programming, and various aspects of hardware installation and maintenance. Depending on the particular organizational structure you work in, you may have other persons and/or departments that are primarily responsible for these tasks. Your job will be easier and you will be able to do your job more effectively if you have some understanding of these other processes.

The sources listed in Table 16.1 will assist you in learning about these many other areas. Each of the areas could well be a full-time job if you tried to learn all the subtleties involved. You certainly don't have time for that. By exploring these areas as the need arises, you can quickly expand your understanding of the system you are supporting.

Table 16-3   Recommended Reading List

Title	Author	Category
The Guide to SQL Server	Nath	SQL Server
A Guide to SQL Server	McGoveran/Date	SQL Server
High Performance Relational Database Design	Kirkwood	SQL Server
SQL Server Survival Guide	Panttaja Consulting	SQL Server
Sybase Architecture and Administration	Kirkwood	SQL Server
The Practical SQL Handbook	Emerson/Darnovsky/Bowman	SQL

Table 16-3   Recommended Reading List (Continued)

Title	Author	Category
SQL Instant Reference	Gruber	SQL
Understanding SQL	Gruber	SQL
Using SQL	Groff/Weinberg	SQL
Client/Server SQL Applications	Khoshafian/ Chan/Wong/Wong	Database Design/Tuning
Database Tuning: A Principled Approach	Shasha	Database Design/Tuning
Handbook of Relational Database Design	von Halle/Fleming	Database Design/Tuning
UNIX C Shell Desk Reference	Arick	UNIX
UNIX—The Complete Reference	Coffin	UNIX
Administrator's Guide to Sun Workstations	Becker/Slattery	System Administration
Essential System Administration	Frisch	System Administration
Solaris System Administrator's Guide	Winsor	System Administration
Information Modelling	Veryard	Data Modelling
Database Programming & Design	Miller Freeman	Magazine
DBMS	Miller Freeman	Magazine
SQL Forum	CSS Inc.	Magazine
Smileys	Sanderson	General

16.1 SQL Server Books

1. *The Guide to SQL Server* by Aloke Nath. Addison Wesley, 1990. ISBN 0-201-52336-1

    Covers the Microsoft version of SQL Server for PCs. This is good background on the differences between the UNIX and PC versions of SQL Server. Covers the product well and will prepare you for the even greater rift developing now between Sybase and Microsoft about their visions of the future of SQL Server.

2. *A Guide to SQL Server* by D. McGoveran with C. J. Date, Addison Wesley, 1992, ISBN 0-201-55710-X

    One of the first books out about SQL Server. It covers the server and related products but at a very high level. Further, the book refers to "System 5" SQL Server, which was never produced—System 10 was the next version after 4.9.x. This makes it confusing at times to read the book, because you don't know if what is being discussed is really in System 10 or was specific to System 5.

3. *High Performance Relational Database Design* by John Kirkwood. Ellis Horwood, 1992. ISBN 0-13-030198-1

    Covers relational database design for performance in general but uses Sybase SQL Server for specific examples. Good general discussion of the issues involved with database performance.

4. *SQL Server Survival Guide* by Panttaja Consulting Group, 1992-1993.

    Getting old, but provides interesting details of the various versions of SQL Server. This information is very hard to find in the current Sybase documentation but is very useful if you are working with a database system that includes servers running older versions of SQL Server. The book's style is very terse, but it covers a lot of ground.

    If you ever get a chance to hear Mary or Jim Panttaja speak, you should pay attention. They are *very* good and have many insights that will help you immediately with your SQL Server problems. They have the rare ability to cut to the chase before the audience tunes out.

5. *Sybase Architecture and Administration* by John Kirkwood. Ellis Horwood, 1993. ISBN 0-13-100330-5

    Covers the basic structure of data and indexes in the SQL Server. Attempts to cover all aspects of the SQL Server but doesn't give lots of details. Good coverage of the server's optimizer. This book doesn't even mention System 10.

16.2 SQL Books

6. *The Practical SQL Handbook* by Sandra L. Emerson, Marcy Darnovsky, and Judith S. Bowman. Addison Wesley, 1989. ISBN 0-201-51738-8

    Covers all the basics needed to learn SQL. Note that this book has the advantage of focusing on Sybase SQL Server and actually works all the examples against the *pubs* database provided with the SQL Server product. This makes the book a very good way to learn SQL while working with the Sybase product. Note that this does mean there is a bias, and you won't see any discussion of how things are handled by other products.

7. *SQL Instant Reference* by Martin Gruber. SYBEX, 1993.
    ISBN 0-7821-1148-3

    Excellent, in an unusual way. It makes clear just how different Sybase Transact-SQL is from either the 1989 or 1992 SQL standards. This is very good reading because it will make you realize just how narrowly focused you can become if all you ever see is the Sybase version of SQL. Very good for reading between server crises.

8. *Understanding SQL* by Martin Gruber. SYBEX, 1990. ISBN 0-89588-644-8

    Good at covering the basics of SQL and how it works. Note that most DBAs won't admit they need to learn SQL, but they do. If anyone tells you they truly understand correlated subqueries involving the compute clause, it's baloney.

9. *Using SQL* by James R. Groff and Paul N. Weinberg. Osborne McGraw Hill, 1990. ISBN 0-07-881524-X

    Very good for learning SQL in general without being tied to a specific vendor's product. You would do well to learn SQL from such a book before you wade into the particulars of one relational database product versus another. Only then can you begin to appreciate how many of the product's features are nonstandard which may lock you into the vendor once your applications are running with these nonstandard features of SQL. This book provides many examples and is very thorough.

16.3 Database Design/Tuning Books

10. *Client/Server SQL Applications (A Guide to Developing)* by Setrag Khoshafian, Arvola Chan, Anna Wong, and Harry K. T. Wong. Morgan Kaufmann, 1992. ISBN 1-55860-147-3

    Provides a very good overview of the process of implementing client-server applications. It also compares the features of the leading vendor's products. Very good reading for the DBA to gain an appreciation for what is involved with getting an application up and running.

11. *Database Tuning: A Principled Approach* by Dennis E. Shasha. Prentice Hall, 1992. ISBN 0-13-205246-6

    Excellent. You must buy it and you must read it, all of it. This book covers general aspects of database tuning better than anything you will see anywhere else. Then it gets even better by comparing the way the leading vendors deal with (and don't deal with) the problems that come up in any multiuser database. You must read this book. Then you must hide it from everybody because they will steal it.

12. *Handbook of Relational Database Design* by Candice C. Fleming and Barbara von Halle. Addison Wesley, 1989. ISBN 0-201-11434-8

    This book is a classic and should be on your shelf next to Homer's works and Groening's *Life is Hell*. This book should be read, even though it will be painful in places, so that you get a true appreciation for just how hard it is to stuff any real-world situation into a relational model. The book covers the process of modeling and laying out the database objects extremely well, to the point that you will thank the forces that be that you are a DBA and don't have to ponder the many-to-many questions of life.

    Barbara von Halle also writes an extremely good column, called "Database Design," in Database Programming & Design magazine. You should read this column religiously to see what the heck those persons do all day.

16.4 UNIX Books

13. *UNIX C Shell Desk Reference* by Martin R. Arick. QED Technical Publishing Group, 1992. ISBN 0-89435-328-4

Excellent for learning the absolutely absurd way that the C shell works. You will need to understand the arcane commands and syntax of whatever shell you are using for your DBA scripts, and this book is excellent if you are using C shell. Good coverage of both the commands and putting them into scripts.

14. *UNIX—The Complete Reference* by Stephen Coffin. Osborne McGraw Hill, 1988. ISBN 0-07-881299-2

A good solid reference for the arcane world of UNIX commands and syntax. Especially good is the coverage of the cron utility.

16.5 System Administration Books

15. *Administrator's Guide to Sun Workstations* by George Becker and Kathy Slattery. Springer Verlag, 1991. ISBN 0-387-97250-1

Covers Sun system administration in particular and is very useful if you are running your SQL Server(s) on Sun machines.

16. *Essential System Administration* by Aleen Frisch. O'Reilly & Associates, 1991. ISBN 0-937175-80-3

Covers UNIX system administration in general, which is very good. Especially good is the explanation of disk partitions and the files that control access to the disk partitions. A very good book for the DBA to read to gain insight into why there are full-time system administrators and why you should be nice to them.

17. *Solaris System Administrator's Guide* by Janice Winsor. Ziff Davis Press, 1993. ISBN 1-56276-080-7

Illustrates very well the differences between SunOS and Solaris. If any of your servers are running on Sun machines, you should read this book as well as the book above because you will be moving to Solaris sooner or later.

16.6 Data Modeling Books

18. *Information Modelling* by Richard Veryard. Prentice Hall, 1992. ISBN 0-13-454182-0

    A very good way to learn how data modelling works in real-life business situations. Good reading for the DBA to see how to pervert real life into a form that runs well in the relational world. The author has it right when describing what the book should have been titled; see the first page of his preface.

16.7 Magazines

19. **Database Programming & Design**
    Database Programming & Design, Miller Freeman Inc.,
    600 Harrison St., San Francisco, CA 94107

    More biased toward the old database world, that is, lots of stuff on IBM, etc. They cover SQL Server issues occasionally, but the real value is in the general coverage of the wider database world. As mentioned, the column "Database Design" by Barbara von Halle is well worth the price of the publication.

20. **DBMS**
    DBMS, Miller Freeman Inc., 411 Borel Ave., Suite 100, San Mateo, CA 94402

    Covers the database world very well with everything from object-oriented yelling and screaming to the history of the relational model. Buy this magazine for Joe Celko's column (and puzzle) if nothing else. His comments are often inflammatory but always worth reading.

21. **SQL Forum**
    SQL Forum, POB 240, Lynnwood, WA 98046-0240

    Has some of the most in-depth discussions of SQL Server issues you will ever find. At times the discussions are a bit too abstract but are still well worth wading through. You will discover solutions to problems you don't even understand. Expensive and well worth it. Can be biased towards the PC world, but almost all of the information is very useful to the UNIX world as well.

16.8 General

22. *Smileys* by David Sanderson. O'Reilly & Associates, 1993.
    ISBN 1-56592-041-4

    Vital to performing your job as DBA. You need to include these guys at the end of your email to users about killing them, stopping their processes, and answering their endless questions. Also useful to interpret the oftentimes bizarre 'smileys' you may get from everyone else, for example, is the sender yelling at you or does he simply want you to know that he has a mustache? (That is, the difference between :-(and :-{ respectively). Finally, { means "a psycho," so I'll leave it at that.

    {

Index

Symbols

;-)

another *vdevno* mess 164
application with no indexes 384
capacity planning for System 10 453
clean dumps 322
creating clustered index 369
cylinder 0 overwritten 241
database no longer mirrored 204
DBA team 226
dbcc checks on DBCC server 304
dbcc runs too long 430
defined xiii
disasters do happen xi
disk init fails, *vdevno* problems 164
dumps, mirrors and professionals 328
fantasy of the small database 427
free space on *master* device 263
Goodwill Tour 76
mirroring 205
must monitor mirrors 205
please buy Replication Server 48
real DBA's 211
Replication Server has many components 63
reserved word conflicts 452
risk sharing 306
SA support 76
server device names 161
server installation documents 75
server machine maximum disk space 389
server performance and mirroring 333
server product files 86
servermap 222
sp_addlogin modified 13
SQL Server Troubleshooting Guide 275
stupid segment stuff 179

su privilege 22
System 10 upgrade and errorlog 464
tape drives 31
the CIO and disk space 359
transaction log dump size 368
upgrade to System 10 507
user-hostile servermap 214
users delete 10 rows 321
very large database (VLDB) 432
Xmas saved by disk mirroring 188
you've been hired 212
your predecessor(s) 211

Numerics

1105 error
and transaction log 251
checking errorlog 238
fixing 323
server device with multiple segments 424
tempdb 323
thresholds in System 10 464
transaction log full, recovery 314
transient 420
verifying and fixing 419
2K page. *See* server device: size
2K pages
sysusages 401
605 error
on DBCC server 304

A

active server device
mirroring 199

E

F

W